Routledge Revivals

The Co-operative Movement in the Punjab

First published in 1937, *The Co-operative Movement in the Punjab* presents a sketch of the development and working of the co-operative movement in the region in its various aspects. With its vast and fertile fields, it's sturdy and assimilative manpower, it's beautiful rivers and its marvelous canal system, the Punjab, the sword-arm of the erstwhile Empire, was the stronghold of co-operation in India.

The book discusses various themes like agricultural indebtedness and aspects of rural credits; co-operation in India; agricultural credit societies; provincial co-operative bank; women and co-operation; milk recording societies; central banks; cattle insurance; stock breeding societies and land mortgage banks in the Punjab. This book is an important historical reference work for scholars and researchers of Indian history, agricultural history, South Asian history, history of Punjab, and history in general.

The Co-operative Movement in the Punjab

Ata Ullah

Routledge
Taylor & Francis Group

First published in 1937
by George Allen & Unwin Ltd.

This edition first published in 2024 by Routledge
4 Park Square, Milton Park, Abingdon, Oxon, OX14 4RN

and by Routledge
605 Third Avenue, New York, NY 10017

Routledge is an imprint of the Taylor & Francis Group, an informa business

Publisher's Note
The publisher has gone to great lengths to ensure the quality of this reprint but points out that some imperfections in the original copies may be apparent.

Disclaimer
The publisher has made every effort to trace copyright holders and welcomes correspondence from those they have been unable to contact.

A Library of Congress record exists under LCCN: 38005973

ISBN: 978-1-032-76094-0 (hbk)
ISBN: 978-1-003-47710-5 (ebk)
ISBN: 978-1-032-76098-8 (pbk)

Book DOI 10.4324/9781003477105

The Co-operative Movement in the Punjab

Ata Ullah
M.A.
Lecturer in Economics,
Muslim University, Aligarh

With a Preface by

C. R. FAY, M.A., D.SC.
Reader in Economic History at the University of Cambridge, and Chairman of the Horace Plunkett Foundation

London
George Allen & Unwin Ltd
Museum Street

FIRST PUBLISHED IN 1937

TO

H. CALVERT, ESQ., B.SC., I.C.S. (Retired)

THE PUNJAB'S RAIFFEISEN

THIS BOOK IS RESPECTFULLY

DEDICATED

PRINTED IN GREAT BRITAIN BY
UNWIN BROTHERS LTD., WOKING

PREFACE

WITH its vast and fertile fields, its sturdy and assimilative man-power, its beautiful rivers and its marvellous canal system, the Punjab, the sword-arm of the Empire, is the stronghold of Co-operation in India. Possessing an honest and suffering peasantry, money-lenders that are rich and rapacious as well as shrewd and powerful, an indebtedness that is practically irredeemable, and an administration which claims—no doubt with a certain amount of justification—to protect the rights of the cultivator (sinking under the weight of illiteracy and debt), it presents a fascinating subject for study from various points of view.

Co-operation is, by universal consent, the only effective lever which can most quickly and easily lift the cultivator out of the mire that threatens to engulf him. Co-operation as a remedy is particularly suited to Indian conditions and has long been, and rightly too, held out to be the Indian peasants' only hope of salvation. It has now been tried for over a generation. It is high time, therefore, particularly in view of the abnormal difficulties with which the peasantry of the country is faced, to take stock of the achievements and failures of the movement, with a view to framing a more fruitful policy for the future.

The Punjab is admittedly the most advanced Province so far as the growth and working of the movement is concerned. In the following pages I have attempted to present a sketch of the development and working of the movement in the Punjab in its various aspects. But for the recent acute and prolonged depression the reader would have been presented with an exceedingly encouraging account of the movement in the Province.

The Punjab owes its position as the premier Province in the matter of growth and working of the movement to its incomparably brilliant and devoted Registrars, each one of whom has left the mark of his individuality and devotion on the system of the Punjab. To Messrs. H. Calvert, C. F. Strickland, and M. L. Darling the Province will always feel grateful.

On the vast problem of agricultural indebtedness of the Province and its varied and intricate aspects I have, wherever necessary, expounded or quoted the views expressed in official Reports—mostly the Punjab Banking Enquiry Committee Report. Those who know the Province, and the conflict of interests that this subject involves, will easily realize the delicacy of the problem. I would, however, wish to make it plain to my readers that I do not find myself in complete agreement with the official views on many aspects of agricultural indebtedness in the Province. My contention is that the problem of agricultural indebtedness in the Punjab, in spite of the Banking Enquiry Committee, has never been studied with that care, minuteness, and thoroughness which it deserves.

I may on some future occasion, nearer or more distant, given the proper facilities, attempt to unveil to the public view such aspects of rural indebtedness in the Province which, unless intelligently and effectively handled, will, to say the least, send the Province insolvent.

The manuscript was completed in the middle of 1935 and originally gave the figures for 1933 only. In December 1935 the Annual Report for 1934 was published and I have attempted to incorporate figures for 1934 in the body of the book wherever possible. I have merely incorporated the figures and not attempted to recast my views in the light of the new Report; for no generalizations of any permanent value can be undertaken merely on the basis of a year's working of the Societies.

The book appears in the "Indian Co-operative Series," a distinction which the Indian Co-operative Institutes' Association has generously bestowed upon me and which I shall always cherish with pride. I owe it in all fairness to the Association to declare that the responsibility for the views expressed in the book is entirely mine.

My warmest thanks are due to a number of friends intimately connected in various capacities with the working of the movement in the Province. To each one of them, including a brilliant lady worker, of whose assistance I desire to make specific mention, I offer my sincere and personal gratitude. I cannot also help making a public reference to the very considerable help rendered to me by Khan Mohd Bashir Ahmad Khan, M.A., LL.B., Secretary, Punjab Co-operative Union and Honorary Secretary All India Co-operative Institutes' Association, Lahore. I wish as well to record my sense of deep indebtedness to Syed Bashir-ud-Din, M.A., Librarian Muslim University, Aligarh, for the never-failing courtesy and promptness with which he arranged to secure for me from the Punjab the large stock of books without which it could not have been possible for me to complete this task.

ATA ULLAH

MUSLIM UNIVERSITY, ALIGARH,
UNITED PROVINCES, INDIA
December 15, 1936

CONTENTS

PREFACE

By C. R. FAY, M.A., D.SC.

Reader in Economic History at the University of Cambridge, and Chairman of the Horace Plunkett Foundation

SINCE 1930 four of the great pioneers of co-operation have passed away, Charles Gide, Sir Horace Plunkett, Henry W. Wolff, and lastly, in June 1936, at Coonoor in South India, Sir Frederick Nicholson, whose Report of 1895–7, on the possibility of introducing Land and Agricultural Banks into the Madras Presidency, was the starting-point of the co-operative movement in India. The staff officers of these pioneers—men like R. A. Anderson, Plunkett's right-hand man in Ireland, and the great Registrars of the Punjab, Calvert, Darling, and Strickland—are themselves approaching the age of retirement. And now it is the task of the third generation to carry forward their good work. The work required of them is two-fold. First, executive work, as servants of the movement, whether paid or honorary; and secondly, educational work, by which I mean not only the instruction of co-operators and co-operative officials in the principles and technique of co-operation, but the awakening of the thoughtful public to the possibilities, limitations, and social significance of the movement. The Punjab has for long held a high place in English thought on account of the vigour of its people and the solidity of its economic achievement; and just because it is so vigorous and solid it has realized fully the value of co-operative education. Shortly before his death Charles Gide established an International Institute for the study of co-operation. It meets every two years in the different capitals of Europe. In 1936 it met at Budapest. Mr. Strickland and I were the representatives from England, and we were endeavouring there to approach our problem in that same spirit of academic fairness, of appreciation combined with criticism, which characterizes the work of Mr. Ata Ullah. He writes from the Muslim University of

Aligarh in the United Provinces. I hope that similar provincial studies will issue from other universities covering the other great Provinces and States of India; and that when this has been done, or while it is doing, Indian teachers and writers on co-operation will form an institute similar to that of Gide for the international study of co-operation in Asia.

I had the honour a short while ago to succeed Sir Daniel Hall as Chairman of the Trustees of the Horace Plunkett Foundation. Our founder was a great Irishman; and happening to read in the same week Mr. Ata Ullah's manuscript and Mr. R. A. Anderson's recently published *With Horace Plunkett in Ireland* (Macmillan, 1935), I was struck with the close similarity between Ireland and India. Both countries were injured in former days by an alien exploitation. Both, being primarily agricultural, were exposed suddenly to the irruption of industrialism. Both have their present problems: in Ireland the gombeen man; in India the money-lender; in Ireland the strife between Orangemen and Roman Catholics; in India communal friction between Muslim and Hindu. But both have met their problem in the same way—technically by the encouragement of an improved agriculture, socially and economically by the promotion of agricultural co-operation. Plunkett came back from the United States in 1889 to start the movement in Ireland. Nicholson went to Europe in 1892 to study co-operative credit. The first meeting of the Irish Agricultural Organization Society, a voluntary non-political body, the child of Plunkett's genius, was held in 1894; and in 1904, after some years of provincial experiment, in which the Punjab was well to the front, the first Co-operative Credit Societies Act was passed by the Government of India. Much has been accomplished since then, but the way has been hard and much remains to do. Plunkett at the Wembley Conference of 1924 told us in his rueful way how "for thirty-five years he had striven to push the monolith of co-operation up the slippery slopes of Irish and some other mountains." And our author, writing as of 1934, observes in his final review, p. 503: "Thirty long years have passed. The movement has grown in volume and variety. . . . But it is time we should fully realize the extreme inadequacy of the movement as a method of revitalizing the peasantry of the Province, which is the pride of our country." He is thus critical, but as the rest of his book makes abundantly clear, he does not despond. And I would remind him that in the deep depression through which the whole world has recently passed it was not to be expected that the co-operative movement should go unscathed. I know Canada well, and I visited India, including the Punjab, last year; and I think I may say of India what I know I can say of Canada, that the co-operative movement stood as a buffer in these hard years between the rural population and social demoralization. I will recall the lines with which Plunkett concluded his inaugural address to the I.A.O.S. in April 1894:

> If what seemed afar so grand
> Turn to nothing in your hand,
> On again, the virtue lies
> In the struggle, not the prize.

To this call the indomitable spirit of the Punjab will, of a surety, respond.

Mr. Ata Ullah will pardon me if I underline what seem to me the most valuable aspects of his book. First of all, he relates co-operation to the distinctive characteristics of Punjab agriculture and Punjab temperament. There was a danger in the suggestion that what India had to do was to find Raiffeisen. What it had rather to do was to know itself. Secondly, he thinks for himself; and where his personal experience conflicts with the official view, he does not hesitate to say why. This comes out, for example, in his spirited defence of the savings clubs, called "Cometi," which the Punjab women have among themselves. He will not allow that they are a gamble and a waste. Knowing the difficulty of bringing women into any contact with the movement, he argues with effect that something of co-operative value may be built out of this institution, which has the great merit of being native to themselves. Thirdly and finally, he has an eye for interesting material. There is an excellent chapter on the Kot Estate Societies, showing what can be done by a chivalrous landlord through the instrument of co-operation; and another excellent chapter on the Consolidation of Holdings, which for me was the most interesting of all. For the red-letter day of my visit to India was that which I spent as the guest of Sir Jogendra Singh, the Minister of Agriculture, inspecting the consolidation at Phillaur—compact holdings, good roads, improved wells, and real men. I talked with the village elders and they seemed to understand me even before my words were translated. I have sometimes wondered whether co-operation was all I constantly claim it to be, whether it really has those spiritual values without which it is a mere statistical parade. That day at Phillaur will not allow me to doubt any more.

C. R. FAY

January 7, 1937.

THE CO-OPERATIVE MOVEMENT IN THE PUNJAB

CHAPTER I

THE PUNJAB[1]

THE Punjab, or the Land of Five Rivers, derives its name from the Jehlum, Chenab, Ravi, Beas, and Sutlej, the five rivers which have proudly traversed their course through the plains of the Province from time immemorial. It constitutes the north-western portion of the Indian Empire with an area of 136,965 square miles and a population of 28,490,857. Its geographical position, climatic conditions, agricultural development, its variety of creeds and communities, its conflict between millions of its painfully patient and profoundly passive sufferers and their heartless exploiters, its incomparably magnificent canal system, its wonderfully industrious but hopelessly poor, recklessly extravagant, and irredeemably indebted peasantry present a many-sided problem which commands a careful and a sympathetic study by every well-wisher of this country.

The following brief account of the different aspects of life will serve as a background for a proper understanding of the pressing problems of the Province.

ADMINISTRATIVE DIVISIONS

The Punjab is administratively divided into the British territory and the Punjab States. The British territory occupies a total area of 99,265 square miles or 72·5 per cent of the total area of the Province. The British Punjab has a population of 23,580,852 or 82·8 per cent of the total population of the

[1] This chapter is based mainly upon the *Punjab Census Report* for 1931 and the *Agricultural Abstract of India*.

Province. The British Punjab is divided into five main areas, each administered by a Commissioner. These areas are further divided into districts. There are twenty-nine such districts in the Punjab. Each district is administered by a Deputy Commissioner. The following are the chief administrative divisions of the Punjab, with the districts under each division:

AMBALA	JULLUNDER	LAHORE
1. Hissar	7. Kangra	12. Lahore
2. Rohtak	8. Hoshiarpur	13. Amritsar
3. Gurgaon	9. Jullundur	14. Gurdaspur
4. Karnal	10. Ludhiana	15. Sialkot
5. Ambala	11. Ferozepore	16. Gujranwala
6. Simla		17. Sheikhupur

RAWAL PINDI	MULTAN
18. Gujrat	24. Montgomery
19. Shahpur	25. Lyallpur
20. Jhelum	26. Jhang
21. Rawal Pindi	27. Multan
22. Attock	28. Muzaffargarh
23. Mianwali	29. Dera Ghazi Khan

The Punjab States occupy an area of 37,699 square miles or 27·5 of the total area of the Province, and have a population of 4,910,005 or 17·2 per cent of the total population of the Punjab. The Simla Hill States are twenty-seven in number and have the Deputy Commissioner of Simla as their Superintendent. The rest of the states have political relations either with the Punjab Government or with the Government of India through the Agent to the Governor-General.

NATURAL DIVISIONS

With main reference to the physical and climatic features, the Province has been divided into four Natural Divisions: the Indo-Gangetic Plain West, the Himalayan, the Sub-Himalayan, and the North-West Dry Area. These divisions form a part of the Natural Division of India.

The four Natural Divisions of the Punjab comprise the following districts and states:

I. INDO-GANGETIC PLAIN WEST

1. Hissar
2. Loharu State
3. Rohtak
4. Dojana State
5. Gurgaon
6. Pataudi State
7. Karnal
8. Jullundur
9. Kapurthala State
10. Ludhiana
11. Malerkotla State
12. Ferozepore
13. Farid-Kot State
14. Patiala State
15. Jind State
16. Nabha State
17. Lahore
18. Amritsar
19. Gujranwala
20. Sheikhupura

II. HIMALAYAN

21. Sirmoor State
22. Simla
23. Simla Hill State
24. Bilaspur State
25. Kangra
26. Mandi State
27. Suket State
28. Chamba State

III. SUB-HIMALAYAN

29. Ambala
30. Kalsia State
31. Hoshiarpur
32. Gurdaspur
33. Sialkot
34. Gujrat
35. Jhelum
36. Rawal Pindi
37. Attock

IV. NORTH-WEST DRY AREA

38. Shahpur
39. Mianwali
40. Montgomery
41. Lyallpur
42. Jhang
43. Multan
44. Bhawalpur State
45. Muzaffargarh
46. Dera Ghazi Khan

CHARACTERISTICS OF THE NATURAL DIVISIONS OF THE PUNJAB

The Himalayan.—This tract contains country on both sides of the outer range of the Himalayas and covers an area of 22,000 square miles. The lower slopes, valleys, and foot-hills are under cultivation. This region is quite rich in fertile tracts scattered here and there. There are numerous mountain streams which are converted into small water-courses by the cultivators and utilized in irrigating the valley and the lower slopes. The tract is rich in fuel wood, timber, and grazing-grounds.

The high mountains are covered with perpetual snow and many of the tracts are separated by the barriers of snow in winter from the rest of the world.

Climatically the Division is mild in summer and very severe in winter. The average annual rainfall is over 60 inches. Kangra claims 120 inches, the highest, and Chamba 37 inches, the lowest average.

The Sub-Himalayan —This Division comprises the narrow strip of country, adjoining the Himalayan, into which run some of the spurs of the Himalaya, such as the Swaliks and the high hills of Kasauli, Dalhousie, and Murree. The land in the vicinity of foot-hills is traversed by numerous hill torrents which add to the fertility of the soil by their rich deposits of silt. The three northern districts of this tract are hilly in character and composed for the most part of broken country. In the rest of the districts the greater portion of the area is a fairly level plain. In this level plain the depth to water is small and wells, therefore, are easy to work. The average rainfall is over 30 inches.

Indo-Gangetic Plain West.—This Natural Division comprises a level alluvial plain. The rainfall in this region is less than in the Sub-Himalayan area and decreases from east to west. A large area of this region is irrigated by perennial canals. The units not receiving canal water as Jullundur and Kapurthala possess an extensive well-irrigation. The districts adjacent to Rajputana border possess a sandy soil, a low water table, and very scanty well-irrigation. The average rainfall in this region is 20 inches.

North-West Dry Area.—The North-West Dry Area has a smaller rainfall and a lower water table as compared to the Indo-Gangetic plain.

Before the area of canal irrigation the region comprised a vast expanse of arid waste and was the favourite haunt of the pastoral people. The construction of canals during the last forty years or so has immensely benefited the Districts of Lyallpur, Shahpur, Jhang, Montgomery, Multan, and Bhawalpur State, so that the arid wastes of a generation ago have been converted into the biggest granaries of the world. Irrigation through wells is also to be found in Multan, Jhang Muzaffargarh, and Dera Ghazi Khan.

POPULATION

The latest Census Report reckons the population of the Punjab at 28,490,857. The rise in population during the last fifty years has been estimated at 37 per cent. The following table illustrates the influence of religion on the movement of population during the last half-century:

Religion	1881–91	1891–1901	1901–11	1911–21	1921–31	1881–1931
Hindus.. ..	9·8	0·7	−15·3	3·4	2·3	−5·8
Sikhs	10·2	11·6	37·0	7·8	31·0	138·1
Muslims ..	10·9	10·4	0·5	5·5	16·5	51·2
Christian ..	70·5	35·5	201·3	70·5	26·0	1394·8
Increase ..	10·2	6·3	−2·4	5·5	13·5	37·0

The rise among the Sikhs and Christians is not due to natural causes alone, but to a considerable extent due to conversions. The rise among Muslims seems entirely to be due to natural increase. The increase in the number of Muslims helps to increase the population considerably. The survival rate is highest amongst Indian Christians and fairly high amongst Muslims and comparatively low for the rest of the population.

AREA AND DENSITY

The density of population for the whole of the Province is 208 per square mile; that for Japan being 439, United Kingdom 489, Germany 358, Belgium 699.

The Punjab has an area of 136,964 square miles, out of which the British territory alone accounts for 99,265 square miles.

The following table gives the area and density of each district:

	Area	Density per Square Mile
AMBALA DIVISION	Square Miles	
1. Hissar	5,215	151
2. Rohtak	2,470	290
3. Gurgaon	2,244	301
4. Karnal	3,125	241
5. Ambala	1,879	330
6. Simla	80	209
JULLUNDUR DIVISION		
7. Kangra	9,858	83
8. Hoshiarpur	2,175	453
9. Jullundur	1,323	627
10. Ludhiana	1,399	403
11. Ferozepore	4,087	246
LAHORE DIVISION		
12. Lahore	2,614	331
13. Amritsar	1,572	527
14. Gurdaspur	1,846	490
15. Sialkot	1,576	546
16. Gujranwala	2,307	272
17. Sheikhupura	2,302	287
RAWAL PINDI DIVISION		
18. Gujrat	2,248	386
19. Shahpur	4,789	153
20. Jhelum	2,773	182
21. Rawal Pindi	2,023	257
22. Attock	4,115	130
23. Mianwali	5,440	69
MULTAN DIVISION		
24. Montgomery	4,424	215
25. Lyallpur	3,128	343
26. Jhang	3,443	172
27. Multan	5,609	100
28. Muzaffargarh	5,609	100
29. Dera Ghazi Khan ..	9,378	49

AGE PERIODS IN THE PUNJAB

(Number per 1,000 of Both Sexes)

Age Periods	Punjab		N.W.F.		Bengal		Madras	
	Male	Female	Male	Female	Male	Female	Male	Female
0–5	82	77	79	78	77	79	71	73
5–10	71	61	75	61	71	63	65	64
10–20	177	96	177	91	108	106	102	103
20–30	95	79	105	86	95	95	83	96
30–40	71	56	77	61	77	61	71	70
40–50	49	39	47	37	49	38	49	47
50–60	33	24	28	21	26	22	30	29
60 & over	29	21	22	15	17	16	23	24

The table indicates that the Punjab has the highest proportion of children as well as old persons, except that females in Madras seem to be longer lived.

Urban and Rural Population.—The essential difference between a rural and an urban population is that the former is mainly engaged in agriculture and the latter in commerce, manufactures, and other occupations. A place having a population of over five thousand would be considered a village if it did not possess urban characteristics. Division of population in urban and rural areas as indicated by the latest census figures is as follows:

	Urban			Rural		
	Punjab	British Territory	Punjab States	Punjab	British Territory	Punjab States
1931	12·4	13·0	9·2	87·6	86·1	90·8

The major portion of the population is still rural. In spite of a considerable rise in the total population of the

Province during 1921–31, the proportion of urban and rural population has fluctuated only within a comparatively small margin.

Of the population roughly one-half is Muslim, three-eighths Hindu, and one-eighth Sikh. Socially, the landed classes stand high; Jats numbering nearly five millions and Rajputs over a million and a half constitute the leading landed class. The Punjab contributed over 400,000 soldiers to the Great War, mainly recruited from rural areas.

COMMUNICATIONS

The total mileage of metalled roads is only 4,073. Some of the roads are in a fairly good condition. Roads under the District Boards are hopelessly poor. In spite of considerable progress during the last thirty years the Province is still definitely poor in the matter of communications. In the rainy season floods cause a good deal of loss and considerable inconvenience, and even within the same district render communications hazardous or impossible. It is now possible, although in some cases in fair weather only, to motor between places such as: (1) Lahore and Mianwali (via Sargodha and Khushab); (2) Lahore and Bhakkar (via Lyallpur and Jhang); (3) Lahore–Multan–Dera Ghazi Khan, and Rakhni; (4) Delhi–Hissar and Malaut; (5) Pakpattan–Multan, Rawal Pindi–Khushalgarh and Kohat; (7) Jhelum–Chakwal–Talagang–Pindigheb and Campbellpur; (8) Jullundur–Hoshiarpur–Dharamsala; (9) Lyallpur–Sargodha; (10) Sialkot–Gujranwala–Pindi Bhatian, and Chinot; (11) Toba Tek Singh–Kamalia Burewala; (12) Jhang and Kabirwala.

The length of unmetalled roads is 20,719 miles. The old type means of transport are represented by pack animals, yakkas, tumtums, tongas, and carts drawn by bullocks.

Mechanical traffic is increasing with astonishing rapidity. Lorry service between important railway stations has proved a formidable rival to the railway, and much of the loss to the railway is directly attributable to this competition. Motorcycles, cars, and lorries have risen from 462 in 1913 to 21,926 in 1931.

Railway Transport.—Motor vehicles are of use in carrying light goods and short-distance passengers, and the railways carry heavy goods and long-distance passengers. The total mileage served by L.W.R. in the Punjab is about six thousand. The total number of passengers who travelled on the North-Western Railway during 1911–21 was 817,380,800 as against 619,909,000 for the decade ending 1931.

In 1924–25 wheat booked from N.W.R. stations to Karachi amounted to 1,105,212 tons and for various reasons dropped to 358,116 tons in 1931–32. With further development of road communications the possibility of road transport acting as feeders to railways is almost unlimited.

The number of post-offices in the Punjab in 1931 stood at 3,778, and the number of letters delivered in that year amounted to 120,229,278. Every town in the Province has a post-office —total number in 1931 being 524—and one out of every 97 villages has a telegraph office. The use of the telephone is extending; in 1931 37 towns possessed telephonic connections.

MEANS OF IRRIGATION IN THE PUNJAB

The Canal System of the Province.—The prosperity of the Punjab depends upon its agriculture, and the fate of agriculture is determined by an uncertain rainfall. Irrigation, therefore, chiefly conditions the prosperity of the Province. The Punjab canals irrigate 728 out of every 1,000 irrigated acres in the Province. The majority of these canals are owned and worked by the Government. The wells, which irrigate 199 acres out of every 1,000 irrigated acres in the Province, are generally private property owned by individuals or groups of individuals. The number of masonry wells in use in the Province in 1930 was 292,102.

The area irrigated by canals in the Punjab has increased from 8,300,000 in 1913–14 to 12·4 million acres in 1930–31.

The following statement summarizes the working of the Punjab's world-famous system of irrigation:

Serial Number	Name of Canal System	Length of Main Line in Miles	Length of Distributaries in Miles	Cultivable Area commanded in Thousands of Acres	Average Area Irrigated Annually in Thousands of Acres
1	2	3	4	5	6
1	Western Jumna ..	335	1,892	2,305	877
2	Sirhind	537	3,446	2,093	1,774
3	Upper Bari Doab ..	341	1,535	1,452	1,304
4	Lower Bari Doab ..	132	1,244	1,532	1,181
5	Upper Chenab ..	173	1,250	1,453	596
6	Lower Chenab ..	471	2,522	2,724	2,530
7	Upper Jhelum ..	128	608	545	332
8	Lower Jhelum ..	181	1,011	1,240	876
9	Upper Sutlej (inundation canal)	—	—	—	337
10	Sidhani	67	253	396	299
11	Indus (inundation)..	441	269	649	236
12	Shahpur (inundation)	116	117	116	67
13	Ghaggar (inundation)	97	33	108	16
14	Lower Sutlej ..	—	—	—	333
15	Chenab Sutlej ..	227	130	386	193
16	Muzaffargarh ..	446	543	647	337
17	Pakpattan Canal ..	200	975	1,103	276
18	Dipalpur Canal ..	157	866	888	391
19	Estern Canal ..	79	377	423	137
20	Mailsi Canal ..	107	643	739	239

NOTE.—The average area shown in column 6 is for the ten years the Lower Sutlej inundation canals the average area is for the years mated with Dipalpur and Mailsi canals respectively, of the Sutlej existence for the whole decade; the average area in their case,

Date of Commencement of Construction	Date of First Irrigation	Date of Completion of Construction
7	8	9
Before annexation 1888—Sirsa Branch	1820, 1891–92	1886, 1895
1867–68	1883–84	1886–87
1849–50	1860–61	1878–79
1906	1913–14	31.3.1917
1905	1912–13	31.3.1917
1884, 1890 *	1887, 1892 *	1889–1900
1905	1915–16	31.3.1917
1897	1901	31.3.1917
Some existed before annexation and some added later, 1855–70	1855, 1884	1858–59, 1885–86
1883–84	1886	1886
(Existed before annexation)	Prior to 1849	1849–50
1862–64	1870	1870–71
1896–97	1897	1898–99
Before annexation	Were in operation prior to the annexation of the Punjab by the British	Some improvements were finished in 1895
Before annexation		Some improvements were finished in 1895
Before annexation		Some improvements were finished in 1896
1923–24	1926–27	31.3.1932
1924–25	1927–28	31.3.1932
1924–25	1927–28	31.3.1932
1925–26	1927–28	31.3.1932

* As an inundation canal system.

1921–22 to 1930–31 inclusive; but in the case of the Upper and
1921–22 to 1927–28. These two systems were thereafter amalga-
Valley Project. The Sutlej Valley Project canals have not been in
therefore, is for the years they have actually been in operation.

PUNJAB CANAL COLONIES

Lyallpur, Shahpur, and Montgomery are the big and Sidhani, Sohagpura, Jhang Chunian, Upper Chenab, and Upper Jhelum the small canal colonies. The agriculturists in these colonies were brought from different districts of the Province. These colonies represent a rare attempt at the economic development of the Punjab. Deserts and waste lands have been rendered cultivable and habitable. The State has earned large sums of money directly and indirectly out of the development of colonies and the Province has prospered considerably. Beautiful and well-planned towns of great commercial value have grown up and the very face of the Province seems to have been changed during the last forty years. The total area colonized is over five million acres, which is more than one-sixth of the total cultivated area of the Province. The Province has about twenty thousand miles of canals and distributaries, which not only insure it against famine but are also estimated to produce crops to the value of 50 crores annually. The recent prolonged economic depression has unfortunately made these benefits and developments a thing of the past. When better times return it is these colonies which will speed up the process and make cultivators forget this disaster which seems to have embittered their souls and disturbed their minds beyond all description.

WATER-LOGGING

While the canal irrigation has, by converting the extensive arid wastes of the Punjab into blooming fields and gardens, very considerably enhanced the prosperity of the Province, it has brought a very acute problem in its wake which virtually threatens even the normal life and vocation of people in rural areas. The continuous flow of canals for years has made water percolate downwards and has brought about a rise in sub-soil water. This rise in the sub-soil water recently reached such uncomfortable limits in certain places that it made life practically impossible at those places. In the Sialkot District I know at places the sub-soil water-level reached and damaged the very foundations of houses and rendered the baking of bread in ovens impossible. Water-logging conditions have appeared in several districts, particularly Sheikhupura, Gujranwala, Sialkot, and Gujrat. Although the area affected so far, however, represents only a small percentage of the total area irrigated by canals, yet as a result of these conditions, quite a considerable area has gone out of cultivation. The Government realized the nature and extent of the problem and the Irrigation Department adopted a number of remedial measures. A portion of the area thrown out of cultivation has been reclaimed. The remedial measures consist of closure of canals for prolonged periods, the running of canals as low as possible, and construction of drains to carry off the seepage water. A cure has as well been found for the reclamation of the *thoor*-stricken area, rendered unfit for cultivation owing to the salts in the soil having been forced up by the rise in sub-soil water. But the remedy is still to be tested for its practical and economical application.

The Government undoubtedly is alive to the seriousness of the problem and has set up a water-logging Board, which consists of the Financial Commissioner and the three Chief Engineers and the Directors of Agriculture and Public Health. The Board holds quarterly meetings, and a conference is held annually under the presidency of the Governor. Water-logging, owing to the defects in the construction of canals, is making its approach felt even in areas where it is not yet recognized as a problem at all. It is hoped that the engineers of the Punjab, who rightly enjoy a reputation of having given the world its most magnificent canal system, will demonstrate their skill in overcoming the difficulty that besets us.

TENURES AND PHYSICAL FEATURES

Linguistically, as well as from the point of tenures, the Province may be divided into two halves, the eastern and the western. The east is the home of the peasant proprietor and the west the stronghold of the landlord. As the Banking Committee put it: "In the east (except in Kangra) men live in villages, and the ancient village community still survives; in the west, to a large extent, they live on wells, and the strongest ties, particularly northwards, are those of the tribe. The east as a whole is the richer of the two, for lying near the Himalayas most of it has a rainfall of 20 to 40 inches, and the soil is surprisingly fertile. On the other hand, much of the west considers itself fortunate if it gets 10 inches in a year, and the districts bordering on Sind do not expect more than 4 or 5. The west would be almost uninhabitable but for its rivers, in the broad shallow valleys of which wells can be sunk with comparative ease. But there are extensive uplands between where wells can be sunk only at a prohibitive cost. Forty years ago this tract, dividing the eastern half of the Province from the western, was the home of a nomad population living a life not very different from that of the Bedouins of Arabia. In the desert *thal* between the Jhelum and the Indus this life still continues. But farther east five million acres have been colonized and brought under the plough, thanks to a system of canals which is without a rival in any country in the world. Here the central areas of the two halves of the Province meet, and landlord, peasant, and nomad live in new-built villages side by side—the landlord is too often an absentee in what is probably the most prosperous agricultural community in India."

SMALL AND FRAGMENTED HOLDINGS

The size and compactness of holdings and security of harvests are, amongst other things, the very essentials of agricultural prosperity. The average peasant proprietor in the colonies owns from 10 to 25 acres as against 5 to 15 in most other parts of the Province. The holdings outside the colonies suffer from extreme fragmentation in addition. Small fragmented holdings with great insecurity of harvests cannot produce a progressive and a prosperous peasantry. The cultivated area of the Province is in the neighbourhood of 30 million acres, and according to Mr. Calvert's estimate there are 3¼ million true agriculturists, over 80 per cent of whom cultivate less than 15 acres. The small area of the holding at the disposal of a cultivator leads Mr. Calvert to conclude that "the Punjab cultivator is essentially the man with one plough."

LAND VALUES

The price of land has risen more than fourfold since the beginning of the twentieth century, and stood at Rs. 420 per acre in 1930–31, but has on account of the recent depression touched a very low figure. As the cultivator borrows not according to his needs but his means as a result of a rise in the value of land his total indebtedness has considerably increased.

VALUE OF CROPS

"The average annual value of the agricultural produce of the Punjab for the three years ending 1928–29 is estimated by the Director of Land Records at Rs. 99 crores. Tea, tobacco, fruit, vegetables, and chillies are not included, since figures for them are not readily available. Even if they were included, the resultant figure would not represent the total gross income of the land. A large sum would have to be added on account of stock breeding—there are over fourteen million cattle in the Province—and such products as eggs, milk, butter, and ghee; timber, fuel, grass, and last but not least, wool" (Punjab Banking Enquiry Report).

(1) CULTIVATED AND UNCULTIVATED LAND

(Acres)

Cultivated—	
Net area actually cultivated	27,549,514
Uncultivated—	
Current fallow	3,221,166
Cultivable waste other than fallow	14,716,694
Not available for cultivation	12,721,012
Forests	1,979,286

(2) AREA UNDER IRRIGATION

(Acres)

Canal (Government)	9,929,217
Private	407,039
Tanks	33,229
Wells	3,766,667
Other sources	130,904

(3) CROPS IRRIGATED

(Acres)

Maize	427,193
Other cereals and pulses	1,629,543
Sugar-cane	403,825
Other food crops	254,192
Cotton	2,014,609
Other non-food crops	3,504,496
Total	8,233,858

(4) AREA UNDER DIFFERENT CROPS

(Acres)

Rice	799,028
Wheat	907,613
Barley	629,480
Jawar or cholum	1,013,634
Bajra or spiked millet	3,232,886
Ragi	14,954
Maize	1,004,431
Gram	5,546,685
Other food grams and pulses	1,495,388
Total	14,644,099

(5) AREA SOWN AND MATURED AND ANNUAL RAINFALL

Year	Area Sown, Acres	Matured Area, Acres	Percentage of Maturity	Average Annual Rainfall, in Inches
1921–22	31,025,796	25,646,616	83	22
1922–23	31,788,857	28,513,062	90	31
1923–24	30,605,406	26,730,513	87	26
1924–25	31,721,487	26,767,204	84	25
1925–26	29,709,855	24,609,965	83	30
1926–27	30,406,941	26,179,323	86	26
1927–28	29,472,581	24,828,661	84	21
1928–29	31,961,745	24,297,824	76	20
1929–30	30,954,237	24,551,255	79	27
1930–31	30,265,208	25,122,601	83	25

(6) NUMBER OF LIVE STOCK, PLOUGHS, AND CARTS

Oxen—	
Bulls	10,659
Bullocks	3,939,231
Cows	2,418,444
Young stock	2,708,481
Buffaloes (1929–30)—	
Male	388,108
Cow	2,727,264
Young stock	2,101,950
Sheep	4,457,786
Goats	3,616,792
Horses and ponies	118,311
Mares	222,966
Young stock	70,541
Mules	31,812
Donkeys	604,641
Camels	279,203
Ploughs	2,323,843
Carts	339,088

(7) AREA ASSESSED AND INCIDENCE OF THE LAND REVENUE ASSESSMENT (1931–32)

Fully assessed area for which figures are available—	
Total	41,608,427
Cultivated	26,624,793
Total revenue from land, excluding cesses	Rs. 4,77,20,468
Total revenue from land per head of population	Rs. 2 5a. 0p.
Land Revenue assessed on fully assessed area	Rs 4,59,51,139
Incidence of Land Revenue on fully assessed area per acre—	
Total Area	Rs. 1 0a. 5p.
For cultivated area	Rs. 1 11a. 7p.

The area sown in the Province is determined chiefly by the character of the rainfall and hence shows considerable fluctuations, being low in a dry year and high in a year of good monsoon.

The percentage of area matured is adversely affected both by the failure and excess of rainfall. The Punjab peasant's ideal rainfall means a daily shower from the middle of July to the middle of August, a good shower every week from the middle of August to the middle of September, and one good shower from the middle of September to the middle of October. The total area under the plough has increased during 1921–31 by 1,309,815 acres or by 4·5 per cent. The limit of cultivation is being reached as much new land is not now available for cultivation.

LITERACY

The ability to read and write a letter is the test of literacy. The number of literates in the whole of British territory is 1,097,044 males and 150,713 females,or 100 and 17 per thousand of the total population aged 5 years and over of each sex respectively. The actual number of illiterates aged 15 and over in British territory (15,608,462) is greater than what it was (14,148,847) in 1921. The distribution of literacy according to Natural Divisions is as follows:

The Sub-Himalayan takes the first place in literacy both of male and female. Plain comes next and is followed by the Himalayan. The North-West Dry Area is the most backward.

Simla is the most literate district. Of the districts in the plains; Ludhiana, Rawal Pindi, Lahore, Jhelum, Amritsar, Ambala, Hoshiarpur, Jullundur, Kangra, Sahpur, and Multan appear at the top in the point of male literacy. The most backward districts in point of literacy are Dera Ghazi Khan, Muzaffargarh, Karnal, Gurgaon, Hissar, and Rohtak.

LITERACY BY AGE, SEX, AND RELIGION

(*Number per thousand who are literate Ages* 20 *and over*)

Religions	Males	Females	Number of Literates Aged 20 and Over
All religions	113	15	—
Hindu	178	20	357,472
Ad-Dharmi	32	4	—
Sikh	151	25	150,695
Jain	608	69	5,851
Buddhist	162	15	—
Zoroastrian	633	534	—
Muslim	62	7	233,541
Christian	154	86	—
„ European ..	706	473	—
„ Indian	86	66	17,017
Jew	500	—	—

On account of greater facilities for the acquisition of education literacy is great in towns, and for the lack of similar facilities incredibly small in rural areas, where one may travel miles around without meeting a person who can read or write a letter.

The education of the rural areas particularly needs a more agricultural bias. The educated agriculturist, however splendid his opportunities, runs away from the land and wishes to seek shelter in Government employment. A large number of agriculturists are sitting idle in rural areas awaiting an opportunity to enter Government service. They are unfortunately a dead weight on the Province, for their education seems to have unfitted them for anything other than a mere clerkship.

PRINCIPAL OCCUPATIONS OF THE PEOPLE

Cultivation, the premier industry of the Province, employs 5,340,486 males and 1,049,228 females; of these 4,537,644 males and 229,878 females are recorded as earners, and 802,842 males and 810,350 females as working dependents, while 466,995 males and 19,486 females follow this industry as subsidiary to some other occupation.

Principal Occupation	Total Actual, 1931	Number of Workers, 1921	Percentage Variation, 1921–1931
Cultivation	6,380,714	5,074,554	25·7
(1) Non-cultivating proprietors taking rent in money or kind	320,673	337,779	−5·1
(2) Estate agents and managers of owners, rent collectors, clerks, etc.	3,546	7,342	51·7
(3) Cultivating owners and tenant cultivators ..	5,320,303	4,265,527	24·7
(4) Agricultural labourers ..	736,028	463,906	58·7

There has been a fairly large increase in the already numerous class of cultivators. Increase in this class is due to (1) increase in population; (2) post-war demobilization, and (3) expansion in cultivation. Jullundur, Karnal, Ferozepore, Muzaffargarh, Kapurthala, and Sirmoor show a decrease. The Census Report remarks: "The conclusion to be drawn is that in these last-named areas the limit has been reached, beyond which the land is unable to yield a return to the labour of cultivators."

Stock-Breeding.—The total number of workers with stock-raising as their principal occupation has increased from 210,116 in 1921 to 256,564 in 1931. In addition to this there are 16,616 earners who are engaged in this work as subsidiary to some other occupation.

PROFESSIONS AND LIBERAL ARTS, 1931

		Variation Percentage as compared with Figures for 1921
Religion	102,252	−14·5
Law	10,237	82·1
Medicine	29,685	86·6
Instruction	39,023	80·2
Letters, Arts, and Sciences ..	32,230	− 8·8

	Actual Workers in 1931	Percentage Variation from Figures for 1921
Banking and exchange	42,479	−2·3
Brokerage and commission agents ..	10,299	−3·0
Trade in textiles	53,478	30·6
Trade in skins	11,222	19·4
Trade in wood	11,334	57·2
Trade in metals	4,160	139·0
Trade in pottery, bricks, and tiles ..	3,034	795·0
Trade in chemical products	5,819	34·7
Trade in hotels, cafés, etc.	12,855	214·8
Trade in pulses and food-stuffs ..	167,788	−47·2
Trade in toilet articles and clothing ..	9,445	14·8
Trade in furniture	2,898	37·9
Trade in building materials	964	88·3
Trade in means of transport	13,864	−35·7
Trade in fuel	7,785	209·3
Trade in articles of luxury	5,973	−11·0
Trade in other sorts	251,721	170·2

The districts with the greatest number are Karnal, Shahpur, Lyallpur, and Multan. Eighty-six persons were returned in 1931 as keepers of birds and bees. Fishing is a spare-time job of Jhiwars and boatmen; 4,653 persons are engaged in fishing and another 990 practice it as a subsidiary occupation.

Exploitation of Minerals.—The number of workers in this class is very small. Rawal Pindi division shows considerable numbers engaged in this class, as coal, salt, cement, and petroleum are to be found in this division.

Industry.—The proportion of population engaged in industry is highest in Lahore, Amritsar, Ambala, Gujrat, Jhelum, and Gujranwala.

The number of factories coming under the purview of the Indian Factories Act and the number of persons employed therein is shown by the following table:

Year	Number of Factories	Number of Operatives
1921	297	42,428
1922	366	46,588
1924	434	50,842
1926	548	52,648
1928	559	51,613
1930	526	49,549
1933	647	—

Class of Factories	Number in 1921	Number at the Close of 1931
Cotton, spinning and weaving ..	3	6
Woollen mills	2	3
Hosiery	—	6
Food, drink, and tobacco	26	59
Chemicals, dyes, etc. (including oil mills, soap factories, etc.)	2	13
Printing presses	8	30
Processes relating to woods, stone, and glass	3	9
Cotton, ginning, cleaning, and pressing	212	298
Minerals and metals (including foundries	7	26
Petroleum refineries and miscellaneous engineering	—	12

The foundry, oil-milling, weaving, and hosiery industries received considerable impetus during 1921–31. The foundry industry is localized at Batala, Ferozepore, Bhiwani, Farrukhnagar, Lahore, Lyallpur, and Amritsar, and is turning out agricultural implements and industrial machinery, including oil engines and parts thereof.

Petroleum wells were found in the Attock district in 1914 and yielded in 1931 oil amounting to 138,943 gallons. The oil-field is connected to the company's refinery at Morgarh, near Rawal Pindi, by a pipe line covering 42 miles.

The cement works are situated at Wah, between Rawal Pindi and Campbellpur. The Managing Company started work in 1922 and produced nearly 70,000 tons of cement in 1929. The Wah cement is consumed within the Province.

The number of joint-stock companies increased from 112 in 1912 to 285 in 1931.

Blankets and woollen rugs are produced in large numbers and the carpets of Amritsar are well known for their quality. Weaving is the most important industry. Workers in gold silver, brass, copper, and earthenware are fairly numerous. Ivory carving is extensively carried on at Amritsar and Leiah, and also in the Patiala State. Wood-work is carried on in a number of districts.

CHAPTER II

AGRICULTURAL INDEBTEDNESS AND SOME ASPECTS OF RURAL CREDIT IN THE PUNJAB

CAUSES OF INDEBTEDNESS

THE following are some of the main causes of agricultural indebtedness:

(1) *Failure of Rains or other Seasonal Calamities.*—Indian agriculture has been called "a gamble in rain." If the rainfall is timely, adequate, and fairly distributed over the country, the peasantry prospers. Whenever harvests fail on account of scanty or excessive rainfall or any other cause, the peasant, who has no reserve funds to fall back upon, has of necessity to incur debt to tide over this period of difficulty.

(2) *Purchase of Occupational Requirements.*—A cultivator stands in need of seed, implements, cattle, etc. He lives from hand to mouth and has to borrow money whenever he has to purchase such requirements of his profession. Loss of cattle due to epidemics or scarcity of fodder is often one of the chief causes of indebtedness in India.

(3) *Improvidence, Extravagance, and Litigation.*—Thrift has seldom been a virtue with the Punjab cultivator. Ceremonies connected with marriages, births, deaths, etc., have acquired almost a religious sanction which for the fear of his *bradri* a cultivator dare not defy. The agriculturist borrows heavily to meet such expenses. Improvidence is ingrained in his nature and he is improvident to the extent of bartering not only his own future but even that of his children. He has developed a love for litigation which he feeds upon borrowed money like the rest of his evils. Even the Co-operative Societies, which discourage litigation, have to lend money for litigation out of sheer necessity.

(4) *Land Revenue.*—Certain thinkers are inclined to believe that the burden of the Land Revenue is telling upon the income

of the cultivator and should be lightened. That the cultivator has to borrow to pay off Land Revenue is recognized on all hands. Members of Co-operative Credit Societies alone in the Punjab borrowed in 1931–32 approximately 16·46 per cent of the loan for payment of revenue.

(5) *Easy Credit.*—With the establishment of peace and order under British rule, there has come about an increase in the value of land. With a fall in the rate of interest the facilities for borrowing have tempted the agriculturists to borrow, not as much as they need, but as much as they can. The money-lender with his vicious system of business always keeps them well in his grip and the great rise in prices and the inflated value of land have increased their power of borrowing.

(6) *Uneconomic Holding.*—The smallness of his holdings, and the manner in which they lie scattered, combined with inefficiency in other respects, make it impossible for them not to run into debt in the absence of some extraneous source of income.

(7) *Loss of Economic Equilibrium.*—The introduction of machinery, import of foreign cheap goods, changes in public tastes, and various other factors have brought about the fall of village industries. The agriculturists find themselves now entirely dependent upon agriculture. This, combined with an increase in their numbers, makes the situation all the more difficult for them.

USURY

Usury may not be recognized as a cause of agricultural debt, but surely it is very greatly responsible for its continuance. Debts are allowed to pile up, the rate charged is such that in most cases even an honest attempt at paying off cannot but fail. We may here cite in passing a case that came up recently for hearing in the High Court, Lahore. A Muslim cultivator in the Attock district borrowed in 1882 a sum of Rs. 500 on the security of land. At the rate of 25 per cent the debt swelled to just under Rs. 2 lakhs, for which the subordinate court granted a decree.

THE EXTENT OF INDEBTEDNESS

Nowhere in India has any serious attempt at finding out the agricultural indebtedness been made. The system and forms of money-lending in India render an accurate estimate impossible. Without going into the methods of such calculation, it is, therefore, desirable to give the estimates available. The agricultural debt of the Province in 1921 was estimated at Rs. 90 crores, 75 of which were considered to be due from the proprietors. For 1929 the Banking Committee's estimate puts the total debt for the Province at Rs. 135 crores.

The two estimates in terms of revenue and cultivated areas compare as follows:

	1921	1929
	Rs.	Rs.
(1) Debts' multiple of land revenue ..	19	27
(2) Debt per—		
(a) Cultivated acre	31	45
(b) Head of those supported by agriculture	76	104

Distribution of Debt.—The mortgage debt stands highest in Ferozepore. In ten years this district has added Rs. 380 lakhs to its mortgage debt. Mortgage debt is rapidly increasing in Lyallpur, where it hardly existed in 1920. Within ten years, after 1920, the mortgage debt has increased in Lahore by 112, in Hoshiarpur by 107, in Ludhiana by 106, and in Gurdaspur by Rs. 105 lakhs.

Increase in Mortgage Debt and its Causes.—The following table shows the increase in mortgage debt of the Province:

For the Ten Years ending	Net Increase in Usufructuary Mortgage Debt	Rural Population (Year to which it relates in brackets)
	Crores of Rs.	Millions
1899	9·95	18·00 (1901)
1909	5·06	17·8 (1911)
1919	10·42	18·5 (1921)
1929	28·75	20·12 (1929)

According to the most reliable authorities the mortgage debt of the Province has increased because a sudden rise in the general standard of living has been followed by a fall in the price of agricultural produce and by a number of poor harvests. To these two factors must be added the great expansion of credit which has been possible because of the rise in value of land and the growing importance of the agriculturist money-lender. The agriculturist money-lender, it must be remembered, advances a higher proportion of value in the case of a mortgage than the ordinary money-lender, because, unlike the ordinary money-lender, his powers of foreclosure are not limited. A high rate of interest is closely connected with increase in indebtedness. High rates of interest can only be paid in good harvests combined with high prices. In seasons of poor harvests and low prices, since payment is not possible, much compound interest is automatically added to the principal.

We may have to take the total debt at some discount on account of a tendency said to be in evidence in some strongholds of co-operation where it is believed to be better business to borrow at lower rates against mortgage than to pay higher rates on unsecured debts, for reasons and notions of self-esteem or social position that weighed with the borrower a generation ago.

PRODUCTIVE DEBT

In considering the volume or increase of indebtedness in the Province we must not forget that a part of the increase in debt has been devoted to productive purposes. During the decade ending 1929, over 27,000 masonry wells had been constructed and in about four years 750,000 acres of virgin land had been brought under cultivation by Punjabi farmers in the Punjab and the neighbouring states. According to a colonization officer's estimate, Rs. 1,000 of capital are required to bring 25 acres under cultivation. On this basis Rs. 3 crores must have been needed for this purpose, and it must have involved considerable borrowings. The same applies to the sum of Rs. 2 crores needed for the construction of wells.

Some people are known to have borrowed for emigration to places outside India. In 1928 nearly four thousand emigrated from Jullundur and Hoshiarpur alone. Such people must have mortgaged their lands before they went. Besides these there may be many other forms in which people must have used their debts productively.

CHAPTER III

MONEY-LENDING IN THE PUNJAB

No genuine and serious attempt has yet been made at studying the various aspects of money-lending in the Punjab with which is bound up in a considerable measure the agricultural prosperity of the Province. Is the money-lender of any real use to the agriculturist or is he a seasoned usurer who is bent upon carrying on his exploitations as far as he can? Is he exacting a share quite out of proportion to the services he renders? Is he indispensable? Should his activities be regulated? These are the problems which are uppermost in the minds of all those who wish the Province every prosperity and desire to ensure fair dealings. But with all their fundamental importance these problems have not been studied with any show of earnestness or any claim to completeness. Whenever any such attempt at regulating any aspect of money-lending is made, the clash of interests divides the Province into hostile camps and the whole show assumes a communal aspect. It is exceedingly unfortunate that the Province splits itself up into Muslims and Hindus over such purely economic measures. This is so because money-lenders are Hindus and borrowers Mussulman as a rule.

I wish scrupulously to avoid expressing any opinion on the various aspects of money-lending which may involve me in side issues only. I claim that the methods of the sahukars have not yet been exposed and the significance of their activities has not been realized and consequently regulation of money-lending has not been undertaken in a straightforward manner. I shall, however, content myself, for purposes of this book, with giving a brief summary of the information available in the Report of the Banking Enquiry Committee.

NUMBER AND IMPORTANCE OF MONEY-LENDERS

According to the Census Report for 1931 there are in the British Territory 30,923 males and 1,191 females returned as bank managers, money-lenders, money-changers, etc. In addition to these there are 4,661 males and 88 females returned as working dependents. Thus the total number of persons engaged in money-lending, etc., as the principal occupation is 36,863. There are, moreover, 11,513 males and 86 females with whom money-lending is a subsidiary occupation, and evidently the majority of these are agriculturist money-lenders. The number of workers in the corresponding group in 1921 was 38,132, which implies a decrease among money-lenders pure and simple. But the Census Superintendent for 1931 remarks that these returns may not be quite complete, as the occupation of money-lending has become unpopular in many places and may therefore not have been returned as such.

The provincial Banking Enquiry Committee, however, gives better and comparatively more reliable figures in this connection. Mr. Calvert made an attempt at finding out the number of money-lenders in 1922. He relied, for his calculation, upon the income tax statistical returns up to 1918. He estimated the number at 40,000. But his estimate, as the Banking Enquiry Committee put it, could have taken little account of the female money-lender and the agriculturist money-lender, because the former has probably never appeared in the income tax returns and the latter has only begun to do so since 1921, when income tax administration became more efficient. Agriculturist money-lenders, excluding those who advance only against mortgage, number about 19,000.

It is not possible to calculate the number of women who practise money-lending, but the evidence of the Inspectors, Co-operative Societies, Punjab, shows that it must be considerable.

"About 5 per cent of the 2,000 members of women's Co-operative Societies apparently makes a practice of it." The Banking Committee ought to have given a little more thought to it.

As I write these lines the Report for 1929 is not with me for a calculation that I wish to make. The Report for 1930 puts the total number of women members of societies at 2,286. Out of this we know that Hindu and Sikh ladies alone are capable of practising money-lending. This number in 1930 was 580. Five per cent is to be calculated not out of the total number but virtually out of 580. Therefore, in 1930 there were 118 members out of a total of 580, i.e. a little over 20 per cent of the Hindu and Sikh ladies, even when members of a Co-operative Society, carrying on money-lending. On this account the Banking Enquiry Committee's calculation of female money-lenders is an underestimate, for in the Province at large the proportion of females in the communities is not the same as in the membership of Societies for women. The Census Report for 1921 indicates a decline in the number of money-lenders. The Banking Committee argues that if we set off the number of women who lend against this decline, we are still left with 59,000 money-lenders. "Tentatively, therefore, but cautiously, we may say that in the Punjab there must be at least 55,000 who depend solely or in part on money-lending."

"*We are upon surer ground when we add that after agriculture, money-lending is the most important industry in the Province, and that in* 1928–29 *it paid* 36 *per cent of the total income tax paid by business and industry.*"

THE URBAN MONEY-LENDER

Though it is often difficult to say whether a money-lender is urban or rural, since he frequently does both types of business, there is a clear difference between the money-lender who lives in the village and his cousin who lives in the town. It is not always easy to distinguish between the urban money-lender and the indigenous banker. Like the banker, the urban money-lender may take deposits and deal in *hundis*, but neither the one nor the other will be an important part of his business, and money-lending itself may be combined with, and even be subsidiary to, some other form of business, such as commission agency. The indigenous banker may also combine business and banking, but in his case banking is primary. This is largely a difference of degree, and other differences between the two are of the same nature.

The indigenous banker finances trade and industry rather than consumption, the urban money-lender consumption rather than trade. Both banker and money-lender advance partly without security, but the banker more often with than without, and the money-lender more often without than with. The money-lender as compared with the banker is less careful of the objects for which a loan is required. Most of the banker's clients pay punctually, and most of the money-lender's have to be pressed. The banker, therefore, can afford to lend at 6 to 9 per cent and rarely above 12 per cent, but the money-lender commonly charges 9 to 12 per cent and goes to 18 per cent.

URBAN RATES OF INTEREST

It is sometimes supposed that rates of interest vary with locality and that they are necessarily lower in the town than in the village. This is only true to a slight extent. The preponderating factor is in both cases the quality of security offered with special reference to the trouble and risk involved in a loan. In both village and town the rates for first-class security range from 6 to 9 per cent and for good second-class security from 9 to 12 per cent, and in both, *when material security is not forthcoming, they rise to almost any figure.*

The Loan Shark.—This class hardly touches commerce and trade and confines itself largely to the smaller type of consumptive loans. Money-lenders of this type deal mainly with those who have little or no security to offer, beyond perhaps a fixed wage or salary or a prospective hope and whose need for money is often too great to permit of any equality of contract, or whose personal extravagance makes them as careless in borrowing as they are reckless in spending; to such these money-lenders dictate the terms. To guard against the risk and inconvenience of default, a much larger sum is specified in the pro-note than the amount advanced, sometimes, indeed, as as much as double, but if the loan is punctually repaid with interest at 12 per cent no more will be demanded. The rate of interest may be anything from 12 to 48 per cent (or more) and varies with the security and need of the borrower.

The Pathan.—Pathan is sufficiently numerous in Lahore. He is the worst type of loan shark, and his avarice is only limited by his capacity to extort. He lends small sums of money to those who are almost too poor to borrow at all and his lowest rate of interest is a monthly charge of 1 anna in the rupee, i.e. 75 per cent a year, and his actual rate may be twice as much. For recovery he depends mainly upon personal intimidation, in which he is greatly assisted by the reputation of his race.

THE MONEY-LENDERS' NET PROFIT

All income tax officers were asked by the Banking Enquiry Committee to submit a return giving various particulars for money-lenders assessed to income tax in 1928–29. The results show that 2,292 money-lenders were taxed upon an income of Rs. 79 lakhs, representing 8 per cent upon Rs. 9¼ crores of capital invested in money-lending. The return represents the net profit after all expenses and bad debts admissible under the Income Tax Act have been deducted or taken into consideration. The Banking Committee believe that on the whole it is unlikely that the average return on respectable urban money-lending is more than 9 per cent. For less reputable types it is more profitable, but no estimate of any value can be attempted.

THE RURAL MONEY-LENDER—THE SAHUKAR

Importance.—He is even more important than the urban money-lender and in 1928–29 represented nearly 20 per cent of the income-tax assessees of the Province. In that year 5,998 were taxed upon an income tax of Rs. 170 lakhs produced by Rs. 13 crores of capital. His stronghold is in the south-east and the south-west, and in three districts—Karnal, Rohtak, and Gurgaon—he constitutes 60 per cent or more of those taxed.

Causes of Decline in his Business.—The reasons assigned to the decline in his business are the following:

(1) The legal protection given to the peasant proprietor borrower, combined with a greater tendency on his part to take full advantage of it;
(2) The rise of the agriculturist money-lender;
(3) The rapid growth of Co-operative Credit Societies; and
(4) The counter-attractions of trade.

As to (1), the agriculturist cannot now "be evicted by a Civil Court without the intervention of the revenue authority; his plough, cattle, implements, and seed cannot be attached; if he is sued, interest charges can be examined, and if necessary reduced, and when he dies his ancestral land is not liable for payment of his debts unless they are charged upon it."

He cannot easily be deprived of his land by a money-lender in payment of his debts owing to the operation of the Land Alienation Act. The land may be taken possession of for twenty years. After the passage of the Land Alienation Act, the sahukar was obliged to rely for recovery largely upon a semi-monopolistic position which made him indispensable to the cultivator, but since then two formidable rivals have begun to menace his position—the agriculturist money-lender and the Co-operative Credit Society.

Migration to the Town and Market.—There seems to be a general impression that here and there money-lenders are leaving the village. The migration began to be of consequence in the great boom after the war, when a large number of sahukars, who, it must be remembered, are generally shop-keepers and traders as well as money-lenders, were tempted to leave their villages and seek their fortunes in the smaller towns and the new colony markets. The migration would probably have been completely arrested by the present commercial depression but for two factors—the feeling of growing insecurity in certain areas, and the increasing difficulties of recovery.

Recovery of Dues.—The Banking Committee remarks: "It

was indeed the universal complaint of those we met that the difficulties (in regard to recovery) were increasing, and that this was prejudicing their business; and we were informed that in many districts they find it advisable to employ an influential zemindar friend, a lambordar or zailadar to assist them."

NET PROFIT—ESTIMATE BY INCOME TAX OFFICERS AND OTHERS

Unfortunately very few statistical data exist for the purpose; if the rural money-lender kept proper accounts the income tax returns would provide an excellent basis for an estimate; but his accounts are notoriously sketchy, so much so that with about two-thirds of the 5,998 rural money-lenders assessed in 1928–29, a flat rate had to be applied to determine their assessable incomes. In the absence of statistical information the income tax officers were asked, as in the case of urban money-lenders, to estimate, in the light of their everyday experience, what net profit a rural money-lender might expect to make over a course of years after allowing for expenses and bad debt. Their replies indicate 15 per cent for Karnal, 18 for Lahore, and 20 for Montgomery.

Five more run from 12 to 15 per cent. The lowest are 6 per cent for Jullundur, and 7 for Rohtak and Gujranwala. Money-lenders were asked at some places and their estimates were widely divergent.

I would like to explain in this connection that no income tax officer can have taken into account the substantial but unwritten gratifications received by the rural money-lenders. At Jullundur when asked by the Banking Committee, the money-lenders put the figure at 6 to 7 per cent. Well, if central banks are paying 7½ per cent on fixed deposits, no money-lender should and would ever advance his money to cultivators.

Banking Committee's Estimate.—The Banking Committee, after weighing all the evidence before it, records as follows:

"For the southern Punjab, then, it may be said that over a period of five or ten years the rural money-lender earns on the average about 12 per cent net upon his capital. In districts where the unsecured loan is more usual than the secured, and where the common rate is 24 or 25 per cent, the net profit is probably as high as 15 per cent; and contrariwise, in districts like Jullundur and Hoshiarpur, where secured debt is commoner than unsecured, and where the money-lender is hard-pressed by competition of his two rivals, it probably runs from 10 to 12 per cent. For the Punjab as a whole, taking into consideration both secured and unsecured debt, we may say that it is probably between 12 and 13 per cent. We say this with the more confidence since the return for the 5,998 money-lenders taxed in 1928–29 gives a net return of 13 per cent."

Present Position of the Sahukar.—The position of the sahukar is not as strong as it was in certain districts, but in others he is reported to be almost as strong as ever, and in the richer parts of Lahore and Ferozepur still to have a tight grip over his debtors. In Rohtak his relations with the zemindars are strained. Owing to agricultural depression the rural money-lender has been hit very hard in the matter of recovery, but his debt keeps on swelling and he is squeezing out whatever he can besides renewals of debt.

THE AGRICULTURIST MONEY-LENDER

One of the most striking features in the rural economy of this Province is the growth of the agriculturist money-lender during the last twenty years. In 1928 there were probably about 19,000 agriculturist money-lenders in the Province (other than those agriculturists advancing only on mortgage) and at least 1,000 of them must be Muhammadans. The tribe that provides the largest number of agriculturist money-lenders is the Sikh Jat, which means that they are most numerous in the central Punjab. Every Sikh village in Amritsar is said to have one or two of them, and the Jullundur and Nawashar tahsils contain many more. In Gurdaspur eight (nearly all Sikhs) are assessed to income tax out of a total of four hundred assessed in the Province. The only non-Sikh district where they are strong is Rohtak, and that is because of the retired soldier, generally a Hindu Jat, who invests his savings in money-lending. The agricuturist money-lender is less in evidence in the soldiering districts of the north as they are almost entirely Muhammadan.

The Mortgagee.—If we include among the agriculturist money-lenders the agriculturist mortgagee who advances only on the security of land—and such advances are a form of money-lending—it is probable that the number of agriculturist money-lenders will greatly exceed 19,000. Seventy-five per cent or more of land mortgaged during the last twenty-five years has been mortgaged to agriculturist tribes and it has been estimated that three-fourths of the total debt of the Province is due to agriculturists. All available evidence tends to suggest that the agriculturist money-lender is increasing in number.

The methods of the agriculturist money-lender are believed to be the same as those of the ordinary money-lender, but his rates of interest are supposed to be comparatively lower. Most agree that he is avaricious and exacting, and that, being to some extent in a stronger position than a sahukar, he recovers a larger proportion of his charges.

Consequences of the Growth of Agriculturist Money-lenders.—What the ultimate consequences of the growth of agriculturist money-lenders may be, the Banking Committee says it is impossible to see. A few, however, begin to be evident. The first is that he is even more of an obstacle to the spread of Co-operation than the ordinary money-lender, for he is just as strongly impelled to oppose it, and, being a Jat amongst Jats, can oppose it more effectively. Secondly, the desire to get hold of other people's land cheaply makes him more of a danger to the peasant proprietor than a creditor who has no power of eviction.

CO-OPERATIVE CREDIT VERSUS CREDIT BY SAHUKARS

ADVANTAGES OF DEALING WITH MONEY-LENDERS

(1) *Facility in Borrowing.*—The money-lender is a business man who desires to reap as high profits as possible. In fact he is out for exploitation of his clients. Shrewd business man that he is, he is ever ready to advance to those of whose capacity and willingness to repay he is perfectly sure. Borrowing from the sahukar, with those persons who enjoy his confidence, is a perfectly simple business. The money-lender would willingly advance to such persons. From others he demands material security. Lending to such people is perfectly safe. To others he lends on the joint security of a number of people. The money-lender advances loans much more quickly than a Society does, and he does not enter into any discussion regarding the use of the loan. Securing a loan from a Society is a comparatively difficult and a protracted affair.

(2) *Secrecy.*—Unfortunately the Punjab peasant dislikes publicity of his borrowings, because indebtedness may disclose an unsound economic position and consequently assign a lower social status. The sahukar flatters his vanity in that respect. The entire business is conducted with thorough secrecy. The peasant does not like the fact of his borrowing announced and discussed in committees. This is his trait of character and peculiar way of thinking, and perhaps most of the educated persons as well will be seen to be suffering from this very defect.

(3) *Facilities in Payment.*—(*a*) *Repayment in kind.*—The cultivator produces corn, and in the payment of his obligations he wishes to give what he produces. Since he lives in a village where money economy has not yet been introduced in its completeness he feels it more convenient to discharge his obligations in terms of what he produces. His workers—menials and labourers—are all paid in kind. The Co-operative Society claims its debts to be paid in cash, and converting corn into cash

does involve a good deal of inconvenience, time, and expense. The sahukar accepts payment in kind because it brings in an extra profit to him on account of the concessional rate at which he gets the corn and because of frauds that he can generally subject the cultivator to. In spite of all attendant evils and losses, the cultivator still likes to repay in kind and the sahukar accepts payment in kind while a Society does not.

(*b*) *Latitude in Recovery.*—The sahukar, as long as he is convinced of the soundness of the position of his clients, is, after exacting as much as he can, willing to postpone recovery of his loans. His relations in this respect at least become personal and he is recognized to be generous when non-payment does not amount to a wilful refusal or inability to pay. The cultivator does recognize it as a favour to him which the Societies in the interest of the spirit which they wish to create cannot afford to do. The recent agricultural depression has given an advantage to sahukars over the Societies in the matter of recoveries. The sahukars' sums are swelling.

(*c*) *Renewal of Loans.*—The sahukar lends money to the agriculturists not for their economic regeneration but for his own profit. The sahukar is not at all concerned with inculcating such moral virtues in his clients as amount to economic assets. Whenever, therefore, the cultivator is unable to discharge his obligation to the sahukar he is made to renew his bond. If he is willing to do it, the sahukar heartily avails himself of the much longed-for opportunity of perpetuating his exploitation. This seeming concession, although a matter of very great and immediate appreciation on the part of the debtor, amounts to injecting a poison into his body which knows no antidote.

It is this renewal of loans which renders an amicable settlement of debts impossible. It may be that a debtor originally borrowed only Rs. 500 and has by instalments paid out Rs. 5,000, and is still in debt to the extent of Rs. 2,000.

(*d*) *Reduction in Debt.*—A sahukar is sometimes willing to reduce the total amount of accumulated debt by a small fraction, often by a certain amount of interest. The sahukar in such cases often has recovered amounts of money quite out of proportion to the money originally lent. Even then such an abatement of any amount of debt or of interest alone, whether real or imaginary, is very much appreciated by the debtors. It is a matter of common knowledge that in most cases this abatement is unreal. But it has a great psychological effect. The Societies can hold out no such prospects, however fallacious the same may be. The sahukar thus scores a point against the Societies.

(4) *No Limit on Borrowing.*—The sahukar has his own definite limits concerning the amount he would advance to each of his debtors. But he keeps no such registers as would make every debtor know the maximum limit of his borrowing. The debtor, in fact, is unaware of any such mental reservation on the part of the money-lender. But it remains a fact that the sahukar does not advance money up to any limit to each one of his debtors. But equally important is his policy of not announcing this fact to his clients. The Society fixes the limit of borrowing for each member for various reasons connected with the objects of Co-operative lending and soundness of the Society. The uncalculating cultivator does look upon his limitation as a disadvantage.

(5) *The Object of the Loan.*—A Society scrutinizes the object of the loan, suggests reduction in the amount to be lent out, and positively discourages borrowing for certain purposes. This is an inconvenience and is sometimes resented as an indignity. The sahukar is supremely indifferent to the purpose of the loan and the debtor delights in this indulgence shown to him and flies from the Societies into the clutches of the sahukar. Due to the undeveloped character and lack of intelligence on the part of debtors, the immediate convenience far outweighs all distant advantages.

Different Rates of Interest.—The sahukar is more fortunate in being able to make a distinction among his clients in the matter of the rate of interest each shall pay. To those who have gained the confidence of a sahukar either on account of their supremely satisfactory economic position or moral reliability, the sahukar can lend on lower rates of interest than he charges to others. But while advancing the argument in favour of the sahukar and against the Societies, even those who should know better seem to forget that the lowest rates charged by the sahukar are generally higher than the highest rate of interest charged by a Co-operative Society. By borrowing from a Co-operative Society, therefore, even the best of the sahukar's clients does not stand to lose.

ZEMINDARS' DIFFICULTIES AND DISADVANTAGES IN DEALING WITH THE CO-OPERATIVE SOCIETIES

(1) *Inadequacy and Delay.*—Co-operative Societies are not mere lending agencies. They represent a moral, educational, and an economic movement. The Punjab peasant, like every one of us, believes in the promptness and adequacy of the help he needs. Borrowing from Societies is necessarily a prolonged process. Nor can all the borrower's unproductive and excessive loan demands be met at the hands of a Co-operative Society. He feels the accommodation he receives is neither prompt nor adequate.

(2) *Rigidity and Harshness in Recovery.*—Borrowing from and repaying to a Co-operative Society has a great moral and educational value which is a valuable economic asset in the long run. The Society insists upon punctual repayment, does not grant extension in the period of repayment with the comparative plundering ease of a sahukar. The borrower is made to feel the necessity of punctual repayment and the power of compulsion exercised by exacting neighbours is felt to be unpalatable. The harshness exercised in recovery of loans by neighbours or officials of the Department is sometimes really unbecoming of this great movement.

(3) *Cash Repayment.*—Payments are received by Societies in cash. The zemindar finds it easier for him to repay his loans in kind, which the sahukar is always willing to accept; of course, not because it is convenient to the cultivator, but because it is more profitable to the obliging *bania*.

(4) *Non-Remittance of Interest.*—The sahukar's debts swell

tremendously. He makes his recovery appear less harsh to the cultivator by always carrying his accounts forward. He may sometimes remit a portion of interest due to him on a loan, the original of which he has recovered many times over. Societies do not and perhaps cannot do so.

(5) Half-yearly recovery of interest and loan is resented, and this repayment is confused with payments under compound interest.

(6) *Unlimited Liability.*—Those who understand the meaning of unlimited liability have not quite an unnatural dread of a Society which may render them liable to pay for the foolishness and mistakes or positive dishonesty of others. Unlimited liability after liquidation of a Society generally tells very heavily upon the well-to-do members.

(7) *Official Visits.*—Frequent visits from the officials of the Co-operative Department cause them a good deal of inconvenience, and the visits of lower officials put them to some expense besides necessitating a sacrifice of much valuable time at particular seasons.

(8) *Dislike of Publicity.*—People do not seem to like that their indebtedness, external and internal, should be so mercilessly exposed before their neighbours and relatives. They say that with such an awful exposure of their indebtedness they endanger the prospects of marrying their daughters and sons.

(9) Members seem to think that the allotment to the Reserve Fund stands at an unduly high figure and they entertain suspicions regarding its indivisibility.

(10) Indivisibility of profits, which is advocated by the Department, is not appreciated by the peasants.

(11) *High Audit Fees.*—The annual audit fee, 10 per cent of the annual net profits, is thought to be very excessive. Referring to the P.C.U. contribution the Registrar admits in his Report for 1933 that even the present rate of contribution is paid none too willingly by Societies.

(12) Insistence on personal sureties for each loan is not always preferred.

(13) Generally the most influential people of the village

manage to get on the committees. The conduct of such people shakes the poor man's faith in the usefulness of Societies.

(14) The sanction of the Registrar for spending money on charitable purposes is in some cases resented by members of Societies. This restriction is of very great importance and is at present absolutely essential to the safe handling and proper expenditure of money.

(15) The greatest advantage of the Societies lies in the fair dealing that they ensure the borrowers. There are no designs upon their property and there are no frauds. Repayment can never be denied, and, unlike a large number of sahukars' receipts, are never refused.

CHAPTER IV

CO-OPERATION

HISTORY AND THEORY OF CO-OPERATION

CO-OPERATION implies an association of individuals for the promotion of some common economic object. The masses all the world over are steeped in supreme difficulties, chiefly due to their economic disabilities. These disabilities are a result of individualistic and capitalistic conceptions and practices of the modern society. The profound selfishness of the average man and the lack of organization among the poor render them liable to a heartless exploitation by those whom inheritance or chance has given a position of comfort and vantage. Co-operation, by combating the causes that are responsible for the present economic disabilities of the masses, seeks to ensure them a better economic life with all its wholesome influences. Co-operative association has a common economic benefit as its objective and is based upon certain well-defined principles. It should, however, be remembered that Co-operation means working together for a common end and not for any single object.

Originally it was the pinch of poverty and the desire for a way out that brought the movement into existence. But Co-operation as a combination does not necessitate extreme poverty as its basis. Its benefits cannot and have never been denied to the comparatively well-to-do people. The first basis of Co-operation is a common economic need among the members and a realization of the fact that honest combination will render the attainment of that object easier and cheaper.

In the second place, members join the movement not as capitalists but as human beings whose chief asset is their character, hence on terms of perfect equality. For the success of the movement it is absolutely essential that the act of association be perfcctly voluntary.

Various definitions are current, but definitions often help to conceal the dimensions of a conception. An assemblage of definitions, justifiable from an academic point of view, may, and I am afraid often does, create an uncalled-for confusion. I will therefore give three of the very simple definitions available. Herrick defines Co-operation "as the act of persons, voluntarily united, of utilizing reciprocally their own forces, resources, or both, under their mutual management to their common profit or loss." Sir Horace Plunkett defines Co-operation as "Self-help made effective by organization." According to Mr. Hubert Calvert, the famous Registrar of the Punjab, "Co-operation is a form of organization wherein persons voluntarily associate together as human beings on a basis of equality for the promotion of the economic interests of themselves."

There are various forms of Co-operation and different countries have, according to their needs, developed the different forms. In a country like India, where a vast majority of the population lives directly and indirectly upon agriculture, it is the needs of the agriculturists that will be felt to be more urgent. Again, in an industrial society a different form of problem will press for solution. Take India alone—the poverty of the peasant and the proverbial rapacity of the money-lender make the provision of Co-operative agricultural credit a fundamental necessity. Again, in the disposal of his produce he is exploited by a number of middlemen to the extent of depriving him of his due share. Co-operative marketing organizations must come to his rescue. Better Farming, Consolidation of Holdings, and Stock-Breeding are some of the other lines along which co-operative organization is the only hope of safety and success. As purchasers, the cottage workers have to pay higher prices for their raw materials or they have to borrow cash at almost prohibitive rates of interest. If they combine co-operatively they can get the raw material or capital on better terms. As sellers they suffer the same disabilities. They have to support a whole class of exploiters who thrive on the worker's ignorance and lack of waiting or reserve power. Co-operative association once again will relieve them of the stifling grips of the middleman.

As consumers all of us suffer many disadvantages. The average retail seller mixes the good and the bad stuff, sometimes mixes dust and dirt with good stuff, raises the prices and earns a high profit for himself, sometimes charges different prices to different people. If a large number of consumers combine in an association they can secure their provisions and other requirements with absolute guarantee as to their quality and price, besides a share in the profits of the bargain. Along these different economic interests of people different forms of the Co-operative movement have developed. There is hardly any line of our common economic interests in which Co-operation has not come to our rescue.

The basis of Co-operation as a movement has been ably described by the Committee on Co-operation thus:

"The theory of Co-operation is, very briefly, that an isolated and powerless individual can, by association with others and by moral development and mutual support, obtain in his own degree the material advantages available to wealthy or powerful persons, and thereby develop himself to the fullest extent of his natural abilities. By the union of forces material advancement is secured, and by united action self-reliance is fostered, and it is from the interaction of these influences that it is hoped to attain the effective realization of the higher and more prosperous standard of life which has been characterized as 'better business, better farming, and better living.' "

Moral Element.—"We have found that there is a tendency not only among the outside public but also among supporters of the movement to belittle its moral aspect and to regard this as superfluous idealism. Co-operation in actual practice must often fall short of the standards aimed at and details inconsistent with Co-operative ideals have often to be accepted in the hope that they may lead to better things. We have in our report been compelled to deal mainly with the Co-operative organization from a business standpoint. But we wish clearly to express our opinion that it is to true Co-operation alone, that is, to a Co-operation which recognizes the moral aspects of the question, that Government must look for the amelioration of the masses, and not to a pseudo-Co-operative edifice, however imposing, which is built in ignorance of Co-operative principles."

PIONEERS OF CO-OPERATION

Co-operation as a formal movement may in a way be said to have begun with the associative philosophy and experiments of Robert Owen. In 1844 twenty-eight poor men, mostly flannel weavers, by small subscriptions, raised a capital of £28 and opened in Toad Lane, Rochdale, a little Co-operative shop which may rightly claim to be the mainspring of modern Co-operation.

The Rochdale Equitable Pioneers began trading in the most modest way. Members would take turns to serve in the shop. Acting upon sound business principles, backed by a spirit of intelligent sacrifice and honesty, the shop did succeed in completely transforming for the better the position of millions of working classes. The shop enabled them to purchase their provisions cheap and unadulterated. It helped them to save money and avoid running into debt. The shop swiftly passed from retail to wholesale trade, and from distribution to manufacturing, building and house-owning, shipowning and banking. Germany has given to the world renowned pioneers of Co-operation in the persons of F. W. Raffeisen, Burgomaster of a group of villages round Neuwied, and Herr Schulze, Mayor of Delitzch. Raffeisen worked for the betterment of farmers and Schulze mostly for that of the artisans.

Luzzatti's People's Banks of Italy furnish us with an idea of the beginnings of Co-operation in Italy.

The chart on p. 70 illustrates the characteristics of these forms of Societies.

ESSENTIALS OF A MODERN RAFFEISEN SOCIETY

The following principles are practised in all modern Raffeisen Societies in Germany:

(1) Limitation of the area of operation.

(2) Low shares.

	SCHULZE An Inhabitant of Prussia (1808 to 1883)	RAFFEISEN A German (1818 to 1833)	LUZZATTI Italian Jew (1841 to 1927)
Position	A judicial officer	Burgomaster	Prime Minister of Italy
Type of Society	Urban. Mostly suited to the needs of artisans, small traders, and the middle class	Rural Societies. Suited to the needs of labourers and poor peasants	Urban Societies. Suited to the needs of the middle class
Shares	Shares were of high value and long duration. Saving was essential. No loans without economy and in absence of close association	There were no shares in the beginning. Shares of nominal value were introduced after some time. Close association and union were essential to the granting of loans	Short-time shares of low value. Economy and mutual association essential to the granting of loan
Liability	Unlimited	Unlimited	Limited and unlimited
Management ..	Societies were organized on pure business principles. Workers are paid because work ought to be paid. Management is in the hands of a managing committee which is supervised by yet another committee	Based on business principles combined with mutual feelings. Service is honorary. Only one committee to run the Society	Based on business principles combined with fellow feeling. Work is honorary. Managing committee and supervisory committee run the Society

Security on the loan	Personal. Movable and immovable property	Mostly personal	Personal. Movable and immovable property
Period of the loan	Loans are granted for short terms—mainly for three months—and can be renewed with proper sanction	Mostly for one year in case of loan for agricultural purposes and for longer periods for land improvement or payment of old debts	For short periods consistent with the nature of the business
Dividend	Dividends are paid. The business view predominates	No dividends are paid. Profits are paid and those, too, for public welfare	Moderate dividends are paid but the idea of earning a dividend is deprecated
Objects	Purely economic	Economic, Moral, and social	Economic, moral, and social
Remarks	Not based on pure co-operative principles	Based on purely co-operative principles	Based on purely co-operative principles

(3) Permanent indivisible reserve fund.

(4) Unlimited liability.

(5) Loans only for productive or provident purposes.

(6) Loans only to members.

(7) Credit for relatively long periods with payment by instalments.

(8) Determination every year by the members of each society of (*a*) the maximum credit of individual members; (*b*) the maximum total of saving deposits receivable; (*c*) the maximum total of loans that may be taken up.

(9) Absence of profit-seeking, dividends if paid being limited as a maximum to the rate of interest paid by borrowers for loans.

(10) Office-holders (except secretary) not paid for their services.

(11) Promotion of the moral as well as the material advancement of members.

ESSENTIALS OF A CO-OPERATIVE CREDIT SOCIETY

(1) Every member must have a knowledge of the principles of Co-operation.

(2) Members must be selected in the first place with due regard to their honesty. "The first essential is the careful selection as members of honest men, or at any rate of men who have given satisfactory guarantees of their intention to lead an honest life in future."

(3) The Society should lend to its members only.

(4) Loans must always be given for productive and never for speculative purposes.

(5) Loans for essentials of daily life, such as necessaries, can fairly be classed as productive.

(6) The borrower must satisfy the members that he is in a position to repay the loan from an increase in his income consequent upon the productive use of the loan, or

(7) That by the exercise of thrift he can effect a margin of

saving which will enable him to repay the instalments of his loan as they fall due.

(8) The mutual watch of all members should ensure that the loan is being applied to the purpose for which it was made.

(9) Whenever a loan is being misapplied it should be at once recalled.

(10) The general supervision of a member or two by making them sureties for the loan. There should be a committee of management with a President and a Secretary for the conduct of the more general matters of the Society's business, elected out of the general body of members, and should render free service to the Society.

(11) The ultimate authority should never be delegated to the office-bearers but should be retained in the hands of the members.

(12) The constitution of the Society should be purely democratic; each member must have one vote only, and all business must be transacted with the maximum publicity within the Society. For example, there should be kept in some place open to the inspection of every member a list showing the loans issued to each member, the names of his sureties and the amount of the loan still unpaid, and each member should be required to know generally how his account stands; general meetings should be frequently held at which the accounts and affairs of the Society are fully discussed and explained.

(13) The express object of the Society should be the development of thrift among its members, with the hope, too, that this idea of thrift will spread in the neighbourhood.

(14) The development of thrift and of a proprietary interest in the Society should be aided by efforts to build up as soon as possible a strong reserve fund from profits.

(15) The Society must also be encouraged to obtain as much as possible of its capital from the savings which its teaching and example have brought among its members and their neighbours.

(16) With all these must go the elementary business principles of honesty, punctuality, proper accounts, diligence, and payment when due.

To ensure all this there must be adequate control from within, increasing vigilance and supervision by office-bearers, and a continuous effort by members in learning the principles of Co-operation, in meeting frequently, in watching others, in working hard and observing thrift, and in punctual repayment of their own loans as they fall due.[1]

[1] Abridged from the Maclagan Committee Report.

CHAPTER V

CO-OPERATION IN INDIA

NEED FOR THE ESTABLISHMENT OF CO-OPERATIVE CREDIT SOCIETIES

WITH the consolidation of British power and administration in India the old economy of the country suffered a violent and an all-embracing change. Growth of population and the decay of joint family system resulted in subdivision and fragmentation of holdings which rendered agriculture an unpaying venture.

The export of agricultural produce brought good profits to the middleman and comparatively little to the producer. The new system of land revenue rendered it imperative for the cultivator to sell his produce without delay and therefore at low prices. The introduction of a new system of law and administration entirely changed the nature of money-lending and created unprecedented opportunities for the exploitation of the needy son of the soil by the cunning sahukar. All this came with a stunning suddenness and seemed to cut into the very bones of the peasantry. Many and various were the convulsions that followed this change. The Government tried a number of measures, such as restrictions on alienation of land, usury laws, and State loans with a view to relieving the distress of the agriculturists, but with not much success.

The situation in the Bombay Presidency assumed an unparalleled gravity in 1875. A large number of the inhabitants of forty-five villages in Poona and of twenty-two villages in Ahmad Nagar showed active and open hostility against the money-lenders. The mob attacked the money-lending classes and forced them to surrender the bonds and other securities and burnt those documents openly. The riots could only be quelled with the aid of the military.

This made the Government realize the gravity of the situation and a number of measures giving assistance to the cultivators and seeking to check the rapacity of the money-lender were passed. But these measures proved highly inadequate. The nature of the problem to be handled and the right solution of it were discussed in the Famine Commission Report of 1901.

Recommendation of the Famine Commission of 1901:

". . . But, owing to causes, which it would be tedious to trace, the sahukar or *bania* has, from being a help to agriculture, become in some places an incubus upon it. The usurious rates of interest that he charges and the unfair advantage that he takes of the cultivator's necessities and ignorance have, over large areas, placed a burden of indebtedness on the cultivator which he cannot bear. Passed on from father to son, and continually swollen in the process by compound interest, this burden of indebtedness has become hereditary and retains the cultivating classes in poverty, from which there is no escape that we can perceive, except through State assistance or the discovery of some other means by which the cultivator may get, on easier terms, the accommodation that he needs. But even the fuller measure of State aid in the shape of *takavi* loans, which we shall recommend, will go but a small way towards removing the difficulties of the whole class.

"Government cannot possibly finance all the cultivators of a district, still less of a province. In the establishment of Mutual Credit Associations lies a large hope for the future of agriculture in India; and from the inquiries we have made there is reason to believe that, if taken up and pressed with patience and energy, such associations may be successfully worked."

The Stagnation of the Lower Classes in India.—The Maclagan Committee Report, attempting to explain the object of the movement, gave the following description of the stagnation of the lower classes as a basis which necessitated the introduction of Co-operation in this country. "As the aims of the movement have not always been clearly apprehended, we consider it desirable to explain at the outset that the chief object of Co-operation in India was to deal with the stagnation of the poorer classes, and more especially of the agriculturists, who constitute the bulk of the population. It was found in many parts of India, as in most European countries, that in spite of the rapid growth of commerce and improvements in communications the economic condition of the peasants had not been progressing as it should have done, that indebtedness instead of decreasing had tended to increase, that usury was still rampant, that agricultural methods had not improved, and that the old unsatisfactory features of a backward rural economy seemed destined persistently to remain.

"The more obvious features of the situation presented themselves in the form of usury and land-grabbing on the part of the money-lending classes, while the agricultural classes either hoarded their savings or, owing to thriftlessness and indebtedness, showed themselves unable to withstand bad seasons and to meet organized trade on equal terms. The depression of the rural classes was further characterized by an underlying absence of any desire for education or advancement and a certain resigned acceptance of oppression from those who, by wealth or social position, occupied a superior position, an attitude which, though often spoken of as 'conservative,' has frequently little of intentional conservatism about it, but is rather due to ignorance, to a traditional subservience in the past, and to an absence of ideals for the future. The peculiar feature of Co-operation as a remedy for stagnation is that it is intended to meet not only the more obvious material evils, but also the underlying moral deterioration to which the poorer classes have so long been exposed."

The miseries and misfortunes of the Indian agriculturists in the form of acute poverty and frequent famines forced themselves upon the notice of Provincial Governments and towards the nineties of the last century developed into a formidable problem which no Government, even in its own interest, could ever afford to neglect. It was the perplexing poverty and increasingly alarming indebtedness of the Madras cultivators that prompted the Government of that Presidency to find a way out of the distress. The Madras Government, grasping the possibilities of Co-operation as a remedy, placed in 1892 Mr. (afterwards Sir Frederick) Nicholson on special duty "to study the theory and practice of Agricultural and other Land Banks in Europe and to suggest means by which a similar movement might be popularized in India." The idea of Co-operation was even then not foreign to the Presidency, as a large number of indigenous societies called the *Nidhis* were working there with a certain measure of success. Madras thus appeared to provide a suitable field for planting Co-operation in India. Nicholson's illuminating and exhaustive report, still invaluable in many respects, saw the light of day in 1897 and 1899.

The Government of the United Provinces, more or less at the same time, deputed Mr. Dupernex of the Indian Civil Service to inquire into the possibilities of establishing Agricultural Banks in selected localities. The result of Dupernex's investigation was published in the form of the celebrated *People's Banks for Northern India* in 1900.

These Reports helped to attract public notice to a cause the gravity of which had already been forcing itself upon the notice of the Imperial and the Provincial Governments in the country. Societies had begun to be established in some parts of the Punjab, the United Provinces, and Bengal either by public-spirited leaders of people or sympathetic district officers. Such Societies were registered, if at all, under the Companies Act of 1892 which, with its 256 elaborate provisions, was utterly unsuited to the growth of that type of Society which it was sought to introduce on an extensive scale. Lord Curzon's Government will always be remembered as the preserver of the ancient and proud architectural wonders of India and the protector of the sturdy, simple, industrious, and much-exploited son of the soil. Lord Curzon's Government was not slow to realize that for introducing Co-operation in India special legislation was essential.

A special committee under the chairmanship of Sir Edward Law was appointed to make suitable proposals to that end after consulting the Provincial Governments and special officers who had acquired experience in that line. Sir Edward Law's Committee came to the conclusion that Co-operative Societies were worthy of every encouragement and of a prolonged trial.

CO-OPERATIVE CREDIT SOCIETIES ACT OF 1904

The detailed recommendations of the Law Committee concerning the management, privileges, working, and supervision of the Societies formed the basis of the Bill which was passed into law as The Co-operative Credit Societies Act of 1904.

The chief provisions of the Act of 1904 as summarized by Dr. Hough are as follows:

(1) At least ten persons living in the same village or town or belonging to the same class or caste could start a registered Co-operative Society for the encouragement of thrift and self-help among the members.

(2) The main function of a Society was to raise funds by deposits from members and loans from non-members, Government, and other Co-operative Societies and to distribute the funds thus raised in loan to the members or, with the special permission of the Registrar, to other Co-operative Credit Societies.

(3) Each Province was to appoint a special officer—the Registrar—to guide and control such Societies.

(4) In view of the concessions granted to Societies and with a view to infusing a confidence in the public in their working, the accounts of each Society were to be audited by the Registrar or by a member of his staff authorized on his behalf.

(5) Rural Societies were to have four-fifths of their members agriculturists; urban, four-fifths non-agriculturists.

(6) Urban Societies were given a choice in the matter of their form of liability, which could be limited or unlimited. In the case of Rural Societies unlimited liability was the rule.

(7) No dividends were to be paid from the profits of a Rural Society, but the profits were to be carried at the end of the year to the reserve fund, although when this fund had grown beyond certain limits fixed under the by-laws, a bonus might be distributed to the members.

(8) In Urban Societies no profit could be paid unless one-fourth of profits in any given year were carried to the reserve fund.

(9) Loans could be advanced only to members usually on personal or real, but not ordinarily on chattel security, although ornaments could be accepted as security.

(10) The interest of any one member in the Society's share capital was strictly limited.

(11) Societies formed under the Act were exempted from fees payable under the Stamp, Registration, and Income Tax Acts.

The object of the Act was set forth as "the encouragement of individual thrift, and of mutual co-operation among the members, with a view to the utilization of their combined credit, by the aid of their intimate knowledge of one another's needs and capacities, and of the pressure of local public opinion," as Sir Denzil Ibbetson put it. It was made abundantly clear that the legislation in case of Rural as well as Urban Societies was meant for the benefit of men of small means and not of capitalists.

After the passage of the Act of 1904 each Province appointed a Registrar for organization, control, and supervision of Societies. Within the short span of two years of the passage of the Act 800 Societies sprang into existence. The number of Societies grew at a rapid pace and experience disclosed that the Act of 1904 was inadequate in certain respects and faulty in others. The Conference of Registrars held in 1909 scrutinized the Act in the light of their experience and future possibilities. The proposals of the Conference for an amendment of the Act were examined by local governments and finally embodied in the Act of 1912.

CHANGES INTRODUCED BY THE ACT OF 1912

(1) *All Forms of Co-operation.*—The Act of 1904 mainly restricted itself to the operations of the Co-operative Credit Societies and neglected all other forms of Co-operation, without the development of which Co-operation could not be expected to produce any lasting results. In fact, it is claimed that the necessity of introducing Co-operation in all its forms in the

country was realized by the legislators, and it was a mere "slip" that the scope of the Act of 1904 had been left so narrow. The Act of 1912 expressly provided for the organization of all forms of Societies in addition to the Credit Society so as to ensure an all-round progress of the movement and consequent many-sided benefits to the people concerned. Under the new Act, therefore, any Society could be registered "which has as its object the promotion of the economic interests of its members in accordance with Co-operative principles, or a Society established with the object of facilitating the operations of such a Society."

(2) *Change in Classification of Societies.*—The old distinction between Rural and Urban Societies was swept away and the new Act classified Societies according to the nature of their liability as "limited" or "unlimited." The original principle that Agricultural Credit Societies should as a general rule be unlimited liability Societies was retained even under the new Act.

(3) *Distribution of Profits made Easier.*—Although the Act of 1904 did not expressly prohibit the distribution of profits in an unlimited liability Agricultural Credit Society, yet it did work against an expansion of the Societies with that object in view. Experience, particularly in Burma and the Punjab, showed that the prospects of ultimately participating in the profits of a Society induced many to join the movement who would otherwise have abstained. The Honourable Mr. Carlyle, in introducing the Bill in 1911, said: "It will, I think, generally be recognized that the inclusion of provisions for the division of profits to the members of unlimited Co-operative Societies tends to bring in influences dangerous to the true Co-operative spirit. We must, however, accept facts, and not insist on pushing too far our Co-operative idealism." It was not intended to encourage the distribution-of-profit type of unlimited liability Society, but to legalize their formation. The sanction of the Government continued essential to the formation of such Societies.

(4) *Formation of Unions and Central Banks.*—The Act of

1904 had not provided for that stage of development in which primary Societies are federated into Unions, and Central Institutions are set up to finance them. The establishment of Banking Unions and Central Banks was provided for under the new Act; unless otherwise directed by the Local Government the liability of Central Societies was to be limited. A number of minor amendments besides the above changes was introduced. A registered Society could, with the Registrar's sanction, after carrying one-fourth of the annual net profits to the reserve fund, contribute up to 10 per cent of the remaining net profit to a wide range of charitable purposes. Shares or interest in Co-operative Societies were given a prior claim to enforce the recovery of certain dues.

Under the impetus of the new Act and with the enthusiasm of a new movement the number of Societies rapidly went up and by 1914 had gone up in the neighbourhood of 15,000, with a membership of nearly 700,000. The Government issued a comprehensive review of the working of these Societies in June 1914, detailing the lessons of the experience and describing the nature and extent of the problems involved. "The sums involved in the movement were becoming very large, the arrangements for financial management in the stages above that of the individual Society were becoming complicated, and the principle for the conduct of inspection and audit remained indefinite and uncertain. It was felt by the Government that it could not take the responsibility of fostering and supporting further growth unless it was satisfied that the movement was proceeding on lines economically and financially sound" (Maclagan Committee Report).

COMMITTEE ON CO-OPERATION

A Government of India Resolution dated October 8, 1914, announced the appointment of a Committee on Co-operation, the terms of reference of which were as under:

"The primary duty of the Committee will be to examine whether the movement, especially in its higher stages and in its final aspect, is progressing on sound lines, and to suggest any measures of improvement which seem to be required. For this purpose the inquiry will be directed primarily to an examination of such matters as the constitution and working of Central and Provincial Banks; the financial connections between the various parts of the Co-operative organization; the audit, inspection, and management of all classes of Societies; the utilization of the reserve and the manner in which reserve funds should be exhibited in the annual accounts. At the same time Government of India do not desire rigidly to limit the scope of the inquiry and the Committee may, at its discretion, consider and make recommendations regarding any aspect of the Co-operative movement." The Report of the Committee on Co-operation presided over by Sir Edward Maclagan, published in 1915, though sadly out of date, still continues the most reliable and standard work on Co-operation in India.

Since the introduction of the political reforms of 1919, Co-operation is a transferred subject in the Provinces, and has gathered both an ever increasing volume and speed.

Burma, Central Provinces, the United Provinces, and Madras have had the working of the Co-operative movement examined by committees of experts. Burma, Bombay, and Madras have passed their own Co-operative Acts to provide for a healthier and more useful growth of the movement.

The main characteristic of Co-operation in India is that it is predominantly an Agricultural Credit movement. It could not perhaps be otherwise.

CHAPTER VI

THE DAWN OF CO-OPERATION IN THE PUNJAB

PROGRESS PREVIOUS TO THE PASSING OF THE CO-OPERATIVE ACT

PREVIOUS to the passage of the Co-operative Societies Act of 1904, it was in Multan and Mianwali, two districts alone, that an effort had been made by officials to induce the people to organize themselves with a view to securing at least the material benefits of Co-operation. Mr. Maclagan, who in 1920 rose to the Governorship of the Punjab, and Captain Crosthwaite founded three Societies in the Multan District in 1898.

These were short-lived Societies. One of these would undoubtedly have succeeded if its sources of official assistance had not dried up. Captain Crosthwaite began organizing Co-operative Societies in the Bhakkar subdivision of the Mianwali District in 1900. At the time the Registrar started work in the Punjab five such Societies were flourishing under the fostering influence of their founders. It was discovered by the Registrar, in 1905, that in Hoshiarpur District a Society had been in existence since 1892. This Society, at the commencement of the Co-operative movement in the Punjab, was found to be the oldest and the most prosperous. One characteristic feature of the Society was that it had never received any official help. A description of this Society appears in the next chapter.

This brief sketch of the activities of the two Punjab officers will suffice to illustrate the fact that prior to the passage of the Co-operative Societies Act the Co-operative movement had been practically non-existent in the Punjab.

Mr. M. S. D. Butler, a Punjab civilian (afterwards Governor, Central Provinces), was appointed Registrar Co-operative Credit Societies, Punjab, and assumed charge of his new office on September 19, 1904. On his taking up an appointment under the Government of India, Mr. Wilberforce assumed charge of the newly created department on October 26, 1904. He spent about the first five months of his term in setting up an establishment and in carefully laying out a plan of campaign. He brought out a short pamphlet describing the types of Societies suited to the conditions in the Punjab besides drawing up model by-laws.

SELECTED DISTRICTS

The Government of India, in their Resolution No. 1–63, dated April 29, 1904, suggested that a few districts in each Province should be selected in which, according to the Provincial Government, the experiment could be tried with the greatest hope of success. In the matter of the selection of Districts for experiment the Government of India added that "an important factor in the choice will be the personal character and influence of the District officer and the probability of his remaining in charge of the district for some time to come . . . it is the latter who must give the first impulse. . . ." Rawal Pindi, Karnal, Hoshiarpur, Montgomery, and Mianwali were selected. In the first attempt at experiment, Rawal Pindi and Montgomery had to be left out because the Registrar did not receive adequate encouragement at the hands of the Deputy Commissioners concerned.

DIFFICULTIES

The Registrar's first difficulty was concerning the lack of information not only regarding the principles of Co-operation, which difficulty still continues to a great extent, but also concerning the Co-operative Credit Societies Act. The Registrar says that a vast majority of the agriculturists had not even heard of the Act and he did not meet a single individual who even if he had heard of it had even read it. Improved means of communication and more frequent contact between the town and the country, no doubt, have created a desire for knowledge, but the ignorance of the Punjab agriculturist is still colossal. This distance of time (thirty long years) has not appreciably improved matters so far as a knowledge of similar measures to-day is concerned. One of the greatest obstacles to improvement of life in India is our love of ignorance. We are still in a stage of civilization when knowledge has got to be pumped into unwilling minds, and the poor Punjab peasant makes no exception to this rule.

Most of the people who know anything about it had merely heard a rumour that the Government was about to relieve their indebtedness. The Registrar, therefore, in the first instance, with a view to introducing the movement, set himself the fundamental task of spreading information about it and correcting such misapprehensions as had been created owing to rumours that had become current on the passage of the Act. The Registrar "held a few large and several small meetings of agriculturists and privately instructed a large number of men of local prominence in the Co-operative idea in general and the types of Societies suitable to their special needs."

As holding of meetings everywhere was not possible and lectures did not ensure a permanent record of the teaching, the Registrar brought out an explanatory pamphlet on the subject with model by-laws, and arranged for its free distribution in large numbers. This was, in fact, the only source of information for District Officers whose active help and genuine sympathy was absolutely essential to making a beginning in this direction.

A Naib-tahsildar was appointed as the Registrar's Personal Assistant and within a couple of years was replaced by an E.A.C. The District Officers were supplied with a copy of the Government of India Resolution No. 1–63, 3, dated April 29, 1904, and all official papers connected with the objects and handling of the movement. The District Officers helped mostly through such of their subordinates as were expected to understand the people concerned fairly well. A very interesting but nevertheless an embarrassing situation was created by the misguided activities of two Tahsildars at Kaithal and Tahnesir in the Karnal District. This episode at this distance of time is, I think, amusing enough to bear quoting. It has its own importance even now, inasmuch the situation has not much altered in many respects during the last thirty years.

AN AMUSING EXPERIENCE

"These Tahsildars received some excellent instructions from the Deputy Commissioner, but entirely misunderstood their purpose. They thought that it was a Government order that Societies should be started everywhere, and without the least comprehension of the nature of the scheme proceeded to take energetic and active measures. The Tahsildar of Kaithal explained to a large meeting of the zaildars and lambardars that the Registrar was arriving shortly and that before his arrival they must each send in applications to be entered. . . . In the other three cases the coerced contributors were practically all in debt and naturally saw no advantage in borrowing Rs. 50 or Rs. 100 at 27 per cent from a money-lender to finance a Society in which they took no interest and of which they had no knowledge. . . . The misguided action of the Tahsildar has to a certain extent discredited the scheme in Thanesar and Kaithal."

CHAPTER VII

TYPES OF SOCIETIES RECOMMENDED

THE PANJAWAR SOCIETY

THE Registrar discovered, during his propaganda tours in 1905, the existence of a Society at Panjawar in the Una Tehsil of Hoshiarpur District. This Society had not only never been fostered by Government officials but had worked quite unnoticed for a whole decade. This Society had been organized by Rajputs at Panjawar, a village situated on the inner slopes of the Sawaliks. The Registrar, in his first Annual Report, gave the following brief sketch of its progress and constitution, which he thought would not be out of place.

The voluntary character and the practical success of the Society gives to this venture an historical significance of its own and the story of the valiant effort well deserves to be retold.

"This Society was formed in 1892 and joined by all the landowners of the village, now fifty-five in number. The cause of the formation of this Society was as follows: The undivided common land belonging to the village consisted of about 1,500 acres. Of this about ninety acres of sandy, stony soil had been recently thrown up on the Panjawar side by the Sohan and was in almost daily danger of being washed away. Light crops were raised on parts of it without any thought of the future. The rest of the common land was exposed to the attack of hill torrents (*chos*) and was being cultivated in the same improvident manner and was rapidly deteriorating. A large part of the village property was thus becoming worthless, and there was every indication that this process would continue. Protective measures were obviously required, and it was equally obvious that even in the improbable contingency of individuals taking such measures disjointed efforts would be wasted. The only chance of any improvement lay in combined action. Fortunately, there was a clear-sighted man in the village, Mian

Hira Singh, the lambardar, who realized the situation himself and considered it his duty to impress it on his improvident neighbours. He also saw an opportunity of relieving the village from its fast increasing indebtedness. Mortgages of over Rs. 10,000 had already been effected.

"He thought out a scheme calculated to counteract both these evils and after much difficulty he induced his fellow-villagers to accept it. His scheme was that the whole of the common land should be handed over to a Committee of Management for a considerable period and that its income should be employed (1) in managing and improving the common land, (2) in making ordinary advances, and generally for the improvement of the village, (3) in taking over the mortgages held by outsiders on behalf of the mortgagors. The whole of the undivided common land was therefore handed over for thirty years to a committee elected by the members for management and for applying the income according to Hira Singh's scheme.

"At the end of thirty years partial or total disruption can take place according to the wish of the majority. It seems certain, however, that a considerable sum will be retained as the capital of a permanent Village Society.

"To begin with the total income was small and was practically all spent on improvements to the common land. In the first year the balance was only Rs. 109, last year it was Rs. 2,200. No cultivation was permitted at first on the land thrown up by the Sohan. Most of this is now under cultivation and improving yearly. For the first few years the Committee, ably led by Hira Singh, spent most of their funds in securing this land by planting *kharkana* grass and trees at the spots most liable to attack. They allowed the land to settle down instead of weakening it by cultivation. The result is that they have made themselves practically secure in the possession of this valuable property. They have in the same way arrested the attacks of the hill torrents and cut down their damage to an extent not attempted elsewhere and have rescued much land which was previously worthless. They have planted altogether 100,000 trees, nearly all *shisham*.

"At the end of the thirty years their value at the lowest computation will be Rs. 3,00,000. Besides these improvements they have taken over all the land mortgaged to outsiders at a cost of over Rs. 10,000 and have now about Rs. 3,000 out on short loans at 6 per cent.

"As their object in taking over these mortgages has been to benefit the mortgagor, they have returned to him at once as much as they can without actual loss to the Society. As a general rule, they have returned nearly half of the land at once. At the end of the period the mortgagors will receive the rest of their land without payment, as their shares of the total funds will certainly exceed the amount of the mortgage. They have also sacrificed a large amount of income; for instance, they have made gratuitous distribution of seed in bad years, and paid Government revenue without asking for repayment. They have also had to meet the expenses of a lawsuit, in which they have succeeded, over the largest of the mortgages. Fortunately, one of their members is a public-spirited vakil who has given his services for nothing.

"All these results have been attained on an income averaging about Rs. 1,500 a year and mainly through the efforts of a man of poor education, though of great organizing ability.

"Partly because the Committee has the practical monopoly of money-lending in the village and partly from the influence which it possessed originally and has since increased, it has been able to control the domestic affairs, including the marriage expenditure of its members. Hira Singh tells me that his interference in the domestic affairs of the village is the Society's most popular feature. His opinion is that there is no one more pleased than the borrower who gets an advance of Rs. 150 when he asks for an advance of Rs. 1,000. . . ."

The Shamlat Society founded by Hira Singh came to a close after a long and a useful life during which it accumulated about Rs. 70,000. The members of the Society collectively received a profit amounting to Rs. 58,000, and the rest of the money was spent on improving the village in various ways. The working of this Society had so demonstrated the fruits of Co-operation that the Shamlat Society was replaced by a Credit Society in 1920. The membership of the Panjawar Credit Society is now over 120 and its working capital has shot up to Rs. 97,000. The Society has so won the confidence of the public that it has been able to attract Rs. 84,000 by way of deposits at the exceedingly low rate of 2½ per cent.

The Society has created a love for thrift, and even women's deposits in the Society amount to Rs. 7,000. The most gratifying part of the story is that S. Rajendar Singh, son of the late Sardar Hira Singh, is now the guiding spirit of the movement. A Banking Union has recently been established at Panjawar which will always be remembered as a monument to the sagacity and great practical common sense and foresight of a Punjab village leader who had received no education in the modern sense.

THE MIANWALI SOCIETIES

The methods of the Mianwali Societies were thought out by Messrs. Maclagan and Captain Crosthwaite in 1898 in Multan and underwent further elaboration at the hands of Captain Crosthwaite in the Bhakhar subdivision of the Mianwali District.

The capital of these Societies was raised by voluntary subscriptions in kind collected at the end chiefly of the *Rabbi* harvest, *Kharif* being of no significance in the district. The value of grain subscribed was credited to the member's account and was not returnable until after the expiry of ten years. A portion of the grain contributions was kept to be utilized as seed advances for the next season and the rest of it was converted into cash to make money available for ordinary advances. The loans in the beginning were advanced only for purchase of seed and cattle and as more funds accumulated loans could be granted for other purposes. Interest charged by a Society varied from 5 to 16 per cent and was generally payable in grain. The Societies' profits consisted of cash interest realized and of the difference between the price of grain at the sowing and harvesting seasons in the case of advances for sowing. These profits form the indivisible capital of a Society which, after registration in 1905, the Registrar thought could be increased by the cash subscription of a few wealthier members who did not intend to withdraw them.

The rules of management were of the usual Raffeisen type. The Registrar keenly appreciated the basis and the working of Societies and wrote as follows: "For a poor Muhammadan community this type of Society is peculiarly suitable. The members learn a splendid lesson in the advantages of thrift and combination for the permanent advantage of the village. As no interest is taken by the subscribers, a great stumbling-block of rigid Muhammadans is also removed."

THE DEPOSIT SOCIETY

The Money Deposit Society advocated by the Registrar was unlike the one in vogue in Germany then. It was of the type contemplated by Act X of 1904. The Society had no share capital. Its capital consisted of the fixed deposits bearing interest, raised chiefly from the members. Money thus collected was advanced to members on a higher rate than the one paid to the depositors. The profits were carried to a reserve fund which was indivisible.

The Registrar recommended the Panjawar type of Society as most suited to villages which possess undivided common land or *Shamilat*. But such villages, owing to constant sub-divisions, were very few. The Mianwali type was recommended for adoption by poor communities who had to create capital. The Money Deposit Society was recommended as best for the more prosperous villages of the Central Punjab.

THE NUMBER OF SOCIETIES STARTED

During the year 1905 much could not be accomplished owing to necessary preliminary requisites of a new establishment and propaganda work. In the Karnal District four Societies of the deposit type were started. In Hoshiarpur District three Societies were started, two of which were of the deposit type and one of the Mianwali type. In the Mianwali District five Societies previously started by Captain Crosthwaite were registered. Montgomery District made a start with only one Society at Syadwala. The total number of Societies started was thirteen.

THE EVOLUTION OF A NEW TYPE OF SOCIETY

For the success of the Co-operative movement in every country experience had proved that due allowance must be made for local conditions, and the Registrar of the Punjab, during the first three years of the movement, attempted to discover a type of Society which would recommend itself strongly to the Punjab peasant. He discovered very soon some glaring fundamental defects in the types of Societies organized in the beginning.

DEFECTS IN THE DEPOSIT SOCIETY

Deposit Societies depended for their working on the capital supplied by wealthier agriculturists at what turned out to be short-term deposits or at best borrowed from outside at the risk of such people. This capital was utilized almost entirely by the poor cultivators of the soil. These Societies worked more like philanthropic establishments rather than as business institutions. The Hindu investor, or, to give him his proper name, the money-lender, could not expect the same return on his capital as he had been used to enjoy. The suggestion of investment in a rival institution appeared quite revolting to his nature. The Mussulman, unswayed by any considerations of return for his deposits, did not like to risk his savings for nothing. As the Registrar remarks, "Mussulman often prefers private to public charity." Capital could, of course, be borrowed from the outside market, but it would have meant an increased liability of the wealthier members, besides all the trouble of management, with little or no profits.

Nor was this all. That being a purely experimental stage, there seem to have been some misgivings as to the repayment of the money deposited by such people as had enough and to spare. But evidently confidence in a Society's power of recovery was lacking. Mr. Wilberforce, the first Registrar of Co-operative Societies, was of the opinion that: "If the Government would be responsible for the recovery of loans such Societies would undoubtedly succeed and soon obtain a monopoly of money-lending."

THE MIANWALI SOCIETY

With its small annual grain subscriptions the Mianwali type of Society appealed only to the backward Muhammadans, who were thus expected to learn creating capital which, if continued, would enable members to accumulate enough to suffice for their scanty needs. Evidently such a primitive procedure giving not very adequate results could not sufficiently recommend itself to "the more intelligent agriculturists of the Central Punjab."

The successful working of a Society depends upon its management. The Mianwali type of Society allowed no interest, even on deposits. This lack of return on investment killed all incentive for the membership of such a Society by the more prosperous and intelligent men without whom management would suffer hopelessly.

An experience of only a couple of years made the Registrar realize: "Neither of these two types of Societies is ever likely to attract the idle capital and large savings of the few wealthy men as well as the small savings of the poor majority. Until a Society can attract the savings of all classes and encourage thrift it is certainly not most suitable for the circumstances."

The new Punjab Society was an adaptation of the Luzzatti model popularized by Signor Luzzatti in Italy. In the new Punjab Society thus evolved every member was required to acquire at least one share. He could acquire more if he was willing, provided his financial position admitted of it. Payment of a share or shares accquired was through annual instalments spread over a period of ten years. The acquisition of a share in a Society would compel a member to show a tangible interest in the welfare of the Society, and the annual payment towards the acquisition of that share would provide an incentive towards saving.

No dividends were to be declared for ten years, after which period three-quarters of the profits were to be divided amongst the shareholders. One-fourth of the profits left after payment to the shareholders was to be transferred to the reserve fund, which would be made available for the general purposes of the Society. (The amount paid for purchase of shares is repayable at the end of ten years, though the interest of shareholders and their rights to receive dividends will continue.)

As confidence in the ability of the Society and appreciation of its advantages increase I hope that this by-law will be altered. These Societies usually lent at about 9 per cent and paid 5 per cent on fixed deposits.

In the new type of Society the whole of the reserve could be used as working capital. The Registrar, while believing this active use of the reserve to be against the spirit of the Act and that of the German Co-operative enthusiasts, found solace in the opinion expressed on this subject by H. W. Wolff. With reference to share banks with or without limited liability he says: "Most Co-operative Banks make their reserve fund available for employment in their own business, and this is perfectly legitimate." With regard to the Raffeisen type of bank he says: "Even their reserve funds are as in the case of share banks rightly held to be employable in loans."

ADVANTAGES CLAIMED FOR THE NEW SOCIETY

The new organization of Society made it possible for a Society to be supported by genuine popular feeling besides being based upon the material interest of the members. The Society enabled the cultivator to borrow at a lower rate than one he had to pay to the money-lender. This tended to increase his material prosperity. But more significant than the enhancement of material welfare is the cultivation of thrift, a virtue which constitutes the greatest failing of the Punjab peasant. The

Registrar, in explaining the attraction of the new share system to the Panjabi cultivators, said: "Depositing his money so as to gradually create a balance in his favour does not attract him. But to become a shareholder in his Society and thereby to create for himself and his family a permanent pension is a totally different matter. He looks on the dividend he will receive after ten years as a pension to obtain which he is willing to forgo all his petty extravagances. If at the same time he is able to help to establish an institution which will finance him at moderate rates of interest, when he desires to borrow, the advantage of his investment is doubled." This new type of Society was devised not by Government officials but by zemindars of Gurdaspur District.

CHAPTER VIII

PRIMARY AGRICULTURAL CO-OPERATIVE CREDIT SOCIETIES

AREA OF OPERATION

MUTUAL knowledge of character, assets, and inclinations of the members of a Society is the very foundation upon which a Society is built. The larger the area which people occupy the smaller is their knowledge of each other. It is desirable, therefore, that the area of operation of a Society should be so suitably confined as to allow members to be mutually acquainted and so situated in respect to each other as to be in a position to exercise an effective mutual control. "One Society to one village and one village to one Society," has been recognized in this connection as quite a sound principle. In certain cases an exception has to be made and we find that with an increase in membership in big villages the Society becomes quite unmanageable.

In a village, therefore, where the volume of population prevents the acquisition of mutual knowledge by members and where, on account of unwieldy membership, there is no hope of success for the Society, or when a village for one reason or another is split up into a number of uncombinable sections and interests, it is justifiable to have more than one Society. In some cases where persons scattered over an area ordinarily larger than that of a village are so bound by some known relation, and are able and willing to be jointly responsible, the law allows the formation of a Society in spite of the largeness of the area.

Societies for separate tribes, classes, castes, or occupations are justifiable on this ground. The Indian Banking Inquiry Committee observes: "We agree with the recommendation of the foreign banking experts that membership of Primary Societies should not be confined to a special creed, caste, or calling or to a certain number of people resident in a certain locality." As far as this recommendation implies uniting people through an economic organization in which all have a common interest, the object is simply commendable.

But so far as it is likely to disturb the quiet working of Societies already in existence or is calculated to hinder the organization of Societies amongst people with whom interests other than the stake in a Society would not permit pooling their resources, it is obviously not of much value just at present. A graduate friend of mine, not very much interested in politics, on learning of the conviction of a Mussulman leader, kept perfectly calm. When I told him that the leader was a Rajput, he was visibly moved, for, he said, "he belongs to my caste; I must feel for him."

Elections are often successfully fought on these indefensible pleas, and this kinship of caste and creed is yet too much with us. Co-operation may break these kinships and extend the boundaries of our interest in our neighbours, but just at present it is feared in some cases these combinations will render Co-operation impossible. Exceedingly unfortunate as it undoubtedly is, it is too strong a factor (just at present) to be neglected.

The Societies of different tribes and classes and creeds are thriving in the Punjab. The essential principle that Societies should normally consist of members who are in so close touch with each other as to be able and willing effectively to undertake the proper working of a Co-operative Society stands.

MEMBERSHIP

The members of a Co-operative Credit Society shall consist of:

(1) Persons who join in the application for registration;

(2) Persons admitted in accordance with the by-laws of the Society.

QUALIFICATIONS

(1) Must be of good character;
(2) Of not less than eighteen years of age;
(3) Not a member of any other Society; and
(4) Substantively employed.

Members are admitted after election by the Managing Committee, subject to the confirmation of the General Meeting. Every member submits an application and specifies the number of shares which he wishes to subscribe. He also specifies in his application for membership a successor or successors in interest whom he wishes to nominate on account of his holding in the Society.

Every member, on admission by the committee, pays an entrance fee of Rs. 1 and takes at least one share in the Society. He then signs his name in the members' Register which contains a list of names, descriptions, and addresses of the members. When a member has paid his entrance fee and the first instalment of his share he is deemed to have acquired all the rights and incurred all the obligations and responsibilities of a member of the Society.

TERMINATION OF MEMBERSHIP

Membership shall terminate by:—

(1) Death;
(2) Ceasing to hold one full share;
(3) Ceasing to be substantively employed;
(4) Withdrawal after one month's notice to the Secretary, provided that he is not in debt to the Society and is not surety for an unpaid debt;
(5) Bankruptcy;
(6) Expulsion by the Society;
(7) Joining any other Society, whether with limited or unlimited liability.

EXPULSION OF MEMBERS

A Society may expel any of its members for:—

(1) Failure to pay the share money or debts due from him to the Society;

(2) Conviction for a criminal offence involving dishonesty resulting in his imprisonment for three months;

(3) Bankruptcy or application for bankruptcy;

(4) Any action which may be held by the Managing Committee and a General Meeting to be dishonest or contrary to the stated objects of the Society or to the interests of Co-operation, such as misapplying a loan, incurring serious outside liability without the Society's knowledge or permission or refusing to give information as to his debts A quorum of two-thirds of the members is required in a meeting which expels any member. Any money due from the Society to such a member may be offset in payment of any sum which he owes directly to the Society or through being a surety for it.

THE SIZE OF A SOCIETY

The size of a Society has a very important bearing upon its working. The small and the large Society both have their advantages; small Societies admit of easier, speedier, and more effective training in Co-operative principles and supervision as compared with large Societies. The chief advantage of a large Society lies in the economy of its management. But too small and too large Societies have each their defects and difficulties. A Society would be reckoned as too large or too small to run safely under any given set of circumstances. Surely under any given set of conditions an optimum size of a Society has to be determined.

The quantity and quality of membership constitute the two most important factors that go to determine the sound working of a Society. The Committee of 1915 laid stress on the importance of small beginnings. "The members of a Society should be few to start with, and increases should be gradual and the ultimate total moderate." Men thoroughly reliable in every respect should be chosen as the foundation members and increases in membership should be cautiously brought about. Admission to a Society must be earned by a candidate and should in no way be treated as a benefit conferred by him on the Society.

A Society in Bombay, when its membership reached about four hundred, was being grossly mismanaged, evidently because it had in this respect overstepped the limit of safety. The Registrar split it up into four different Societies, three of which showed remarkable improvement within six months of their reorganization. Mutual knowledge of the character, assets, and inclination of each other is the very basis of the success of a Society. When the membership becomes unwieldy all these essential characteristics of membership vanish, with the result that a Society degenerates into an aimless crowd. When the ideal is lost sight of and the members become too numerous for effective and honest mutual association, the fate of the Society is sealed, and the sooner all is over with it the better.

There has been in recent years a noticeable decline in average membership of Primary Agricultural Societies in India. The general average for the country as a whole was 41 in 1912–13, and a recent estimate puts it in the neighbourhood of 34. The average figure for the membership of Agricultural Societies in the Punjab was 31 in 1930. The average, in spite of very great efforts during the last four years, has not appreciably increased; the latest estimate putting it at a little over 32.

MIXTURE OF OCCUPATIONS

If a primary Credit Society is composed of members representing different occupations, it is claimed that the funds of the Society will never be lying idle, for the seasonal demand for funds by members of different occupations will be fairly distributed. The Committee on Co-operation expressly stated that such mixed Societies, wherever started, had not been a success.

In practice a tendency has been noticed on the part of non-agriculturist members of such Societies to take loans at the same seasons and for the same periods as agriculturists. The Committee of Co-operation wisely stated that on the whole more is to be gained by respecting the general limits indicated by the occupations of the members and securing community of interest. The fact of the matter is that in Punjab villages you do not come across people other than agriculturists who stand in need of joining a Co-operative Society as independent artisans or workers. Within a Primary Society, therefore, a mixture of occupations is not to be encouraged, but a mixture of Societies on an occupational basis affiliated to a Central Bank is obviously desirable.

THE METHOD AND BASIS OF REGISTRATION

The Sub-Inspector of the Department visits a village, calls together a number of influential residents, who help him to organize a public meeting in the village. The Sub-Inspector addresses this public meeting and impresses upon the people the necessity and advantages of Co-operative organization. He explains to them the implications of such an organization as well as the broad outlines of the working of a Society and the principles underlying it. The inhabitants of the village are then asked to consider the desirability of organizing a Co-operative Society. The Sub-Inspector may have to pay repeated visits to a place in order to mobilize the forces for action. When the people begin to evince sufficient interest in the movement to express a wish for organizing a Society, papers for registration of a Society are compiled and sent to the Assistant Registrar, who, after satisfying himself as to the genuineness of the demand, sends these papers for the Registrar's final approval. With the Registrar's approval the Society comes into being. The minimum number of members is put at ten.

In principle it is absolutely necessary for the Registrar not to undertake hasty registrations, for in most cases if a Society comes to grief in its early years, it is due to faulty organization. It is expected that before registration thorough and detailed inquiries are made.

The Registrar is expected to have full information about and absolute satisfaction concerning at least the following important aspects of the organization of Societies.

(1) Have the organizers really assimilated the broad principles of Co-operation?

(2) Are the intending members so heavily involved in debt as to hinder the successful working of the Society? The statement showing assets and liabilities of the intending members is to be scrutinized carefully.

(3) Is there an adequate supply of capital available for financing the new Societies?

(4) Are the applicants men of good character and is the village as a whole free from the taint of litigiousness?

(5) Are the means at hand for satisfactory supervision of the Society in the process of formation?

(6) Are the office-bearers of the Society and the Managing Committee able and reliable? These and other important questions are to be thoroughly thrashed by the Registrar before he gives his sanction for the registration of a new Society. Co-operation will not succeed amongst a people who lack honesty, managing ability, industry, and a spirit of mutual association.

TEACHING OF CO-OPERATIVE PRINCIPLES

A broad outline of the principles of Co-operation is given to the intending members of a Society. Teaching of the principles is the very basis upon which the entire edifice is to be raised. When registration has been sanctioned an effort has once again to be made by the organizing authority to instil into the minds of the members the principles of Co-operation.

Every member ought to be able to memorize the important principles so as to make these principles a part and parcel of his mental and moral being. Most of the Societies that come to grief reveal a lack of grasp of the main working principles of the movement. In Burma, the Registrar has laid down ten simple rules for action which every member is expected to learn and understand thoroughly. The Committee on Co-operation was much impressed with the results of this method of training in the efficiency of Societies. It is advisable, however, to recall in this connection the verdict of the Committee on Co-operation in Burma (1928–29). Says the Committee: "The teaching was mainly confined to the 'Ten Main Principles,' and so seems never to have progressed beyond what may be described as the kindergarten stage. We found everywhere a sad lack of knowledge of all that is meant by Co-operative Banking; the teaching seems to have stopped short at the memorizing of the Ten Principles, and the whole structure of rural credit was not understood and not explained. The meaning of credit, the extreme danger of credit in the hands of anyone untrained to its use, and the need for the strict control of its use, do not appear to have been adequately taught. The meaning of the Act, Rules, or By-laws were insufficiently known even to the staff. Not once did we meet anyone who knew all the rights a member possessed within a Society, or what powers he could wield against a bad chairman or a bad committee. . . ." ". . . The 'Ten Main Principles' seem to have acquired a sanctity which prohibited alteration, with the result that teaching seems to have become crystallized in the very elementary stage reached before the Maclagan Report, and there has been no adequate advance." It is exceedingly desirable that the organizer must have a very clear idea of what to explain and how to explain it. It will be more effective if simple rules are laid down, and after being explained to each member a printed form containing these rules is given to every member. The heads should vary according to local needs, but should, in the opinion of the Committee on Co-operation, include the following points:

(1) That the object of Co-operation is as much to encourage saving as to grant loans on reasonable terms;

(2) That the success of a Society depends on the mutual knowledge of the members and the exclusion of bad characters

(3) That the liability of the members is joint and unlimited,

(4) That loans must be properly used for the objects for which they are sanctioned;

(5) That repayments must be punctual and genuine;

(6) That the powers of control vested in the General Meeting should be known to the members; and

(7) That the source of funds and the constitution of the Central Financing Agency, as well as its relation to the Society, should also be understood by them. Every Punjab Society is given an Urdu copy of the above rules which form the basis of teaching in the Punjab.

This much of the knowledge concerning the working of a Society should be required of the members not only at the time of the organization of a Society, but throughout its existence ever afterwards.

THE PURPOSE OF THE LOAN

The illiterate, ignorant Indian peasant lacks most of the virtues that make for success in life. Wise use of money is a virtue that most people lack, but unreasonable and unproductive expenditure is inexcusable in a poor man who borrows at exorbitant rates and barters his future. In Europe a Co-operative Society invariably lends for a productive purpose.

In India the poor peasant lacks so much of mental, moral, and social equipment essential to life that undue strictness in granting loans for productive purposes only will invariably make a cultivator quit his Society once for all, hence a concession to weakness and ignorance has to be made. Members who are unable to get accommodation for ceremonial purposes will of necessity have to go to sahukars, whose clutches grip the very souls of these people. It is, therefore, advisable not to rule out unproductive debts altogether. Care must, however, be taken by the Committee to see that the accommodation asked for is inevitable and not excessive.

This policy has had a very salutary effect in bringing about a real change in the outlook of the borrowers in the matter of the object of the loan. People have curtailed their expenses on ceremonies simply because the social will as expressed by the Society suggests such curtailments.

The following points have to be kept in view while sanctioning a loan: (1) Is it absolutely essential? (2) Is it being incurred for productive investment? (3) Is the borrower well qualified for the venture in which he intends to invest his loan? (4) Is there anyone more deserving of the loan than he is? (5) Is the amount adequate for the purpose for which the loan is being advanced?

PERIOD OF THE LOAN

Primary Credit Societies have only recently realized the distinction between short-term and long-term loans. These Societies are not fitted for advancing long-term loans. For ceremonial purposes loans should not as a rule be granted for more than two years. In the case of expenditure incurred on a son's marriage, part of the loan can and should easily be realized out of the *Neota*.

In the case of loans for productive purposes the period of the loan should be so long as to allow the borrower to pay out of the proceeds of his investment. If a cultivator borrows for seed he must be made to repay the loan after he has harvested and sold his crops. In Burma loans have been classified, and the period of loan has been specified in the by-laws of the Society. Loans for the purchase of cattle, land, redemption of old debt, etc., must be granted for particular specified periods.

The newly organized Societies should not lend for long periods, for, by their very constitution, they are unfitted to bear such a burden. The Madras Committee on Co-operation has discovered a relation between the period of the loan and the prosperity of Societies. Healthiest Co-operation is to be found in those localities where most stress is laid on short-term loans, and in places where long-term loans are granted the cultivators are deeper in debt than formerly.

A Primary Agricultural Society, in the interests of its members, should not grant long-term loans. The Punjab by-laws have the periods fixed for different classes of loans.

THE AMOUNT OF THE LOAN

Every Society maintains a *Haisiyat* Register, showing details of each member's assets—an estimate of the value of his house, land, cattle, and property in any other form. New limits are thus annually fixed for each member. The Property statement is revised and brought up to date usually once a year. On the basis of this statement a Society determines the maximum borrowing capacity of a member. In Societies property is in reality not a basis for such a maximum; it is the normal requirements for a member's means of livelihood which form the real basis. Property is merely a check. The sum of normal requirements of members should approximate closely to the maximum credit limit fixed by Societies. In the words of the Central Banking Enquiry Committee: "In fixing the individual maximum borrowing power of the members fair latitude is allowed according to their needs. Such maximum bears a definite proportion to the individual assets of the member and does not ordinarily exceed 50 per cent of the value thereof. The purpose of the loan and the repaying capacity of the borrower constitute important factors in determining the amount of the loan within the prescribed limit of the borrowing power."

The Society in advancing loans should always remember that within the credit limit of a member, the reasonable needs of a member should be satisfied in full. If he has no money with him and wants to borrow Rs. 50 for the purchase of a bullock, why grant him Rs. 30 only and thus compel him either to purchase a worthless animal or be driven to the money-lender once again for a legitimate need? The average loan per member in the Punjab was Rs. 141 in 1932.

REPAYMENT OF THE LOAN

The loan is to be repaid in easy instalments and every reasonable facility should be granted to the members in repayment. Once the instalments have been agreed to no effort should be spared in getting the loan repaid at the proper time, for it is exceedingly important in the interest both of the member and of the Society. A tendency is noticeable in some places amongst members of not paying the instalments regularly. Sometimes it happens that an influential member defaults and others follow suit. All such cases reveal that the principles of Co-operation have not been assimilated. Although it is highly desirable that every possible measure and precaution should be adopted to ensure prompt payment of instalments due, yet proper regard must be had for any change in normal circumstances that has rendered the borrower unable to pay in time.

Insistence and undue pressure upon the borrower that compels him to sell his cattle or land or to go to a money-lender once again is to be deprecated very severely, for it is calculated to make a member develop a hatred for the movement. If default is not wilful and dishonest it must be honoured by granting reasonable extensions for repayment. The Central Banking Committee says: "When the borrower is unable to pay on account of any just cause, like failure of crop, a suitable extension of the period of repayment is made and no undue pressure is brought to bear on the borrower."

A tendency to effect book adjustments is noticeable at some places. The loans due are shown to have been repaid and new loans are shown to have been issued. Whenever repaying and re-issuing of loans are shown simultaneously there must be strong suspicion that mere book adjustments have been made, for the time of repayment is just the time when members normally have not to borrow.

ANALYSIS OF LOANS IN THE PUNJAB

The following table gives an analysis of the objects for which loans were advanced by two thousand Societies in the Punjab during 1933:—

Purpose	Number of Loans	Approximate Percentage	Approximate Percentage in Five Previous Years
Cattle	5,297	17·06	17·97
Fodder	565	0·87	1·18
Seed	1,306	2·61	2·67
Implements	164	0·48	0·32
Carts	88	0·24	0·27
Rent	117	0·41	1·04
Revenue	4,817	14·33	11·79
Household	708	1·67	1·69
Grain	1,432	2·17	2·08
Debt	3,978	21·46	24·97
Wells	310	1·38	1·14
Land improvement ..	144	0·63	0·86
Land cultivation	102	0·31	0·81
Land redemption	147	1·16	1·3
Land lease	104	0·71	0·48
Land mortgage	87	0·67	0·75
Land purchase	853	7·5	5·6
Building	1,129	7·05	4·57
Education	139	0·56	0·94
Trade	1,832	9·81	10·4
Ceremonies	1,367	6·36	8·0
Litigation	97	0·34	0·14
Miscellaneous	384	1·34	0·96
Total	25,157	—	—

CHAPTER IX

PRIMARY AGRICULTURAL CO-OPERATIVE CREDIT SOCIETIES—*continued*

THE SECURITY FOR THE LOAN

IN a Primary Co-operative Credit Society security for a loan should as a rule be personal, for the very object of the movement is to awaken in the members a desire for a better economic position based upon honesty, industry, and mutual help. When a loan is being granted in accordance with the spirit and law of Co-operation and when the borrower is a reliable man the loan is as safe as the borrower's sense of honesty and honour.

But notions of individual honour and respect for personal contracts do not always count with bankers. Co-operation in India must place the sound and successful working of a Society above all lofty principles. The Committee on Co-operation, as the following observations make clear, insist upon sureties for every loan:—

"It is a well-known and distinguishing characteristic of Co-operative credit that the primary security for all loans is personal. By this it is meant that it is to the man himself and to his sureties rather than to his property that regard is paid when a loan is given, but in some quarters we find that this principle is interpreted to mean that a debtor should alone be responsible for his loan, and that no sureties need be demanded from him . . . we consider that there are advantages in interposing all such securities as are available before endangering the Reserve Fund. By the provision of such securities recovery is facilitated and a further safeguard is obtained against the grant of excessive loans or the mis-application of money borrowed. The practice is almost universal in Europe and we consider that it should be made the rule in India."

NON-MEMBERS AS SURETIES

It is open to a Society to accept non-members as sureties on the assumption that such a practice widens the area of liability. This view enjoys the support of no less an authority than Mr. Wolff. "It is not necessary, as some Indians stipulate, that the surety enlisted should be a member of the Society. It will be quite sufficient to know that he is good. If not a member, he will, by his liability engaged, be adding a new outside buttress to the fabric of the Society, pledging more money for its liabilities." But this is a risky course to adopt in spite of its advantages, inasmuch as outsiders are neither amenable to the discipline of the Society, nor can they be dealt with under the arbitration procedure allowed under the Co-operative Societies Act. The conclusion of the Committee on Co-operation is:—

"It will therefore be advisable as a rule that sureties should be members, and we consider that so long as a member does not become responsible on behalf of himself as principal and of others as surety for more than he can be relied on to pay, there is no objection to members being mutually responsible for each other, either in groups of three or otherwise. We would further lay stress on the importance of making sureties realize their responsibility. We have come across cases of default in which the officers of a Society held that it would be cruel in cases of default to proceed against 'the poor surety,' and we hold strongly that there should be no hesitation in making recovery from sureties, when the debtor fails to pay, before having recourse to any ulterior form of recovery. Without such action it is impossible to maintain in members the sense of mutual responsibility which is the main safeguard of the movement."

ECONOMIC POSITION OF SURETIES

It is not adequate that sureties be merely solvent. They must be known to be good for the amount for which they are accepted as sureties. A man may have plenty of means, but his liabilities in different forms may be equally or even disproportionately large. Moreover, the point to be kept in view in accepting a surety is not the sum that can be squeezed out of him by distress and sale, but the amount which he should be able to pay without serious consequences. In assessing a man's value as a surety, his liability as a borrower to the Society must be deducted. It is believed to be a safe rule to assess a man's value as a surety at one-tenth of his assets.

TANGIBLE SECURITY

The Committee on Co-operation observe: "It is a central principle of Co-operation that security should be personal; that is, that it should depend primarily on the man and his sureties and not on his property. The idea of personal security, however, implies the power of a member to repay, and this in its turn depends on his capacity as a worker, his honesty of character, and the amount of his property. A Co-operative Society differs from an ordinary money-lender in that it takes cognisance of all three factors, while the latter looks at the last only. There is nothing unco-operative in the hypothecation of unmovable property, so long as it is recognized that personal security must be given and that the borrower's property is only a secondary or collateral protection. It follows from this that, when tangible property is accepted as security for a loan, it should be taken in addition to the instruments executed by the borrower and his sureties, and not in place of them; and we think that the existence of a pledge or mortgage should not absolve Societies from taking sureties also or from proceeding in case of default against the sureties before taking action." The Committee on Co-operation recommended that wherever necessary, mortgage should as a rule be without possession, its chief object being the prevention of the alienation of property.

THE RATE OF INTEREST

The table on p. 114, taken from the Central Banking Inquiry Committee Report, gives in a consolidated form the rate of interest charged to the cultivator along with the rates that the lending agencies have themselves to pay.

The rate of interest charged to the cultivators by the Primary Societies is the most intelligible index of the usefulness of a Society to its members. If the Society supplies money to its members on the same rate of interest as is charged by the sahukars, the manifold moral, educational, and social benefits of the movement will fail to appeal to the cultivators.

But a Co-operative Society, even when it charges the same rate of interest as a sahukar does, besides its numerous other advantages, bestows greater financial benefits on the cultivator. When we remember the unwritten charges of a sahukar over and above his utterly unsatisfactory and often unreliable methods of account keeping, combined with his willingness to let loans swell to large proportions, we can easily realize that a loan from a Society means a positive financial advantage to the borrower. All these subtleties, alas! will not count with him.

But when he once joins the movement it is obviously the duty of those responsible for the spread and popularization of the movement to make the ordinary cultivator see that the movement is beneficial to him in every respect. A lower rate of interest charged by the Society in comparison to the rates charged by other agencies is the most fundamental advantage that a member seeks, and in the beginning perhaps the only one he can properly appreciate. A rate higher than the prevailing rate of the market from which a cultivator usually borrows is out of the question, for the moment you ask for such a rate, if he has any intelligence left in him, he will revolt and bolt away. When the rate of interest charged by a Society to its members is the same as they are required to pay elsewhere there is no hope of the Society surviving the positive disinclination of prospective and the profound indifference of the actual members.

RATE OF INTEREST

Province	Primary Societies		Central Banks		Provincial Banks		
	Rate charged to Cultivators by Primary Societies	Rate paid on Deposits	Rate paid to Central Banks	Rate paid on Deposits	Rate paid to Provincial Banks on Loans	Rate on Deposit	Rate on Accommodation to Imperial Bank
	Per cent	Per cent	Per cent	Per cent	Per cent	Per cent	Per cent
Ajmer-Merwara ..	9–12	4–8	6–9	$1\frac{1}{2}$–$7\frac{1}{2}$	—	—	—
Assam	$15\frac{5}{8}$–$18\frac{3}{4}$	8	11	8	$8\frac{1}{2}$	$7\frac{1}{2}$	7
	Generally $12\frac{1}{2}$						
Bengal	$7\frac{1}{2}$–$15\frac{5}{8}$	$4\frac{11}{16}$–$9\frac{3}{8}$	$9\frac{3}{8}$–$12\frac{1}{2}$	2–$8\frac{1}{2}$	7–8	4–$6\frac{1}{2}$	Bank rate
Bihar and Orissa ..	$12\frac{1}{2}$–$15\frac{5}{8}$	7–9	$10\frac{1}{2}$–$12\frac{1}{2}$	$4\frac{1}{2}$–6	6	2–5	11
Bombay	$9\frac{3}{8}$–$12\frac{1}{2}$	2–8	6–8	$1\frac{1}{2}$–$7\frac{1}{2}$	$5\frac{1}{2}$–8	2–$4\frac{1}{2}$	No accommodation available at present
Bruma	15	6–12	10	6–9	10	5–$7\frac{1}{2}$	
Central Provinces	Generally 12	3–10	9–10	3–7	6–$6\frac{1}{2}$	2–$5\frac{1}{4}$	7
Delhi	—	6–7	8–9	4–$6\frac{1}{2}$	—	—	—
Madras	$9\frac{3}{8}$–$10\frac{15}{16}$	3–$6\frac{1}{2}$	$7\frac{1}{2}$–8	2–$5\frac{1}{2}$	6–$6\frac{1}{2}$	2–$4\frac{1}{2}$	$6\frac{1}{2}$ Overdrafts
North-West Frontier Province ..	—	6–7	8	$4\frac{1}{2}$–$3\frac{1}{2}$	—	—	—
Punjab	$9\frac{3}{8}$–$12\frac{1}{2}$	6–7	8–9	5–$6\frac{1}{2}$	$6\frac{1}{2}$	$3\frac{1}{2}$–$5\frac{1}{2}$	Bank rate
United Provinces	15	9	12	6–7	—	—	—

What is a fair rate of interest that a Society may charge? No set answer, irrespective of other considerations, is possible. The rate to be charged will be determined by a number of factors. A rate very much lower than the rate charged by other agencies is open to the following objections.

(1) *Not Possible.*—The Co-operative movement cannot afford to be a cheap financing agency. For its growth and expansion it needs must be conducted, so far as finances are concerned, on business principles, for it cannot thrive on the philanthropy of the few. The credit that the movement needs has to be raised at the market rate of interest, which implies a rate of interest at which capitalists are willing to advance money for the movement not out of philanthropic but mere business principles to such institutions in whose stability they have a perfect confidence. Societies, therefore, cannot in their own interest charge very much below the prevailing rate.

(2) *Reckless Borrowing and Re-loaning.*—If the rate of interest is very low, reckless borrowing will be encouraged. We have always to remember that the cultivator needs not more but controlled credit. The rate of interest must not be so low as to encourage reckless borrowing. Imprudent borrowing inflicts a greater injury upon them than the high rate of interest. A lower rate of interest may tempt some members to borrow large sums in order to lend them to borrowers outside the Society at higher rates. So far as the present-day cultivator in India is concerned the danger is merely of an academic interest. If money-lenders join Societies, of course with their sharp wits they will not hesitate to exploit the resources of a Society in this way.

(3) *Reserve Fund.*—Continuous and considerable reduction in the rate of interest charged by a Society is in popular expression the test of the real benefits conferred by a Society upon its members. But that is not in the interest of the Society and, therefore, of the members. A Society's first effort should be directed towards building up of a strong reserve. According to the Maclagan Committee half the difficulties experienced by Central Banks in financing Societies arise from the fact that

the rate of interest charged on the loans to members has been pitched too low or has been reduced prematurely.

(4) *Societies of Rich Persons.*—The Government of India, in its Resolution of 1914, observed that as long as the rate charged by a Society was below that of the outside market it could not be regarded as excessive. If the rate of interest were to be pitched relatively very low the organizers may develop a tendency to organize Societies among persons quite well off to the utter neglect of those to whom the benefits of the movement are indispensable. Rich persons once in power in a Society can as well easily refuse admission to poor persons.

(5) *Imprudent.*—Very low rates of interest are imprudent because they are not likely to let the Society thrive. A Society has normally to provide for bad and doubtful debts besides meeting its expenses of management. To live and continue its useful activity a Society stands in need of keeping the rates of interest not very much below the level of the prevailing market rate.

(6) *Creation of Overdues.*—If the disparity between the sahukar's and Society's rate is considerable, those members who are indebted to sahukars will be tempted to pay off their debts to the money-lenders and let the Society's overdues accumulate.

In the Punjab in most Societies the rate charged is 12½ per cent. In comparison with the market rate it is not a high rate, but it is a pity that from the Provincial Banks' 5½ per cent maximum, passing through the Central Banks and the Society to the real borrower, the rate should swell to 12½, a more than twofold increase against the person whose very existence depends on cheap credit. Surely this must be mended. The disparity between a Society's borrowing and lending rate in Europe rarely exceeds 1 per cent. In the Punjab it is 5 per cent in case of deposits and 3 per cent in case of loans from a Central Bank.

A REASONABLE RATE

If the financial accommodation that a Society gives to its members is to be of any lasting benefit to them it must be available at more moderate rates of interest. Neglect for the moment the present state of depression. Is it at all possible for the peasant proprietor in the Punjab, with his multifarious limitations, to make his industry yield him more than 12 per cent profit? Surely not. Is such a help, then, of any use to him? As long as a borrower is being charged a rate higher than the rate of profit his investment brings him, so long there is no hope for him. It is on account of this basic difficulty and uneconomic charge that he borrows from the Society to pay the sahukar. In turn he is being tossed from one to the other and for no fault of his. It is, therefore, of the utmost importance so to lower the rate of interest that it can honestly be made the basis of a better reorganization of his economic life. All the academic and theoretical objections have to be brushed aside. If a Society is Co-operative in all other respects a lowering of the rate of interest will accelerate its progress and not clog its operation. In practice a high rate of interest will take all the charm and grace out of the movement.

What constitutes a reasonable rate is determined by a number of factors at any given time.

Although no industry in India, even when organized on the most up-to-date lines, is expected to make even 12 per cent, yet the Central Banking Inquiry Committee seems well satisfied with 12 per cent. This Committee observes: "We consider that if a Rural Society charges its members a rate higher than 12 per cent per annum, it should form the subject of careful inquiry by the Provincial Government and the Provincial Bank concerned, and steps should be taken to reduce the rate of interest."

SUGGESTIONS FOR REDUCTION IN THE RATE CHARGED

The suggestions made to the Central Banking Committee for further reduction in the rate of interest charged by Primary Societies may appropriately be brought out here.

(1) Punctual repayment of loans by the members of the Society and effective reduction of overdues, thereby making

the Central and Apex Banks financially sounder and consequently able to get money at cheaper rates.

(2) Reduction of the working expenses of Central Banks in some Provinces where they are now unduly high. While for instance in the Punjab their working expenses in 1928–29 were less than ½ per cent of their working capital, in Bihar and Orissa, on the other hand, the percentage was as high as 2·37.

(3) Borrowing by Central Banks at cheaper rates for short terms and utilization of urban slack money.

(4) Establishment of more intimate relations between the Provincial Banks and the Central Banks so that the latter may follow the lead of the Provincial Banks in the matter of the regulation of their deposit rates. The Provincial Banks must be vested with certain powers of control and supervision over the Central Banks, of course with the willing consent of the latter and with due safeguards for ensuring a predominant voice to the Central Banks in the management of the affairs of the Provincial Bank.

(5) A direct tapping of savings by Rural Societies wherever it is possible.

RELATION WITH MONEY-LENDERS

The question whether members on admission to a Credit Society should be prohibited from dealing with money-lenders is one of supreme importance. Undoubtedly as long as members of a Co-operative Credit Society continue their dealings with the rapacious money-lenders, so long they cannot be said to have thoroughly imbibed the spirit of Co-operation. Any legal provision prohibiting the members from having any dealings with the money-lenders involves a moral obligation on the part of the Societies to provide all necessary credit to the members. This, even after a generation's working of these Societies, has been found impossible of performance. The Co-operative Societies in Bombay supply only 7 per cent, and in Madras about 5 per cent, and in the Punjab a very small fraction of the total annual agricultural credit needs of the people. The Maclagan Committee on Co-operation recommended "that all necessary steps should be taken to meet the needs of members by adequate and proper financing within the Society itself, and we may remark that the best solution of the difficulty is, wherever this may be possible, to induce

PERCENTAGE OF MEMBERS OF CO-OPERATIVE CREDIT SOCIETIES WHO BORROW FROM MONEY-LENDERS AS WELL AS SOCIETIES

District	Class A and B Societies	Class C Societies
(1) Hissar	5–10	40–45
(2) Mianwali and Attock	25	60
(3) Amritsar	Nil	40
(4) Jullundur	16	29
(5) Multan Montgomery	25	48
(6) Lahore	10	60
(7) Ludhiana and Ambala	5	25
(8) Rawal Pindi and Jhelum	5	30
(9) Ferozepore	33	55
(10) Muzaffargarh and Dera Ghazi Khan	25	70
(11) Lyallpur and Jhang	30–40	45
(12) Colony area Jhang (non-colony) area	30–40	90
(13) Hoshiarpur	10–15	12–18
(14) Rohtak and Karnal	30	70
(15) Gurdaspur	10	40
(16) Sialkot	30	47
(17) Kangra	20	50
(18) Gujranwala and Sheikhupura	50	80
(19) Shahpur and Gujrat	20–30	60–70
(20) Gurgaon	30–40	70–80

the money-lender to lend through the medium of the Society by becoming himself a depositor, or to convert a previous debt due from a member into a deposit with the Society at a reduced rate of interest and with possibly a reduction also in the capital amount of the claim."

The above table, reproduced from The Punjab Banking

Enquiry Committee's Report, gives us an insight into the dealings of the members of Co-operative Credit Societies with money-lenders in the Punjab.

In order properly to appreciate the significance of this table we have to remember in the first place that members are extremely reluctant to disclose their dealings with the money-lenders, and, secondly, that in the Province by far the largest number of Societies is classified as C. In 1933, the classification of Societies stood as follows:

A	B	C	D
302	1,722	12,149	1,786

This is enough to indicate that members of Co-operative Societies in the Punjab borrow from money-lenders considerably and that only a very small percentage of the members is free from the money-lender's debts. It seems unfair not to quote the Punjab Banking Committee's conclusions in this respect. "There is a general concurrence of opinion amongst those qualified to judge that the evil is due not to any want of funds in the movement, capital is more than sufficient, but to the inefficiency and selfishness of many Management Committees, and to a lack of understanding of Co-operative principles in the general body of members. Where committees are inefficient delays occur in making loans and urgent needs have to be satisfied elsewhere. And when they are selfish, they are apt to borrow more than they should themselves and, like all who do this, to default when the time for repayment comes. Others follow their example and money ceases to circulate freely."

PAYING OFF MONEY-LENDERS' DEBTS ON ADMISSION TO A SOCIETY

Is it advisable to pay off the entire debts of a member to his creditors when he joins a Society? The one very evident objection to such a course is the impracticability of the suggestion. The movement as a whole is incapable of paying off the entire debts of those who have joined it.

Moreover, such a course amounts to relieving a man of his obligations without any effort on his part. But such a suggestion has not the remotest chance of even a serious consideration when the member in question is too far involved in debt to render his extrication possible.

When such a possibility is backed by the member's character and assets, the Maclagan Committee suggest that the best plan would be to arrange to clear off a member's debts at an early date, though not necessarily on admission. How long will it take the member to pay off his debts if they are transferred from the money-lender to the Society? Can the member hope to pay off the Society? Will he not, while in the process of paying his debts to the Society, revert to the money-lender once again? How can we overcome certain administrative difficulties that are likely to arise? All these problems have to be borne in mind before we attempt an answer to the question. We must at the same time remember that this is the speediest method of bringing about the regeneration of the farmer. This has been practised on a large scale, almost universally in the Kot Estate Societies, with the most convincing results. It is, however, exceedingly doubtful if the benevolent supervision of the movement and the sympathetic handling of a farmer's problems is equally possible elsewhere.

That it must be attempted goes without saying. We will do well to recall the Maclagan Committee's judgment on this question. "If the creditor is troublesome and threatening there is no help for it but to clear off the debtor's debts at once. Otherwise we consider it is best to pay off a part of the debts at a time, as funds can be spared for the purpose, those paying highest interest being chosen first, and the mortgage debts and others bearing less interest being kept over till the debtor has been sufficiently long in the Society for his qualities to be appraised and for the receipt of contributions from himself towards his extrication. We think that a procedure of this kind has a better educative effect than the immediate and wholesale clearing off of debts on admission."

CO-OPERATION AND INDEBTEDNESS

The average indebtedness of the members of the Agricultural Co-operative Credit Societies is indicated by the following table:

Year	Average Indebtedness per Member Rs.
1920	78
1930	143
1931	144
1932	141

An inquiry was conducted in 1929 on behalf of the Banking Inquiry Committee into the state of indebtedness of the members in 3,341 Societies.

The following is the summary of the results arrived at:—

Total number of members	112,358
Percentage of members—	
(*a*) entirely free from debt	13
(*b*) who did not borrow in 1928–29	46
Average number of loans per member taken during the year	1·4
Average loan	Rs. 88
Average amount of loan outstanding at the end of the year per member—	
(*a*) indebted to his Society	Rs. 177
(*b*) whether indebted or not	Rs. 152

The Department believes that these figures are fairly typical. Thirty-six per cent of these Societies belonged to A and B classes, against 19 per cent for the whole of the Province. The Registrar remarks as follows: "On the whole they suggest that Societies are not financing their members fully; only 13 per cent of the members were entirely free of debt, yet 46 per cent did not borrow at all during the year. . . . The explanation of this is probably the fact alluded to below . . . that a large proportion of members deal with both Society and money-lender." It should, however, be made clear that non-borrowers must have included amongst them those who were defaulters and could therefore get no loans and those who, having reached their credit limits, could not have applied for more.

For a number of years the Department had been collecting information concerning the number of members entirely free of debt in cases of Societies which complete their ten years. Such figures, the Department feel, were very reliable. The last published figures relate to the year 1928 and indicate that 43 per cent of the members were entirely free from debt. The excessive increase in the agrarian indebtedness of the Province was, according to the Banking Inquiry Committee, due to excessive borrowing, carelessness in repayments and high rates of interest. Co-operation has provided capital to the agriculturist at the lowest rate consistent with safety, it has served to check his love of borrowing, and has attempted to instil in him the virtue of punctual repayment. Not only that, it has taught him the right and wise use of money. As the Banking Inquiry Committee remark: "A scheme of Government or Joint Stock Bank finance might reduce the rates of interest, but only Co-operation can teach the peasant to borrow at the right time and in the right amounts and for the right ends, and to repay on the right date; and only Co-operation can teach him to save so that he may not have to borrow at all." If the results achieved fall short of the high standard expected it is the ignorance and illiteracy of the Punjab peasant that is to blame, and as long as his ignorance continues so long must every attempt at his betterment meet with severe reverses, and, if at all, with disappointing successes. Sir Daniel Hamilton has well said: "The Indian ryot carries on his right shoulder a mountain of debt and on his left a mountain of illiteracy. Relieve him of the mountain of illiteracy and he will soon become strong enough to stand erect and throw off the mountain of debt. Education will teach him Co-operation, and Co-operation will free him from the incubus of indebtedness."

CHAPTER X

PRIMARY AGRICULTURAL CO-OPERATIVE CREDIT SOCIETIES—*continued*

SOURCES OF CAPITAL

THE capital of a Society is composed of:

(1) Shares;
(2) Deposits from members;
(3) Deposits and loans from non-members;
(4) Realized profits.

ENTRANCE FEES

In most Provinces in India it is customary to levy a small entrance fee from members on admission to a Society. The charge varies from 4 annas to R.1. The object of the fees, besides recovering preliminary expenses, is to make the members realize that they are being admitted into a position of privilege which is well worth making a little sacrifice to obtain. In the words of the Committee on Co-operation, it serves "as a proof that a member, by a definite and voluntary act of payment, undertakes the rights and liabilities involved in his admission and to discourage withdrawal by making it entail the loss of a small sum."

The Maclagan Committee did not think it of much importance whether the entrance fee was levied or not. It does appear to me that admission fees are necessary, particularly in those Societies which have no share capital.

SHARE CAPITAL

Every member must hold at least one full share. A member admitted after the first year is required to pay all instalments of shares on account of past years, together with interest at

6½ per cent per annum, before exercising any of the rights of a member. But generally the payment of shares continues its normal course when a new member joins a Society. No member can hold shares the nominal value of which exceeds Rs. 1,000, or one-fifth of the total share capital actually subscribed. Shares may be withdrawn without profit after ten years. Share capital is now an important source of the working capital of Societies with limited and unlimited liability. Share capital amounts to an advance payment by members to meet their unlimited liability.

THE SHARE SYSTEM IN THE PUNJAB

The framers of the original Act had clearly the Raffeisen type in view. In the Punjab this model has been varied to the extent that a substantial portion of the capital of a Society is contributed by members as a share capital. The value of a share is generally Rs. 10 and it is paid up in the course of ten years in the form of small half-yearly or annual instalments. During the period of payment all profits are indivisible. The Local Government rules allow the Societies after the completion of this period to decide upon alternative courses. The shares, if the members so choose, may be returned and the profits voted indivisible for ever, or the shares may be retained and three-fourths of the profits credited to the members as new shares in proportion to the old shares held. In succeeding years, three-fourths of the annual profits may be divided amongst the members. Dividend is limited to 10 per cent.

The share system and indivisible profits are expected to make a Society very nearly if not completely independent in the matter of funds. In 1933 the members of agricultural Societies owned Rs. 1,10 lakhs as share capital and Rs. 2,30 lakhs as reserve fund, and Rs. 34 lakhs as profits. This means that the Societies in that year owned 46 per cent of their working capital. In view of the above figure we are justified in sharing Mr. Strickland's belief when he says: ". . . so that it is only a matter of time before all villages possess a common fund from which the legitimate needs of their members may be met. The drain of interest to the usurer will no longer be felt. All profits resulting from business will remain in the village. and the benefits of thrift will be obvious to everyone."

In some Provinces shares or instalments of them are obtained through deductions from loans advanced to members. The Maclagan Committee did not object to this practice on the ground that shares even in this way are paid up out of the members' own profits. It does remain a fact, however, that payment of shares out of direct savings instead of as a part of loan has a greater educational and moral value.

ADVANTAGES OF THE SHARE SYSTEM

(1) The share system insures a rapid accumulation of capital owned by the members, and helps to swell the working capital of a Society. The larger the working capital the greater will be the amount of interest earned on the money lent. This will help to swell the profits.

(2) A Society needs money for the use of its members. The larger the Society's own capital the lesser is its dependence on outside sources for the supply of credit. A self-supporting and independent Society is a great success.

(3) An increase in a Society's owned capital enables the Society to reduce the rate of interest charged to members at a very much earlier stage than can be possible in the case of Societies with no share capital.

(4) Societies with a share system enjoy a great financial strength which enables them to stand panics and disturbances in the money market much more comfortably than Societies having no share system.

DANGERS OF THE SHARE SYSTEM

(1) The share system cannot be dissociated from a hunger for earning dividends. Once we introduce the share system the dividend hunter is bound to creep in. He is tempted to

join a Society and to purchase shares of the Society not because he is generous enough to let the poor have the benefit of his money nor because he wishes to borrow from the Society. His sole aim is to reap rich dividends out of his investment and all his position and intelligence in the working of the Society he uses to that end. "The share is regarded as a share in a company and not as an effort towards thrift nor as an attempt to strengthen rural credit."

(2) The big shareholders in particular, with a view to swelling dividends, combine to oppose any reduction in the rate of interest.

(3) The share capital, combined with the swollen undivided profits, may shoot up to an amount very much in excess of the needs of the members. The mere fact of money being available will tempt the members to borrow more than their needs warrant.

DEPOSITS

The Maclagan Committee on Co-operation recommended that it should be the care of a Primary Society to raise as much of its capital from local deposits as possible. The Society should work cautiously so that it inspires confidence in the movement in its immediate surroundings. Unless Societies as a class attract sufficient local capital as deposits the movement cannot be said to have succeeded in one of its very important objects. The Committee on Co-operation suggested that members of a Society may be allowed a higher rate on their deposits than non-members.

The Committee did not approve of the compulsory deposits from members. "A certain proportion of the members' deposits consists in some Provinces of compulsory deposits which the members are required to make at stated intervals. These differ from compulsorily subscribed shares in that they carry no liability and their interest is secure. The justification of such deposits is found in the view that thrift should come before credit; but in practice almost all members join to borrow and have at first no money to deposit. As a means of inculcating thrift and building up an owned capital we consider that small instalment shares are preferable to a compulsory deposit system. The Committee also suggested that only fixed deposits should be taken at least for one year, for as a rule Rural Societies are unable to handle current accounts." Members and non-members make deposits with the Primary Agricultural Credit Societies in the Punjab.

DEPOSITS WITH PRIMARY AGRICULTURAL CREDIT SOCIETIES

(*Lakhs of rupees*)

	1928	1929	1930	1931	1932	1933	1934
Members ..	30	30	33	35	34	35	32·76
Non-members	27	32	36	39	41	42	43·50

It is mainly in Jullundur that Agricultural Societies attract large deposits; the amount of such deposits, Rs. 10·90 lakhs, represents nearly one-third of the entire deposits in such Societies in the Province.

An analysis of the depositors and their circumstances would have been of great use, but unfortunately it has not yet been attempted. "One example may, however, be given. A member of a Society in Talagang, a tahsil where deposits are rare, deposited Rs. 800 with his Society, and when asked why, replied he had done so to escape having to lend the amount to impecunious relatives who would probably not repay." No information concerning any other aspect of such deposits is available from the annual reports.

LOANS FROM THE CENTRAL BANK

The Societies borrow heavily from Central Banks to meet their members' demand for loans. The loans of the Central Banks to Banks and Societies were over Rs. 3,38 lakhs in 1932 and over Rs. 3,54 lakhs in 1933.

THE RESERVE FUND

The Reserve of a Primary Society was defined by the Committee on Co-operation as all indistributable surplus profits after payment of expenses, including as expenses in Societies on the share system the portion of the profit to which the shareholders are entitled. Section 33 of the Co-operative Societies Act of 1912 states:

"No part of the funds of a Registered Society shall be divided by way of bonus or dividend or otherwise among its members. Provided that after at least one-fourth of the net profits in any year have been carried to a Reserve Fund, payments from the remainder of such profits and from any profits of past years available for distribution may be made among the members to such extent and under such conditions as may be prescribed by the rules or the by-laws:

"Provided also that in the case of a Society with Unlimited Liability, no distribution of profits shall be made without the general or special order of the Local Government in this behalf."

An Unlimited Liability Society seeks to erect a buffer between the members and the ultimate possibility of the worst coming to the worst. The Co-operative principle of charging the members just the cost of the service is varied a little to their advantage. The Society lends to the members at a little higher rate than it borrows. The surplus thus created is pooled into a common fund known as the Reserve.

The surplus secured through charging a little more on the loans than the Society pays is "generally used as working capital and so accumulates rapidly at compound interest." It cannot be divided for ten years, if ever, so there is gradually built up a good Reserve Fund which adds to the credit of the Society (it is a tangible security to the creditors) and protects the members against the risk of being called upon to make good any deficit. This indivisible Reserve Fund will gradually grow in importance as years roll on. It is the real capitalization of character inasmuch as its existence means that members are not throwing any burden upon it by defaulting. "At present imperceptible, its influence will gradually transform the whole economic aspect of village debt and credit, for it is only a matter of time before there will be accumulated a sum sufficient for all the current needs of the members, and thereafter interest on loans will no longer constitute a drain on the community."

The total working capital of the Primary Agricultural Credit Societies in 1933 was Rs. 8,40 lakhs, which means that in that year the Reserve represented over 27 per cent of the working

GROWTH OF RESERVE FUND IN THE PUNJAB
(*Lakhs of rupees*)

	1929	1930	1931	1932	1933	1934
Reserve funds ..	1,40	1,63	1,84	2,06	2,30	2,69

capital. It is very creditable when we recall that it was only 4 per cent for the Raffeisen Societies of Germany a few years ago.

Concerning the employment of the Reserve Fund the Committee on Co-operation observed as follows:

"In some Provinces the surplus assets are used in loans made by the Societies to members; in some the surplus assets are placed in deposit with other Co-operative institutions and are thus ultimately utilized in the same way; in others they are separately invested wholly or partly in outside securities, while in one Province they are invested in Government paper which is deposited with the Provincial Bank under an arrangement which makes the total of such Government papers available to the Provincial Bank as pledge to support its own credit, and, consequently, that of the whole movement. In the case of the majority of Primary Societies we think that, assuming that they are secure in respect of their fluid resources, everything points to the desirability of a Primary Society using its surplus assets in loans to its members. If we assume that a Central Bank and Societies affiliated to it have jointly to keep a certain amount of money as fluid resource, then (except so far as three-fourths of the Central Bank's profits liable to division in dividends and such outgoings are lost to the movement) it makes no practical difference to the movement as a whole whether the Societies use their surplus assets in loans while the Central Bank provides the fluid resources or whether the Societies pool their surplus assets with the Central Bank and allow it to use them for fluid resources. Whatever profit goes to the Central Bank is lost to the Societies and vice versa. In deciding whether the profits should go to the Central Banks or to the Primary Societies, we should be guided by the fact that our object is to strengthen the financial and moral position of the needs of the Primary Societies rather than vice versa.

"In this matter, as in all others, we regard the benefit of the Primary Societies as the main object, the Central Banks and other such institutions being merely a machinery accessory to it. The object should be to free the Primary Societies as far as possible from recourse to their Central Banks, and this can only be done by enabling them to build up their own capital sufficient for their needs. This can best be achieved by allowing Primary Societies to use their accumulated net profits or surplus assets in loans to members, on which they get high rates of interest compared with the rates received on Government paper.

"In brief, therefore, a Primary Society is concerned with the Reserve Fund mainly in the form of surplus assets, and so long as proper provision is made for the necessary fluid resources these surplus assets may properly be employed in the business of the Society. The object of a Society should be to accumulate a Reserve Fund of this character until it obtains a capital of its own sufficient to meet all its needs, and thus becomes independent of outside assistance. Until this stage is reached, the margins on which it works should be as large as is compatible with the successful maintenance of the Society, and it is only when this stage is reached that any reductions (other than those essential to meet outside competition) should be effected in the rates of interest charged by the Society on its loans to members."

The Reserve Funds are generally invested by Primary Societies in Central Co-operative Banks. In some Societies loans are advanced to members out of this Reserve Fund. The question whether Societies should be allowed to use a portion of their Reserve Fund as their working capital becomes one of great importance when we remember that the Central Banks pay a low rate of interest on the Reserve Fund to Societies, but charge higher rates on loans advanced to Societies.

The observations of the Central Banking Inquiry Committee may be quoted with advantage. "The Townsend Committee recommended that Central Banks should lend to Societies at concessional rates sums up to the extent of the Reserve Fund in deposit with them, and that after the Reserve Fund of a Society aggregates to an appreciable percentage of the Society's total working capital the excess may be permitted to be used in the Society's business. We recommend the former proposal for the consideration of the authorities concerned. In the present stage of the development of the movement it is safer to keep the Reserve Fund invested in the Central Banks and not to permit the Societies to lend it to their members."

Under the Punjab rules and by-laws:

1. The Reserve Fund of a Society may, unless the Registrar by special order directs it to be invested as provided in section 32 (*a*), (*b*), (*c*), (*d*), be utilized in the business of the Society.

2. The Reserve Fund shall be indivisible and no member shall be entitled to claim a specified share in it.

3. On the dissolution of a Society, the Reserve Fund shall be applied to discharging the liabilities of the Society and to the repayment of the share capital.

Any sum that may remain may be applied to such object of local and public utility as may be selected by the Committee and approved by the Registrar. If within three months of the dissolution of the Society the Committee fails to select an object that is approved by the Registrar, the latter shall credit the balance of the Reserve Fund and any other surplus funds to the Co-operative Society to which the Society was affiliated or shall deposit the amount in some other bank until a new Co-operative Society with a similar area of operations is registered, in which case it shall be credited to the Reserve Fund of the new Society.

CHAPTER XI

PRIMARY AGRICULTURAL CO-OPERATIVE CREDIT SOCIETIES—*continued*

LIABILITY

MEMBERS of an Agricultural Co-operative Credit Society are jointly and severally liable without limit for all debts incurred and all loans and deposits taken by the Society in pursuance of its stated objects. This is known as unlimited liability.

Limited liability implies that the obligation of a member towards payment of the debts of a Society is limited to the value of his shares in the Society. In case a Society goes into liquidation, a member who has purchased shares in the Society worth a hundred rupees and has paid up the full value of shares purchased will not be liable for the payment of debts of this Society anything over and above what he has already paid in the form of full value of his shares.

Under unlimited liability a member's liability towards payment of the debts of the Society may extend to the last penny of his fortune. Under limited liability a member undertakes to meet the debts of a Society to the extent of the full value of his share or shares, and no more. But unlimited liability in a Co-operative Society virtually implies unlimited liability to make contributions at the order of the liquidator to make good any short-fall in assets. No creditor can enforce it if there is a liquidator appointed. An outside creditor can sue the Society and get a decree against the Society (i.e. against its assets, which are mostly bonds of the members for their borrowing). He cannot touch the unlimited liability; only the liquidator can do that. The same applies, of course, to a Joint-Stock Company of unlimited liability. The Court in the one case and the Registrar in the other is responsible for the appointment of liquidators.

A good deal of controversy has raged around the question

of liability. In order properly to understand the meaning and significance of unlimited liability we have to carefully study the interpretation put upon it by the Committee of Co-operation in 1915. It was held by Sir Edward Laws' Committee of 1901 to be the form of liability best suited to Agricultural Credit Societies, and under the existing law an Agricultural Credit Society must in the absence of the special permission of the Local Government be based on unlimited liability.

With a few isolated exceptions all the Primary Agricultural Credit Societies in India are Societies with unlimited liability.

"The law does not specify definitely the character of the liability, nor have we any data before us to show the interpretation put upon it by the courts. No difficulties have hitherto arisen in connection with the enforcement of this liability, but should it hereafter be found necessary to define it more clearly we should suggest that it should take the form of 'Contributory unlimited liability,' that is to say, that where there is deficit in the engagements of a Society to its creditors, this deficit should after the full payment of shares (if any), be recoverable by a series of *per capita* levies upon the members up to the full extent of their property, direct proceedings by a creditor against individual members being forbidden. Hitherto it has been generally understood that the unlimited liability of a society is intended to imply the liability of the whole of the property of the members of a Society for the debts due by the Society. Some of the less well-informed members are under the impression that it entails the liability of the whole of the property of each member of a Society for the debts due by the other members to the Society, but the practical difference between the two aspects of the liability is perhaps less than might at first sight appear, and in any case the members of Societies when they think of the liability at all appear to think of it merely as unlimited, and accept it willingly as such. We have not found that the adoption of this form of liability, where the safeguards against loss are properly understood, has any appreciable effect in keeping out the richer peasants, nor have we met with any demand for the substitution of a limited responsibility. The unlimited liability is not understood to involve any obligation against the alienation of property by members, and although the material basis for the liability is thus rendered somewhat fluctuating and indefinite, we do not consider that an arrangement which would in effect impose an indefinite charge on all their existing property would be either practicable or desirable. The unlimited form of liability as it now stands has, contrary to the anticipations of many, been unreservedly accepted by the people, and we have evidence before us to show that it constitutes an important factor in the confidence reposed in Societies both by the Central Institutions inside the movement and by the Joint-Stock Banks outside it. We see every reason, therefore, for adhering to the principle that Agricultural Credit Societies should be Societies of unlimited liability, whether they are with or without shares. In either case the ultimate liability of all the members is in the last resort unlimited, and the advantage of share capital is that, if in case of liquidation the share capital is sufficient to meet any deficit that may be found to exist, there is no need of any further levy to meet the liabilities of the society." This was written twenty years ago when the Societies were hardly a decade old, and the risk under unlimited liability principle had no opportunity to display itself. It may here be pointed out that it is not wholly correct to say that "the law does not specify definitely the character of the liability." The law provides for it under the powers of the liquidator; it is contributory unlimited liability as the liquidator can order the contributions under the Act.

HOW RISKS OF UNLIMITED LIABILITY ARE MINIMIZED

Membership of an Agricultural Co-operative Credit Society involves, undoubtedly, the assumption of an unlimited liability for the debts of the Society. But does it in reality imply that the entire property of any one member or the whole property of all the members is at stake? Theoretically it is. In practice, however, the constitution and working of a Society make it possible to get the maximum benefit out of this moral obligation of the members, and help to suppress all dangers of that ultimate collapse of the Society which may expose the members to the risks of unlimited liability.

Having accepted unlimited liability in view of the great financial and moral benefits it brings with it, the members adopt the following measures and restrictions with a view to confining their actual liability within limits of great safety.

(1) *Limitation of the Maximum Borrowing Power of the Society.*—They safeguard their unlimited liability, in the first instance, by limiting the maximum amount the Society may borrow from outside sources. They keep in view the limit of safety, and do not thus let such a situation arise as may involve them in any serious financial embarrassment.

(2) *Limitation of the Maximum Borrowing by an Individual.*—Having in the first instance restricted the total borrowings of a Society within limits of perfect safety, the members of a Society undertake to fix the maximum amount that each member may borrow. The total assets of a member are put down in the *Hasiyat* Register. The amount that he is allowed to borrow is very much less than his assets. By limiting the amount that each member can borrow it is sought to make each member's liabilities to the Society realizable from his assets alone.

(3) *Needs and Profitable Investment.*—Within the above limits of safety a member is not allowed to borrow at his sweet will. He is allowed to borrow to meet urgent and pressing needs, and only up to amounts reasonably sufficient to meet those needs. He is not given the choice to borrow up to his maximum credit limit for any and every purpose. The idea is not to advance him up to the limit at which he can be sold up without loss to the Society. Profitable employment of the amount to be borrowed is an important consideration with the Society. It is sought to teach him the benefits of intelligent investment.

(4) The risk of unlimited liability is further limited by: (*a*) The extreme care displayed in the selection of members

whose economic, social, and moral positions are taken into consideration.

(*b*) The careful scrutiny of the purpose of the loan—loans are not as a rule granted for unproductive or speculative purposes, or for such businesses as the borrower is incompetent to take up.

(*c*) A careful supervision over the use of the loan.

Whenever a loan has been secured fraudulently, or is being misapplied, it is recalled.

(*d*) Theoretically at least the entire risk of unlimited liability is minimized when the Society insists upon the security of one or more respectable persons for every loan.

The masterly exposition of unlimited liability as given by Mr. Calvert has been reproduced by the Central Banking Enquiry Committee, which well bears quotation in full:

"In a registered Society, unlimited liability, whatever may be its implications in strict legal theory, amounts in co-operative practice merely to the contributions which a liquidator may levy in the process of liquidation: in other words, it is an ultimate contributory liability which arises when a Society is wound up. It does not mean that any or all the creditors may sue any member for the debt due to them. As explained clearly by Mr. Calvert, the loss in a Co-operative Society will fall *firstly* on the member, *secondly* on his sureties, *thirdly* on the reserve, *fourthly* on the share capital, *fifthly* on the unlimited liability of the members, and finally on the creditors of the Society."

Besides the above, Mr. Calvert has the following precautions which must be and usually are adopted for safeguarding against the risks of unlimited liability:

(1) Members must be selected, as obviously every one wants to be sure that a new member will be able to bear his share of the common burden; (2) Members must be formally admitted, so that there will be some proof that they accepted legal liability for the debts of the society as they stood on the date of admission; (3) members must be allowed to withdraw in case they find the Society incurring a heavier liability than

they desire to share in; (4) the liability of past members must continue for a period so that surviving members have opportunity to proceed to liquidation if they consider that in consequence of withdrawals, the liability is becoming too great for them; (5) members must not be allowed to transfer their shares or interest to any one they please, but must only transfer to or through the Society, for the survivors must be sure that the transferee is fit for his liability; (6) the members must be able to expel anyone whose liability is worthless, or who has pledged it in another Society of unlimited liability; (7) the list of members is the list of persons liable, and so must be kept up to date; the date on which anyone ceases to be a member must be carefully entered, as from this date commences the period of liability of a past member; (8) accounts must be strictly kept and duly audited so that the extent of the liability can be definitely established, and all members must have the right to see the accounts; (9) amendments to by-laws must require a considerable majority of the members, as an amendment may alter the liability; (10) the members in general meeting must settle the maximum liability they are prepared to undertake; and (11) must have full power over the employment of funds; (12) a reserve fund is desirable to protect the liability, as any loss will first fall on the fund; accordingly (13) a limitation of dividend is desirable so as to leave more for reserve; (14) members must have the right to secure independent inspection of the accounts, and in the long run (15) to bring about the liquidation of the Society, and so definitely close their liability.

ADVANTAGES OF UNLIMITED LIABILITY

(1) Owing to joint responsibility and unlimited liability the members as a rule do not admit anyone to their society in whose honesty, integrity, business ability, industry, and character they have not the fullest confidence. Each one of the members of a Society will help only that person to secure admission into the society in the soundness of whose position

in every respect he has as much faith as in his own. Thorough mutual knowledge is essential.

(2) Loans will only be granted for productive purposes and up to limits of entire safety.

(3) The members will keep a mutual watch so that in case money is being misused the loan will be cancelled and recalled. No money will thus get lost, and arrears will not be allowed to accumulate.

(4) The greatest benefit of the unlimited liability of members, besides ensuring a sound working of the Society, is that it inspires perfect confidence among the creditors of the Society which is thus enabled to raise the needed funds at quite a low rate of interest. Unlimited liability is the cheapest and the only form of security which can be developed in a poor community. "Schulze Delitzch considered this unlimited liability indispensable at the beginning, in order to put all on guard in an association composed of persons not yet accustomed to forethought in financial matters. It would oblige each to watch his associates as well as himself. Later on, when the members have become better trained and acquainted with each other, and lenders appreciate their credit value, they might limit their responsibility."

(5) The greatest advantage of the unlimited liability is, however, a moral one. It teaches people to exercise their discretion in the selection of members, and to place every confidence in their honesty, and when need be shake them up to a sense of responsibility.

Mr. Wolff has very aptly pointed out that, "Raffeisen adopted unlimited liability in order that the Society should stand on no etiquette with candidates, consider well whether such are eligible, and unsparingly supervise them." The spirit that pervades unlimited liability has been well brought out. It is well to remember, however, that whatever the theoretical basis of the adoption of unlimited liability by Raffeisen, it remains an historical fact that limited liability as a privilege was then unrecognized by law. The greatest advantage of unlimited liability, however, is that it teaches a man to honour the confidence that his companions have placed in him. Observance of joint responsibility is in itself a great moral virtue of immense economic significance.

DISADVANTAGES OF UNLIMITED LIABILITY

Whatever the theoretical basis and practical advantages of the unlimited liability principle it does present certain well-founded difficulties. People are as a rule unwilling to shoulder responsibilities for the acts of others, particularly when those responsibilities are without limit. Unlimited liability virtually means putting at stake your entire fortune for the deeds or the misdeeds of others. This very few people are bold enough to undertake willingly.

In every country well-to-do people have withheld their association with undertakings involving unlimited liability. The feeling of each prudent man of fortune has been so well expressed and backed up by the weight of Professor Carver's conclusion. "It is possible that the Raffeisen system might be of use in a few cases where there are very poor and struggling farmers. But the principle of unlimited liability would absolutely prevent its being even seriously considered by fairly prosperous, property-owning farmers.

"That is to say, a farmer who owns considerable property would not enter into any scheme where all his property would be liable for the debts of the organization should it become insolvent.

"Among a few very poor farmers, no one of whom owns more than a very few hundred dollars' worth of property, and all of whom are about equally wealthy (or poor), the principle of unlimited liability is essential in order to secure credit on favourable terms, and is no serious drawback from the standpoint of the individual farmer. But there is no reason why Co-operative credit associations, with limited liability, should not have considerable development in this country." Professor Carver's statements no doubt carry the weight of his authority and command the respect of us all. Professor Carver seems here to have taken "unlimited liability" too literally. The number of safeguards and protections enumerated practically take all the sting out of it. Of course fairly prosperous property-owning farmers, whom Professor Carver is thinking of, would be able to subscribe to good shares probably in excess of any sum ever demanded from a member under unlimited liability. Assume for a moment that the Society has fixed its maximum borrowing limit at Rs. 10,000, and it has fifty members; these may either have unlimited liability, or have limited liability, each member taking one share of Rs. 200, of which fifty may be fully paid-up and 150 reserve liability. Of course in the latter case, shares must be non-withdrawable so long as there are loans owing to the outsiders. The "unlimited liability" is limited at once by a resolution fixing the maximum borrowing power.

It is exceedingly desirable that the implications of unlimited liability be carefully explained to members of Co-operative Societies. Indian village life is in some respects quite a tribal association in which people are absolutely willing to shoulder the joint responsibilities contemplated by the unlimited liability principle.

The liability of a past member for the debts of a Society as they existed at the time he ceased to be a member continues for two years after the date he severed his connection with the Society. The liability of the estate of a deceased member continues for a year after his death.

The danger from unlimited liability depends upon the degree of mismanagement of the Society. There is absolutely no danger in a Society which is under first-class management. "But there is grave risk if the management is slack or reckless, as many a rueful former member of a liquidated Society has been made to realize. The real liability, of course, is in inverse ratio to the size of the Society's reserve, the steady building up of which is required in all the Acts."

The Central Banking Inquiry Committees' conclusion in this respect is quite weighty:

"Co-operators find that with the observance of these precautions, and the restriction of loans to members selected for their honesty, the unlimited liability is of great practical value in raising and dispensing Co-operative rural credit, instead of being a danger or a snare. We have, however, no objection to limited liability Societies being encouraged in places where the Co-operative Movement cannot make a great headway under the unlimited liability system."

CHAPTER XII

PRIMARY AGRICULTURAL CO-OPERATIVE CREDIT SOCIETIES—*continued*

WORKING OF THE SOCIETY

THE supreme authority vests in the General Meeting, which comprises all the members of a Society. The General Meeting is held at the time of the annual audit, or as soon after as may be practicable. A General Meeting may be summoned by the Registrar or the President, or by the committee of their own motion, or at the written request of not less than six members. The presence of at least one-third of the members is necessary for the disposal of any business at such meetings, provided that where the total number of members exceeds one hundred, thirty members suffice. In a General Meeting of a Co-operative Credit Society the following business is transacted:

(1) the election, suspension, and removal of members of the Managing Committee, including a President and one or more Vice-Presidents;

(2) the election of a Treasurer to keep the money of the Society;

(3) the consideration of the annual statement of accounts and balance-sheet, and of the auditors' report, and the inspection note of the Registrar and the Inspector;

(4) the disposal of profits in accordance with the Act, the notified rules and by-laws;

(5) the confirmation of the admission and expulsion of members, and of the transfer of shares;

(6) the fixing, subject to the approval of the Registrar, of the maximum liability to be incurred during the following year in loans or deposits from non-members;

(7) the fixing of a maximum credit for each member which shall not be exceeded without the sanction of the Registrar;

(8) the amendment of the by-laws, subject to the sanction of the Registrar;

(9) amendment of the by-laws shall only be carried out by a majority of a meeting at which not less than two-thirds of the members are present. All other questions before the General Meeting shall be decided by a majority of votes. When the votes are equal, the chairman shall have a casting vote.

(10) Each member shall have one vote, irrespective of the number of shares held by him. No proxies are allowed. No member in arrears with his share instalments is allowed to vote. All business discussed or decided at a General Meeting is recorded in a proceedings book, which is signed by the chairman of the meeting.

MANAGING COMMITTEE

The Managing Committee usually consists of at least five members, including a President and one or more Vice-Presidents. The members of the Managing Committee are elected for one year, and are eligible for re-election. A member of the Managing Committee ceases to hold office when he ceases to be a member of the Society; applies for insolvency, or is declared insolvent; becomes of unsound mind; is convicted of any offence involving dishonesty, or is imprisoned for three months; accepts any office or place of profit under the Society, or receives any honorarium; lends money on his own account.

Meetings of the committee are held whenever necessary. The attendance of at least three members is necessary for the disposal of any business. At a meeting of the committee, the President, or Vice-President, or in their absence one of the members presides. Each member has one vote, and the chairman has a casting vote.

The committee exercises all the powers of the Society except those reserved for the General Meeting, subject to any regulations or restrictions duly laid down by the Society in a General Meeting, or in the by-laws. The committee has in particular the following powers and duties:

(1) to observe in all their transactions the Act, the notified rules, and the by-laws;

(2) to maintain true and accurate accounts of all money received and expended, and all stock bought and sold;

(3) to keep a true account of the assets and liabilities of the society;

(4) to keep a register of members correct and up to date;

(5) to prepare and lay before the annual General Meeting a profit and loss account and a balance sheet;

(6) to examine the accounts, sanction contingent expenditure, and supervise the maintenance of the prescribed registers;

(7) to consider the inspection notes of the Registrar and the Inspector, and take necessary action;

(8) to elect new members, to issue new and transfer old shares, subject to the confirmation of a General Meeting;

(9) to arrange for the recovery of share instalments;

(10) to summon General Meetings;

(11) to contract loans subject to any restrictions imposed by the General Meeting or by the Registrar;

(12) to decide the terms on and the periods for which loans are to be given, to approve or reject the security, to arrange for the recovery of loans and profit, and to sanction renewals when necessary;

(13) to decide the terms on, the periods for, and the rates of interest at which deposits are to be received, and to arrange for the payment or return of deposits;

(14) to decide the terms of purchase and sale of agricultural requirements and produce;

(15) to watch that loans are applied to the approved purpose for which they are made;

(16) to assist the inspection of the books by any person authorized to see them;

(17) to appoint, suspend, or dismiss employees;

(18) through any member or officer or employee of the Society or any other person specially authorized to institute, conduct, defend, compromise, refer to arbitration, or abandon legal proceedings by or against the Society or committee or

the officers or employees concerning the affairs of the Society;

(19) to acquire on behalf of the Society shares in registered Central Co-operative Societies;

(20) generally to carry on the business of the Society.

In the conduct of the affairs of the Society the committee is required to exercise the prudence and diligence of ordinary men of business, and is responsible for any loss sustained through acts contrary to the law, the notified rules and by-laws. All business discussed or decided at a meeting of the committee is recorded in a proceedings book, which is signed by the chairman of the committee and all members of the committee present.

THE STAFF OF THE SOCIETY

The Secretary.—The Managing Committee appoints a Secretary, who, if he is not a member of the committee, may receive pay or an honorarium with the sanction of the General Meeting. The powers and duties of the Secretary are as follows:

(1) to maintain correctly and up to date the prescribed papers and registers;

(2) to procure from borrowers the due execution of bonds with security;

(3) to prepare all receipts, vouchers, and documents required by the notified rules or the by-laws, or called for by the committee;

(4) to sign on behalf of the Society and conduct its correspondence;

(5) to summon and attend General Meetings and meetings of the committee;

(6) to record the proceedings of such meetings and have them duly signed;

(7) to prepare the annual statements;

(8) to certify copies of entries in books.

The observations of the Maclagan Committee on Co-operation concerning the duties and qualifications of the Secretary are of fundamental importance.

"The Secretary may be a member of a Society or not, and, where necessary, there is no objection on Co-operative grounds to paying him some remuneration on a strictly limited scale. He should, if possible, be a local man and not an outsider. We think a local Secretary, capable of performing the duties even in an inferior way, is preferable to a more competent man brought in from outside. The village accountant does not make as a rule a suitable Secretary, but we see no objection to the village schoolmaster being appointed Secretary when the Education Department allows him to undertake the work.

"The functions of the Secretary differ in different parts of India, and we do not press for uniformity, but it is essential that as far as possible he should be kept to purely clerical work, such as writing accounts and minutes, and should not be allowed to take into his own hands any of the functions of the committee. For this reason we view with some distrust the system prevailing in some provinces in which one Secretary does the work of a group of Societies in tracts where societies are small and backward. Such a system tends to give the Secretary too much power, and though we recognize that in many cases there is no alternative, we look on this course as a temporary expedient which should be abandoned as soon as opportunity offers.

"In some places we do not come across a literate person to take up the duties of a village Secretary throughout a whole range of villages. Hence paid group Secretaries have to be employed. An efficient and an honest Secretary is the very foundation upon which to build a Society, hence the training of Secretaries receives special attention in the Punjab. By 1926 over ten thousand Secretaries had received training. As a rule there is experienced a good deal of difficulty in finding in our villages competent and reliable persons to act as Secretaries. The village *mullah* and the schoolmaster are found to be working as Secretaries in quite a large number of Societies. The movement owes these gentlemen a debt of gratitude, for many of them are working honorarily, and the rest are receiving a very modest allowance for their services."

The figures for such Secretaries are available only for 1928 and 1929.

Year	Number of Societies	Secretaries
1928	1,188	Schoolmasters
	877	Mullahs
1929	1,383	Schoolmasters
	963	Mullahs

The Circle Secretary.—The Assistant Registrar, Mianwali, wrote in 1930:

"There are a number of villages where for miles round we cannot find a single literate man to work as Secretary." This difficulty, which is peculiarly common in all the remoter and more backward tracts of the province, is met through the appointment of Circle Secretaries, or the use of the local Sub-Inspector as Secretary. A Circle Secretary is a paid Secretary who works for several Societies in a group of villages situated within a convenient circle. The employment of Circle Secretaries or the use of local Sub-Inspectors are both exceedingly undesirable arrangements, and are only resorted to whenever utterly unavoidable.

Year	Number of Societies having Circle Secretaries	Number of Societies employing Sub-Inspectors as Secretaries
1930	1,228	3,393
1931	1,045	2,988
1932	1,426	3,035
1933	1,608	3,105
1934	1,393	3,478

The Department is out to discourage such arrangements, but the evil will take time before it can be eradicated with any hope of ultimate success.

Treasurer.—The Treasurer shall take charge of all money received by the Society from the Central Bank, from members, and from others, and shall make disbursements in accordance with the directions of the committee. He shall sign the cash book in token of its correctness, and produce the cash balance whenever called upon to do so by the committee or auditor. In Societies where grain is accepted in payment of shares, or in any other manner, the Treasurer shall have the charge of the grain in stock and shall have one key of the go-down, the President shall have the other key.

Lack of suitable persons to fill up these two posts separately compels the committee of the Society to appoint and the Department to accept one person who combines the two offices in him. The Report for 1932 observes:

"It is however satisfactory to state that a common source of embezzlement, the combination of the office of Secretary and Treasurer in a single individual, is rapidly disappearing. There are now 26 societies with this infliction; there were 215 in 1929. The offices of Treasurer and President are still combined in 133 societies."

CHAPTER XIII

CENTRAL SOCIETIES. THE PUNJAB CO-OPERATIVE UNION LIMITED, LAHORE

THE Punjab Co-operative Union is the chief non-official Co-operative institution in the Province. It was registered in July 1918. It can now rightly claim to be the biggest and the most successful institution of its type in India. The successful working of this institution is an unimpeachable proof of the growth of Co-operation in the Province. It is a matter of very great pride and profound pleasure that in running such a big Co-operative institution the Punjab non-official co-operators have in their own way fully repaid the labours of official leaders of Co-operation whose rare abilities and wide sympathies have made the Punjab the envy of other provinces in the matter of soundness and rapid growth of Co-operation. Co-operation for its success in India needs leaders and workers of the right type, and the Punjab Co-operative Union, Lahore, is fortunate in having secured for its management the services of an able and a devoted Secretary.

The Union for the proper performance of its functions maintains the following staff:

I. Sub-Inspectors doing—	
(*a*) audit and supervision	70
(*b*) supervision only	348
(*c*) audit only	188
(*d*) miscellaneous work in connection with training, milk recording, mortgage banks and commission shops ..	9
II. Sub-Inspectors for women's societies ..	11
III. Auditors for Central Banks	3
Total	629

OBJECTS OF THE UNION

The objects of the Union as set forth in its by-laws are as follows:

(1) To promote and extend Co-operation, to work for the common good of all co-operators, to aid in the conduct of Co-operative business; and to act as agents on behalf of its members, and to develop and strengthen Co-operative organization.

(2) To take measures for the audit, as required by law, of all registered Co-operative Societies which contribute to the funds of this Union.

(3) To establish and maintain a provident fund for all employees of this Union, of all Central Banks, and of all other registered Co-operative Societies in the Punjab.

(4) The funds of this Union shall be applied to the promotion of the objects stated in By-law 3, and in particular to:

(i) the entertainment of a staff for the promotion and extension of the Co-operative movement, and for the audit of Societies;

(ii) The purchase, printing, and publishing of literature for the instruction of the staff and of the members of registered Co-operative Societies, and other measures for the diffusion of a better knowledge of Co-operation.

MEMBERSHIP

The membership of the Union is open to (*a*) such Central Co-operative Banks, Unions, Commission Shops, and Mortgage Banks operating over a tahsil or larger area, registered in the Punjab by which the application to register made to the Registrar is signed, and those (*b*) admitted by the committee in accordance with by-laws, and (*c*) the Registrar, Deputy Registrars, Assistant Registrars, and Financial Adviser to the Co-operative Department, Punjab.

The Registrar is the *ex-officio* President of the Union. The total membership of the union stands at 188, of which twenty-six individual members represent the entire gazetted staff of the Department.

LIABILITY

Each Co-operative Bank of the Union, which is a member, shall each year be liable for any loss sustained to the extent of ½ per cent of its working capital as it existed at the end of the previous Co-operative year.

FUNDS

The funds of the Union consist of:

(1) Contributions to the audit and provident fund.

(2) Other contributions towards the general purposes of the Union.

(3) The loans and deposits.

GENERAL MEETING

The General Meeting is the supreme body of the Union. Every member Society elects a representative to the General Meeting of the Union for every hundred members or fraction thereof. General Meeting is usually held twice a year, in summer and winter. The summer session of the General Meeting is the Budget Session. It undertakes the final consideration of the annual statements of accounts and balance-sheet, and of the Auditor's report. Members of the Executive Committee, including one or more Vice-Presidents, are elected during the winter session.

All important questions concerning the movement in the Province are discussed in, and all future programmes adopted by, the General Meeting. Mr. Strickland wrote in 1927: "General Meetings are attended by representatives from all parts of the Province, who exercise a healthy control over policy, and are learning to avoid interference in the smaller executive matters. Discussions are intelligent and good tempered, official recommendations are frequently modified and occasionally rejected, and the confidence that their decisions, though possibly disapproved, will be accepted by the Registrar if they don't conflict with the law, imposes a sense of responsibility on the members."

The General Meeting is empowered to amend by-laws subject to the sanction of the Registrar. Amendment of the by-laws is carried out only by a majority of a meeting at which not less than two-thirds of the members are present, or, in the case of member Societies, are duly represented, provided that amendments previously approved by the Registrar may be adopted by a majority consisting of two-thirds of those present at a General Meeting, at which due notice of the intention to discuss such amendments has been given. All other questions before the General Meeting are decided by a majority of votes.

EXECUTIVE COMMITTEE

The supreme power vests in the General Meeting, but for a speedy and satisfactory conduct of business all necessary powers have been given to a smaller body called the Executive Committee. The Executive Committee consists of thirty-two members. Each district containing two hundred or more registered societies sends one representative to the Executive Committee. Twenty-eight members are thus elected. Three more are nominated by the Registrar, who is an *ex-officio* President both of the General Meeting and the Executive Committee. The Executive usually meets four times in a year.

The meetings of the Executive Committee are always well attended, and the members, who are staunch and experienced co-operators of the Province, give the best of their consideration to the problems under discussion. A knowledge of the fact that upon the deliberations of this body depends the future of Co-operation in the Province, and a scrupulous regard for maintaining the esteem with which the Registrar greets the decisions of this body, makes each member realize his responsibility very keenly. Membership of the Executive

Committee of the Punjab Co-operative Union is an honour that any co-operator in the Province may well be proud of.

The Executive Committee may appoint from amongst its own members a small working committee, and may delegate to such a working committee, or to any officer of the Union, such of its own powers as may be prescribed by a General Meeting.

THE AUDIT OF CENTRAL BANKS AND PRIMARY SOCIETIES

In the beginning the audit of Central Banks and Unions was undertaken either by Inspectors or professional paid auditors. The Union employed three professional auditors for the audit of Central Banks in 1925. All Central Banks and Unions, the working capital of which is Rs. 4 lakhs or more, are audited by firms of professional paid auditors. The audit fee is paid by the Union. Inspectors audit such Unions and Banks the working capital of which is less than Rs. 4 lakhs. In February all Central Banks and Unions the working capital of which is Rs. 4 lakhs or over are audited by Inspectors. The P.C.U. auditors audit all Mortgage Banks, the four Central Banks the working capital of which is less than Rs. 4 lakhs, and all Unions, the annual audit of which had been done by the Inspectors. This ensures for every Central Bank and Union advantage of the experiences of the auditors and the Inspectors, for the auditors emphasize the methods of account keeping, and the Inspectors emphasize principles of Co-operation. The Registrar has, after satisfying himself as to the fitness of the Sub-Inspectors, authorized them to audit all Primary Societies on his behalf.

MEANS OF PROPAGANDA

Propaganda forms the very basis of the success of any movement. The P.C. Union has always from its very commencement devoted every attention to propaganda in favour of the movement. Various agencies have been employed by the Union to make propaganda yield good results.

Sub-Inspectors.—A Sub-Inspector as the Union prepares him for his task is propaganda personified. Propaganda is a part of his duty, and it is he who prepares the ground for the establishment of Societies. The success of the movement is, however, now itself the most effective means of propaganda. The people in rural Punjab now run after the officers of the Department for the establishment of Societies.

The Co-operators' Day.—The International Co-operative Alliance, London, suggested the celebration of Co-operators' Day in 1923. The Co-operators' Day was celebrated in the Punjab for the first time in July 1927. The celebration of the day has now been shifted to November in view of the extreme unsuitability of weather and *business* of the zemindars in the Punjab in July. This day is celebrated in the Punjab under instructions from the Punjab Co-operative Union. The writer of these lines was in 1927 invited to address a huge gathering at Sialkot, and still treasures that letter of thanks and appreciation sent by the authorities that arranged for it.

"*Co-operation.*"—The Union deserves to be congratulated warmly for its appreciation of the fact that propaganda, to be effective, must be carried on in the language of the people. *Co-operation*, the Urdu journal of the Union, is to my mind an expression of one of the finest ideas which any Government Department in India has ever had the distinction to appreciate. This journal, devoted as it is to the cause of Co-operation in the Province, was started in 1924, and commands a fairly large circulation. It is running at a loss. With a little more of attention it should be raised to a still higher standard, where it should in reality be counted as an outstanding achievement of the Punjab Co-operative Union.

Films.—The Union got two films prepared for it at a cost of Rs. 11,000. One deals with credit, and the other with improvement of stock. The film dealing with credit is of very great value as a means of propaganda in favour of Co-operation, but unfortunately is now not being shown on account of the hostile attitude of the sahukars and their well-placed friends.

Two more films have also been bought by the Union.

Magic Lanterns.—Every Assistant Registrar has been supplied with a magic lantern and some useful slides. These lanterns were once extensively used, but are practically out of use now. The Inspectoress has been supplied with a gramophone for purposes of propaganda amongst women.

Pamphlets and Charts.—The Union publishes and distributes free of charge a number of pamphlets dealing with the various aspects of Co-operation in the Province. It prepares charts which have a great propaganda value. The following are some of the important pamphlets published and distributed in large numbers, free of charge, by the Union: (1) *What is Co-operation?* (2) *Co-operation in the Punjab.* (3) *Co-operation in India.* (4) *Growth of Co-operation.* (5) *Co-operation and Education.* (6) *Co-operation and National Prosperity.* (7) *Thrift.* (8) *Compulsory Education Societies.* (9) *Adult Education.* (10) *Stock Breeding.* (11) *Arbitration.* (12) *Commission Shops.* (13) *A Key to Wealth.* (14) *Consolidation of Holdings.* (15) *The Money-lenders' Defeat.*

Translation of Standard English Works.—The management of the Union, with an admirable insight into the requisites of its success, has displayed its originality and soundness of judgment in yet another form. Preliminary propaganda will awaken in the people a desire to study the movement. Arrangements must therefore be made for meeting the demand for more knowledge than the preliminary propaganda creates. Not only that. The Sub-Inspector is the very foundation of the movement. He cannot adequately add to his knowledge through a study of the movement in English. Study through the medium of Urdu is more profitable, and takes less time. The Union, therefore, for making a knowledge of the movement available to a large number of people in and outside the movement, has brought out Urdu translations of a number of standard works on Co-operation and Rural Economics. Urdu versions of the following books are available:

(1) *Wealth and Welfare of the Punjab*, by Calvert.
(2) *Studies in Co-operation*, by Strickland.

(3) *Co-operation and Agriculture*, by Wolff.
(4) *Co-operation and Burma*, by Barreto.
(5) *Denmark a Commonwealth of Co-operation*, by Hoe.
(6) *Rural Economics*, by Carver.
(7) *Rural Credits*, by Herrick.

A number of other books are in the press.

Libraries.—A number of Central Banks and Unions have been persuaded to establish libraries on Co-operation. The Union undertakes to supply books and pamphlets for such Libraries in order that all those interested in the movement may have an easy access to the literature available on the subject.

There are two chief sources of the income of the Punjab Co-operative Union, namely, the Punjab Co-operative Union contribution paid by every Society at 10 per cent of its annual net profit, and the Government grant. An incidental source of income to the Union is the Reserve Funds of liquidated Societies credited to the Punjab Co-operative Union. Interest on investments also yields a moderate income to the Union.

The main heads of expenditure of the Union are the following: (1) Audit, Supervision, and Propaganda; (2) Training of Staff; (3) Audit of Central Institutions; (4) Provident Fund; (5) P.C.U. Fund, etc. The following table will give an idea of the revenue and expenditure of the Union for the last five years:

Year	Revenue	Expenditure
1929	4,77,681	4,60,523
1930	6,42,354	5,26,397
1931	6,73,337	6,04,130
1932	7,31,315	6,52,275
1933	7,74 lakhs	7,21 lakhs

The Report for 1933 reveals that with the fall in the profits of Societies the P.C.U. contribution has begun to show a decline, and is a real cause for anxiety.

CHAPTER XIV

CENTRAL SOCIETIES. THE PUNJAB PROVINCIAL CO-OPERATIVE BANK

THE Punjab Provincial Co-operative Bank was registered in December 1924. The Bank undertook to arrange the transfer of funds from such central institutions as had more than they wanted to such central institutions as needed more money. This function before the registration of the Provincial Bank was performed by the Registrar. The Provincial Bank undertook as well the function of dealing with the financial institutions of other provinces. The number of shareholding Societies in 1925 came up to five thousand.

As early as 1926 the Bank executed an agreement and a trust deed, according to which the Punjab Government guaranteed 6 per cent interest for twenty-five years on Rs. 20 lakhs of debentures which the Bank wanted to issue. The Bank in its turn undertook to carry all profits to a sinking fund. In 1927 debentures worth Rs. 5 lakhs were issued, and the loan was over-subscribed. This was a loan for Mortgage Banks secured by Government guarantee.

By 1928 there was witnessed a considerable increase in the working capital of the Bank, chiefly on account of the prohibition imposed on Central Banks making any further loans to each other. Before this, Central Banks with surpluses to invest were allowed to lend to other central institutions through the agency of the Provincial Bank. As long as the demand for money was greater than the supply of surplus funds seeking investment, such a course presented no difficulty, but with the great increase in deposits by 1925 the supply of money for investment far out-ran the demand for it. Under the changed conditions, then, it became a problem how to reconcile their conflicting claims.

The Bank decided to meet the situation by declaring its willingness to accept money on deposit from its affiliated

Societies at fixed rates without limit of amount. It thus became a balancing centre for the whole movement, and the Central Banks were thus finally stopped from making deposits with each other. This system insures investment for the surplus money in the movement at a uniform rate which, consistently with the object of the Bank, is as high as possible. This rate sets a standard for the larger Central Banks, and puts a stop to their competition for deposits by offering rates higher than the market conditions warrant.

THE CONSTITUTION AND WORKING OF THE BANK

Objects.—The objects of the Bank are to facilitate the operations of registered Co-operative Societies by:

1. the carrying on of banking and credit business;
2. the issue of debentures in order to afford financial assistance to such Societies;
3. the supervision of interlending between such Societies;
4. the provision of educational assistance and training to the staffs of such Societies;
5. other measures designed to improve the work and to extend the usefulness of such Societies.

MEMBERSHIP

Membership of the Punjab Provincial Co-operative Bank is open to all societies registered in the Punjab under the Co-operative Societies Act. The Registrar of Co-operative Societies, Punjab, is an *ex officio* member of the Bank, without holding a share or incurring any liability.

Liability.—The liability of each member is limited to the nominal amount unpaid in respect of his shares.

CAPITAL

The working capital of the Bank is composed of:

1. An unlimited number of shares of the value of Rs. 100;
2. Deposits from members and from the public;

3. Loans as sanctioned by the Registrar;
4. The proceeds of debentures sold by the Bank;
5. Accumulated profits.

Shares, subject to the confirmation of the Executive Committee, may be transferred to existing shareholders, or to registered Co-operative Societies in the Punjab. The disposal of the shares of the liquidated Societies depends upon the discretion of the Committee. Shares are ordinarily to be paid up at the rate of Rs. 10 for every year of the life of the shareholding Society, but any shareholder may pay up the full value of the share at any time.

GENERAL MEETING

A General Meeting is held annually soon after the annual audit. The Registrar and the committee can summon the meeting. A meeting may be convened if at least one hundred shareholders send a written requisition. Seven days' notice of a General Meeting is to be given to every member. Each member has one vote, irrespective of the number of shares held by him. A registered Society which has acquired a share may appoint any one of its members as representative for the purpose of voting on the affairs of this Bank. No other proxies are allowed. All matters before the General Meeting are decided by a majority of votes. In the event of votes being equal the chairman has a casting vote.

With such a large membership (over 13,000) as the Provincial Bank commands, it is impossible to hold a General Meeting of the shareholders at Lahore. Within a couple of years of the establishment of the Bank it was realized that such General Meetings would not be possible, and it was consequently decided to hold the General Meeting in sections at such places which may be the headquarters of a Central Co-operative Bank or a Co-operative Banking Union. Such sectional meetings are held at 110 places at present. It was proposed that at such sectional meetings members of the Provincial Bank who are affiliated to such Central Banks or Banking Unions may attend and vote. An identical agenda is circulated for purposes of sectional General Meetings, and questions discussed at such meetings are decided by counting all the votes recorded at all the meetings. In the absence of the President or a Vice-President, the Chairman at all sectional meetings is elected by the members present. The following business is transacted at a General Meeting:

1. Election, suspension, and removal of members of the Executive Committee, including one or more Vice-Presidents;

2. The consideration of the annual statement of accounts and balance-sheet, and of the Auditors' report;

3. The disposal of the profits, as disclosed by the audited balance-sheet;

4. The confirmation of the admission of new shareholders and the transfer of shares;

5. The amendment of the by-laws, subject to the sanction of the Registrar.

All questions before the General Meeting, except that of amendments of the by-laws, are decided by a majority of votes. Amendments of the by-laws previously approved by the Registrar may be adopted by a majority consisting of two-thirds of the members present at a General Meeting. A previous notice to discuss such amendments must be given. The Registrar of Co-operative Societies, Punjab, is the *ex officio* President of the Bank.

EXECUTIVE COMMITTEE

The normal working and immediate care of the Bank is entrusted to an Executive Committee, a smaller body capable of meeting more frequently and easily. The Executive Committee consists of the Registrar and thirty-one other representatives of the shareholders duly elected. These members are elected for one year, and are eligible for re-election.

The Executive Committee has appointed from its own members a small working committee, and delegated to it some of its powers. Similarly the Executive Committee can delegate some of its powers to the officers of the Bank. Transfer of such powers needs the sanction of the General Meeting. For the disposal of business at least six members of the Committee must be present.

POWERS AND DUTIES OF THE EXECUTIVE COMMITTEE

Amongst other powers and duties of the routine type, the Executive Committee is required:

1. To maintain the accounts of all money received and expended;
2. To maintain true accounts of the assets and liabilities of the Bank;
3. To issue new and transfer old shares; subject to the confirmation of a General Meeting;
4. To fix with the sanction of the Registrar the credit of Societies, and to alter it as required;
5. To decide the terms on, the periods for and the rates of interest at which loans are to be given, and to arrange for the recovery of loans and interest;
6. To decide the terms on, the periods for, and the rates at which deposits are to be received, and to arrange for the repayment or return of deposits;
7. To decide the terms of purchase and sale of agricultural requirements and produce;
8. To contract loans with the sanction of the Registrar, or raise other capital as directed by the General Meeting;
9. To buy, sell, endorse, assign, pledge, or otherwise negotiate securities of the Government of India, Local Governments, and other trustee securities;
10. To appoint, dismiss, suspend, or punish salaried or unsalaried employees of the Bank.

INSPECTION

The by-laws provide that the constitution, working, and financial condition of the Bank shall be examined by the Financial Adviser to the Registrar of Co-operative Societies,

Punjab, at least once in each co-operative year. A copy of the inspection report is submitted to the Punjab Government.

Membership of the Bank is not open to individuals. All Co-operative Registered Societies in the Punjab, irrespective of the form of activity they may be engaged in, are eligible for membership. No direct advantage is derived by Primary Societies through their affiliation to the Provincial Bank. The indirect benefit, however, is real, and is best felt in a time of financial stringency. The Provincial Bank, as a matter of policy, does not deal directly with the Primary Societies, whose balancing centres are their own District or tahsil Central Banks.

All Central Banks and Unions are affiliated to the Provincial Bank. No regular maximum credit limits are fixed for Central Banks by the Provincial Bank. The only form of supervision exercised by the Provincial Bank over the working of the Central Banks and Unions is the calling of monthly statistical returns from these bodies.

The Provincial Bank, in collaboration with the Punjab Co-operative Union, organizes annual training classes for the benefit of the staff of Central Co-operative Banks and Unions more or less on the lines of the Inspectors' Refresher Course. The scheme has both the practical and theoretical aspects. The Lahore Central Co-operative Bank and the Provincial Bank provide the training ground on the practical side, on the theoretical side lectures are arranged on banking law, bank book-keeping, and important circulars of the Registrar bearing on policy and procedure of the Central Banks in matters of finance, audit, and supervision.

The Bank has given a subsidy to the Punjab Co-operative Union, which is primarily responsible for propaganda and education in the principles and benefits of Co-operation. One of the most important functions of the Punjab Co-operative Union is the training of the staff and of office-holders and members of the Co-operative Societies. It is carrying out this function in a very satisfactory manner, as is apparent from the system of Co-operative training in the Punjab described elsewhere in these pages.

The Bank is a member of the Indian Co-operative Banks' Association, and keeps accounts with other Provincial Banks.

DEPOSITS

The Committee on Co-operation remarked in their Report that: "Provincial Banks will no doubt have occasion more frequently than Central Banks to raise short-term deposits to meet particular needs, but as in the case of Central Banks, efforts should usually be made to obtain deposits fixed for the longest possible terms. The money is required for loans to Central Banks, and it would only embarrass them if it was granted for shorter terms than were required by the Societies borrowing from them."

The Punjab Provincial Bank is at liberty to receive deposits at or without interest, and at call or payable after notice, provided always that the Bank keeps in hand either invested in Promissory Notes of the Government of India or in other securities approved by the Local Government and in cash an amount which shall be equal to 40 per cent of the amount deposited with the Bank for the time being payable on demand. The latest rates allowed on fixed deposits are as follows:

FIXED DEPOSIT

Period	Rate allowed to Central Banks	Rate allowed to Public
12 months ..	$2\frac{3}{4}$ per cent	2 per cent
6 months ..	2 per cent	Acceptance of deposits for periods less than a year has been discontinued
5–10 years ..	$\frac{1}{2}$ per cent more than the rate allowed by the banks to their deposits, subject to a maximum of 4 per cent per annum	Long-term deposits are not accepted from the public

The minimum sum for a current deposit is Rs. 100. This relates to deposits by individuals. For the Central Banks no limit is fixed, whether maximum or minimum. Interest at 1 per cent p.a. on daily balances is allowed on current account of constituent central institutions. No interest is allowed on current accounts of individuals. Current accounts are attended with greater risk in a time of crisis as compared with fixed deposits or Savings Bank accounts. Maintenance of a high percentage of fluid resources is compulsory in the case of current accounts. Besides, encouragement of thrift is best promoted by fixed and Savings Bank accounts rather than current accounts.

FIXED DEPOSIT RULES

(1) No sum below Rs. 500 is accepted.

(2) Charitable or educational institutions, widows, and orphans may be allowed a higher rate than usual.

(3) Interest is payable on application half-yearly on February 1st and August 1st upon presentation of the deposit receipt to the Bank. The payment of interest will be endorsed on the receipt. No compound interest will be allowed if the amount of interest is not drawn.

(4) All deposits will cease to bear interest after the expiry of the term of notice of withdrawal.

(5) Payment of Fixed Deposit can only be made on presentation of the Bank receipt duly endorsed.

(6) Fixed Deposit Receipts are not transferable, nor can the amount be drawn before due date.

(7) Fixed Deposit accounts can be opened in one or more names payable in case of more than one name, either jointly, or to any one of them, or the survivor or survivors. No account can be opened in the name of a minor, except through his guardian.

(8) The accounts of the *purdahnashin* ladies may be operated only on a duly attested authority.

SAVING BANK DEPOSITS

The Provincial Bank accepts Savings Bank deposits. Both individuals and Societies can start these accounts. The minors' accounts can be opened by the guardians. To open an account the minimum amount acceptable is Rs. 10. Subsequent deposits may be Rs. 5 or over. No single account may exceed Rs. 10,000, exclusive of interest. The rate of interest allowed on these

LOAN AND DEPOSIT ACCOUNT OF THE PUNJAB PROVINCIAL BANK

(*Lakhs of rupees*)

	1929	1930	1931	1932	1933	1934
Loans and deposits held	10·95	11·54	12·25	20·87	16·52	18·52
Central Banks and Unions	40·00	56·59	68·43	109·43	134·32	115·48
The Punjab Government (for Mortgage Banks) ..	14·12	16·74	15·00	13·26	11·52	9·90

deposits at the present time is 2 per cent p.a. on monthly minimum balance of Rs. 10, or multiples of Rs. 10. Withdrawals are allowed twice a week, but the aggregate amount drawn in a week may not exceed Rs. 200. For withdrawal of sums over Rs. 200 the Bank requires a notice of at least seven days, and the duration of the notice increases as the amount of withdrawal rises. An amount of Rs. 500 or over standing in the Savings Bank deposit may at any time be transferred to Fixed Deposits for a period of not less than six months. The Bank reserves to itself the right of reducing the rate of interest or of closing any Savings Bank account after giving two months' notice either by public advertisement or private intimation.

LOANS

The by-laws lay down that the funds of the banks shall be utilized primarily for the purpose of granting loans to Co-operative Societies registered under the Co-operative Act, and which are members of the Bank. No loan to a Society which is not a member can be advanced without the sanction of the Registrar. Although Primary Societies are affiliated to the Bank, the Bank as a matter of policy does not directly advance any loans to such Societies. The Bank lends money to Central Banks, Mortgage Banks, and the Banking Unions.

In the case of Central Banks and Banking Unions the terms of transaction are very nearly similar. According to the by-laws every loan advanced by the Bank to a Co-operative Society shall be made payable at the end of a period which shall not exceed ten years from the date of the loan, provided always that the Bank shall be at liberty to renew any such loan at the expiration of the original term for such further period as the Bank shall think fit, but so that such renewed period also shall not exceed ten years in any case. But in practice the Bank lends to Central Banks and Banking Unions on a demand pro-note on the understanding that the loan would stand out for one year. In the case of mortgage banks the loan is advanced for ten years. The loan is to be repaid in twenty half-yearly instalments. The rate of interest charged to all these three Societies is the same, and stood at 6½ per cent in 1930. The Bank does not usually lend to any Society more than twelve times its paid-up capital and all its reserve put together. No fixed percentage of the total loanable amount is reserved for distribution among the Central Banks, Banking Unions, and Mortgage Banks. But to the Mortgage Banks the Bank lends only what it has realized on long-term debentures and that which it borrows from the Government.

For financing Mortgage Banks, the Provincial Bank has borrowed Rs. 18 lakhs from the Government and has raised Rs. 5 lakhs on debentures for twenty-five years. The Government loan of Rs. 18 lakhs is for fifteen years.

In 1930, in the case of Central Banks, it was decided that the rate charged on loans by the Provincial Bank for punctual payment of instalments would be 6½ per cent, which in case of delay in repayment was to go up to 6¾ per cent. In the case of Mortgage Banks the conditions were all the more stringent. In the case of a Mortgage Bank delay in repayment by one month would make the rate charged go up to 8 per cent.

This penal clause, however, has never been enforced. In

(*Lakhs of rupees*)

Year	Fixed Loans granted to Central Banks and Unions		Cash Credit Loans to Central Banks and Unions		Fixed Loans to Mortgage Banks		
	Amount Granted	Total Outstanding at the end of the Year	Total Limits Granted	Amount Drawn	Provincial Bank's Liability	Amount Granted during the Year	Amount Outstanding at the end of the Year
1929	20·94	10·93	19·84	4·07	15·77	7·85	18·46
1930	36·98	28·54	29·09	5·09	24	2·83	19·09
1931	32·68	46·11	33·29	6·55	26·74	1·20	19·06
1932	51·88	50·88	6·77	1·21	5·56	—	17·94
1933	28·24	24·02	6·82	0·65	6·17	—	16·93
1934	33·40	20·88	3·82	1·26	—	—	16·45

1933 the committee of management decided that the Provincial Bank should advance loans to a Banking Union only if the Central Bank in the area for any reason could not do so. It was felt that the parent Central Bank would thus be more closely in touch with Unions, and should as well be a better judge of their needs and financial position. In the same year it was further decided that central institutions borrowing from the Provincial Bank should in future be required to make repayments in six monthly instalments in consonance with their demand on member Societies. These repayments are expected to be made in full. Fresh loans to the Central Banks are to be granted at the time when money is being advanced by them for seasonal needs. These suggestions were made with a view to enabling the central institutions to employ their funds with less waste, besides giving the Provincial Bank greater control over the money lent.

RATES CHARGED AND PAID

Rates charged and paid by the Provincial Bank have been varying with market conditions in recent years. The following table illustrates this.

Year	Interest paid to Central Banks on their Fixed Deposits	Interest charged to Central Banks on Loans Advanced by the Provincial Bank	Rate on Cash Credit Advances
	Per cent	Per cent	Per cent
1930	5	6½	6½
1931	6	6¾	—
1932	Minimum, 5	Maximum, 7½	—
	Maximum, 6¾	Minimum, 6	—
1933	Maximum, 5	Maximum Bank rate	—
	Minimum, 3½	Minimum, 5	—

The rates for fixed deposits offered to Central Banks, with a view to encourage their investments, are higher than those granted to individual depositors.

CURRENT ACCOUNTS

The Provincial Bank has opened current account business with the Central Banks and the Unions, and to a negligible extent with the public. The Bank merely seeks to increase this type of business with the members only.

RECOMMENDATIONS OF THE CENTRAL BANKING ENQUIRY COMMITTEE

"It has been suggested that as the failure of a Provincial Bank might very seriously affect, if not destroy, the whole Co-operative movement in the Province, it is desirable to transform the existing institutions into special registered institutions with part of the share capital subscribed by the Provincial Government. We are not in favour of such transformation. We recommend that Provincial Banks should continue to be bodies incorporated under the Co-operative Societies Act. Provincial Banks are best suited for linking up the Co-operative credit organization with the general money market and Commercial Banks, and should be managed on ordinary business principles with due regard to the special requirements of Co-operation. These banks should not deal directly with primary credit Societies, and should consolidate and strengthen their position as financing agencies and balancing Central Banks. We consider it desirable that the executive head of a Provincial Bank should be a thoroughly trained banker with competent knowledge of the principles and practices of Co-operative Credit."

CHAPTER XV

CENTRAL SOCIETIES. CENTRAL BANKS

UNSUITABILITY OF A JOINT-STOCK BANK TO FINANCE CO-OPERATIVE CREDIT SOCIETIES

JOINT-Stock Banks are not suited to help the Primary Credit Societies on account of the following reasons:

(1) *Nature of Security.*—Co-operative Societies place a very high value, and in fact base their entire transactions, upon the moral security of the borrower. A Joint-Stock Bank on principle recognizes entirely or chiefly the material security, and refuses to recognize immaterial security, even when backed up by unlimited liability, as sufficiently safe basis for advancement of loans.

(2) *Period of the Loan.*—The Joint-Stock Banks are accustomed to transactions in short-term loans in the commercial sense. These loans are usually for two or three months, and afford a much more rapid turnover than can ever be possible in case of loans applied to agricultural purposes. No Joint-Stock Bank will, besides, be prepared to lock up its entire capital in financing agricultural Societies.

(3) *Not under Co-operative Control.*—Although the Registrar's object is to make institutions able to get on without his guidance and control, yet in a large number of cases the interest of the movement for some time to come requires that every agency connected with it should be under the guiding control of the Registrar. No Joint-Stock Bank could afford to work under the Registrar's control.

(4) *Inadequate Control.*—An institution that advances money to Primary Societies, by the very nature of things, if it is not to come to grief, must devote considerable attention and be adequately fitted to exercise a direct control over the working of the borrowing Societies. For this type of work a Joint-Stock Bank is ill-equipped and reluctant to undertake.

These drawbacks of the Joint-Stock Banks have in every country necessitated the establishment of Co-operative Central Banks, which, as the Committee on Co-operation, puts it, will appreciate the special conditions under which Co-operation works, and act in sympathy with those conditions.

TYPES OF CENTRAL BANKS

(1) *The Capitalist Central Bank.*—In the Capitalist Central Banks membership is either entirely confined to individuals, or is open to Societies as well exactly on the same basis as to individual members. In such banks there is neither any special provision for securing the representation of Societies on directorates, nor is any definite portion of the share capital reserved for the Societies. There is in such banks no restriction on the distribution of profits to the shareholders. Such banks may be of some use to the movement as long as they do not undertake such banking business as brings them in line with other Joint-Stock Banks, and when they undertake to lend to Societies alone. But if such banks are allowed to lend to Societies their transactions must be carefully scrutinized by the authorities of the Co-operative Department, for in absence of any such control they are likely to degenerate into mere money-lending agencies with all the rapacity of individual money-lenders. The old Capitalist Bank, with only individual members, is now rarely to be met with. In spite of its enormous and evident disadvantages, the U.P. Banking Enquiry Committee has recommended the extension of such rural banks through which money-lenders combine to lend to neighbouring Societies. This experimental extension has been recommended in view of the success of one such bank. Although such a bank, from a co-operators' point of view, falls very much below the ideal, yet its establishment with proper safeguards will help to mitigate the evils of private money-lending which flourishes as it impoverishes the country. Any measure that is likely to make money-lending more humane and honest is to be wel-

comed in this country, even if it has many superior alternatives elsewhere.

(2) *The Pure Co-operative Bank.*—Membership of purely Co-operative banks is confined to Societies alone, and the management is entirely in their own hands. This type has its own advantages. Such banks represent institutions in which not only the clash of interests is avoided, but in which there is a complete identity of interests of the lender and the borrower. This unity of interests helps to diminish the costs on the staff engaged for the verification of the credit limits of borrowers, or for effecting recoveries. In the case of such banks, as the Committee on Co-operation remarked, there is no need of earning dividends, since the profits out of which they come are derived from the very institutions which would receive them.

Amongst the defects of this class of banks is the difficulty in finding representatives fitted to become successful Directors.

(3) *The Mixed Banks.*—The membership of this class of banks is open both to individuals as well as Societies. In these banks not only a certain proportion of the shares is reserved for the Societies, but a specific representation of the Societies on the directorate is reserved. This representation of the Societies insures a controlling influence to them. There are restrictions on the distribution of profits. The Maclagan Committee thought that provision should be made to enable the bank by degrees to become more Co-operative by diminishing the number of its non-working individual shareholders, either by lapse or by redeeming their shares, or by confining all fresh share issues that may be found necessary to Societies alone.

CONSTITUTION AND WORKING OF A CENTRAL BANK

Objects of a Central Co-operative Bank.—According to the Punjab by-laws, the objects of a Central Co-operative Bank are to facilitate the operations of registered Co-operative Societies by:

(1) The carrying on of banking and credit business;

(2) The purchase and sale for common account of agricultural implements and produce;

(3) The supervision and audit of registered Co-operative Societies;

(4) The provision of educational assistance to members of such Societies;

(5) Other measures designed to improve the work and extend the usefulness of such Societies.

The funds of Central Co-operative Banks may be applied to the furtherance of these objects, to the maintenance of a staff for the supervision of the Societies within the working area of the bank, and so spreading knowledge of the benefits of Co-operation.

MEMBERSHIP

The membership of a Central Co-operative Bank is open to registered Co-operative Societies and Unions within the District, and to such persons who join in application for registration or may be approved by the Managing Committee. The Deputy Commissioner of the District, in which the bank is situated, is in some cases an *ex officio* member without holding a share. Every other member must hold at least one full share. Members are admitted after election by the Managing Committee subject to the confirmation by the General Meeting on the payment of the nominal value of one or more shares. Under this provision some Central Banks admitted individuals to membership, allowing the payment of shares by instalments. The Registrar has recently abolished this concession in the case of individuals, while favouring its retention in the case of Societies. No individual can, therefore, now be a member of a Central Bank unless he has paid the full value of his share or shares.

The representatives of Societies, by themselves, do not always furnish a bank with such a directorate as will ensure its success. Central Banks, therefore, in practice have had to allow membership to individuals, which concession has been of immense practical value. Individual members possessing influence and ability by devoting their time and attention to the working of these banks have substantially contributed to their success. At least fifty per cent of the shares of a Central Bank are reserved for Societies.

GENERAL MEETING

A General Meeting is held usually after the annual audit. The meeting can be summoned by the Registrar or by the Committee of their own motion, or at the written request of not less than one-fifth of the shareholders. For the disposal of business at a General Meeting not less than ten members or representatives shall be present in person.

In a General Meeting the following business shall be transacted:

(1) Election, suspension, or removal of members of the Managing Committee, including a President and one or more Vice-Presidents;

(2) The consideration of the annual statement of accounts and audited balance-sheet, and of the auditors' report;

(3) The disposal of the profits;

(4) The confirmation of the admission of new shareholders, and of the transfer of shares;

(5) The amendment of by-laws subject to the sanction of the Registrar;

(6) The election of representatives to the Punjab Co-operative Union, Limited.

Amendments of the by-laws shall only be carried out by a majority of a meeting at which two-thirds of the members are represented; except model by-laws or amendments previously approved by the Registrar, which may be adopted by a majority consisting of two-thirds of the members present at a General Meeting, in which due notice of intention to discuss such by-laws or amendments has been given. All other questions are to be decided by a majority of members. Each member in a General Meeting has one vote, irrespective of the number of shares held. A registered Society which has acquired a share in a Central Bank may appoint as its proxy for the purpose of voting in the affairs of this bank any of its members. No other proxies shall be allowed.

MANAGING COMMITTEE

The Managing Committee consists of a specified number of members, including a President and one or more Vice-Presidents. The members, except the President, retire in rotation, one-third retiring annually. For the first two years the retiring members are selected by lot. Retiring members are eligible for re-election. In the case of a vacancy occurring during the course of the year, the Managing Committee may co-opt a member till the next General Meeting. A member of the committee ceases to hold office if, amongst a number of other things:

(1) He ceases to be a member of the bank or of the Society which he represents;

(2) Is, or applies to be, adjudicated insolvent;

(3) Holds any office or place of profit under the bank, or receives any honorarium;

(4) Fails, without any excuse approved by the Committee, to attend three consecutive meetings;

(5) Defaults in payment of the principal or interest of a loan.

The committee shall include representatives of shareholding Societies in the proportion of not less than 50 per cent of its membership. Every tahsil having fifty affiliated Societies or more shall have at least two representatives, otherwise at least one. The representatives are elected by the General Meeting; but, in the case of tahsil representatives, no one shall be elected unless he is (*a*) resident in the tahsil in question, and (*b*) proposed or seconded by representatives of shareholding Societies in that tahsil. Representatives of shareholding Societies must be members of a shareholding Society, but need not be members of the bank. The committee may appoint from among its members a small working committee, and may delegate to it or to the officers of the bank such of its own powers as may be prescribed by the General Meeting. At a meeting of the committee each member shall have one vote, and the chairman a casting vote.

The committee shall have the following powers besides those essential to the discharge of the routine type of work:

(1) To maintain the accounts of all money received and expended, and all stock bought and sold;

(2) To maintain true accounts of the assets and liabilities of the bank.

(3) To examine the maximum credit of Societies sanctioned by the Registrar, and to reduce it if necessary.

(4) To decide the terms on, the periods for, and the rates of interest at which loans are to be given, and to arrange for the recovery of loans and interests;

(5) To decide the terms on, the periods for, and the rates of interest at which deposits are to be received, and to arrange for the repayment or return of deposits;

(6) To decide the terms of purchase and sale of agricultural requirements and produce;

(7) To contract loans with the sanction of the Registrar, to raise other capital as directed by the General Meeting, and to pledge the bank's credit for such purposes;

(8) To examine the accounts and supervise the maintenance of the prescribed registers;

(9) To facilitate the annual audit, and to prepare and submit to a General Meeting the annual report and audited balance-sheet;

(10) To arrange, if necessary, for the audit of the accounts of Societies within the working area of the bank, and to administer any audit fund under its control.

In their conduct of the affairs of the bank the committee shall exercise the prudence and diligence of ordinary men of business, and shall be responsible for any loss sustained through acts contrary to the law, the notified rules, or by-laws.

THE STAFF OF THE CENTRAL BANKS

The staff usually consists of the Secretary, the Manager, and the Treasurer. The Treasurer is appointed by the committee to take charge of all money entrusted to him by the bank, and to account duly for the same, and make such payments as those in charge of the bank may order in accordance with their powers. The powers and duties of the Secretary and of the Manager under his control are according to the by-laws as follows:

(1) To superintend the working of the office, and to be responsible for the proper and punctual maintenance of the accounts, including a cash book and a ledger showing the accounts of every shareholder, depositor, creditor, and borrower, and a stock register;

(2) To maintain correctly and up to date the register of members, the share list of persons nominated under by-law;

(3) To grant loans to Societies up to the maximum credit fixed and to procure the due execution of the bonds;

(4) To receive deposits and issue receipts as prescribed by the committee;

(5) To buy and sell agricultural produce and requirements as directed by the committee;

(6) To receive money due to the bank and give receipts;

(7) To pay money due from the bank;

(8) Generally to conduct the current business of the bank, and to perform all duties entrusted to him by the committee.

THE WORKING OF A CO-OPERATIVE CENTRAL BANK

The Co-operative Central Banks lend to member Societies and to individuals only on the security of their deposits. The maxim credit limit of a Society is fixed in accordance with rules by the Assistant Registrar. Whenever a Society wants to borrow money the committee of the Society decides upon the sum to be borrowed, and one of the office-holders of the Society goes personally to the Central Bank with which it is affiliated and gets the money. The Central Bank advances money to the Society on the execution of a Cheque Bond. The advance is usually made in the form of cash credit, and repayment is in instalments, the repayments being made to follow the payment of instalments to the Society by the borrowers. Central Banks may recall a loan at any time. Some Central Banks engage Sub-Inspectors to supervise the working of Societies in order to insure their solvency, but normally all such supervision is undertaken on behalf of the banks by the staff of the Co-operative Department. If a Central Bank scents some danger to a debtor Society, it can refer the case to arbitration, or may request the Registrar in a friendly letter to cancel the registration of the Society. As a matter of right, however, a Central Bank may insist upon an inquiry which may lead to cancellation of the Society.

Central Banks are audited twice a year. The first audit is done by Inspectors of the Department from September 1st to February 28th, the second is undertaken by professional auditors from March 1st to August 31st each year.

The Central Banks organize meetings and carry on occasional propaganda in favour of Co-operation. No special and lasting efforts have as yet been made by the banks in this direction.

Not much is attempted by the Central Banks in the matter of serving the Societies or cultivators in spreading a knowledge of improved agriculture, or the use of first-class seed and up-to-date implements. During the Great War and a little after that some banks did render valuable services to the cultivators in the matter of improvement of agriculture and the provision of necessaries like salt and standard cloth.

No Central Bank has ever failed during the last twenty-seven years. If a Central Bank fails and the accumulated share capital, the Reserve, and the bad and doubtful debt funds prove inadequate to meet its liabilities, the shareholders shall be asked to contribute to the extent of the unpaid value of their shares. The depositors will suffer only in the last resort. The Central Bank will meet, first, its liabilities to secured creditors, and the ordinary creditors' claims will be considered only after the first class of creditors has been paid up.

The total liability attaching to shares, whether held by individuals or Societies, is ordinarily limited to their face value. The Central Banking Enquiry Committee state: "In order to protect the depositors, and to create confidence in the minds of the public and of the commercial banks that have dealings with Co-operative Banks, it has been suggested that the limited liability of the shareholders in Central Banks should be coupled with a reserve liability of about five to ten times the share capital. Though we agree that the reserve liability may be permissible in the case of shares held by Societies, we do not approve of the suggestion in so far as it applies to individuals who are members. Even in the case of Societies, we consider that such reserve liability should be restricted to the face value of the shares, and not to some multiple of it."

CAPITAL OF A CENTRAL BANK

A Central Co-operative Bank derives its working capital from four chief sources:

(1) Share Capital; (2) Reserve; (3) Deposits; and (4) Loans.

Loans can generally be secured from the Imperial Bank of India, Joint-Stock Banks, and the Provincial Co-operative Bank. Surplus funds of Primary Societies, as well as their contributions to the Reserve Fund, also constitute important sources from which the Co-operative Central Banks derive their capital. The reserve funds of Primary Co-operative Societies are not held by Central Banks in the Punjab.

RESOURCES OF A CENTRAL BANK

The top table on page 182, gives us an idea of the resources of Central Banks in the Punjab.

Deposits in their different forms, such as fixed, current, recurring, provident, and savings constitute an important factor in the resources of a Central Bank. Deposits are made by individuals as well as Societies. Fixed deposits are for specified periods, and are most frequent. Savings bank accounts have been recently started in some of the banks. Current

(*Lakhs of rupees*)

	1929	1930	1931	1932	1933	1934
Working capital ..	6,64	7,05	7,09	7,09	7,15	6,86
Owned capital ..	59,50	72	79	86	97	1,05
Invested in Government Securities	1,00	1,07	91	99	100	1,12
Deposits of—						
(*a*) Individuals ..	4,92	5,31	5,11	5,02	5,15	4,93
(*b*) Societies ..	47	44	56	59	62	59

(Owned capital includes share capital, reserves, and undistributed profits.)

account business is at present not undertaken by all the banks. An idea of the savings bank accounts may be had from the following table:

Years	Number of Accounts	Balance of Savings Bank Accounts
		Rs. (lakhs)
1931	11,874	43·19
1932	14,430	41·12
1933	16,879	58·06
1934	19,029	70·84

The nature of the sources of deposits in Co-operative Central Banks is disclosed by the top table on page 183.

The latest report gives figures for the deposits of large landlords and small farmers not previously recorded.

Large landlords' deposits amounted to Rs. 31 lakhs, and those of small farmers to Rs. 10 lakhs in 1933. It is significant that in most of the Central Banks, as the evidence of the Managers and Secretaries indicates, the zemindars had no deposits at all. As is clear from the table the deposits of local bodies and pensioners are steadily increasing. The fall in deposits from

(*Lakhs of rupees*)

	1929	1930	1931	1932	1933	1934
Local bodies	53	57	60	62	72	72
Other institutions ..	83	1,05	1,16	1,07	—	—
Officials and pensioners (Civil and Military)	53	52	44	48	34	—
Professional men (other than officials and pensioners)	53	52	44	48	34	—
Persons engaged in trade and commerce ..	62	68	63	60	47	—
Women	45	51	52	50	44	—
Minors	32	36	31	32	34	—

traders, women and minors, and professional men is due to the general diminution of income.

The duration of fixed deposits usually varies from one to ten years.

(*Lakhs of rupees*)

	1929	1930	1931	1932	1933
On deposit for—					
(*a*) Ten years or more ..	8	7,93	12,50	2,87	5,51
(*b*) Five years or more, but less than ten years ..	54	69	71,54	9,52	8,82

With a view to encouraging saving amongst the Societies, usually Societies are offered higher rates on deposits than are allowed to individuals.

SAVINGS BANK ACCOUNTS

Most of the Central Banks in the Province have recently opened savings bank accounts. The savings bank accounts were not started simultaneously in all the Central Banks in the Punjab, and maybe there are some Central Banks even now where savings bank accounts have still to be introduced. The lowest amount accepted as initial depost in savings bank accounts varies with different banks.

The Rohtak Central Bank accepts Rs. 10 for the first deposit, and Rs. 2 for every subsequent deposit as the minimum. The Central Bank at Montgomery accepts even one rupee as the minimum deposit. The minimum for first deposits ranges generally between Rs. 5 and 2. The Provincial Banking Enquiry Committee record as follows in this connection: "To encourage the use of accounts amongst persons of limited means, whom Co-operation is expressly designed to help, we recommend that the limit should be reduced to one rupee. In Russia, before the Revolution, deposits of one kopek (about a pice) were accepted by the largest Co-operative Bank in the country.

The maximum to be kept under this account also varies with different banks. While the Central Banks at Lyallpur and Bhiwani accept up to Rs. 10,000 in the savings bank account, those at Rohtak and Montgomery, like a number of others, have fixed the maximum at Rs. 5,000.

In some of the banks this type of business is increasing, in spite of a fall in the rate of interest allowed. The Co-operative Central Bank, Lahore, granted on savings bank deposits a uniform rate of $4\frac{1}{2}$ per cent. This rate has now, like the rates on fixed deposits, been lowered by every Central Bank.

The Central Co-operative Bank, Lahore, restricted in 1930 the withdrawals to twice a week. The same bank in the same year decided to calculate interest on monthly balances only, and discontinued calculating interest on the basis of daily balances.

A word must here be said as to the classes of people who participate in the savings bank accounts of the Central Banks.

It is mostly Government servants, vakils, and others who have opened such accounts. The Banking Enquiry Committee repeatedly asked if zemindars were among the classes that took up this type of business with the banks, and the invariable answer was a decided "No!"

Although there is no specific provision in the rule and regulations of the Central Banks debarring illiterate persons from starting savings bank accounts with such banks, yet it is unfortunate that no illiterate person has been allowed to open such an account with a Central Bank, Lahore Central Co-operative Bank being an exception in this respect. The staff of the banks seems to disapprove of the idea of having to deal with persons who cannot sign their names. Signatures can be identified quite easily, whereas thumb impressions cannot at all be identified by the bank staff. When depositors are willing to come personally, I feel it is unfair to the development of the country to refuse permission to the illiterate to start any type of accounts with any class of banks.

CURRENT ACCOUNTS

The Committee on Co-operation did not favour the starting of current accounts in Central Banks because the funds so raised could not be suitably employed, and that fluid resources provision would leave little margin of profit. At the back of this suggestion was the lurking fear and suspicion that the acceptance of such deposits may be resented by commercial banks. This is an old story now, and Central Banks throughout the country accept current deposits. In the Punjab current accounts have only very recently been started by Central Banks, and even then not by all. Current account business was started by the Central Bank, Lahore, in 1925. The number of such accounts rose from 77 in 1925 to 315 in 1930.

DEMAND BILLS AND CHEQUES

The collection of demand bills and cheques and the sale of demand drafts is done by the central institutions only in towns where there are no commercial banks. The banks adhere to the restrictions laid down, and are doing this work efficiently. The following figures, which on account of duplication in calculation must be allowed 30 to 50 per cent discount, show the volume of such transactions in 1933:

	Number	Value, Rs. (lakhs)
Demand drafts sold	4,051	13,32
Demand bills and cheques collected ..	14,811	45,84

The permission granted to central institutions for collection of demand bills and cheques and the sale of demand drafts is subject to the following restrictions:

(*a*) Only banks in towns where there are no commercial banks are permitted to collect;

(*b*) For their own customers;

(*c*) For other persons at such places as the commercial banks of their town, having no agents, are unable to collect.

Restrictions as regard the issuing of drafts are similar. The object in granting this permission and putting such restrictions upon the Co-operative Central Institutions is simply to give facilities to the public at large which would be lacking otherwise. Any competition with the existing commercial banks is to be discouraged.

BRANCHES

Branches of Central Banks in the Punjab are limited to only three. Gujranwala Central Bank has its branch at Hafizabad, and Ambala Central Bank has two branches, one at Nariangarh and the other at Jagdhri.

LOAN AND DEPOSIT TRANSACTIONS OF CENTRAL BANKS

The rate paid on deposits and charged on loans has varied considerably during the last five years on account of the acute depression. In the Punjab the most usual rate in normal times was 6 to 7 per cent on deposits, and 9 to 12 per cent on borrowings. Owing to the depression rates paid on all types of deposits have gone down considerably.

PAYMENT OF LAND REVENUE THROUGH CENTRAL BANKS

Mr. F. L. Brayne, Deputy Commissioner, Gurgaon, initiated an experiment in the payment of land revenue through the Central Bank at Rewari. Substantial payments of revenue were made through the bank as long as Mr. Brayne held charge of the District, but payments have now dwindled to mere insignificance.

In 1928 the Government instituted a general inquiry with a view to ascertain whether facility for payment of land revenue through Central Banks should be extended to the whole of the Province, or failing that to such Co-operative Banks alone as were situated in places where there was a branch of the Imperial Bank. Payment of revenue through Co-operative Central Banks was practically universally condemned, and the second part of the suggestion had to be dropped as premature. The Punjab Banking Enquiry Committee feel that if the Government wishes to encourage the banking habit amongst the rural classes, an obvious way of doing so is to allow payment of its dues through a bank, wherever it is possible. The Committee suggest that a further experiment should be tried at places where there is a branch of the Imperial Bank and where Co-operation is well established. Jullundur tahsil is suitable in both respects.

PAYMENT OF MILITARY PENSIONS

Nearly Rs. 140 lakhs are annually paid in the Punjab by way of military pensions. The payment is made through the Post Offices, and it is a pity that nothing is done by the Postal Department to encourage saving of any part of these pensions. At the instance of Mr. F. L. Brayne, the Registrar discussed with the military authorities the desirability of making such payments on the option of the pensioner, through the Co-operative Societies. The suggestion did not materialize, for it is impossible at present to make payments through Village Societies, and the Adjutant-General in India did not approve of the use of Central Banks as an experimental measure. If the habit of saving and investment is to be encouraged among the rural population of this country it is of the utmost importance that such opportunities should be availed of without much further delay.

PROGRESS OF THE CENTRAL CO-OPERATIVE CREDIT SOCIETIES IN THE PUNJAB

Years	Numbers	Members	Working Capital (In lakhs of rupees)
1918	45	4,866	56,16
1919	57	5,701	71,75
1920	80	7,476	92,42
1921	98	8,963	130,68
1922	110	10,454	166,13
1923	110	11,548	188,80
1924	113	12,441	222,79
1925	111	14,108	295,81
1926	111	16,149	379,17
1927	116	17,991	502
1928	118	20,151	607
1929	120	21,678	664
1930	118	22,400	706
1931	119	22,770	709
1932	119	22,950	709
1933	118	22,288	715
1934	118	23,093	686

COST OF MANAGEMENT OF CENTRAL BANKS

The Banking Unions and the Central Banks have in recent years shown a remarkable increase in efficiency of management.

Nearly all central financial institutions now call upon their clients for confirmation of loans, savings bank, and current accounts half-yearly or annually, and most seek such confirmation in case of fixed deposits too. The establishment of a Central Bank is often very small because these banks do not as a rule engage persons for supervision of the Primary Societies and popularization of the movement. Generally the establishment consists only of a Manager, an Accountant, Clerk, and a Treasurer. The Report for 1933 records that the working expenses of the forty-eight Central Banks represent 0·6 per cent of working capital.

PROFITS OF CENTRAL BANKS

According to the by-laws, not less than one-quarter of the net profits is to be carried to the Reserve Fund. The remainder of such profits and of any profits of past years available for distribution may be applied as follows:

(1) To the payment of dividend not exceeding 10 per cent;

(2) To the formation of a depreciation fund, building fund, or fund for the equalization of dividends;

(3) Not more than 10 per cent to pay to any purpose referred to in Section 34 of the Act, and approved by the Registrar, namely, relief of the poor, education, medical relief, and the advancement of any other object of general public utility except one relating exclusively to religious teaching or worship; or to a common good fund to be devoted to any of these purposes.

VOLUME OF PROFITS

In recent years the profits of Central Banks have shown a tendency to increase owing to the reduction in the rates paid for money and an expansion in the volume of business. The tendency has unfortunately been severely counteracted by (1) depreciation in the market value of Government securities in which Rs. 107 lakhs had been invested by these banks. Quite recently these securities have much appreciated in value and are now many lakhs above the book value, and hence the Central Banks and the Provincial Bank have a large hidden reserve. (2) The delay in the payment of large amounts of interest due from borrowing Societies on account of the fall in agricultural prices, or other similar reasons that tend to lower the earnings of the agriculturists. The profits for 1932 amounted to Rs. 10,38 lakhs, and fell to 9,82 in 1933.

The figures for 1933 indicate that the lowest amount earned as profit by a Central Bank stood at Rs. 166, while the highest profit which was earned by the Lahore Central Co-operative Bank amounted to Rs. 1,12,806.

DIVIDENDS

The average dividend paid by Central Banks for the three years ending 1931–32 was 5·4 per cent. Twenty-two banks paid a dividend for 1931–32 in 1933, seven during 1931–32 paid a dividend for 1930–31, nineteen paid no dividend for 1931–32. The Report for 1933 records: "That banks, generally in the south-east of the Province, are precluded from paying dividends until the large amount of interest is recovered which has accrued on Societies' loans and not been paid. This will not be possible until harvest conditions in this area become normal."

FLUID RESOURCES

Central Banks are required to maintain adequate fluid resources to meet the depositors' claims. The standard of such resources is fixed by the Registrar, and is generally fixed according to rules of prudent banking. The Central Co-operative Banks in the Punjab are required to keep 12½ per cent of fixed deposits maturing within twelve months, 25 per cent of savings bank balances, 50 per cent of current account balances, and the total of statutory reserve account. Fluid resources are maintained in the shape of (1) cash balances on hand, (2) undrawn cash credit with the Imperial Bank of India and with the Provincial Co-operative Bank, and (3) Government of India promissory notes.

BAD AND DOUBTFUL DEBTS

Loans from D Class Societies and from Societies under liquidation are automatically classed as "Bad and doubtful debts." Bad and doubtful debts must occur as the movement expands. It is gratifying to note that during a whole decade, 1920–30, central banking institutions had to write off only Rs. 57,954 as irrecoverable, and this sum includes Rs. 21,536 of interest. The recent depression has hit hard the cultivator and his Society, and consequently the central banking institutions.

BAD AND DOUBTFUL DEBTS OF THE CENTRAL BANKING INSTITUTIONS IN THE PUNJAB

(*Lakhs of rupees*)

	1931	1932	1933	1934
Percentage of owned capital	52	64	—	—
Total amount of bad and doubtful debts	40,89	54,68	64,63	76,53
Due from D Class Societies..	32,09	42,4	48,28	59,25
Due from Societies under liquidation	8,80	12,28	15,95	17,28
Reserve fund against bad and doubtful debts	8,33	10,47	15,83	18,24
Amounts written off—				
Principal	—	—	1,982	4,035
Interest	—	—	7,952	16,995
Total written off from the commencement of the movement—				
Capital	—	—	51,713	60,970
Interest	—	—	24,663	47,398

BAD AND DOUBTFUL DEBT FUND

All Central Banks create Bad and Doubtful Debt Funds out of their profits as special reserve against such debts. The banks aim at making this fund equal to at least half of the amount these Societies owe to the banks. By 1931 some banks had attained, or even passed, that standard. On the whole, at least the amount of the Fund, as the latest figures indicate, has not even reached 25 per cent. The total of Bad and Doubtful Debt Fund in 1933 being Rs. 15,83 lakhs, against Rs. 64,63 lakhs due under this head from Societies.

Banking Unions.—There are in addition to the Central Banks 64 Banking Unions operating in the Punjab. The unions are Central institutions operating as a rule within a radius of 10 to 15 miles, whereas banks are either district or tahsil institutions. The Punjab is rightly proud of its prosperous Banking Unions.

CHAPTER XVI

WOMEN AND CO-OPERATION

THE mistress of the house everywhere virtually controls the expenditure, and being practically always in our country more ignorant than the master, has generally no idea at all of organization or house economy. It is accepted as a truism in the Province that, other things remaining the same, the frugality or spendthriftness of a wife makes or mars a home. All unjustifiable expenses on ceremonies are vigorously defended by women, even when men declare themselves to be thoroughly sick of all those silly things. It is, therefore, of very great importance that the problem be attacked at the very source of it. Make women thrifty and you make a nation thrifty. Only the barest beginning has yet been made. In view of the colossal magnitude of the task to be attempted, the extremely insignificant efforts yet made do not justify our feeling that we have reached, as the Registrar put it, "the experimental stage." One Inspectress, helped by ten Sub-Inspectresses, constitute the frailest of fleets in a limitless ocean. Continued efforts will certainly bring better results. The Department has given us no inkling into the distribution of Societies in rural and urban areas. Evidently Women's Thrift Societies are formed more in towns than in villages, but are needed more in villages than in towns.

In villages, on account of the tremendous ignorance and universal illiteracy of women, besides other adverse factors, a thrift society will hardly be a success. But women have their own characteristic ways of doing things. In Jhelum women are stated to be "better members than male members in credit Societies." In certain places women have not only joined men's Societies, but have become their office-holders. There is every hope that more effort will yield still better results. The Sub-Inspectress has to face countless difficulties in a Province like the Punjab, where Muhammadan girls have to observe purdah.

Their life is one of real hardship, particularly when they are in camp. Defective means of communication and unsatisfactory arrangements concerning their board and lodging when in camp present insurmountable difficulties. All credit to those who are working under these conditions.

THE "COMETI"

The Punjab woman has her own method of effecting compulsory savings. It is known as "Cometi." It is essentially the same system as flourishes in Japan and China under different names. A brief account of its working will not be out of place, for it is this indigenous system of saving which at once resists the growth of Co-operation among women, and which in certain respects will serve as the foundation upon which the edifice of Co-operation can be erected with the greatest and the surest chance of success. A number of women, ten or more, generally the number is above ten, come together and decide to organize a Cometi. The members of a Cometi always are known quite intimately to each other. Each member undertakes to subscribe an equal and a specified sum each month. This contribution is to be paid for as many months as the number of members of the Cometi. The monthly subscription is deposited with or paid to the Secretary, who enjoys the confidence of the members, and is often elected for having taken the initiative in organizing, or, as I should like to put it, for floating the Cometi.

The amount so subscribed is advanced to one member on a fixed date after all members have paid up their instalments for that month. This accumulated amount is paid out or advanced by the consent of a number of members to any member who has already orally applied for it on account of some pressing need. In case a number of claims are put forward simultaneously, decision is taken by throwing the lot. Every member has to be paid her claim only once. Generally at the completion of the first term, if it proves a troublesome affair the organizer's enthusiasm dies out, and the Cometi vanishes into thin air. If, owing to the co-operation of and discipline among members, it has worked with smoothness and satisfaction, it may with the addition of falling out of some members prolong its existence for yet another term. The contributions in case of poor people amount to only one or two annas a day.

Through this organization some very real needs of the people are met without getting into debt. Not only that, the great economic advantage besides promotion of the habit of thrift is the saving in the form of payment of interest to the sahukar, the high rate of which in the Punjab is the most fundamental cause of the exploitation of the poor and perpetuation of indebtedness. It is through some compulsory savings and investments that a poor widow manages in a term of years the expenses of the marriage of her daughter. It is through the Cometi that some women come to possess ornaments which serve as their reserve for the rainy day, and it is again through this system that women can meet all types of pressing needs without making any payment in the form of interest, or without getting entangled in the meshes of a money-lender. One woman I know had through participating in the Cometi system within a number of years saved a sum of Rs. 300, which she spent in paying the initial expenses of sending a brilliant son to the Law College, Lahore. The young man is an old pupil of mine, and will no doubt feel a little amused at the manner in which I am using this information about him.

A word about the working of this system. On the whole it works admirably well, but, like all other systems, it has its own disadvantages. The disadvantages, to my mind, are not inherent in the system, but ingrained in human nature. Some members when they are refused an advance carry their resentment too far, and sever their connection with the organization. This is quite disgusting, but it is there nevertheless. In such a case all instalments which the member has paid to the Cometi have to be returned to her, and in the normal course of events it is a little inconvenient to arrange this repayment. Sometimes the organizers advance money at first to their friends and relations, which is resented by others. Very rarely a member may refuse to pay for some time, but the social pressure is too great for anyone to resist payment successfully for any length of time. The Registrar, Co-operative Societies, Punjab, in his Report for 1926, concerning the working of this institution, remarks as follows: ". . . the total collection is paid over in each month to the member on whom the lot falls. Nothing can be more pernicious, or more attractive to the unreflecting mind. It is a gamble, and the monthly prize is ordinarily wasted." This remark was made by Mr. C. F. Strickland, one of the Registrars, whose name will for ever be ingrained in the grateful memories of the people in the Punjab. I wish I could understand this remark better than I do. From the original in the report which I have before me I am inclined to believe that it is not the Cometi as an institution that Mr. Strickland is pleased to style a "gamble." On the face of it, it is payment to members by lot which he refers to when he talks of a gamble. The great moral standard which the ideal co-operator wishes to attain may perhaps find a "gamble" in making payment by lots. As far as I can see, there is no gambling about it. In our enthusiasm for Co-operation in its truest spirit, let us not close our eyes to the reasonableness of the methods adopted by others. Throwing the "lot" is, where all accept it, if not the fairest, the only practical method of taking decisions in such cases. The process followed in the Punjab is as follows. The names of all the members are written on slips of paper. These slips are put in a pot and well mixed up. An equal number of slips, only one of which bears the word "Cometi," the rest being blank, is put in another pot and well mixed up. A child is asked to take out of these pots one slip each at the same time.

This process is continued till the child has in one hand the name of a member and in the other the slip marked "Cometi." The payment for that month is made to that member. I feel there is nothing pernicious in it, and I see no reason why the chief among the co-operators should call it a "gamble." Maybe nothing is "more attractive to the unreflecting mind," but it remains a fact that all the originality of reflecting minds has as yet failed under similar conditions to devise a more satisfactory method of taking decisions. As to this monthly prize being "ordinarily wasted," I can simply say that this, even if taken for granted, is in no way a fault of the system but of the individual. Have all co-operators learnt the wise use of money? He must be a brave man who can answer this question in the affirmative. A study of the Report for 1927 reveals Mr. Strickland's mind in perfect unambiguity. "Every scandal in the rival 'Cometi' societies is a point in our favour. These gambling clubs are still popular, and no plan has yet been evolved to divert them on to Co-operative lines; their essence is risk, with undeserved loss and gain, for which Co-operation has no place." If a man's thoughts can be studied from his books, I think I am advancing a very modest claim when I say that I have made every effort to understand the working of Mr. Strickland's mind as well as it was possible for me to do. My impression is that he was a born co-operator, and whenever he lifted his pen in support of Co-operation he wrote with an inherent and honest conviction, and not merely out of a sense of duty associated with the head of the Co-operative movement in a Province. Such extra strong condemnation of the Cometi makes me feel that these remarks are born of misinformation. Not only are these Cometies not gambling clubs; they are founded upon the joint and several honesty, thrift, mutual confidence, and all such moral qualities which form the very stuff of Co-operation. The success of these Cometies is the surest indication of the Co-operative sense of the women in the Punjab. If no plan has yet been evolved to divert them on to Co-operative lines, why get annoyed over it?

This should, however, in no way be treated as a defence of the "Cometi" as opposed to the Co-operative Thrift Society for women. I believe if an earnest effort were made along the right lines it would be possible to capture whole Cometies and transform them into Thrift Societies for women. The average women in the town is now on account of greater demands upon her reserves anxious to save more, and no one is more conscious of the worries that a "Cometi" involves.

If she is approached in the right spirit and along sound lines there is no doubt that a mere diversion of the course will make the stream of her savings flow with greater force and rapidity. A Co-operative Thrift Society, in point of view of the soundness of its working, the perfect safety of its contributions, and its freedom from frauds and ill-feelings, is far above the "Cometi," which can only be tolerated in the absence of any other thrift-promoting organization. Hardly had an attempt been made for a year by an Inspectress, who undertook "to convert five million women of the Province," before the Department seemed to have exhausted all its stock of patience. "Their essence is risk, with undeserved loss and gain, for which Co-operation has no place." In these words have the Cometies been denounced. When and if a loss occurs it surely is undeserved. Are we to understand that a loss when it occurs in a Co-operative organization is fully deserved? But how is the gain undeserved? There is no gain. What one saves over a number of months one receives back in a lump sum. If it be so, as undoubtedly it is, and the Department with all its love for Co-operation and the proverbial blindness of love cannot have the courage to deny it, I should like to know how and where the element of "undeserved gain" comes in when a member of a Co-operative Society with unlimited liability renders himself liable to payment for the sins of others. Surely it is an indefensible case of undeserved loss. I repeat once again that the Cometi is an exceedingly safe and sound foundation upon which to build Women's Societies. Surely these can be diverted to Co-operative lines, but as long as we fail to devise such means for their diversion or conversion let us be more chivalrous adversaries.

Miss Ahmad Shah, B.A., a Christian lady, after completing her training and passing her test at Gurdaspur examination, set her shoulder to this task of stupendous importance. Regarding women in the Punjab, the Registrar's opinion was that "they are not unfriendly to the Co-operative idea, but cannot in the mass be described as either progressive or courageous." With an admirable insight into the foundations of individual and national prosperity the Department's line of attack was "to preach thrift." Four months' efforts brought into existence fifteen Women's Thrift Societies. Efforts in the first year were almost entirely confined to the Lahore division. The difficulties in the path of the worker were in the beginning and remain up till now quite abnormal.

DIFFICULTIES IN ORGANIZING AND RUNNING SOCIETIES FOR WOMEN

(1) Sub-Inspectors cannot undertake any actual or even propaganda work on account of purdah and other restrictions imposed upon us by our modes of life.

(2) Sub-Inspectresses whose services are secured demand high salaries with poor qualifications.

(3) "Husbands may be hostile, either fearing that enlightenment will make their womenfolk more expensive and less submissive, or finding them so perfect and enlightened that no improvement can be conceived. Sometimes husbands who do not object to their wives joining the Societies in the beginning, seem to realize, and do actually complain afterwards, that 'the Society was a nuisance.' "

(4) "Women are also self-satisfied, no less than the rest of us, and are confident that their views are correct."

(5) They are hopelessly unpunctual as a class.

(6) They are not capable of giving sustained attention and continued interest.

(7) Their meetings can have no air of seriousness and business.

The Inspectresses' description of their meetings is simply exquisite, besides being wonderfully true to life: "The Inspectress draws a distressing picture of meetings which resemble a *mela*, with babies howling, youngsters quarrelling, and their mothers chattering and wanting only to be amused."

(8) In most of the Societies, members are thoroughly

illiterate, and the first difficulty after organizing a Society presents itself in the choice of a Secretary. That Society is supposed to be lucky in which even a single member is literate.

(9) It is equally difficult to find a Treasurer to fill an office which, in reality to be adequately occupied, needs higher qualifications than those necessary for Secretaryship. These two difficulties are surmounted by resorting to the exceedingly undesirable, but under the circumstances utterly unavoidable, practice of combining the two offices in one member. It is on account of lack of literacy and the prevailing unbusinesslike habits that the Department does not always find it "possible to keep the Societies strictly within the by-laws." It is apprehended that any "insistence on strict compliance would scare them out of existence." "There is no check over what is done between two visits of the staff. So we have to make a virtue out of a necessity, and are guiding them with a light hand." In 1930, in twenty-one Societies the local Sub-Inspectress had to work as Honorary Secretary for want of any member competent enough to take up that work. In 1929–30, "the Inspectress inspected all but eighteen Societies, and in the case of sixteen she reports that inspection was impossible, because members obstinately refused to take any interest whatever in the Societies. These will have to be closed. The other two Societies were not inspected because in one case the President went to the hills for the whole summer and the books were not obtainable in her absence, and in the other no accounts had been kept."

(10) Meetings have often to be postponed on account of religious and social obligations.

(11) Prejudices and suspicions of different kinds have to be faced. "One Society, after being registered, refused to work owing to a rumour that the Inspectress belonged to the Criminal Investigation Department." In some cases women are mentally incapable of understanding the Sub-Inspectresses' earnestness in organizing such Societies. They seem to feel that somehow or other it is the Sub-Inspectress that will be the gainer and not the members themselves. Some women honestly suspect

that the Government may at any time take possession of their money. Some really believe that the Inspectress by coming into contact with them can find out their real economic position, which knowledge may involve them in some additional payments. There is no end to such suspicions. It does happen that a number of women agree to organize a Society. The Sub-Inspectress's persuasion has succeeded. The next day the Sub-Inspectress sees all her fond hopes dashed to the ground. Something has made all the women to go back upon their own decision. The Sub-Inspectress, poor frail worker, has to invite help from other quarters. The Sub-Inspector of the circle comes to her help and persuades the male members belonging to the families of prospective lady members of a Society. The birth of a Women's Society is a painful and a laborious process.

(12) In some Societies the low rate of interest on deposits, 7 per cent in 1928, did not seem sufficiently attractive. A Society consisting of Hindus refused to consider anything less than $37\frac{1}{2}$ per cent. Mussulman women display a still harder prejudice against charging of interest.

(13) In some cases, "a rival association formed," according to the advocates of Co-operation, "on more gambling lines . . ." the Cometi, succeeds in enticing away the members of a Women's Society.

(14) One circle Registrar remarks that Women's Societies are "always overshadowed by a danger of party faction among the husbands of their members. If the husbands fall out, the Women's Society ceases to function."

(15) Failures of the members to pay their monthly contribution is an exceedingly disappointing feature of Women's Societies. In 1929–30 no less than 528 members, i.e. about one out of every four, had to be expelled, mostly for non-payment of monthly contributions.

(16) Women are more susceptible to suspicion, and their faith therefore can be more easily shaken in anything at any time. In 1929, in the words of the Registrar, "the political situation produced an atmosphere of doubt which led many to demand back their money, and Rs. 45,892 were withdrawn

as against Rs. 9,550 the year before," while the amount of withdrawals, due obviously to a shaken confidence, during 1931–32 rose up to Rs. 88,192. This withdrawal on the basis of the working capital for 1931 works out at over 63 per cent. This needs no elaboration or comment.

OBJECT AND METHOD

In the words of Mr. Darling, the aim of the movement among women "is to make these Societies a means for opening women's

Year	Societies	Members	Working Capital	Withdrawals Rs.
			Rs.	
1928	112	1,691	16,285	9,550
1929	128	1,977	90,319	45,892
1930	146	2,397	1,03,105	—
1931	164	2,871	1,39,701	—
1932	171	2,889	1,59,049	88,192
1933	189	3,393	1,86,000	87,550
1934	218	3,955	2,33,000	1,15,701

minds to the possibilities of a better life." Workers among women have of necessity to do more than mere organization of Societies. I quote the two following instances from the Annual Report for 1928 as typical of the way in which this problem is being handled. "As a step in this direction a club or women's institute for social and educational activities was started at Gurdaspur two years ago, and during the year it was able to purchase books, magazines, and a badminton set with the proceeds of an exhibition of articles made by its members. It is arguable whether an institution of this kind should be registered under the Co-operative Societies Act, but it certainly owes its existence to the co-operative spirit, and is an example of the influence of this spirit upon women.

"Another example is the action of the head mistress of a Sikh girls' school, who has formed a committee of her teachers to preach the cause of better living amongst the women of the surrounding villages. The stimulus in this case was the Thrift Society in the school." The following figures give an idea of the growth of Societies for Women, as an offshoot of which Children's Societies are being started. Like mothers and children they have been grouped together.

Out of 189, Thrift Societies number 183, five are Children's Thrift Societies, and one a Better Living Society.

LOCALITIES

A large majority of these Societies is situated in towns and villages of Sialkot, Gujranwala, Gujrat, Lahore, Amritsar, Gurdaspur, Kangra, Jullundur, and Ludhiana.

COMMUNITIES

Most of the Societies are Societies of women belonging to one community only. About half the number of members are Muslim women, and Hindus and Sikhs form only one-third. The number of Christians is considerable, and a sprinkling of sweepers is met with. The former practice of organizing Societies by communities is rightly being given up, and the new Societies draw their membership from all communities. In fourteen Societies for Women membership is open to men as well.

CONTRIBUTIONS

The sources from which contributions are derived were analysed in 1932 as follows:

	1932	1933
Salaries	734	Out of 3,393, 892 pay out of their own salaries
Miscellaneous occupation	250	361 from income of industries and occupations
Household savings ..	1,905	2,140 from household savings

SOCIAL POSITION OF MEMBERS

The following table, prepared in 1932, indicates the social position of the members of such Societies, and the table indicates the callings of the men-folk.

Lawyers	119
Business men	427
Doctors	57
Services	764
Zemindars	440
Labour	176
Crafts	852

The funds of the Societies are deposited in Central Banks, Unions, Credit Societies, and Thrift Societies. The deposits are in either fixed or savings bank account.

CLASSIFICATION

At the end of the year 1932 Women's Societies were classified as follows:

Year	A	B	C	D	Unclassed Registered	Unregis-tered	Total
1932	27	73	25	9	20	17	171
1933	37	66	32	21	10	23	189

In 1930 we were told that the standard of classification adopted was not the same as for Men's Societies. The Registrar's remark concerning the classification made in 1932 is very significant. "This classification, if at all accurate, is surprisingly good." In the classification for 1933 increase in D class is according to the Registrar "probably due to stricter classification rather than to actual deterioration."

The position of a woman in society differs with the status of men of the family to which she belongs. Amongst the educated and the rich it is a fashion these days to let women have this satisfaction. People who belong to the lower grades of society seem actually to grudge women ownership in any form, for they seem to feel that ownership of property in the name of a woman is derogatory to the honour of man. It is on account of this feeling that Children's Societies were started. The Registrar records in his Report for 1932 as follows: "By-laws for Children's Societies are being drafted. The need for these Societies is ascribed to some reluctance on the part of their menfolk to allow women to save in their own names, whereas men will subscribe for their children's savings with alacrity." To capture the active support of the ladies in a house for any scheme, particularly one regarding expenditure, is the surest method of carrying it through. But children as future masters and mistresses of homes must learn to cultivate the virtue of thrift along with all the manifold moral and business lessons that the membership of a Society brings. The Inspectress, therefore, did only what was right in extending her scope of experiment. In 1929 two Children's Thrift Societies were started. Membership was thrown open to children of both the sexes and of all ages. These Societies are run mostly with the help of the mothers of the members.

The following table shows their growth:

	1929	1930	1931	1932	1933
Number of Children's Societies	2	8	9	7	5

The monthly contributions of the members are deposited in the Mother's Thrift Societies. Although men showed a greater willingness to let money be deposited in the name of their children than they did in the case of their women, yet even this effort seems to have been in vain.

CHAPTER XVII

EDUCATION OF THE STAFF

EDUCATION is the very basis of all progressive life. Co-operation as a movement rests upon education, but in its turn and in its own way promotes the growth of general and business education. But in a country like India, where both the standard and percentage of literacy are hopelessly low, the growth of the Co-operative movement must needs be slow and uncertain. A healthy development of the movement must rest upon a thorough knowledge of the theory and working of Co-operation, Rural Economics, and all allied subjects by those who are responsible for the working of the Department. Education in Co-operation for members of the staff of this Department is like the technical or professional education so essential to success in every walk of life. Since the members of the staff of the Department possess a high standard of general education, it is not difficult for them to acquire a fair working knowledge of Co-operation and of the allied subjects.

The education of the staff of the Department, in the Punjab, owes its origin to that shrewdness and sagacity which Mr. Calvert combined with practical knowledge and an insight into the future requirements of the movement. The object and scope of the education of the staff is best brought out in the Annual Report of the Department for 1920 by Mr. Calvert:

"The first duty of every member of the staff is to secure for himself a thorough education in the meaning of Co-operation, the application of its principles to various problems, its achievements in different countries, and its place in modern agriculture. His next duty is to teach his subordinates and the members of the Committee, and through them the public in general. But that is not all. Inspectors are directed to make a close study of the causes of the common ills, and then to try to devise some remedy on Co-operative lines, that is to say, they are to show the people how to help them to this end."

It was with this object in view that education of the staff was put on a permanent basis. A detailed curriculum in Rural Economics and Co-operation was drawn up and an Educational Inspector was appointed in 1920. The education of the staff is now conducted along the following lines:

INSPECTORS' CLASS

Candidates for this class are selected from amongst new applicants, who must be graduates in Economics or Agriculture, and should preferably belong to the agricultural tribes in the Punjab. A number of students to this class are elected from amongst the Sub-Inspectors in the Department.

Every year an Inspectors' class is held at Gurdaspur. The period of training, formerly three months, now extends from November to February, four months each year. Inspector candidates undergo theoretical training for the first three months and then they are posted as Sub-Inspectors. They are required to undergo training for one month in a Central Bank, and for another in the office of a Circle Registrar. After this they have to attend the Inspectors' class. This class enjoys the best attention of the Department, and besides the Inspector candidates from the Province is attended by students, and even officials from the N.W.F. Province, Delhi, Ajmere, U.P., and a number of Native States.

The courses cover a description of the rural life of the Punjab in most of its aspects, particularly of those which in one way or another are related to the economic life of the people. Besides this, the course includes the Law and Principles of Co-operation. The practical side of the question is not neglected even here. Students are given some practical training. Inspector candidates, nowadays, are mostly very well equipped young men, and their qualifications have enabled the Department to proudly proclaim its achievements in this direction, and the Province richly merits the distinction of leading the rest of India in the matter of education of its staff.

The syllabus is an elaborate one, and a general complaint

against these classes is that too much is sought to be pumped into the aching heads of the Punjab graduates. After completion of the course they are subjected to a fairly stiff examination, which by the time they leave their colleges they learn thoroughly to abhor. This written and oral test is conducted by the highest officials of the Department. The educated young man in the Province, like the cultivator, has an infinite capacity for undergoing all sorts of sufferings quite patiently. A Punjabi young man will surely suffer all this necessary spade work for the reconstruction of a prosperous Province. The lot of these graduates, who on entering this Department court a rough life which their education unfits them to face, excites nothing but pity. I feel constrained to remark that the hardship of the initial stages of the life of an Inspector candidate should be mitigated at least by the grant of a more liberal allowance than is sanctioned at present.

SUB-INSPECTORS' CLASS

The Sub-Inspector is the very pivot of the Department. It is his work that will make or mar the movement anywhere. He is the man on the spot, and represents the spirit and methods of the Department. He must be a man of the right type, and he must have had a good general education, and a thorough training for the profession he decides to enter. Special attention is therefore paid to the education of the Sub-Inspector. A Sub-Inspector candidate is required to undergo field training with a Sub-Inspector and under an Inspector. When the candidate has completed six months' field training he is sent to the Sub-Inspectors' class. This class lasts for two months, and is generally held twice every year in the divisional jurisdiction of a Deputy Registrar. Teaching is undertaken by the Educational Inspector and the Educational Assistant. The syllabus prescribed is not very much different from that for the Inspectors' class, but with a view to making things more intelligible lectures are delivered in Urdu.

Occasionally this class attracts some graduates. The standard of understanding and teaching displayed in this class is fairly satisfactory. Candidates studying in this class are subjected to a test, after the completion of the course, and no candidate who fails to pass this test is posted as a Sub-Inspector.

CLASS FOR SUB-INSPECTORESSES

Miss Ahmad Shah, B.A., Inspectoress in charge of Co-operation among women in the Punjab, received her training at Gurdaspur, and passed the required test. The Punjab pioneered the establishment of Societies for women. For the working of such Societies the services of Sub-Inspectoresses are needed, and the success of the movement depends in the first instance upon the education and training of the workers. Whenever necessary a separate class is opened for the candidates. The first class was started in 1928 at Gurdaspur. The class for 1933 was held at the Model Town, Lahore, for a month.

SECRETARIES' CLASSES

A Secretary is an office-holder in a Society. The success of a Primary Society depends upon the ability and honesty of the Managing Committee. But the Secretary of a Rural Primary Society is the guiding spirit and leader of the movement, and Societies in a large measure owe their success or failure to the ability and honesty of the Secretary. The interest of the movement demands that a Secretary should have a thorough knowledge of the entire working of a Society. Since 1926 classes for Secretaries are held each year at different places. As a rule, a class lasts for a week. Those attending the class are given stipends, and prizes are awarded to those who attain some distinction.

Through these classes it is hoped so to improve the standard of book-keeping in Societies as to inspire greater confidence and infuse more honesty in the working of Societies. Apart from that, these classes, it is hoped, will make Secretaries take greater interest in their work, and so broaden their outlook as to render them an extremely useful and reliable link between members of the Societies and officers of the Department. An efficient and an honest Secretary is the first requisite of a healthy Society, and a successful Society is the soundest, safest, cheapest, and the most effective form of propaganda for the popularization of the movement. Over ten thousand Secretaries, by this time, have had their training through this class. As a result of this training rules are honoured, and book-keeping has considerably improved.

CLASS FOR SECRETARIES OF UNIONS

The Secretary of a Union is a man whose sphere of work and responsibility is wider than that of the Secretary of a Primary Society. Classes for the Secretaries of Unions are held three times in a year, generally in Lahore, Gurdaspur, and Hoshiarpur. Every class lasts about three weeks. The auditors of the Punjab Co-operative Union are in charge of these classes. The Financial Adviser also inspects these classes. The Department of Co-operation very much appreciates the usefulness of such classes.

CLASSES FOR THE STAFF OF CENTRAL BANKS

Everyone connected with the Co-operative movement must receive training for the adequate discharge of his duties. The staff of a Central Bank must be trained in the different branches of work which the running of such a bank involves. It was in 1927 that such a class was started for the first time in Lahore. Thirty-two men joined, but all failed. The second class of its type was started in May 1930, and the third in 1931. This class was not held in 1932, owing to paucity of students. The syllabus of the class deals with methods of keeping accounts, the Co-operative Societies Act, Negotiable Instruments Act, Departmental Circulars concerning Central Banks, the Daily Working of a bank, the Practical Working of a bank, etc.

REFRESHER COURSE

The candidate entering the Department is subjected to an intensive training, and rightly so. But when a man has been on field duty for years together he cannot be expected to remember all the theory he had mastered while under training. The temptation of showing the volume of work accomplished by him may make him neglect in practice certain essentials and fundamentals of the movement. The man on field duty experiences certain difficulties in the working of the movement of which the lecturer in Theory of Co-operation has not the faintest idea. The teacher and the worker are like the inventor and the operator of a machine. The principles of the machine are understood by the inventor, but it is the actual operator who knows the flaws in the working of the machine and can suggest improvements. The operator can as well stress the necessity of adaptation to conditions of which the inventor had no knowledge. Just as the meeting of the inventor and the operator is necessary for the perfection of a machine, similarly the field worker and the teacher of Co-operation must meet in the interest of the smooth working of the movement. The theoretical teacher must know the pitfalls in the working of the movement, and the man on field duty must not be allowed to forget or ignore under the stress of adverse circumstances the very theory and spirit of the movement. Refresher courses were started in 1920 for the first time. Generally two Circle Registrars combine and hold such a class that lasts for about a week, and is attended by all the Sub-Inspectors and Inspectors in those two circles. Through these classes new knowledge is imparted to those whose active work leaves them no time for study. The practical difficulties experienced by the field workers are detailed, and their solutions are evolved through discussions.

In these classes some questions of the highest importance are discussed, and stress is laid on the practical side of the work. In 1932, amongst others, the following subjects were discussed:

(1) Co-operative Credit has done more good than harm.

(2) Recoveries can be improved better by persuasion than by pressure.

(3) The present economic depression is a boon in disguise for the farmer.

(4) Co-operation, especially credit Co-operation, is the most effective remedy for the removal of indebtedness.

According to the Report for 1932, "Among the controversial points discussed at the classes during the year were problems such as the swelling of overdues of interest, the problem of recoveries, the attitude to be taken with regard to D Class Societies, the difficulties in liquidation, execution and the like."

THE CLASS IN AGRICULTURE

The Punjab is an agricultural Province, and the co-operator has at every step to come in contact with agriculturists. Mere provision of credit will be of little avail. The co-operator who seeks to improve the lot of the cultivator must of necessity be in a position to advise him in respect of betterment of his methods of production and business. With this object in mind, Sub-Inspectors in the Department are sent for training to a class in agriculture. This training class for the Department was started about twenty years ago. This class in Agriculture is held for six months at Lyallpur and Gurdaspur, under the auspices of the Agricultural Department. But the sending of Sub-Inspectors as candidates to this class has for the present been stopped as a measure of retrenchment.

SECTIONAL CONFERENCES

The colossal illiteracy in the country is detrimental to the growth of every beneficial movement. General education is the very foundation upon which any movement can thrive. But education will be slow in coming. It is no use quarrelling with the tools. Those who join the Co-operative movement are well looked after. Occasional sectional conferences are held, and co-operators come together to receive education in Co-operation and problems that affect them. Elaborate arrangements for making a success of these conferences are made. Officers from other Departments, e.g. the Public Health, Veterinary, and Agriculture, give every help and assistance. A perusal of reports of the proceedings of such conferences will convince everyone of the extreme usefulness of these conferences.

The Educational Inspectors, or their Assistants, deliver lectures at Normal Schools. The Co-operators' Day, celebrated throughout the Province, is an attempt at enlightening the general public, and at awakening universal interest in the movement.

There are three Educational Inspectors, each one of whom has an Educational Assistant.

In 1935 the Government of India sanctioned a grant of about Rs. 15 lakhs for the training of office-bearers and members of Co-operative Societies. A portion of this grant was given to the Punjab, which has enabled one Educational Assistant Registrar, three additional Educational Inspectors, and three Educational Assistants to be appointed for five years.

CHAPTER XVIII

STOCK-BREEDING SOCIETIES

THE Punjab is essentially an agricultural Province, and the importance of a good stock in such a Province is fundamental. We have a fairly large number of cattle, but their quality is far from satisfactory. Cattle mortality, as in the rest of India, is very high in the Punjab. Although no reliable data are available the general impression is that the quality of milk as well as of plough cattle has deteriorated as compared to the quality of stock half a century ago. Prices of cattle have gone up in spite of this deterioration. Cattle are needed for use as the source of motive power in agriculture, and as a source of milk supply. The Punjab farmer cannot till his land if he has no bullocks, but he is practically done for if he gets no *lassi* or curd. A conscious and an organized effort is necessary to improve the stock in the Province. To a very considerable extent the prosperity of agriculture is bound up with the quality of the stock our farmers possess. Two bad cows cost more and yield less than one good cow. The Sahiwal, Hariana, and Dhanni cattle are of very superior quality, and bulls bred at the Hissar Farm are excellent, and were once in great demand outside India, but in the interests of the Province their export has now been stopped. The Punjab is a Province eminently suited for the breeding of good stock. Breeding by the average cultivator for milk or slaughter is practically unknown. Breeding for milk is carried on in Hissar Farm and in Montgomery, where grants have been given for breeding Montgomery cattle with a fine milk strain. A farmer keeps usually more cattle than he can adequately feed and look after. There has come about a great increase in demand for milk and ghee in the Province, but the average yield of cows and buffaloes is very low, and has certainly not increased. If the Punjab farmer is to be extricated out of his misery and poverty he must improve the stock of his cattle. Scientific stock control in Denmark has doubled the yield of milk and trebled that of butter in about half a century. Selection in Lyallpur has done much the same at the Agricultural Farm. Colonel Matson also enormously improved the yield of his famous Montgomery herd at Ferozepore Military Dairy Farm. The Punjab farmer can do it. He will have to do it, and of all other forms of Co-operation this must appeal to him most. The Department of Co-operation unaided cannot reasonably be expected to achieve much.

All must combine to make the Punjab peasant realize the benefit of stock-breeding, and all must undertake to give him every help and encouragement. Deputy Commissioners can do much if they take some little interest in the material welfare of the people. Nothing appeals to the Punjab farmer more than the interest taken in him by the immediate Government officials.

ADVANTAGES OF STOCK-BREEDING SOCIETIES

(1) The villager is full of inertia, and even when he is convinced of the usefulness of a scheme, he seems unable for one reason or another to take the initiative, or make any sustained effort. The Stock-breeding Societies have demonstrated to him the advantages of keeping an improved stock of animals. The demonstration has been of very great use, and as a result of it, as one of the Registrars once put it, "the villager is beginning to think."

(2) *Prizes and High Prices.*—The tangible evidences in the form of prizes won by the cows owned by the members of Stock-breeding Societies and high prices realized by young stock of approved parents have convinced the cultivator of the usefulness of good stock. At each District fair, where enlisted cows are sent, they are invariably declared as "the best cows in the fair." In 1925 the enlisted cows won 150 prizes, and in 1926 the value of prizes won by registered cows and bulls amounted to Rs. 2,000.

(3) *Breeding for Special Purposes.*—The one great advantage of Stock-breeding Societies has been the realization by the

cultivator that breeding for special purposes is essential. These Societies have taught him that breeding for milk, for plough, and in the case of sheep for wool and mutton, must be undertaken on definite lines.

(4) *Agreeable to Castrating.*—Strong, healthy, and beautiful progeny cannot be supplied by the pigmy-sized detestable creatures that we call cows and bulls. The cultivator's chief difficulty in this respect is the "scrub" bull that roams about in the herds and serves to perpetuate a race of abominable animals; castrating such useless bulls is like striking at the very root of the evil. But the religious sentiment of the Hindu makes this difficult of attainment. As a class the cultivator does realize that castration of useless bulls is essential in the interest of future generations of the stock. The Stock-breeding Societies have helped to spread the movement for castration with a view to eliminating the most fundamental source that works for perpetuating the worthlessness of the stock. The introduction of the Burdizzo castrater has gone a long way in popularizing castration of bulls. In fifteen Cattle-breeding Societies of Lyallpur 244 bulls were castrated in 1925, and during 1926 in eleven villages of the same district no less than 534 bulls were similarly treated. Religious scruples of Bishnois still stand, and two Societies in 1928 positively forbade castration of bulls. Wherever Hindu sentiments prevail bad young bulls likely to damage the future stock are segregated in Gowshalas, or are sold out of the village before they reach maturity. Mussulmans as practical farmers show no such scruples.

(5) *A Liking for Better Stock.*—Stock-breeding has helped to develop a liking for better stock. That criminal indifference as to the quality of the stock to be kept has been shaken in the case of a large number of members of such Societies. Hariana, Hissar, Dhanni, and Montgomery breeds are preferred.

FAULTS OF THE STOCK-BREEDING SOCIETIES

(1) *Indifference.*—The Punjab farmer lacks character in its broadest sense. By habit he is incapable of putting in any

sustained effort even for his own good. He lacks the foundation upon which the prosperity of a people rests. It is surely no cause for wonder for those who know the Punjab farmer and his outlook on life that some of the Cattle-breeding Societies have shown complete indifference to their objects and ideals.

(2) *Breach of Agreement.*—The farmer has been found guilty of a breach of undertaking given by him. He is either negligent of his duties and unmindful of his promises, or the facilities at his disposal are not inviting enough. Whatever the cause, it remains a fact that in some Societies approved cows are not always covered by approved bulls.

(3) *Over-working of Bulls.*—Strange as it may seem in the light of the preceding paragraph, it remains a fact that in a number of Societies bulls and rams are heavily overworked. The remedy for this defect lies in bringing about a considerable increase in the number of bulls and rams.

(4) *Non-realization of Dues.*—The by-laws prescribe a fee to be charged on the birth of calves, and a commission to be levied on the sale of young stock. In practice these commissions and fees are seldom realized. *Basakhi* fair at Amritsar is famous throughout the Punjab, and people from every part of the Province flock there to sell and purchase animals. Members of some Stock-breeding Societies attended that fair in 1926 with a view to purchasing three hundred cows, but actually purchased only thirty, rejecting the rest of the stuff as below their standard.

KEEPING OF BULLS

The Stipend System.—In areas like the Dhanni tract, where the local stock fully meets the requirements of the standard, the District Board pays a monthly stipend to the owner of an approved bull. This bull is utilized in covering the enlisted cows. The advantage of the stipend system of maintaining bulls is that the animals are well looked after by their owners. This system, however, suffers from a very serious defect. The owner is at liberty to sell his bull whenever the offer of a high price is tempting enough for him. Either the greed or the sheer necessity of an owner may deprive a whole Society of an approved bull which is not always easy to replace.

Purchase of Bulls.—In certain tracts like Hariana, the District Board buys the bull and lends it to the community. Part of the price of the bull is contributed by the village. Under this system of maintaining approved bulls the village is sure of the possession of the animal. But this system of maintaining the bull is exceedingly disadvantageous, inasmuch as the animal is not well looked after because it belongs to everybody, and yet to nobody. In certain areas a number of villages collect grain annually, and appoint one man to feed and look after the animal. But a knowledge of our village life makes us realize that this voluntary and charitable arrangement, being extremely uncertain, is exceedingly undependable.

WORKING OF THE SOCIETIES

The object of a Stock-breeding Society is to improve the breed of milch cows in the possession of the small man, and to persuade him to enter the lists as a breeder. Sheep and Goat Societies as well were started with the same object, but have unfortunately now ceased to exist. Every member gets his cows registered, and promises to get them covered by the approved stud bulls maintained by the Societies. The Cattle-breeding Societies gave some promise of success in the beginning, and their objects and ideals have certainly given an impetus to breeding of improved stock, but of late these Societies have not been working with any measure of satisfaction.

As models of what Stock-breeding Societies should be, these Societies in the Punjab, in the words of the Registrar, "leave a vast amount to be desired." In 1929, 14 per cent of the members had no cows, this percentage rose to 24 in 1930, and fell for 1931 to 18, and once again rose in 1932 to 21 per cent. An ever-increasing number of Societies does nothing in a corporate capacity. The Report for 1931 records: "It must again be stated that Cattle-breeding Societies are, as such, largely illusory. They are, of course, meant to substitute, for a rich man interested in cattle, with a desire for improving the breed, and possessing a herd, a combination of a number of poorer men, each owning one or two head, and interested in the improvement of the breed, as being dependent on the strength of good cattle for their livelihood. Briefly, they practically never work in this way." According to the Annual Report for 1932: "A great number of these Societies are a little more than nominal Societies. Madras, Bengal, Ajmer, and Baroda have taken to cattle- and sheep-breeding on a very small scale. The Punjab still leads the rest of India, and with the return of prosperous times it is expected the Department will infuse more life into Societies that exist, and will start more of such Societies. That must be done, and now that a beginning has been made there ought to be no slackening of the pace."

CATTLE-BREEDING SOCIETIES

Year	Number of Societies	Number of Societies maintaining Stud Bulls	Percentage of Members who have no Cows	Number of Sheep Societies	Number of Prizes won by Registered Animals
1923	20	—	—	7	—
1924	36	—	—	—	—
1925	44	—	—	6	150
1929	160	103	14	—	—
1930	150	115	24	2	536
1931	145	103	18	—	485
1932	139	109	21	—	—
1933	136	—	—	—	—
1934	146	—	—	—	—

CHAPTER XIX

CATTLE INSURANCE

THE Punjab is an agricultural Province, and in the present stage of its economic development cattle constitute an indispensable factor in the prosperity of the Province. In 1929–30 the Punjab possessed 10,659 bulls, 3,939,231 bullocks, 2,418,444 cows, 2,708,481 calves, 388,108 male buffaloes, 2,727,264 cow buffaloes, 2,101,950 young stock, 4,457,786 sheep, 3,616,792 goats, 118,311 horses, 222,966 mares, 70,541 colts and fillies, 31,812 mules, 604,641 donkeys, and 279,203 camels. The animals are not well looked after in the Punjab. The fodder given to animals for the greater part of the year is of a very low quality. During winter the animals are huddled in dark and dingy cells which are almost proof against ventilation. In villages no care at all is taken in regard to the water supplied to the cattle for drinking. Usually the cattle drink at the village pond, which is a huge receptacle for all kinds of filth. The water in the pond may be dirty beyond all belief, but the cultivator very seldom feels that it will injure the health of his animals. By his manner of keeping the cattle the Punjab farmer invites disease. But his behaviour is no better when his cattle actually fall ill. He is a fatalist. He feels this illness of his cattle is God sent, and if it pleases God his animals would recover, otherwise no human effort will be of any avail. He has not the remotest of notions concerning the cause and cure of diseases. He does not believe in infection or contagion. He is not to blame for it. He is born in superstition, bred up in complete ignorance, and buried a confirmed fatalist. When his animals fall ill what does he do? He takes scant notice of it in the beginning. When he begins to think about the ill and its cure, what does he do? Whom does he consult? What is the nature of the treatment? The first person is any old man in the village whom age seems to have invested with all authority on cattle disease. He is to prescribe, and his prescription is followed if the medicine he suggests is easily available. Simultaneously, or even prior to the use of the prescription by any idiot or at best a quack in the village, the village Mullah or the priest is approached with a request to move in the matter. He usually chants something over kneaded flour, which is then given to the sick animal. If the owner is in a hurry and wants speedy recovery, clipping of ears or branding of the animal is resorted to. When a man has done all this he has exhausted all human resources, and all this medical aid rendered to the animal is in most cases worse than no aid. The farmer has his own difficulties, even when he knows that a veterinary hospital is situated at some distance from his village. As a matter of fact, these veterinary hospitals are situated in cities and towns, and for the villager living many miles away from such hospitals any medical aid is out of the question. The villager is helpless even when an epidemic breaks out. He does not know whom to inform, and often cattle die by the thousand before any medical aid is rendered. The villager's attitude in case of such preventive measures as the Doctor suggested is thoroughly disappointing. It takes a very great effort to persuade zemindars to get their cattle inoculated. They apprehend some injury to their animals, and refuse to listen to any argument, and are very hard to persuade. All this makes for a very high cattle mortality in the Punjab as in the rest of India. In rural India, arrangements for medical aid in cases of human illness are very nearly the same. Either for the love of his cattle or as a painful realization of the loss the death of an animal involves, the zemindar bewails and bemoans the death of a cow or an ox just as he would the death of a near relative. The loss is felt very keenly, and the whole family goes without food for a couple of days or so. Reliable figures of cattle mortality are not available. An idea of the annual loss through cattle mortality and the relation of cattle mortality to the cultivators' indebtedness may be had from the fact that members of Co-operative Societies alone borrowed Rs. 17 lakhs for purchase of cattle during the last three years. In such a

Province, the necessity for insurance of cattle is of the greatest importance.

The cattle insurance experiment was initiated as a result of a conference of the Departments of Agriculture and Co-operation held at Lyallpur in 1917. Actual work was started in 1918 at Beri in Rohtak District. Chowdhri Baldev Singh was put on duty as special Inspector in charge of this branch. Within a couple of years it became abundantly clear that what little progress the experiment had been making was due to the personal influence of the Inspector and not to any proper appreciation of the need for such a measure. The Department persisted in giving this experiment time enough to judge of the chances of its success. The Annual Report for 1923 records: "There is no indication that the idea of insuring cattle is gaining in popularity, while opinion within the Department is strengthening in favour of abandonment of the effort to introduce this measure." This was a signal, and the Report for 1926 records: "All the Cattle Insurance Societies except one, which was overlooked, have been cancelled, as well as the Reinsurance Union." The following are the chief features of the Punjab Cattle Insurance system:

A Society accepts for insurance only healthy plough and draught bullocks, buffaloes, and cows between the ages of four and eight years. Five per cent of the value of the animal insured is charged as premium in six-monthly instalments in advance. Each payment covers insurance for six months only. If the insured animal dies, two-thirds of its insured value is paid as indemnity. Insurance ceases when the insured animal has completed its twelfth year. In such cases no insurance claim is paid on the death of the animal, but a bonus may be given if the committee approves of it. The start was, as in most other forms of Co-operation, full of promise. But the results achieved ultimately not only belied all expectations, but turned out exceedingly disappointing. At the end of 1919 there were eight registered Societies with 301 members, who had insured 372 animals, the insured value of which stood at Rs. 29,270. The total number of Societies reached 41—

32 in Rohtak, 2 in Gurgaon, 4 in Shahpur, and 3 in Jullundur.

During their working these Societies insured 2,560 animals, the insured value of which amounted to Rs. 2,51,685, and a sum of Rs. 11,162 was collected as premiums.

In all, 34 animals were lost, and Rs. 1,735 were paid in claims.

The surplus of the cancelled Societies has in most cases been deposited in the local Credit Societies as a reserve, but a part of the same has also been employed on the following subjects: (1) Purchase of bulls, (2) Purchase of improved agricultural implements, (3) Pavement of village streets, (4) Clearance of water-courses to a village pond, or (5) has been transferred to Cattle-breeding Societies.

THE REINSURANCE UNION

With a view to reinsurance of the risks to the increasing number of Cattle Insurance Societies, a Reinsurance Union was established in 1920 at Beri in the Rohtak District. The Punjab Government undertook to advance loans to the Union in case of emergency to an amount equal to Rs. 10 per head of the cattle insured in the affiliated Societies on the preceding December 31st. The Government undertook to advance this loan free of interest. The recovery of the loan was to begin two years after the grant of the loan, and was to be spread over five annual instalments. The Government, in view of this promise, demanded that no alteration in the by-laws calculated to increase the risk undertaken by the Union be made without the sanction of the Government. The Union in return for one-half of the premium paid to Societies by their members was liable to contribute in the same proportion towards their payment of indemnities. Thirteen Societies were affiliated to the Union, which reinsured 735 cattle to the extent of Rs. 33,012 and Rs. 1,461 was collected as premiums. The Union contributed Rs. 237 for eleven reinsured animals lost during its life. The Union had no occasion to borrow from the Government. The surplus of the general fund of the Union,

Rs. 1,109, has been deposited in a Co-operative institution, and from its proceeds selected bulls will be distributed to the group of villages which were affiliated to the Union.

CAUSES OF THE FAILURE

Causes of the failure of the Cattle Insurance movement in the Punjab were various:

(1) In most cases interest in this aspect of the movement was short-lived. The recurring need for insurance and the payment as well as collection of premiums was felt to be wearisome.

(2) The movement was in the first instance started in a tract where, on account of the low mortality of the cattle, the need for insurance was not very intense. Over and above this, "the area was very backward in education, and the people very seriously lacking in foresight."

(3) The Rohtak agriculturist usually sells his mature stock after every six months at local fairs, and then begins lavishing his cares on the young stock. This change of cattle after every six months offered a very great hindrance to the success of the scheme.

(4) The tract is dependent upon rain, and is consequently frequently exposed to drought. Even the Co-operative Society had not been well established in this area. The uncertainty of income always leads to irregularity in payment of premiums.

Cattle insurance in no country has made much headway, except for stud animals. In England a good bull may be worth hundreds of pounds, and is so insured; a good stallion may be worth twenty thousand pounds and so that is insured, but the ordinary animal of the farmer is usually nowhere insured.

CHAPTER XX

MILK-RECORDING SOCIETIES

As in most other forms of Co-operation, the Punjab set a very high standard in the matter of starting Milk-recording Societies. Two Assistant Registrars and six Inspectors attended the dairying course at Bangalore, besides a group of Sub-Inspectors, who received a somewhat simpler training at the Punjab Agricultural College, Lyallpur, and at the Karnal Farm. Thus well equipped with technical knowledge, a beginning was made in milk recording in 1926. A number of recording machines were supplied. Both cows and buffaloes were enlisted, and in the very first year thirteen Societies with four hundred animals were registered, and nineteen Societies with five hundred animals were reported as ready for registration. Some progress was made, but the difficulties have proved too much, and it appears that the Veterinary and the Co-operative Departments have in this case at least, like too many cooks, spoilt the broth.

Advantages of Milk-recording.—There is no dearth of cows and buffaloes in the Punjab. But these animals, though a little superior to the stock in some of the other Provinces, are not of the quality that will satisfy everyone. The cow and the buffalo not only supply the motive force for Agriculture, but supply *lassi*, the one thing that sustains the Punjab farmer. Curd forms an indispensable item in the diet of the Punjab farmer. The Punjab needs not more, but better cows and buffaloes. The amount of milk yielded by cows and buffaloes is exceedingly small. To get more milk the farmer keeps more animals. The larger the number of animals a cultivator keeps the smaller is the share of attention and fodder that each animal receives, and consequently there has been, it is feared, a progressive deterioration of the quality of cattle in the Punjab. So far as cows and buffaloes are concerned, and so far as these animals are kept for the supply of milk and ghee, the first step towards improvement is an accurate knowledge regarding the yield of each animal kept by an owner. The breeding of better animals and the elimination of the unfit is only possible when data regarding the yield of each animal are kept by an owner.

ADVANTAGES OF MILK-RECORDING

(1) By comparing the yield of milk by different animals the owner can differentiate between good and bad animals. Cows and buffaloes with lower yield cost just the same as better animals. Milk-recording makes it possible for the owner to eliminate cows and buffaloes of inferior quality, and thus to earn more profits and incur less costs. One good cow will cost less than two bad cows to keep, and will yield more milk. Unless a record of the yield is kept the vague opinions regarding the quality of the cows and buffaloes often turn out to be exceedingly erroneous. A cow's daily yield may be very large, but its total yield may be less than that of one the daily yield of which is low, but the lactation period of which is comparatively very long. The Punjab farmer has no insight into the business side of his profession so far at least as this aspect is concerned.

(2) The quantity and quality of rations for each animal can be regulated much more accurately than otherwise. Useful information can be collected by each farmer regarding the nature of different crops as fodder. When milk yield is being recorded every day the differences in yield dependent upon the use of different types of fodder are easily detected.

(3) Experience has shown that when an owner begins recording the yield of milk, he forthwith commences taking an all-round interest in the animal.

(4) Illness of the animal is detected much more readily and surely. The yield of sick animal falls. When illness is thus detected at the very outset, it means a less expensive and more effective treatment.

(5) A record of the yield, whenever it is trustworthy, will

enable the owner to realize a higher price for his cows and buffaloes than would be otherwise possible.

(6) When once a farmer has realized the significance of it, he will naturally discard the worthless stuff, and will thereby be improving his herd.

Difficulties that Beset the Workers.—If the Punjab farmer could be made to realize the importance of many beneficial measures the Co-operative Department has suggested to him for adoption, and if he could seriously act up to the advice given him, he would soon be a different man. But steeped in ignorance as he is, he fails to profit by the most beneficial advice of those so highly interested in his welfare. The Milk-recording Societies have suffered the following disadvantages:

1. *Ignorance and Indifference.*—There is a good deal of ignorance as to the object of these Societies. The farmer does not clearly understand why some people should get interested in the measurement of the milk that his cow yields. In most cases he is mentally incapable of the true appreciation of this measure. Wherever his ignorance is conquered his indifference steps in and matters are not improved at all.

2. *Superstition.*—Many illiterate persons living in cities believe that the measurement of milk is ill-omened. Milk is known as "God's Light." God's light is too august to be subjected to any worldly measurement. This is a genuine objection with the average farmer. But those living near cities who undertake to sell milk measure "God's light" with a vengeance, and are known often to dilute this light by the addition of water, not from wells but from ponds, for they seem to realize that the specific gravity of muddy water is the same as that of milk.

3. *Secrecy.*—Ignorance is the spring of all superstition, and the Punjab farmer is no exception to this rule. Ignorant and illiterate persons are prone to believe that an announcement of the quantity of milk yielded by an animal, particularly when it is large enough, will invite the evil eye; on the other hand, if the yield is small they rightly seem to believe that

an announcement of the yield jeopardizes the chances of securing a high price for the animal when it is to be sold.

4. *Shyness of Women.*—One very great practical difficulty is that women who usually do the milking feel shy of appearing before officials in charge of these operations. The cow has at least once a week to be milked in the presence of a Sub-Inspector. This difficulty was experienced so keenly in Hissar that work had to be stopped simply because of it.

Milk-recording Societies made good progress in Montgomery, where the members live in close association with each other and hold grants of land from Government on cattle-breeding conditions. A progressive decline in Societies of this type is noticeable, and the attempt seems to have been given up as lost. The Annual Report for 1931 records: "Milk-recording is still on the decline. For as the utility of the Societies of this sort in Rawal Pindi was far from certain, and their unpopularity and expense were undisputed, they have now been converted into Cattle-breeding Societies. The group of Societies around Shergarh, in Montgomery District, among the cow-breeding grantees of the colony, still continues, under the control of the Veterinary Department, in spite of the fact that people concerned do not like it or milk-recording at all. As far as spontaneity and a conscious desire to get better cows by this method go, the conglomeration of cow owners is not a Co-operative Society at all. I am doubtful whether the so-called Society ought to be continued any longer, especially as the returns do not seem to indicate any improvement, and the work is done purely for the Veterinary Department." This should have from the very beginning formed a part of the activities of the Stock-breeding Societies. For a long time to come there does not appear to be any chance of success in this venture. An idea of the quality of our cows may be had from the following figures recorded in the Annual Report for 1930.

	Best Cows	Worst Cows
Period of lactation	275 days	176 days
Average daily yield for—		
(*a*) Period of lactation	24·3 lb.	6 lb.
(*b*) Wet and dry period	18 lb.	4 lb.

CHAPTER XXI

SILT-CLEARANCE SOCIETIES

WATER is the very life-blood of a farmer. Irrigation of his fields he believes to be as necessary as the circulation of blood in his own body. But his ignorance and lack of training render him unmindful of the colossal waste of money and energy which is almost criminal. Certain forms of waste cannot be checked by individual and unorganized efforts. Accumulation of silt in the channels presents a problem that baffles any individual solution. The channels get silted, and the flow of water is blocked and delayed, besides a good quantity of it getting absorbed in the silt itself. When the channel is cleared of the silt the loss of water in transit is minimized, and it flows to its destination much more rapidly. The clearance of silt makes for efficient irrigation. The farmer individually takes to very few things seriously, and in such a case an individual effort has little hope of success. Cultivators were therefore organized co-operatively and collectively with a view to carrying on silt-clearance. A Silt-clearance Society seeks to replace a haphazard style of clearing the channels by an organized system worked by an elected committee, with powers to allot work and get it done either by a member or at his cost.

ADVANTAGES OF SILT-CLEARANCE

(1) *Increase in Area Irrigated.*—Silt-clearance, particularly on the inundation canals, ensures an "earlier running of the channels and a better supply of water." The working of twelve Societies in 1922, it is estimated, increased the area irrigated from 2,100 acres to 5,800. The working of these twelve Societies was estimated to have benefited each individual of these Societies to the extent of Rs. 430. Ten Societies, in Gujrat and Shahpur Districts, through silt-clearance, increased the area

irrigated from 663 to 3,125 acres, and reaped a profit for their members estimated at Rs. 50,000 in 1922.

(2) *Advantages of Joint Action.*—The cultivator is often oppressed by those who in one way or another come into contact with him. The zemindar in the canal irrigated areas harbours manifold grievances against certain classes of petty officials of the Irrigation Department. The formation of these Societies has been of very great real use to the cultivators in the matter of making representations to the Department of Irrigation. Complaints and requests made by the cultivators individually cannot and do not possess the force of a collective representation made by members of a Society.

(3) *Surplus Water.*—One Society at Shahpur was enabled in 1929 to extend its channels by about a mile, and took to selling its surplus water to outside cultivators. This increase in the quantity of water and its consequent sale were the direct outcome of silt-clearance.

(4) *Increased Incentive to Work.*—Man's job in life represents an attempt at conquering the obstacles put in his way by Nature. As one exercises his powers with success, and "something attempted something done" results in an increased incentive to further work.

(5) *Settlement of Disputes.*—Water is as essential to farming as it is to the maintenance of human life. The Punjab farmer understands it as well as anyone else, hence he loses all self-control when anyone stands between water and his fields. This results in serious and sometimes fatal quarrels and perpetuates disputes. Wherever there is a Silt-clearance Society there is an arrangement for an amicable settlement of disputes, which would otherwise involve expense and loss of time without any benefit to anyone.

FAILURE OF THE ATTEMPT

The Silt-clearance Societies represent the failure of yet another beneficial form of Co-operation. Even in the beginning these Societies were successful only at those places where the supervision of the Department was very effective. The chief cause of failure is the cultivator's inertia and inability to exercise sustained effort. After the Silt-clearance Societies had been at work only for five years the Registrar had to record: "The success of these Agricultural Labour Societies depends at present on sympathetic supervision. Where that is available, and where the cultivators are not excessively backward, well-timed reminder prompts them to put in hand the clearance of their channel; elsewhere they all fall into inertia." The Registrar in his Annual Report for 1931 says: "It would be a pity if such useful Societies, which work on the well-understood principle of mutual help in the village, should provide a bitter commentary on village community life." Silt-clearance Societies, it must be recorded, were much discouraged by the underlings of the Irrigation Department and some others of the money-lending castes higher up. The following table shows the growth and decline of the Silt-clearance Societies in the Punjab:

	Number of Societies		Number of Societies
1921	3	1928	26
1922	12	1929	24
1923	18	1930	16
1924	23	1931	14
1925	23	1932	11
1926	25	1933	10
1927	26		

CHAPTER XXII

BETTER FARMING SOCIETIES

THE NEED FOR BETTER FARMING SOCIETIES

THE Punjab is predominantly an agricultural Province, and its most pressing problems are agrarian.

The cultivator is hemmed in by difficulties and disadvantages on all sides. Any improvement in the cultivator's position must involve an increase in efficiency of all the factors of production. The Punjab is poor in spite of the proverbial richness of its resources. The problem admits of a very simple solution so far as rural development is concerned. The Punjab produces 9 maunds of wheat per acre, England 24, and Denmark 32. Denmark has doubled its cows' yield of milk, and trebled that of butter in less than half a century. Milk yield of cows in such dairy farms in Great Britain where records are kept has risen from 599 gallons per annum in 1918 to 670 gallons in 1925. The average for all cows per year is 450 gallons. All these results, however, embody years of hard, honest, and intelligent labour and thrifty life. The soil of England is less of a natural and more of a man-made soil. The Punjab cultivator must do the same to get the same results. The soil has to be improved. Better cattle mean better farming. The cultivator knows the value of better cattle, but he has to be made to conquer such defects in his surroundings and character which have hitherto rendered such attempts unsuccessful. To make his occupation profitable he needs capital on more humane and reasonable terms than those on which the rapacious money-lenders advance to him at present. The Punjab peasant must be redeemed to the possibilities of a happier and a more prosperous life. Stoppage of all waste and leakage and better farming must be our starting-points.

OBJECTS

The objects of a Better Farming Society are to promote the economic interest of its members, and more particularly to arrange for:

(1) The adoption of better methods of agriculture among the members;

(2) The supply of good seed and improved agricultural implements;

(3) The demonstration of the more recent improvements in agriculture and practical assistance in their application;

(4) The creation of funds for loans to members for purchase of improved implements, manure, and good seed;

(5) The purchase or sale for common account of improved implements, seeds, and members' produce;

(6) Other measures designed to encourage in the members the spirit of thrift, mutual help, and self-help.

All owners or tenants of land in the village are eligible for membership. Every member pays a small admission fee, and signs an agreement to the effect that in consequence of being a member of the Better Farming Society he will adopt such improved methods of agriculture as the general meeting may direct, and in the event of the breach of this undertaking he will pay the Society such fine not exceeding Rs. 50 as the committee may impose. The liability of each member is limited to Rs. 50 only. The capital of the Society is composed of:

(1) Such contributions as may from time to time be determined by members in the general meeting;

(2) Deposits from members;

(3) Deposits and loans from non-members;

(4) Fines and penalties;

(5) Government grants;

(6) Profit.

The acceptance of deposits and loans from non-members is subject to the restrictions which the Registrar may impose.

No profits are at any time divided among the members.

Seven-and-a-half per cent of the net profits of any year may be applied to any purpose referred to in Section 34 of the Act, and approved by the Registrar, namely, relief of the poor, education, medical relief, and advancement of any other object of general public utility except one, relating exclusively to religious teaching or worship; or to a common good fund devoted to any of these purposes. The profits, which are indivisible and are carried to the reserve fund, may be utilized in the business of the Society unless the Registrar directs its investment in accordance with Section 32 of the Act.

Manure Pits and Boundary Walls.—Most of the members of Better Farming Societies in Pakpattan, Ferozepore, Gujranwala, Sheikhupura, and Hissar took to digging of manure pits. In Pakpattan all members protected with a boundary wall such of their fields as were near the village. In Sirsa 37 acres were cultivated by two tenants under the direct supervision of the Agricultural Adviser with astonishing results—with a solitary exception all cultivators in the village took to the use of improved variety of cotton and wheat. Sialkot with twenty-four Societies in 1930 took to the growing of vegetables and planting of fruit-trees.

SOME NOTABLE SOCIETIES

The Fruit Growers' Association, Lyallpur.—This Association began work in 1930, and in that year sold 9,000 plants to its members at Rs. 7 per hundred, as against the bazaar price of Rs. 10. This Society seems to have worked only for a year. The Report for 1931 makes no mention of its activities, and the Report for 1932 tells us that it is only a little more than a nominal body. Even the books of the Society could not be found for inspection. We were told in 1933 that the Association was still in a state of coma. A similar fate has overtaken the Montgomery Association of Fruit Growers.

Murree Plantation Societies.—Two Fruit Plantation Societies were started in Murree Hills in 1930, and in the course of the year supplied their members with 305 young plants—peaches, pomegranates, vines, apples, and almonds—all obtained from

Government fruit farms. The number of Societies grew to 14 by 1932. During 1931 these Societies imported over two thousand plants, and an inquiry disclosed in 1932 that 60 per cent of the plants imported were planted successfully. These Societies now number 16, and in 1933 indented for five thousand plants. These Societies are most active.

Land Reclamation Societies.—Hill torrents in Hoshiarpur and Ambala Districts sweep away land under cultivation. Land Reclamation Societies were started in Hoshiarpur (4) and Gurdaspur (1) in 1930. By 1932 the number of Societies in Hoshiarpur increased to five. The Societies in Hoshiarpur by 1932 got a total income of nearly Rs. 9,000, and reclaimed 265 acres in all. The Report for 1933 makes no mention of these Societies, and maybe they no longer exist.

Protection of Trees.—In Una Tahsil of the Hoshiarpur District was registered a Society at the end of 1930 for the protection of chil and sal trees of the village. The Society sought to consult the Forest Department in the matter of felling, planting, and protecting of trees. The Registrar wrote in 1931:

"If it succeeds it will be a very useful example to all villages similarly situated, and a benefit to the villages that lie at the foot of hills, for it may well save them from extinction." The Registrar tells us in his Report for 1932: "The Una Tahsil Society, organized for the protection of chil and sal trees in a large area near the foothills, has come to grief. Rights in *Shamilat* are so many and complicated that disputes are inevitable, have not proved susceptible to co-operative solution, and only fan long-standing animosities."

Tarkwal Better Farming Society.—A Better Farming Society was founded in 1933 at Tarkwal, Rawal Pindi District, to work on a collective basis. The Society has leased 50 acres of barani land, which it cultivates collectively; daily wages are paid to members who work on the land, and the amount of these wages is deducted from their shares when proceeds of the harvest are finally shared out.

Sugar Societies.—Some Societies for manufacture of white

sugar have been started in Ambala, and are helping the spread of knowledge for the better methods of manufacturing white sugar.

Dullewala Society.—This Society at Kasur specializes in the production of potatoes, sweet potatoes, melons, cucumbers, tobacco, and vegetables.

Lac Societies.—Three lac Societies were started in Hoshiarpur

BETTER FARMING SOCIETIES

	1929	1930	1931	1932	1933	1934
Number of Societies ..	119	118	—	109	—	147
Membership	3,036	3,097	—	3,060	—	—
Sale of improved seed (maunds)—						
(*a*) Wheat	—	688	1,411	603	—	—
(*b*) Cotton	—	423	1,621	636	—	—
Improved implements—						
Ploughs	—	70	129	—	—	—
Harrows	—	9	3	—	—	—
Horse hoes	—	4	20	—	—	—
Cultivator hoes ..	—	4	—	—	—	—
Drills	—	4	—	—	—	—
Chaff-cutters ..	—	1	17	—	—	—
Persian Wheels ..	—	—	3	—	—	—
Ploughshares ..	—	—	17	—	—	—
Gujrat hoe	—	—	3	—	—	—

in 1930. Owing to fall in price of lac and the difficulties experienced in composing old feuds and factions these Societies have done no work at all.

Mango Planting Societies.—Eight Societies have been started in the Muzaffargarh District, within a radius of five miles from Kinjhar. These Societies have undertaken the plantation of mango trees under the directions of the Government Fruit Specialist.

These Societies need to be revived to activity, for it is by their means that improvements can be made to spread through Punjab villages.

CHAPTER XXIII

CONSOLIDATION OF HOLDINGS

THE Punjab is a land of small peasant proprietors. The prosperity of agriculture in any country is, amongst a multiplicity of factors, determined by the size of holdings. For any set of other factors the size of holding may be too large or too small to be cultivated with the maximum profit. Kentings defines an economic holding as *one which allows a man a chance of producing sufficient to support himself and his family in reasonable comfort after paying his necessary expenses.*

The following table summarizes the results of an inquiry into the size and distribution of holdings in the Punjab, conducted under the supervision and guidance of Mr. Calvert, embracing 2,347 villages in the Province.

Owners of the Cultivated Land	Average Size of Holding	Percentage of the Total Area
Percentage of Total Owners		
17·9	Less than 1 acre	1·0
40·4	1 to 5 acres	11·0
20·2	5 to 15 acres	26·6
11·8	15 to 50 acres	35·6
3·7	50 and more acres	25·7

The unit of holdings in the Punjab is admittedly smaller than in the West. Outside India, in most countries, wherever the holding is smaller than in the Punjab the farmer enjoys other advantages, such as paying subsidiary occupations which make for his prosperity. In the Punjab, not only are the holdings very small but their fragmentation makes the situation exceedingly difficult for him, and the complete absence of any relieving factors renders his prospects so thoroughly hopeless. "In most districts of the Province, and more especially in the central districts, holdings have been subdivided into numerous fields, not contiguous, but scattered throughout the village area. Numerous instances could be given of villages consisting of a thousand or more fields of which the average area does not exceed one quarter of an acre (2 kanals); in several villages the average area of the field is not more than one-eighth of an acre (1 kanal); of their fields some are too small to be cultivated, others are so narrow that it is not easy to plough crossways" (*Wealth and Welfare of the Punjab*).

CAUSES OF SUBDIVISION AND FRAGMENTATION OF HOLDINGS

Fragmentation is the direct outcome of subdivision of holdings. The following are the causes of subdivision and fragmentation of holdings in India.

(1) *Spirit of Individualism or the Decay of Joint Family System.*—Joint family system was a prominent characteristic of national economy in India. This system is being rapidly supplanted by the growth of a spirit of individualism. Even now family life in India is cemented together more than in many advanced countries. But the spirit of individualism is swelling, and is responsible for the break-up of the joint family system. Insistence on partition of ancestral property in land is much more marked than it was a century ago. Joint cultivation is rapidly becoming a thing of the past. When ancestral property in land is divided the size of the holding goes on decreasing.

(2) *Laws of Inheritance.*—Hindu and Islamic laws of inheritance, particularly Islamic laws, make for subdivision of holdings, which in its turn brings fragmentation as well. Unlike many other advanced countries, the property of a landlord in India is generally divided equally amongst all his sons. Islam prescribes a share to daughters as well. Wherever such laws of inheritance prevail there will be subdivision of holdings. But a subdivision of ancestral property in land is normally accompanied by fragmentation as well. When a father's property is to be divided amongst, say, his four sons, all his land which may not already be in a compact block is

first divided into a number of plots according to its fertility. Each class of land is then divided into four equal parts, and the result in a few generations appears in the form of contemptibly small strips hopelessly scattered at considerable distances. An idea of the hopelessness of the whole affair may be had by looking at the maps showing fragmentation and consolidation of holdings.

These laws of inheritance have been in force for a long period, but subdivision and fragmentation have only been accentuated during the last half-century. The only explanation for this phenomenon is to be found in the fact that the spirit of individualism has dismembered the joint family system, and has consequently brought these laws into vigorous operation.

(3) *Increase in Population.*—Other things remaining the same, an increase in population would lead to further subdivision of land. As long as more land can be brought under cultivation to accommodate the increasing population it is not so difficult a problem. But when the area of cultivable land ceases to increase and a number of causes tend to bring about its partition the size of holdings will decrease and their fragmentation will intensify. The increase of population works by forcing men to cultivate plots which hitherto had remained uncultivated: such plots are naturally scattered about, some within the old area and some on the outside of it. It is this steady cultivation which is one of the main causes of fragmentation.

(4) *Purchase by Money-lenders.*—The money-lenders have in the last sixty years bought numerous small plots of land from owners up and down the village area, and so have assisted further fragmentation.

(5) *Grant to Industrial Castes.*—The industrial castes have been allowed to secure small plots of land in the village in order to keep them from leaving the village. Here again is a cause of fragmentation.

(6) *Decline of Subsidiary Occupations.*—With the advent of machinery and import of foreign goods in India our cottage industries have decayed. Handicrafts mostly supplied subsidiary

occupations to agriculturists in India. The decay of these industries has thrown back upon the land even those whom they supported in part or completely. There are different aspects of the relation between decline of cottage industries and subdivision of land. But we are safe in concluding that "in so far, however, as the handicraftsmen were turned into tenants, their demand for cultivable land must have resulted in greater subdivision and fragmentation of cultivation."

Agricultural indebtedness and investment in land have also been responsible for the ever-increasing fragmentation of land.

DISADVANTAGES OF FRAGMENTATION

While talking of disadvantages of fragmentation we must refer primarily to fragmentation of cultivation. Half the land is cultivated by the owners; so that fragmentation of owner's land means fragmentation of cultivation as well.

(1) *Makes Cultivation Costly.*—Fragmentation serves to increase the cost of cultivation per unit of area. If one acre of land is divided into twenty different fragments its cost of cultivation will be more than the cost of cultivation of a compact block of one acre. "It is calculated that expenditure of cultivation increases by 5·3 per cent for every 500 metres of distance for manual labour and ploughing; from 20 per cent to 35 per cent for transport of manure, and from 15 to 32 per cent for transport of crops. It is obvious that fragmentation adds to expenditure in all these ways."

(2) *Waste of Time and Energy.*—Fragmentation involves great loss of time and energy, inasmuch as labourers and cattle have got to be constantly shifted from one plot to another.

(3) *Checks all Improvement.*—Fragmentation makes efficient farming impossible; supervision of one compact block of land is easier and less costly than that of an equal unit of area scattered at different places in a number of plots. A compact block of land can be easily irrigated, and a well can be dug up for improvement of such a block. When land is divided into small parcels and lies scattered anywhere and everywhere,

even when the combined area is large enough for a number of wells, fragmentation makes this enterprise impossible. There cannot be a well for each patch of land. Since even the combined return of all patches of land fails to repay any effort at improvement, the incentive for improvement is gone.

(4) *Loss in Boundaries and Increased Chances of Disputes.*—A compact field of ten acres will not lose much land by way of its boundaries. If the same area gets fragmented into a hundred pieces the loss in this form by way of boundary lines is alarming. Fragmentation and subdivision render fencing of boundaries impracticable and practically useless. Not only that. Fragmentation with its enhanced boundary lines is a fruitful source of litigation.

(5) *Renders Cultivation Impracticable.*—Subdivision and fragmentation may be carried so far as to make cultivation impracticable. The Agricultural Commission tells us that in some parts of India agricultural holdings have been reduced to a condition in which their effective cultivation is impossible. Dr. Mariss sums up the evils of subdivision and fragmentation as follows: "This destroys enterprise, results in an enormous wastage of labour, leads to a very large loss of land owing to boundaries, makes it impossible to cultivate holdings as intensively as would otherwise be possible, and prevents the possibility of introducing outsiders with more money, as tenant farmers or purchasers of good agricultural property."

REMEDIES ADOPTED IN OTHER COUNTRIES

Subdivision and fragmentation of holdings are by no means peculiar to India. The experience of France, Switzerland, Germany, Belgium, Denmark, and Japan has proved the futility of voluntary agreements at repartition. Remedial legislation based on the following principles has been adopted.

1. Compulsory expropriation of existing holders.
2. Compulsory reconstitution of holdings at the instance of a certain fraction of landholders, or in some cases without it.
3. Subsequent indivisibility of reconstituted holdings.

4. Exemption of the holdings from seizure for debts.

5. Prevention of the reconstituted holdings from being combined with other holdings. Besides the above legislative measures the evils of subdivision of holdings and fragmentation may be checked by a joint management of holdings, and may completely be avoided by following the law of primogeniture, which implies an annulment of our laws of inheritance. The law of primogeniture is too manifestly unjust to be acceptable to Indian feeling. No improvement in agriculture will compensate the economic and moral injustice it involves. Voluntary Co-operative consolidation of holdings is the only course that has been followed with success in India. The movement was initiated in the Punjab in 1920 by Mr. Calvert, once the illustrious Registrar of Co-operative Societies in that Province. The process of consolidation consists in bringing together into one solid block, or as small a number of blocks as possible, the large number of scattered holdings of land belonging to any one individual. When carried on for a large number of individuals it aims at giving compact blocks of land to each individual as close to each other as possible, instead of his small and scattered holdings.

THE WORKING OF A CONSOLIDATION SOCIETY

Nothing will make a zemindar agree to put into practice a scheme likely to affect his possession or ownership of land. It was, therefore, essential to demonstrate to him the advantages of consolidation. The experimental stage was very wisely designed to meet all possible objections by and to allay all fears of the zemindar.

According to the original scheme every member of a Consolidation Society agreed to abide by any method of repartition of land approved by two-thirds of the members. Every member relinquished possession of his land in the first instance for four years, in accordance with any plan so approved. He further agreed to refer all disputes in regard to repartition to arbitration. The possession given for four years was a mere cultivating possession, and during that period transfer of ownership was permissible. It was hoped that four years of the cultivating transfer would bring home to all concerned the great economic advantages of repartition, and that the members would without further argument agree to convert the cultivating possession into permanent exchange of ownership. The realization and demonstration of the advantages of consolidation proved, even at the very outset, so keen and vivid that in some cases owners expressed willingness to accept permanent change straight away, but the Department never pressed for it. At the end of four years, if the members unanimously accepted the permanent transfer of ownership consolidation became an accomplished fact. In case unanimity of decision was lacking the old possession was to be restored. This goes to the credit of the Punjab cultivator, that in no case had the lands to be restored after four years' trial.

AS IT IS NOW

Every member of a Consolidation Society signs a statement that he:

(1) Agrees to the principle or rearrangement of scattered holdings so as to secure more compact blocks of fields for each owner;

(2) Agrees to submit to any arrangement approved by two-thirds of the whole number of members in a General Meeting;

(3) Agrees to permit the rearrangement of his lands in accordance with any such scheme, and to give possession in accordance therewith for ever;

(4) Agrees to submit to arbitration all disputes touching the business of the Society (including disputes as to rights, boundaries, rents, responsibility for land revenue and cesses and possession of the lands affected by any such scheme) that may arise during the existence of the Society;

(5) Agrees to submit to any arrangement approved by two-thirds of the whole number of members in a General Meeting

in case of any future partition or rearrangement of the consolidated area in which he may be concerned.

All transfers of possession in accordance with any such scheme of repartition shall be permanent. A Government paid Sub-Inspector is posted in the area to assist in the repartition and prepare necessary papers.

The Managing Committee prepares a scheme or schemes for the rearrangement of holdings in accordance with the principle adopted at a General Meeting, and submits the results of such a scheme or schemes to a General Meeting for approval. Societies are now kept alive even after consolidation has been completed, with a view to providing for an amicable settlement of all future disputes connected with the process, for which, of course, there will always be a chance.

METHODS FOLLOWED

The following two methods of consolidation are adopted. The first method comprises a system of mutual exchange of fields with a view to bringing the scattered fields of each owner into blocks as near to one another as possible. The second method of repartition consists in treating all land offered for consolidation as common land and dividing it up into suitable compact blocks corresponding to the interests of the several owners of the common land to be consolidated.

ADVANTAGES OF CONSOLIDATION

(1) *Reduction in Disputes and Litigation.*—Very few people outside India can ever form an adequate idea of the large number of disputes which in this country take the form of endless quarrels and frequent fights due to intentional or unintentional encroachments upon the boundaries of adjacent fields. In the Punjab these direct encroachments are at first fought out in the fields, not only by the owners concerned but by a whole lot of factions in a village. These pitched battles give the parties broken ribs and bleeding skulls, and result

sometimes in fatal casualties. It is always after this bloody stage of this drama that litigation begins and brings ruin to many a farmer. If figures for litigation which may be traced to fights and disputes over encroachments upon adjacent boundaries were ever collected for a number of years the world would marvel at the immensity of litigation on this account. It is impossible to have an adequate idea of the waste of time, money, and energy that such large-scale and prolonged litigation involves. There is little hope of, and still less cause for, people devoting themselves to improved farming as long as this perpetual cause of trouble is not effectively stopped. Consolidation of holdings minimizes the chances of such disputes and quarrels, which often assume alarming proportions and constitute a perpetual menace to the peace of rural areas, and are detrimental to the growth of rural prosperity. Consolidation lessens disputes by lessening the points of contact; while a person's fields lie scattered in thirty different places chances are that he will have a fairly large number of neighbours who may not be, to say the least, well-disposed towards him. When through consolidation his thirty strips are converted into one or two blocks, he has a fairly good chance of finding himself surrounded by less quarrelsome, if not most friendly and congenial, neighbours. Under consolidation, even if he is hopelessly unfortunate in the matter of his relations with his neighbours, the reduction in their number renders more possible an adjustment with them. The fewer the number of neighbours, the fewer the chances of friction amongst them, other things remaining the same.

History of consolidation in the Punjab amply illustrates its advantages on this behalf. Some of the specific instances may with advantage be cited here. In 1923, in one village, a long-standing boundary dispute between Sikhs and Mussulmans was amicably settled by so consolidating the land as to give each party a separate block of land. In such cases consolidation avoids not only a mere dispute between two quarrelsome neighbours, but nips in the bud a potential communal riot. In 1924 consolidation was adopted to minimize friction between

Sikhs and Mussulmans under similar conditions. Another quarrel in the Sialkot District over the possession of $1\frac{1}{2}$ acres, which had cost the parties Rs. 600 and was still pending in court, was amicably settled through consolidation. In 1926, "A whole series of partition cases were dropped from the file of a revenue officer, the disputes having been decided by the Sub-Inspector." In a big village in Ferozepore District, consolidation brought about, under the then existing circumstances, an ideal repartition. All the occupancy tenants were given blocks of land on one side of the village, and two large landowners were assigned land in a block by itself. The rest of the land under cultivation was allotted to the cultivators belonging to the middle class. Consolidation brought about peaceful and a speedy settlement of a dispute, over an insignificant pathway in Rohtak District, which had found its way to the High Court.

(2) *More Efficient Irrigation.*—An adequate supply of water is as essential to farming as the circulation of blood is to the maintenance of human life. Under fragmentation of holdings an adequate supply of water for farming becomes increasingly difficult and costly. After fragmentation has reached a certain stage, irrigation of fields becomes not only an economic but also a physical impossibility. Each fragment of land cannot have a well to irrigate it, for in the first instance the cultivator has not the means to construct a well for each fragment, and in the second, even if he could accomplish the fact at no cost to him, it would turn out to be an uneconomic bargain. Under fragmentation of holdings a number of owners may decide to work a well for irrigating a number of surrounding fields. A successful working of such a joint well presupposes an abnormal and a many-sided adjustment amongst owners, which is conspicuous by its absence. Wherever irrigation through canal water is possible, fragmentation of holdings renders it, in some cases, most difficult and often wasteful, and therefore very expensive.

Consolidation of holdings has been a source of immense benefit to the Punjab farmer, because it has enabled him to supply water to his thirsting fields by constructing new wells to irrigate the consolidated blocks of his land. Again, it is consolidation alone that has enabled the Punjab farmer to repair and put into use the old discarded wells which extreme fragmentation of land had rendered unfit for use. The total of new wells sunk on consolidated blocks since the commencement of this movement has, according to the latest figures, gone up to 1,420. Three hundred wells that had fallen out of use have been repaired and brought under use once again. In all, therefore, 2,020 wells, solely due to the consolidation of holdings, are contributing to an increase in the agricultural produce in the Punjab. If the use of a well enhances the product by Rs. 100 only, the consolidation of holdings on one account has increased the annual agricultural product in the Punjab by two lakhs of rupees.

A good deal of water lifted out of wells at a high cost gets lost in the transit on account of bad water-channels, which, besides absorbing considerable quantities of water, give way at a large number of points, and so frequently that they become a source of colossal waste of water and a cause of ceaseless vexation to the farmer. Granting that the farmer realizes this loss and has the means and intelligence to check this waste of water, which means waste of time, money, and energy, fragmentation of holdings does not let him move in the matter at all. Once he has got his land consolidated into one or more blocks of adequate size, he is in a position to make pukka water-channels, the advantages of which are quite evident. A number of owners have therefore built pukka water-channels after consolidation of their land. In one village in Hoshiarpur District, a landowner constructed a drain for conducting water to his fields measuring 1,000 yards. In Jullundur, consolidation of holdings rendered possible the installation of two centrifugal pumps. In areas irrigated by canal water the advantages of consolidation in the matter of consumption of water have been equally evident and great. Even in the primary stages of the movement the farmers realized that bigger and less scattered fields economized the use of water by checking waste. In consolidated areas experience has brought home to the farmer the truth that the same quantity of water is used with better results than under fragmentation of holdings. Consolidation has, therefore, helped to supply water to the land thirsting for it, and has as well rendered possible a more efficient use of water wherever the supply was previously adequate but not economically utilized.

(3) *Increase in Area Under Cultivation.*—Under fragmentation of holdings a good deal of land is lost to cultivation in the form of numerous boundary lines and endless pathways. Sometimes the scattered strips of land are so small that they of necessity go out of cultivation. From the very commencement of the movement in the Punjab reports concerning more land coming under cultivation had begun to pour in. For some time the Co-operative Department kept a record of such increase in the area under cultivation brought about through consolidation of holdings, but the attempt was soon given up. We have it on record that in one village alone, in 1923, 62 acres of an old waste were brought under cultivation. In 1924 as many as 2,700 acres, formerly uncultivated owing to excessive fragmentation, were brought under cultivation. Similarly, in 1929 a total of 5,206 acres of waste land was brought under the plough—a considerable quantity of land which in case of fragmentation of holdings is lost in the form of numerous boundaries of different fields. If 10 acres of land lie scattered in one hundred fields and get consolidated into ten fields only it is obvious that the land lost as boundary lines in a hundred fields will be economized by about 90 per cent. Consolidation of holdings made it possible to save some land from erosion through the planting of trees and weeds. A landowner in pasrur tahsil of Sialkot District, finding his 10 acres of land split up into eighty-four fields, gave up cultivation as hopeless. He went over to Lyallpur and settled as a tenant. When through consolidation his eighty-four fields got compressed into two blocks only, he came back to his place, bought a well to irrigate his holdings, and thus the land which had been lost to cultivation through fragmentation was once again brought under

the plough. This is an example which may at any time and place be quoted as a proud accomplishment of the movement, but let it be remembered that it is by no means the only case of its kind. In the words of the Annual Report for 1929, "Zemindars who have hitherto had to till the lands of others in neighbouring villages have been able to give up this practice and make a living out of their own land alone, now that it has been consolidated." In certain places, the new adjustment of land has so considerably increased the area under cultivation that the farmers have generously set apart tracts of land for "the digging of manure-pits, for grazing-grounds, for gardens, for school buildings, and for school playgrounds." "In Jullundur a village added 3 acres to its graveyard, another set aside ½ acre for a school, and a third 2 acres for a playground, 4 acres for grazing, and 2½ for manure-pits."

(4) *Enhancement of Rent.*—Consolidation makes for more efficient farming, which implies an increase in the income of the farmer, other things remaining the same. This increase in the income of the tenant makes for an enhancement in the amount of rent paid to a landlord. This enhancement of rent consequent upon consolidation of holdings was amply illustrated even in the earlier stages of this movement. In one village the tenants agreed to pay one-half instead of one-third of the produce. As far back as 1926, a Professor in the Khalsa College, Amritsar, could secure from his tenants 80 maunds of grain against 55 before consolidation. In Ghangi village, consolidated in 1922, the rent of the area treated rose the very next year from Rs. 500 to Rs. 1,000. In most of the villages so treated rents are reported to have risen approximately 25 per cent. In Ghazi Kot, an owner had his 31 acres divided into forty fields. He received Rs. 6 by way of rent per acre. After consolidation he got his land in one solid block, and his tenants offered to pay him Rs. 10 per acre by way of rent, and expressed their willingness to sink two wells and to "recoup the cost by annual deductions from the rent."

(5) *Enhancement of Revenue.*—Consolidation of holdings, besides making agriculture more efficient, actually increases

the area under cultivation. Thus, other things remaining the same, the volume and value of produce increase which renders possible an increase in revenue. In one village in Gurdaspur the cultivated area "as a result of consolidation rose from 615 to 1,372 acres, and the land revenue from Rs. 2,059 to Rs. 2,938" (Report for 1933). Recently an inquiry was made in forty villages of the central Punjab, where land revenue is assessed on the cultivated area each harvest. It was found that the average land revenue paid each year in these forty villages was Rs. 6,507 more than before consolidation.

(6) *Better Implements.*—Fragmentation of holdings obstructs progressive agriculture at every step. Consolidation makes possible the use of better and improved implements.

DIFFICULTIES IN THE WAY OF CONSOLIDATION

Internal Difficulties.—The Punjab peasant is ignorant and illiterate, and very richly shares all the weaknesses born of poverty and ignorance. The movement for consolidation for its success requires certain very high qualities of character. That measure of success which has been achieved so far we owe mainly to a glaring realization of the multifarious disadvantages of fragmentation, coupled with practically untold advantages of consolidation. In a village we find the rich and the poor, the weak and the strong, living side by side. It is only natural, owing to the peculiar circumstances under which we live, that the weak and the poor should entertain apprehensions as to the designs of the rich and the strong, particularly when they live in perpetual fear of a conspiracy on the part of their influential fellow-villagers and petty Government officials to the disadvantage of the poor and the weak. These veiled apprehensions may, and often do, take the form of endless excuses for not joining the movement. Mortgagees and minors often present extremely difficult problems for solution. "Occupant tenants," says an annual Report, "discern a trick to deprive them of their cherished rights." This feeling is perfectly legitimate in view of the colossal ignorance that prevails.

But I am afraid in most cases this feeling is born of the suggestions of an interested Patwari who can always in perfect confidence whisper in the ear of any one of them with every chance of credence. There is the problem of a cultivator's passionate attachment to his ancestral plots of land. Old men, with their inherent love of the old order of things and their mental incapacity to appreciate anything new, resist the growth of this movement. Young men may be taken in with the brilliant prospects pictured to them by the Departmental propagandist, but they are guided by their elders who, in spite of their stupendous stupidity, may and often do pose as sages, and whose only argument is a volley of abuse, of the offensive nature of which they are thoroughly ignorant, and whose only authority lies in the possession of land coupled with the respect that age irrespective of merit so greatly commands.

Sonless Proprietor.—Curious are the ways of man. He will not be moved to acceptance of even a useful scheme when there is unfortunately no son to succeed him in the enjoyment of benefits he may create. Sonless proprietors, particularly when not hard pressed by circumstances, face the movement for consolidation of holdings with the supreme indifference of a hermit. The lack of interest in the welfare of the next generation makes them indifferent to the prospects of an improvement in their surroundings. They will not give their consent to any scheme. One Inspector reported that "persons in possession of land unlawfully try their utmost against repartition work."

The cultivator is swayed by fear and lack of confidence in his own understanding. He may be converted to join this movement only after all human powers of persuasion and direct appeals to his personal interests have been exhausted. But a mere whisper by any interested idiot: "This is a trap, giving your consent amounts to digging your own grave," lo, the cultivator loses his hard-established mental equilibrium once again. He revolts against the scheme, and his deep-seated prejudice now will not let him be easily drawn into argument. As an Inspector puts it, "In many cases the landowners refuse to accept the fields approved by them the day before." It is not so difficult to convince a peasant of the usefulness of consolidation, but to make him put some confidence in his own understanding, and the honesty of those who press him to accept the scheme, is an uphill task.

EXTERNAL OPPOSITION

Strange though it may seem, nevertheless it is a fact that there was vehement external opposition to the repartition of land, which will go down in history as one of the most beneficial and revolutionizing forms of Co-operation. In the Punjab the village patwari is an all-powerful and the most influential official. He is the very power and authority personified. This immediate official with whom the villagers have to come into contact every day, to say the least, being low paid and living away from headquarters, does not display a high standard of honesty. In consolidation of holdings he felt a blow aimed at his authority, and hence a reduction in the chances of his illegitimate gratifications. Not only that. Shrewd fellow that he often is, he soon found out that a decrease in the number of fields would ultimately result in a proportionate unemployment in his class. It is not therefore to be wondered at that this clever petty official should have summoned up all his tricks and influence against consolidation of holdings. Rewards had to be offered to the patwaris in order to enlist their active and honest support in the repartition work. But it remains a fact that as a class the patwaris worked against the movement.

For very obvious reasons the revenue staff, in some cases even above the rank of a patwari, was openly and secretly hostile to the scheme. A tahsil quanungo is reported to have said: "I will not let this movement succeed." It is indeed a very poor consolation for the Registrar to record that four Societies, embracing an area of 1,000 acres, were organized in the very tahsil where this proud petty official lived and ruled. A revenue assistant, who visited a village, tried to dissuade the people from accepting mutation. We can form an idea of the hostility of the revenue officials and of the helplessness of the Co-operative Department from the following extract of the annual Report for 1923: "We regard this result as disappointing, and I trust that it will not be understood as an attempt to thrust the blame on to others if I record our opinion that the main cause of slow progress is the opposition of the tahsil staff at Batala. In that tahsil there appears to be the brightest prospect of success: but it has become necessary to bring certain matters to the notice of the Deputy Commissioner."

FAILURES

So long as human nature is what it is, so long as the Punjab cultivator is ignorant, so long as he is being guided by his impulses, and so long as he is misguided by those who make a living out of his ignorance, failures will be inevitable. Consolidation of holdings as a movement has met with many failures. In the year 1926 a dozen villages had to be abandoned in despair after a good deal of time and energy had been fruitlessly invested in the effort. In one case the situation was rendered hopeless by the refusal of a single individual out of 264. His objection was, however, finally overcome. According to the Report for 1927: "Even in the most favourable districts disappointments have to be faced. In Ludhiana a non-agriculturist mortgagee and in Hoshiarpur a retired Sub-Inspector of Police held us up through mere perversity, and in Jullundur no less than eight apparently completed villages failed at the last moment and were abandoned. The unsatisfactory progress of the movement, and in some cases its failure in canal-irrigated areas like Lahore and Amritsar, is to be attributed to the unwillingness of owners to give up the advantages of nearness to the source of water. Such painful and sad experiences the Co-operative Department endures every year. Whole villages have to be abandoned as hopeless, after putting in a good deal of work for months together. The eleventh-hour hitch always comes as a bolt from the blue. In a number of cases in Jullundur, civil courts were invited to upset arrangements previously consented to." A study of the Report for 1932 supplies some cause for real alarm in this direction. "While," according to this Report, "some satisfaction may be expressed at the steady enlargement of blocks after consolidation, the increase in the number of Societies cancelled in despair is a testimony partly to the alarm now being felt by vested interests, and partly to the failing powers of persuasion in districts where the novelty has worn off, and the critical standard of the countryside is getting higher. Four of these disappointments come from Ferozepore. 'There was party feeling in the village, and the inferior revenue staff put obstacles in the way,' says the Circle Registrar. Ambala contributes a quota of three, where the reasons given are quaintly enough 'the absence of natural confidence and the presence of neighbourly jealousy,' sad and significant words. . . . Jullundur, in spite of its 77,000 acres consolidated since Mr. Calvert began the work, reports the abandonment of six villages. The Assistant Registrar, who clings firmly to the faith that all men are deceitful, notes briefly 'factions, party feelings' as a theme which requires no elaboration. It nevertheless has to be noted that these disappointments are a common feature, previous Reports have understated their extent."

THE COST OF CONSOLIDATION

According to the latest information the out-turn of work per Sub-Inspector is increasing, and the cost per acre consolidated which stood at Rs. 2–0–7, in 1932 fell to Rs. 1–13–1 for 1933. Practically all districts indicate a decrease in cost, which is different for different districts, ranging from Rs. 3–7–9 in Hoshiapur to Rs. 0–14–2 per acre in Gujranwala. The entire cost since the beginning of the movement is being borne by the Government. The fundamental weakness of the system, from the viewpoint of Co-operative principles, is that the whole cost of consolidation, of which surveying is responsible for a considerable part, has been borne by the Government. The Registrar remarks that "people nowhere seem sufficiently keen on consolidation to pay for it." The members of a Society must, as a rule, be prepared to pay the cost of this great agricultural reform. But in a country like India, where the illiteracy of the cultivator breeds suspicion as to the object of the best of the beneficial movements, the slightest suggestion concerning payment of cost by the cultivators would have frightened them out of the movement began over a decade ago. The advantages of consolidation have been now very adequately realized, and much of the time and money wasted over propaganda is now being saved. People seem eager to join Consolidation Societies, and are in a measure willing to contribute towards its cost. Ambala, Ludhiana, Jullundur, and Hoshiarpur have credited to a special fund a sum of nearly Rs. 16,000 for defraying the cost of consolidation. There is now a brisk demand for consolidation even in villages where no propaganda has ever been carried on. Applications from about a hundred such villages were received during 1933. The Registrar, in the Annual Report for 1933, observes, "I am inclined to think that insistence on a deposit before work is started would be perfectly feasible, and would not have a killing effect on demand." The Registrar further believes that "insistence upon partial cost of consolidation would serve to expedite work, for villagers, while willing to spend months disputing and deliberating when the staff is paid by Government, would be more inclined to an early settlement of their differences when delay would mean more expense to themselves." The Department proposes in the near future to refuse to consolidate a village unless villagers pay at least 8 annas per acre.

Consolidation of holdings has the proudest of achievements to its credit. The table given opposite will indicate the annual collective results of the movement. Individual cases showing the marvellous results of consolidation are too numerous to be mentioned. The Annual Report for 1933 records: "Ten villages belonging to the rich and influential

CONSOLIDATION OF HOLDINGS

Year	Societies			Societies Cancelled for Members Refusing to Exchange Possession	Area Consolidated (in Acres)	Number of Blocks of Land		Average size of Stocks increased		Number of Owners concerned	Villages in which Work was proceeding	Number of Staff employed by the Government	
	Registered	Unregistered	New			Before Consolidation	After Consolidation	From	To			Inspectors	Sub-Inspectors
1920	20	—	—	—	—	—	—	—	—	690	—	—	—
1921	60	31	—	—	6,350	10,783	2,044	0·75	4	1,698	—	—	—
1922	107	—	—	—	—	—	—	—	—	3,397	—	—	—
1923	133	—	—	—	—	—	—	—	—	5,255	—	—	—
1924	154	—	—	—	—	—	—	—	—	7,078	—	—	—
1925	174	—	—	—	10,411	17,707	3,255	0·6	3·75	8,412	—	—	—
1926	—	—	67	3	18,414	32,059	6,108	0·6	0·3	—	—	—	—
1927	—	—	81	4	38,071	45,165	8,861	0·85	4·3	—	—	7	70
1928	—	—	122	8	64,699	55,655	8,883	1·16	7·3	5,168	199	8	85
1929	—	—	115	3	48,709	87,942	14,667	0·55	3·3	7,630	204	8	115
1930	—	—	113	4	50,105	97,645	16,760	0·51	2·9	7,651	194	10	128
1931	—	—	142	4	72,281	117,982	21,627	0·61	3·3	12,512	208	10	134
1932	—	—	119	15	60,348	102,059	—	0·58	3·5	10,762	186	8	124
1933	—	—	101	5	62,062	91,545	15,432	0·67	4·02	9,284	162	8	104
1934	—	—	99	—	56,148	—	—	—	—	—	—	—	—

(but quarrelsome) family of choudhries of Kathlaur in the Pathankot tahsil have been consolidated, the area consolidated (4,173 acres) being reduced from 1,099 blocks to 58. The villages were spread over an area 9 miles in diameter, and every owner had holdings in every section; now each one has a separate village with a separate water channel. One of them had his 875 acres scattered in 194 blocks over ten villages; he now has a single block in one village."

The Director of Information Bureau, Punjab, recently issued a statement on consolidation of holdings, in which we come across the following lucid account of the result of consolidation in one village. This account it is difficult to resist quoting in full.

"To give a picture of what happens as the result of consolidation, a brief description of the work done in one village may be given. Gharkar is a small unknown village, 6 miles from Samrala, in Ludhiana District. The farmers, though mostly illiterate, had for years been successfully working a Co-operative Credit Society, and learnt and appreciated the benefits of united action. They took up this scheme with eagerness when explained. The result was that the whole village, consisting of 177 farmers, joined the Co-operative Society, and offered 820 acres of their land, scattered at 2,534 places, for consolidation. The Panchayat was elected, and the formal proceedings started on December 13, 1933. The task was difficult, and it took seven long months to reconcile the jarring interests. Thanks mainly to the indefatigable efforts of the Panchayat and the stoic patience of Government officials the scheme emerged successful at last. The results achieved have been simply marvellous. In place of 2,534 blocks scattered in all corners around the village, the land has been divided into only 239 compact holdings, and all are happy at the result. But the happiest of all is one Kirpa Singh, who had his land scattered at sixty-five different places, and is now the king of a compact farm at one place. He will stay in the farm, keep his cattle there, and work there the whole day. If you talk to him, you will learn the extent of his joy. Equally happy is Ram Chand, who had his fields scattered at fifty-seven places, which have been consolidated in two compact blocks.

"There are many like these, and there is none who does not believe that he has received the maximum benefit. Fomerly, they had to cross each other's fields to reach their land and to carry the cattle through. The result was free fights and quarrels. Now, under the resettlement scheme, each farmer has been provided with a road direct to his farm, and can travel to his fields and take his cattle along uninterrupted. Then each gets a place near the village for his manure-pits, and a vacant plot of land for building houses in the event of extension. Last, but not the least, a common plot of land has been left near the village for the future school, the possible Gurdwara, and a playground for children."

Out of the Government of India grant in 1935, a sum of Rs. 10,40 lakhs was set apart for speeding up the pace of consolidation of holdings in the Province. A Consolidation of Holdings Bill was drafted by the Department and recently submitted to the Government for consideration. The decision "reached by those in authority was that the time is not ripe for such legislation." This decision the Registrar very much regrets, and his regret is shared, needless to add, by all well-wishers of the peasantry and of the Province.* The programme for 1936 indicates also that increasing attention is being paid by the Department to the furtherance of the work of consolidation.

* The Consolidation of Holdings Bill was introduced in the Punjab Council in October 1936.

CHAPTER XXIV

MARKETING IN THE PUNJAB

THE methods and problems of marketing in the Punjab have been surveyed, firstly, in two special inquiries conducted by two Assistant Registrars of the Co-operative Department, and, secondly, in the village surveys conducted by the investigators of the Board of Economic Enquiry in the Punjab. This is the material upon which the Punjab Banking Enquiry Committee based its description of the marketing methods and framed its conclusions. This chapter, abridged from the Punjab Banking Enquiry Report, supplies the necessary background for a proper understanding of the marketing methods in the Province, upon which must be based the much-needed solution of this knotty problem.

SALES IN VILLAGES

The Shahpur inquiry brings out the fact that the grower generally sells his produce in the village. Hardly 10 per cent of the 117 persons concerned took their produce to the market, and only one of these was a small-holder. All available information tends to show that sales of agricultural produce are mostly local. In Shahpur itself it is estimated that 85 per cent of the growers sell their produce in the village. An investigation into the finance and marketing of cultivators' cotton in the Punjab, conducted in 1927–28, showed that 8 per cent of the cotton is sold locally. The village surveys all tend to strengthen this conclusion.

REASONS FOR LOCAL SALES

(1) *The Influence of the Creditor or mere Convenience*—The cultivator is in most cases obliged to sell through his creditor, who is generally the village shopkeeper as well. The average

grower prefers to sell in the village even when he is not indebted at all. He does so because it is in many ways more convenient to him than taking his produce to a market.

(2) *Bad Roads.*—The Punjab villages have no roads leading towards cities. Tracks and pathways do not admit of quick and cheap means of conveyance. The man who has much to sell may be willing to put up with bad roads, but the small-holder, who is the commonest type in the Punjab, may not think it worth while. Of the eighty-two small-holders dealt with in the Shahpur inquiry, only one took his produce to the market. The use of motor-lorries has made transportation over long distances both cheap and quick, but this facility can only be enjoyed by the middle-man. Even these adventurers are not able to approach Indian villages, in spite of the recklessness of lorry drivers; and this state of affairs will continue as long as each village does not possess a road leading to the nearest city or market.

(3) *Lack of Information Concerning Rates.*—The cultivator's information concerning prices is hopelessly inadequate. The Cotton Enquiry Committee records: "There seems no doubt that growers are very much in the dark as regards fluctuations in the rates, and that such information only filters through to them very slowly." Much, no doubt, depends upon the distance from the nearest market. In Shahpur, where eight out of eleven villages under inquiry were ten miles or more away, it was found that the cultivator had little knowledge of prices, but in chak 73 G.B., which is eleven miles from Lyallpur, and in Dalowali, which is three miles from Sialkot, the cultivator is said to be in daily touch with the market. Here the Banking Enquiry Committee seems to forget that in the case of the canal colonies, cultivators have enough to sell, and have by their very efforts at colonization given proof of qualities not conspicuous in the average cultivator of the Punjab.

(4) *System of Settling Rates.*—The cultivators have a legitimate distrust of the secret system of settling rates. Mr. Darling's note on marketing describes the secret settlement of rates as follows:

"In every market, except Sonepat, bids are registered secretly. The seller brings his produce to the market, and if it is grain unloads it on the platform before his agent's shop, and if it is cotton leaves it standing in the cart that has brought it in. Once a day, often in the afternoon, the brokers go the round of the market, and passing from shop to shop strike their bargains with the commission agents. They indicate their bids by taking the agent's hand under a cloth and making hidden signs with their fingers. After taking the bids, and consulting the seller if he happens to be present, the agent declares the highest bid, and the bargain is struck. Cotton is sold in the same way, except that after being sold it is taken off to the factory to be weighed; whereas grain is weighed there and then."

This method of sale, the Provincial Banking Enquiry Committee state, appears to be customary in all colony markets. The Banking Committee believes that the open bidding system prevalent at Sonepat is better calculated to inspire confidence in the cultivator.

(5) *Deductions.*—More serious are the deductions forced upon sellers of cotton by factory owners, often without sufficient reason. The commission agents of Montgomery admitted before the Banking Committee that such deductions were made on 80 per cent of the cartloads of cotton brought to the Montgomery market. The Cotton Enquiry Report concerning these deductions remarks:

"It is a common practice for buyers to offer high rates in the market and then to cut down these rates when delivery is being effected on the ground that the *kapas* in the centre of the cart is dirty or inferior in quality to that exhibited outside.

"Such complaints are invariably made when it is too late for the seller to take his produce elsewhere, as a portion of it has already been weighed and mixed with other *kapas* in the purchaser's godown. The seller has, therefore, no option but to accept the reduced rate. Such actions on the part of buyers must engender very bad feelings, and constitute another reason why growers are so loath to market their own produce.

It is reported that such deductions usually vary between annas 2 to 12 per maund, but in some cases they may be much more." An example illustrating this practice is quoted in a subsequent chapter. It is interesting to note that the Indian Cotton Committee believes that the abuse by the cultivator and village trader is of minor importance compared with the malpractices carried on in the ginning factories. In this there appears to be a reference to the much-debated practice of mixing short with long staple cotton and watering.

(6) *Commission Agent and Broker.*—The final reason given by the Cotton Enquiry Report for the grower's preference for village sales is that the commission agent acts chiefly in the interest of the buyers. The Linlithgow Commission thought that the broker was "more inclined to favour the purchaser, with whom he is brought into daily contact, than the seller, whom he only sees very occasionally." The Cotton Enquiry Report suggests that this is true of the commission agent, even when he is ostensibly acting for the seller.

In all the markets considered, with the exception of Sonepat, a broker as well as a commission agent is employed. The commission agent acts for the seller, the broker for the buyer, and this is found to be a satisfactory arrangement. In Sonepat the commission agent acts for both parties, and this, too, is reported to work well, because sales are by public auction, and prices determined by the highest bid.

(7) *Market Organization.*—The Colony Market Enquiry Committee suggests that a powerful factor in deterring cultivators from marketing their own produce is the way the ordinary market is organized. It is dominated by the trader, and the cultivator when he goes there can hardly help feeling himself an alien. He has no voice in the control of market arrangements, say in the fixing of market dues, no representation on market panchayats, and little or no means of ascertaining outside prices. He is often in debt to the dealer, and generally divided from him by religion or caste. He is mulcted in contributions to charitable objects in which, if a Muhammadan, he takes not the slightest interest: and he has frequently to submit to

other exactions which he is powerless to resist. The grower goes to the market wherever he is well treated, as at Chak Jhumra.

The way the ordinary market is organized weighs less with large growers than with the small. The large grower often has some education, and can hold his own; but the small is usually illiterate, and feels himself at the mercy of dealers he does not know, and of conditions he does not understand. Men of this type prefer to stay at home and deal with the local shopkeeper whom at least they know and often trust, and I should like to add that such a trust is more often than not quite misplaced.

WEIGHTS AND SCALES

A difficulty which applies as much to the village as to the market is the general inaccuracy of weights and scales. Out of 1,407 scales tested in five districts 69 per cent were found to be incorrect, and of 5,907 weights 29 per cent. How far inaccuracy and fraud go hand-in-hand it is not possible to say, but village survey reports suggest that it is not uncommon. Inaccurate weights appear to be so general that it is difficult to deal with the evil. In regulated markets the Linlithgow Commission recommended that the provision of a weighbridge should be made compulsory.

But something more than this is needed, and on paper a good deal has been done. Sixty-five local bodies have passed by-laws to control the weights and measures within their areas, and to provide for their inspection; but with most this has been merely a gesture, for few have furnished themselves with weights and measures, and without them the by-laws are useless. A serious difficulty is that a set of standard weights at the Mint costs Rs. 534,1,0, which most committees regard as prohibitive. Even when weights are acquired, the by-laws are not necessarily enforced.

EFFECT OF INDEBTEDNESS ON MARKETING

One of the old unwritten laws of marketing was that a debtor must deal with his creditor. The grower who is in debt to his shopkeeper must sell through him, and the village shopkeeper who borrows from a commission agent must use him as his agent. The rule is not so strong as it was, but it appears still to be more often observed than not.

The question arises, how far it affects prices. As between one trader and another, it probably affects them very little, for it is then a case of a Greek meeting a Greek, and debt is usually not so large that it cannot be repaid or transferred if good service is not given. As between trader and grower, the Linlithgow Commission held it established "that, where the cultivator is in a position to dispose of his produce in a market, however limited its scope, he obtains a much better price for it, even when the cost of transport is taken into consideration, than when he disposes of it in his own village." In the Punjab this appears to be true only in case of the remote and more impoverished tracts, such as Gurgaon, Muzaffargarh, and Dera Ghazi Khan, for remoteness and poverty together put the cultivator at the mercy of the dealer.

But reports of some surveys do suggest that the moneylender exercises a considerable influence over fixing prices, and it is difficult to believe that in normal circumstances the seller is not prejudiced by being in debt to his dealer, if only because equality cannot subsist between debtor and creditor.

PAYMENT OF LAND REVENUE

Where the indebted cultivator probably suffers most is in having to sell part of his produce directly it is harvested to meet his obligations, for then prices tend to be at their lowest. One of the most important of these obligations is the payment of land revenue. Since all have to pay at the same time, a very large amount of produce must come into the market at the same time and depress prices.

VILLAGE AND MARKET PRICES

It is generally supposed that even when not in debt, the cultivator loses by selling his produce in the village. The Banking Enquiry Committee suggests that the evidence at their disposal does not altogether justify this view. Undoubtedly the evidence is scanty because the field of inquiry was quite narrow. One witness, a merchant of long experience, stated that the grower does not get a full value, since he is not upon an equality with the buyer either financially or educationally. One has only to go to a market to realize that the grower is a mere nobody there, and the brokers and commission agents know how to fleece him as much as he will stand.

BETTER ORGANIZATION OF MARKETS

The Linlithgow Commission recommended the establishment of well-regulated markets, for these tend to create in the mind of the cultivator a feeling of confidence and of receiving fair play, and this is the mood in which he is most ready to accept new ideas and to strive to improve his agricultural practices. "At present he is an infinitely small unit," and even if fairly treated is likely to harbour doubt and distrust. This point is well illustrated by the inquiry of 1928. In six markets it was found out that less than 3 per cent of the shops were in the hands of agriculturists, and not a single local body had more than three agriculturist members. Co-operative Commission Shops provide a remedy, but their progress and success is a painfully slow process. Consequently, the Punjab Banking Committee believes that something more effective is needed to establish a proper balance between the interests of cultivator and traders, and suggests that some kind of organization, in which the producer is adequately represented, is required for the control and regulation of markets. In some of the markets of the Province associations have been formed for the settlement of disputes and the control of market business. The rules and regulations made by these associations and panchayats are reported to be just. But, however just they may be in principle, in practice so far as prices, charges, and deductions are concerned, "buyers invariably have things entirely in their own hands." The Banking Committee, therefore, stresses the necessity for the establishment of regulated markets.

THE COMMISSION AGENT

A commission agent's functions are of the most miscellaneous character, touching money-lending at one end and inn-keeping at the other. His charges, the Banking Committee believes, seem to be fair, but some, notably those connected with charity, would doubtless be out of place under more modern conditions, and with more efficient regulation others might be reduced or eliminated.

HOLDING UP OF PRODUCE

The ordinary cultivator has neither the ability nor the desire to hold up his produce for any length of time. The Cotton Enquiry showed that less than 6 per cent of the cotton under investigation was held up for sale after January 31st for a rise in prices; and the Village Survey Reports generally suggest that the holding up of produce for long periods on this account is unusual except amongst the larger and better-to-do holders. Amongst these the rise in prices after the war led to a marked strengthening of the tendency to hold, but the fall in prices after this period has tended to discourage this practice. It may not be to the individual cultivator's advantage to hold, but it is certainly to the general benefit that some should hold.

Though the ordinary cultivator does not hold up his produce for any length of time, he will not sell it as soon as it is harvested, unless he is seriously involved. This appears to be one of the more marked changes of the last five or ten years.

POOLS AND SALE SOCIETIES

The best single remedy for the grower's marketing difficulties is Co-operation. A number of Co-operative Commission

Shops have been established in the Punjab, the operations of which will be reviewed in the next chapter.

STORAGE

Before produce could be much more extensively held up in the village, the storage accommodation would probably have to be considerably increased and also improved. In Lyallpur village report it is said that for want of proper accommodation the cultivators think it better to sell their grain without much delay. If this is the case in Lyallpur, one of the most advanced districts in the Province, we may assume that it is generally the case elsewhere. Big landlords and the more substantial owners in the colonies frequently have godowns, sometimes very carefully built, for storing large quantities of produce. And in the more insecure tracts provision is often made, though in much simpler fashion, for storing a year's, if not two years', supplies against a period of prolonged drought. In Rohtak. the grain is stored in rooms with sanded floors, or in large gunny bags, and to prevent damage by insects the grain is given a mixture of sand, and in monsoon it is usually aired and put out in the sun to dry. Whereas in most of the Province holdings are small and conditions not particularly insecure, storage accommodation is largely determined by the consumption of the family.

Opinion is divided as to whether storage facilities in town and market are sufficient. The Banking Committee thinks them generally sufficient in quantity, though possibly not adequate in quality. There are convincing figures to prove that in the matter of quantity accommodation for storage is sufficient. It has been calculated that thirty-two towns and markets have a storage capacity of nearly 13 million tons.

In most towns produce is stored in more or less primitive godowns or kothas, and in both town and market produce is freely pledged as security for loan. It is impossible to say what proportion of total produce is stored.

The following estimate of storage in some of the markets is

believed to be fairly reliable. Montgomery *mandis* store 40 to 50 per cent of wheat and only 5 per cent of cotton, and the Gojra *mandi* 20 to 25 per cent of the produce. For Amritsar it has been estimated that only 25 per cent of wheat sold is stored in the villages.

LICENSED WAREHOUSES

Though there is ample storage accommodation in the Punjab, it must be admitted that most of it is of a very primitive character. It would therefore be an advantage if well-built godowns could be provided. With this object it is suggested by some that licensed warehouses on the American model should be established, and it is claimed that, if this were done, their managers could issue certificates as to grade and quality which would be useful instruments of credit, and in time become negotiable.

MARKETING FINANCE

From the village to the *mandi* the marketing of produce is largely financed by the village shopkeeper, who is generally also the village money-lender, and to a lesser extent by the commission agent and the Co-operative Society.

The village shopkeeper works principally with his own capital, but often—75 per cent, it is said, in Shahpur—supplements it by advances from the commission agents. These advances are made less with the object of practising money-lending than for attracting business. Occasionally, indeed frequently in Rohtak, the village shopkeeper helps to finance the commission agent by lending him his spare cash at 9 per cent or less.

In the *mandi* the commission agent finances the storage and sale of the produce till it is actually paid for, by, or on behalf of, the purchaser. He works mainly with his own capital, but adds to it such modest deposits as he can attract from a relative or a neighbour. When he requires more, if in a small way of business, he goes to a more substantial commission agent, who charges him from 9 to 12 per cent, and if in a large way to an indigenous banker or a commercial bank, which charges from 6 to 9 per cent according to the security offered. When the security is grain, possession of which is delivered, the charge, as we have seen, is only 7 or $7\frac{1}{2}$ per cent, and this security is being increasingly used. But when it takes the form of house property the charge goes up to 9 per cent; and if the borrower is not entirely reliable, up to 12 per cent. In the slack season rates are lower, and may fall to 6 per cent. From market to port or Indian destination finance is mainly supplied by the commercial banks, notably by the Imperial Bank, and to a lesser degree by the big exporting firms, indigenous bankers, and guarantee brokers.

This finishes the summary of information so far available. The appointment of the new provincial marketing officers and the surveys they are likely to undertake will, it is hoped, throw more light upon these problems and facilitate their solution so as to ensure remuneration to all commensurate with the services they render. Regulated marketing is as necessary as regulated money-lending. The cultivator's problems require a simultaneous handling.

CHAPTER XXV

COMMISSION SHOPS

Object.—The object of a Co-operative Commission Shop is to promote the economic interest of its members by:

(1) The purchase and sale on commission of seed, agricultural implements, and other requirements of its members;

(2) The sale on commission of the agricultural produce of its members;

(3) The provision of agricultural assistance to its members;

(4) The use of pure and improved varieties of seed by members;

(5) Other measures designed to encourage in the members the spirit and practice of thrift, mutual help, and self-help.

Commission shops being in their infancy frequently seek to promote the economic interest of their members merely by undertaking to sell on commission their agricultural produce.

Membership of a Co-operative Commission Shop is open to individuals as well as registered Co-operative Societies. Every member of such a shop must be either an owner or cultivator of land, mortgagee, or leaseholder.

Liability.—The liability of members for the debts of the Society shall be limited to double the nominal value of their shares.

Capital.—The capital of a Co-operative Commission Shop shall be composed of:

(1) An undetermined number of shares of the value of Rs. 50 each; (2) deposits from members; (3) deposits and loans from non-members; (4) realized profits. The acceptance of deposits and loans from non-members is subject to such restrictions as the Registrar may impose.

General Meeting.—The supreme authority is vested in the General Meeting. The General Meeting, amongst other business routine, transacts the following business:

(1) The election, suspension, and removal of the members of the Managing Committee;

(2) The fixing of the commission to be charged by the Society;

(3) Considering whether the site of the Society, its godowns, scales, and other dead stock are satisfactory, and proposing any necessary alterations;

(4) Inviting the members to make suggestions for increasing the quantity of produce for sale, improving the methods of receiving, storing, and grading of produce if necessary, and for paying the proceeds to members. All questions before the General Meeting, except amendment of by-laws, are decided by majority of votes. The chairman has a casting vote.

Managing Committee.—The Managing Committee usually consists of at least six members—individuals and representatives of Societies—including the Chief Director, the President, and one or more Vice-Presidents. The members of the Managing Committee are elected for a year, and are eligible for re-election.

The Committee generally exercises all powers of the Society except those reserved for the General Meeting, in particular it exercises the following duties and powers:

(1) Maintains true and accurate accounts of all money received and expended, and all stock bought and sold.

(2) Keeps true accounts of the assets and liabilities of the Society.

(3) Prepares and lays before the General Meeting a profit and loss account and a balance-sheet.

(4) Decides the terms on which agricultural produce shall be sold, subject to the provisions of the by-laws.

(5) Supervises the sale conducted by the Manager.

(6) Leases or buys land required for the business of the Society, and leases or erects godowns and an office with the previous sanction of the General Meeting.

(7) Decides the terms on, the periods for, and the rates of interest at which deposits are to be received, and arranges for the payment or return of deposits.

(8) Watches and guards against the adulteration of produce sold through the Society, and the evasion of the duty of members to sell through a Society all their saleable produce, and in either case imposes a fine on the culprits.

The Committee in the conduct of its affairs shall exercise the prudence and diligence of ordinary men of business, and shall be responsible for any loss sustained through acts contrary to law, the notified rules, and the by-laws.

The Committee may appoint from among its own members a Chief Director, and may delegate to him or to other officers of the Society such of its own powers as may be prescribed by a General Meeting.

Officers of the Co-operative Shop.—The Chief Director will:

(1) Control the grading of the produce according to quality in the case of sale or auction;

(2) Appoint, suspend, or dismiss employees other than the Manager or the munim;

(3) Control the paid staff of the Society;

(4) Be responsible for the proper maintenance of the accounts;

(5) Supervise and control the current business of the Society, and perform all duties entrusted to him by the Committee.

Manager.—The duties of the Manager shall be:

(1) To receive deposits and issue receipts as prescribed by the Committee;

(2) To advance loans;

(3) To sell agricultural produce, and to buy agricultural implements and other requirements as directed by the Committee or the Chief Director.

He is the most important officer of the Society, and much depends upon his ability and honesty. The appointment of the Manager shall be subject to the approval of the Registrar, and the Registrar may require the Committee to dismiss a Manager for any reasons which may appear to him to be good and sufficient.

Rules of Business.—(1) All transactions shall be strictly on cash terms, subject to the practice of the local market, which allows two days' grace for payment from the date of weighment. No credit shall be allowed except to a Government servant purchasing on behalf of Government.

(2) Sale shall ordinarily be by private treaty, but if the owner or owners so desire it may be effected by public auction.

(3) Every member shall be bound by the rules or instructions of the Managing Committee as to grading of his agricultural produce in respect of its quality and bulk.

(4) Every member delivering his produce for sale may, on the discretion of the Chief Director or Manager, be given an advance not exceeding 75 per cent of the estimated market value of such produce; the balance of the account shall be cleared on the sale of the produce. Interest at 12½ per cent shall be charged on such advance. The Chief Director or Manager may at any time order the immediate sale of the produce deposited if he considers that, owing to the deterioration of the produce or a fall in the market price, the advance given to the depositor is not sufficiently secured.

(5) The Society may charge such commission on sale as may be fixed from time to time in General Meeting for members and non-members respectively.

COMMISSION SHOPS

Causes of Failure.—The following difficulties have been experienced in the running of the Commission shops in the Punjab:

(1) *Boycott at the Hands of Ahrtees.*—The setting up of a Co-operative Commission Shop implies a stunning and a crushing blow directed at the manifold unlawful, unjustifiable, and in many respects the criminal methods of the ahrtees. There is nothing strange or extraordinary about it. No one will quietly submit to a rival whose activities are to all outward seeming calculated to injure his interests, even when the gain sought to be thus protected is born of abominable and criminal practices. The ahrtees as a class have, therefore, done all in

their power to injure the Commission shops. They organized boycotts of the Commission shops. Sangla, Jalalabad, Gujranwala, Jaranwala, Toba Tek Singh, and practically every shop had to face an ahrtees' boycott. There are two classes of commission agents. The agent with limited resources usually acts as the seller's agent, and does practically no storing. He is said to be carrying on *Kachhi Ahrat*. The agent with ample resources who usually acts as the buyer's agent and buys for himself and freely stores for export, is said to be carrying on *Pucci Ahrat*. Co-operative Commission Shops had no foreign relations or agencies to which the grain could be exported, hence the shops bought produce only to resell it locally. The ahrtees' boycott of the shop consisted in their refusal to purchase produce for export from the Co-operative Commission Shop.

In some cases the failure of Co-operative Commission Shops cannot but be attributed to the after-effects of boycott. Causes of the boycott, apart from professional jealousy, are at times quite interesting. Sometimes the ahrtees shifted the blame of their misdeeds on to the broad shoulders of the Congress. The Jaranwala shop was boycotted because in the municipal election the Muhammadan changars (men who keep the grain platforms clean) refused to vote for a Hindu candidate and were dismissed by all the shops in the market except the Commission shop. Another shop was boycotted because the Muhammadan Manager abducted a Hindu girl. One Assistant Registrar writes that, whatever the ostensible reason for a boycott, the real cause is always the same, to ruin a rival. People in charge of the shops, in order to save them from the after-effects for an actual or expected boycott, spend large sums of money in making arrangements to meet such boycotts. The Sangla Hill shop advanced a very big sum to a zemindar in order to shield itself against a boycott. This big advance hastened the disaster, which could have been perhaps otherwise averted.

(2) *The Seller's Preference for the Ahrtee.*—The seller of agricultural produce is incapable of judging aright. Lifelong

association with the ahrtee has reconciled him to all the disadvantages of dealing with the ahrtee. He does not therefore very willingly break away from the ahrtee. A certain amount of the cultivator's reluctance to join a Commission shop is that of a business man who will naturally hesitate to join an undertaking the success of which is at best uncertain. Nothing succeeds like success, and the successful working of a Commission shop will always constitute an irresistible recommendation to people to join it, or to start similar new shops. No pains should ever be spared to save a Co-operative Commission Shop from coming to grief once it has been started. Failure of a Co-operative Society of any type reacts adversely upon the growth and success of the movement in its various aspects. The personal connections with the ahrtee, coupled with the lurking suspicions as to the ultimate success of the shop, make the cultivator show preference to the ahrtee over the shop.

(3) *Disloyalty of the Members.*—Members of a Commission shop have been frequently found guilty of a lack of loyalty to the shop inasmuch as they too, frequently, prefer to sell in the village rather than to bring their produce to the shop. It appears to me that this reluctance on their part is not extraordinary. They are to blame if they bring their produce to the market and sell it to the ahrtees and not to the shop. Selling in the village is convenient to them even when it does involve some financial loss. It is no use quarrelling with them. Arrange to get the zemindar's produce from his village as your rival does, or make it sufficiently attractive for your member to bring his produce to your shop alone.

(4) *Apathy of Buyers.*—In the canal colonies the produce purchased by the Co-operative shops has to be sold mostly through the agents of a big firm. These agents are of the same caste as the ahrtees, and with their characteristic and instinctive sympathy with their caste-fellows patronize the ahrtees and wilfully neglect the Commission shop. Ultimate disposal of the produce is thus delayed, and the shop suffers. In fact, those connected with the working of the shops believe that this was the most oppressive difficulty met with. They are still

of opinion that if, as at one time it was intended, a connection with foreign firms for disposal of the produce is established, the Commission shops will be an unqualified success.

(5) *Zemindar's Competition.*—Wherever a zemindar sets up his own shop the Co-operative shop has to contend with a formidable rival. He has his personal relations with the sellers. The seller blindly places every confidence in him. The tragedy of it is that sometimes an office-holder of a Co-operative Commission Shop severs his connection with the shop only to set up a rival shop close by. He succeeds in enticing away a certain number of people.

(6) *Lack of Business Training.*—Members of the Managing Committees, the Directors, and the staff—all the workers—had no previous business training in this line of Co-operative work. Even when they combine to work honestly and devotedly the lack of business training may, and often does, bring about an unexpected disaster any moment. The Managing Committees cannot stick to their decisions. By-laws are not strictly enforced. In order to gain popularity loans to members are advanced far in excess of the limit allowed. Again it is this lack of business training which makes the general committees forget the importance of regular supervision. Irregularities of management can be remedied only when the Directors take greater pains in the discharge of their duties and leave the Manager no choice except a genuine and a willing enforcement of by-laws. But in this matter, as the Registrar puts it, "There is far too much trust in Providence and not enough in human precaution." Chichawatni shop in Multan Circle advanced Rs. 6,000 to a Jullundur trader on the security of produce said to be in Karachi. The joke of it is that the trader had ordinarily no dealings with the shop.

Agents of the Zemindar.—Sometimes the zemindar does not accompany his produce to the market. He sends it through porters or other people who serve as carriers, who have a dread of the people other than the ahrtee, whom they have known for quite a long time.

Heavy Investments.—In the case of some shops the initial

investments proved too heavy a burden to allow them to work their way to success. In anticipation of success, which it appears was taken for granted, huge sums of money were invested in the purchase of sites and ambitious construction of spacious godowns. This turned out a dead loss in a number of cases. The attitude of the Government is far from satisfactory in this respect. As has been explained elsewhere, the Government in this country should do more than Governments in other countries. The Registrar rightly observes in one of his Reports: "Government itself can hardly escape criticism on the charge of lack of sympathy in the matter of sale price of land, etc. Certainly I know of no other Government which drives such hard bargains with Co-operative Sale Societies, usually valuable concessions are granted to encourage them."

(7) *Advances by Dealers.*—The corn-merchant in a mandi combines in himself a corn-dealer and a money-lender. Where-ever Co-operative shops are started the money-lender in the corn-dealer is aroused to action with all his ways and methods. A corn-dealer ordinarily makes advances to a cultivator, and consequently acquires a prior claim over the purchase of his produce. This device works with greater intensity when it is sought to kill a rival in the form of a new Co-operative shop. Advances of very large sums are made to a large number of cultivators on the express condition that the cultivators must sell their future produce only through them. "The mandi dealer," as the Registrar puts it, "is less of a commission agent than a money-lender in disguise." When for one reason or another a member of a Commission shop is in the grip of the money-lender-corn-dealer, how can the shop be a success? Ordinarily the shop cannot afford to make such advances.

(8) *Default of Buyers.*—Sometimes a Commission shop comes to grief on account of the default of buyers. Much of this default is often due to the slackness of the management. Lyallpur suffered some losses in 1926 owing to the default or insolvency of a few buying firms. Commission shops can successfully meet such defaults by allowing a discount on cash payments. The mere drawing up of an approved list of

buyers will not go very far in securing the shop against defaults, for there is nothing to prevent the failure of one on the approved list.

(9) *Dishonesty.*—Managers and employees of a Co-operative shop are sometimes found guilty of dishonest practices. Such examples of dishonesty have been witnessed quite frequently even during the short history of the sale movement in the Punjab. One Manager was suspended for misappropriation in 1926. "Embezzlements in the Lyallpur, Jaranwala, and Gojra shops have had a damaging effect on the shops at large. A sum of Rs. 2,466 had to be written off as bad debts, and the estimated amount of bad and doubtful debts incurred in a variety of ways is some Rs. 23,000. One of the main reasons for the troubles which have fallen upon the Lyallpur shop was the practice of the late Manager doing business with the Society's moneys and purchasing bad stuff and mixing it with members' produce. The President of the shop, after failing to attend any meeting, has become a sadhu" (Report for 1932).

Hafizabad shop lost Rs. 295 in 1928 over the boycott in that year owing principally to the carelessness of the Manager. During the year 1928 three Managers had to be dismissed for dishonesty. In 1927 an employee of the Hafizabad shop disappeared after misappropriating Rs. 2,000. In 1928 the munim of the same shop absconded with Rs. 1,040, and the next year it was the Manager's pleasure to disappear with a sum well over Rs. 5,000. In this respect the Commission shops have been particularly unlucky.

ADVANTAGES OF SALE THROUGH COMMISSION SHOPS

The Co-operative Commission Shops bring manifold advantages to the sellers of agricultural produce.

(1) *Fair Dealings and Minimum Charges.*—The seller is not cheated of his dues in any way, and the minimum necessary charges are made. The ahrtee befools and cheats the cultivators by intentional miscalculations, false weights, and very high

incidental and religious charges imposed by his class simply because the producer must sell through them. One of the charges that the seller is made to pay is known as Gowshawla, i.e. payment for maintaining useless cows. Hindus are interested in giving protection to such cows which old age or sickness, barrenness, or any other disease has rendered unfit and uneconomic to be kept by individuals. The sellers of agricultural produce are mostly Mussulmans, and not at all interested in giving protection to such useless animals, but they must pay the Gowshawla charge if they are to sell their produce to the Hindu ahrtees. They pay it, and in Lyallpur alone the annual payment amounts to nearly Rs. 30,000.

(2) The ahrtee very seldom makes payment immediately. All shopkeepers in dealing with cultivators as a matter of practice seldom pay on the stipulated date. If a merchant owes another merchant Rs. 500 he must make payment on the specified date, otherwise he will have to pay interest on the debt. But if the same sum is due to a cultivator, the merchant delays payment as long as is possible, for the use of this money will mean some gain to him. One promising Mussulman merchant at Sialkot, who sold his goods to Hindus, explained his difficulty to me; and in view of his unwillingness to accept interest, wanted me to suggest a way out. The Hindu merchants print their terms of sale of goods on their business notepaper. "Non-payment by the appointed date will render the entire amount liable to interest at 5 per cent." This is one of the terms of sale. The Mussulman merchant in question felt the difficulty very much, as his religious scruples would not permit him to allow the above condition of sale to be printed on his business-form. "All right," I said, "you can put down a penalty for non-payment by the due date instead of interest." The young man felt greatly pleased at the suggestion. The Commission shop is in a position to make more prompt payments than ahrtees, for one reason or another, are willing to do.

The charges paid by sellers of grain vary from Rs. 2-2-3

per cent at Gojra to Rs. 2–14–6 at Chichawatni. Charges for sale of grain at Lyallpur amount to Rs. 2–5–6, and are according to an inquiry conducted by the Department of Co-operation made up as follows:

	Rs.	a.	p.
Commission	0	12	6
Weighment	0	3	9
Palladari (paid to the Palladar who fills the scales and does other miscellaneous work)	0	3	9
Brokerage	0	1	3
Shagirdi (for agents' apprentice) ..	0	1	3
Miscellaneous charges in kind ..	0	13	6
Dharmao (for religion)	0	1	3
Gaushala	0	0	3
Total	2	5	6

The charges in kind are made up of small payments of a few ounces per bag to weighmen, water-carriers, sweepers, cooks, and coolies. The usual commission is Rs. 1 per cent, and the Commission shops charge only eight annas. It has been calculated that the sellers save at least 50 per cent over all charges when they sell through the Co-operative Commission Shop. It has been estimated that if grain were sold through Co-operative shops at Gojra, Toba Tek Singh, Okara, and Chichawatni, the annual saving to the zemindars on this account alone would come up to about Rs. 2 lakhs.

Watta.—The price of cotton is fixed while it stands in cartloads in a market or outside the ginning factory. Cotton is then taken into the factory to be weighed. While cotton stands loaded in carts, the quality of the upper layer of the load can only be seen. When the entire quantity of it is unloaded it may be found to be adulterated with inferior qualities of the material or dust. The deduction to be made in price for this difference in the quality of cotton is known as *watta*. This is quite legitimate, but even this provision is used to coerce the seller into accepting a very much lower price for his material than he deserves. Mr. Darling in his note on marketing submitted to the Punjab Provincial Banking Enquiry Committee, says: "It is freely alleged that buyers offer high rates in the market and subsequently reduce them on the ground that cotton in the centre of the cart is dirty or inferior in quality to that displayed above. If the cultivator disputes this, all he can do is to reload his cart and take it off to some other factory; or, what is even more troublesome, journey back to his village with, no doubt, weary bullocks along a heavily rutted *kachha* road. As sales often take place in the afternoon, it may even be too late to do this. Caught between the devil and the deep sea, he is virtually forced to concede the claim." As an example of this coercion, Mr. Darling has given the following example. "A tenant took his cotton to Sargodha and spent three days there before he could sell it to his satisfaction. It was then taken to the mill to be weighed. When weighing was in progress, the millowner insisted upon a deduction from the agreed price on the ground that the produce was not of uniform quality. The tenant's only remedy was to load up his cart and go elsewhere, but his patience was exhausted, and he conceded the claim." Continuing the above note, Mr. Darling remarks: "The Assistant Registrar estimates that it is levied in one sale out of five without tangible reason, and that there is some foundation for this is suggested by figures for four shops in Chichawatni. In the cotton season of 1927–28 *watta* was deducted in 40 per cent of the sales at rates varying from annas 1 to 20 a maund, while in the Co-operative Commission Shop it was deducted in only 12 per cent of sales, and at annas 1 to 8 a maund. The difference is probably due to more straightforward dealings on both sides, and it is a marked advantage of all truly Co-operative enterprises that it encourages men to deal fairly with each other."

WEIGHTS AND SCALES

The Board of Economic Enquiry, Punjab, undertook a detailed investigation into the accuracy of weights and scales in eleven different districts of the Province. The result of investigation in some of the districts was as follows:

	Montgomery	Shahpur
Number of shops whose weights were checked	74	305
Shops with all their weights correct ..	2	70
Number of weights checked	572	2,555
Number of weights found correct ..	243	174
Number of scales checked	139	494
Correct	16	146

Of 2,777 weights checked in Amritsar, Gujrat, and Muzaffargarh Districts 42 per cent were found to be incorrect.

Weights and scales were examined in the course of village surveys conducted on behalf of the Punjab Economic Enquiry Board. The results in some of these villages were as follows:

In Jullundur village the weights and scales of four shopkeepers were tested. "The scales were correct, but not the weights, except in one case, where they had been recently purchased. One shopkeeper had a weight of four seers which was one-eighth of a seer too heavy. He had inserted lead into the hollow at its base, and admitted that he used it when purchasing wheat, cotton, and *gur* from women, and when weighing produce bartered for goods. Another was using a half-seer weight which was one chhatak short, and it is said that he used it only for selling. The third had a weight of 4 chhataks which was one-quarter of a chhatak short. More serious is 'the clever and dishonest weighing of goods,' from which, says the investigator, the consumer loses most of all. In Gaggar Bhana the weights and scales of three shopkeepers were examined. Two had incorrect scales, and the third incorrect weights. One of the latter, said to be equal to six rupees, weighed seven. It was apparently used for weighing the grain given by women and children in exchange for goods. In the Lyallpur village some of the shopkeepers are said to keep two sets of scales and weights, one for buying and the other for selling."

These are examples of what prevails on a large scale in the Province.

(3) Both the ahrtee and the money-lender in various ways misappropriate what the cultivator offers for sale. When the ahrtee and the money-lender combine in one—well, the cultivator is done for. The opening of the Commission shops effectively checks the rapacities of the money-lender ahrtee.

(4) *Educational Value.*—The working of a Commission shop has its own high educational value inasmuch as the Commission shop introduces a zemindar to an important branch of his business, and he realizes how even in the last stage of his business people organize to rob him of his due share in produce.

COMMISSION SHOPS

Year	Number of Shops	Members		Value of Produce Sold in Lakhs of Rupees
		(a) Individuals	(b) Societies	
1925	6	—	—	14,50
1926	13	—	—	25
1927	18	—	—	23,50
1928	19	2,558	985	35
1929	24	3,286	1,273	47
1930	24	3,339	1,288	41
1931	25	3,595	1,280	30
1932	25	3,463	1,415	24
1933	23	338	269	19
1934	22	—	—	19

CHAPTER XXVI

THRIFT SOCIETIES

NON-AGRICULTURAL THRIFT SOCIETIES

Object and Operation.—The sole object of a Thrift Society is the encouragement of thrift amongst its members. The Society undertakes to collect contributions by receiving general deposits. Members sometimes undertake compulsory deposits for special purposes, e.g. buying of a shop, or the making of a house. Despite a provision in the by-laws, generally loans are not at all given to the members. In some Societies, where a member may borrow to the full extent of his contribution, interest is charged.

A beginning was made in 1921, when two Thrift Societies were registered. The Department of Co-operation in launching this experiment started with great enthusiasm and high hopes. The Annual Report for 1921 records: "The Army scheme has already been mentioned. It is intended to approach all heads of departments and offices, all employees of labour, and as many wage-earners as possible in the current year. Whatever the difficulties, if this Province is to make progress there must be thrift."

Propaganda for thrift was carried on amongst Indian troops, but the post-war reduction of officers and a general fear of demobilization rendered any progress impossible of achievement. But the Department placed two Assistant Registrars on special duty, who worked hard to promote these Thrift and Savings Societies, but after a year's work they reported: "So far wage-earners, whether in offices or in factories, show little appreciation of this form of Co-operation: saving to spend is not attractive when borrowing is so easy." Another year of work brought quite encouraging results. The number of Societies shot up to seventy-two. These Societies were mainly organized amongst patwaris, tahsil and district board staff and Indian Christians, notably in Sialkot City, petition writers, and pleaders. The sphere of Thrift Societies kept on expanding till it now embraces the following classes of people: patwaris, tahsil and district board staff, sub-overseers, pleaders, policemen, schoolmasters, railway employees, factory hands, office clerks, and soldiers in regiments.

The working of these Societies was checked in the beginning on account of the law requiring as high as 25 per cent of the profits to be placed to reserve, but this difficulty was got over by a special order of the Minister-in-Charge of the Department. With a view to encouraging the formation and working of Thrift Societies, the Punjab Co-operative Union charges only 1 per cent as its audit fee, whereas the charge for other Societies is 10 per cent of their net profits.

These Thrift Societies had been making very satisfactory progress, but the recent depression has told very adversely on some of them. The following are some of the most important Thrift Societies:

School Societies.—The schoolboy of to-day is the leader of to-morrow. The State and the Society must not let slip any opportunity of inculcating in him all such virtues that go to make a country prosperous. Most people work hard and win an honest living, but they are always in need, for they have had no schooling in thrift. Most of the non-agricultural Thrift Societies in the Punjab are in one way or another connected with schools. Every effort has been made to persuade boys and their teachers to join School Thrift Societies. But in spite of all such efforts, in view of the tremendous magnitude of the task, a mere beginning has been made. Societies of schoolmasters predominate, but the success of all School Societies depends upon the person and attitude of the head master towards the movement. The following are some of the causes of the unsatisfactory progress made by these Societies:

(1) Thrift as it involves a restraint upon man is naturally unpopular with every class of men, particularly those who lack foresight, and the schoolmasters in the Punjab make no exception to this rule.

(2) In the case of School Centre Societies, the members live apart at different places, and consequently the Societies lack that cohesion which is so essential to the success of a joint undertaking.

(3) Transfers of teachers are inevitable, and a teacher usually withdraws all his savings and ceases to be a member of a Thrift Society on his transfer from one place to another.

(4) Irregularity in the payment of salaries to schoolmasters employed by local bodies and other non-Government schools.

(5) The effect of agricultural depression has been very unwholesome on the working of the School Thrift Societies. According to the Report for 1931: "The Societies are not altogether free, however, from the effects of the fall in prices, for many masters are also agriculturists, and have often been constrained to withdraw savings in order to make good their losses on their fields."

(6) In some of the Districts some schools have been closed as a measure of retrenchment. When a school is closed down, the teachers dismissed, the Society is no more.

Penny Banks have been started for boys in some schools. The object of a Boys' Thrift Society is not so much accumulation of funds as the teaching of thrift to the future generation now in the making.

The success of Thrift Societies of schoolmasters, as has already been said, depends upon the head master. Organized effort at all points will tremendously increase the amount of savings. In Jullundur the total savings during 1931 went up by Rs. 10,000 to Rs. 54,000, although withdrawals during the same period amounted to Rs. 29,000. For the year 1931 the monthly contributions of the Thrift Society in the Khalsa High School at Sirhalai Kalan, District Amritsar, amounted to Rs. 1,125, and the total collections to Rs. 62,000.

POLICE SOCIETIES

The Border Military Police Society in Dera Ghazi Khan, in 1931, owned Rs. 25,412, and claimed 251 members. The two

Police Societies started at Jhang and Lyallpur worked quite satisfactorily as long as "Mr. Conner, the founder and the guiding spirit," had not been transferred. In 1932 these Societies were objecting to the deductions of contributions before payment. The Report for 1933, just issued, makes no mention of them, and it is safe to conclude that these Societies no longer exist.

THE FAUJI BANK

The Fauji Bank for military pensioners was started in 1927 and had been till lately working fairly well. It was expected that this example would be followed at other places, and it had even been announced that one such bank would be started at Rohtak. A peculiar difficulty over assignment of pensions is responsible for the undesirable state of affairs to which the bank had fallen. A study of the Report for 1931 would have enabled anybody to foresee that all would be over with the bank within the next year. The Report for 1932 confirms this forecast by maintaining a dignified silence as to the affairs of the Fauji Bank.

MILITARY SOCIETIES

The quiet workers of the Department of Co-operation were bold enough to invade the army, and we all know they conquered. Regimental Societies were formed. "The Societies in Probyn's Horse at Lahore and in the 6th D.C. Lancers at Sialkot are working well. The former has 375 members; the actual savings received by it during the year amounted to Rs. 11,900, and these together with profits and other deposits amount to Rs. 73,000." There are certain cases in which the advances of the Department met with no response.

A railway coolie saved Rs. 900 and deposited the same in a Union. A daily labourer in Multan saved Rs. 275 and deposited it in a Society. A Mirasi in Dera Ghazi saved Rs. 250. A barber collected Rs. 300 for buying a shop.

AGRICULTURAL THRIFT SOCIETIES

In 1925 it was decided not to restrict these Societies merely to non-agriculturists. Agriculturists in the Punjab need such Societies more than any class of population in urban areas. With a view to extending the usefulness of the Co-operative movement to a class which should mould its very life in the

PROGRESS OF THE NON-AGRICULTURAL THRIFT SOCIETIES

Year	Number of Societies	Number of Members	Amount of Savings
			Rs.
1923	72	1,164	25,000
1924	179	2,767	63,571
1925	334	5,574	1,36,000
1926	556	9,000	2,80,000
1927	740	12,500	4,38,000
1928	874	15,000	6,00,000
1929	962	16,932	7,73,000
1930	1,002	18,251	9,56,000
1931	1,048	19,848	11,83,000
1932	1,087	20,563	12,87,000
1933	1,146	21,708	13,89,000
1934	1,195	22,560	16,3 lakhs

spirit of this movement a group of Thrift Societies was organized in the Montgomery District for cultivators. Contribution in grain was accepted, and these were known as Grain Thrift Societies. An average peasant proprietor in the Punjab seldom owns any cash. He is generous in the giving away of what he has. Starting of Thrift Societies for the agriculturists and acceptance of grain by way of contribution to the Society is perhaps the wisest measure ever adopted by the Department. Grain was collected from the members, and the proceeds were deposited in a Central Bank. The by-laws of the Montgomery Grain Thrift Societies permitted a variable contribution in accordance with the quality of the harvest. Grain Thrift

Societies are to be found in Lahore, Sheikhupura, Shahpur, Montgomery, and Multan.

The chief forms of the Agricultural Thrift Societies are the Crop Failure Relief, Land Revenue Redemption, and the Grain Banks.

Grain Banks are at present confined to Muzaffargarh and number eighty-two. Shares of these Societies are collected in grain. Loans are advanced in the form of grain, to be repaid at the next harvest plus 25 per cent. The local money-lenders' charges amount to 50 per cent. Although difficulties in the form of collection, grading, storage, and distribution of grain are immense, yet this is the only form suited to the local conditions in the District, and is working satisfactorily. Land Revenue Redemption Societies number only eight, and are equally distributed in Jullundur and Gurdaspur. These Societies demand a contribution at each harvest in order to form a fund which would ultimately redeem the entire land revenue of a village. Contributions have to be paid until the interest on the total every year is sufficient to pay the land revenue of the year.

The Crop Failure Relief Societies, according to the latest information available, number seventy-one, and with a single exception all are to be found in Hoshiarpur District.

All these various forms of Agricultural Thrift Societies give every promise of progress, but the prevailing agricultural depression has adversely affected so many of them.

WORKING OF AN AGRICULTURAL THRIFT SOCIETY

Savings may be in kind or in cash as previously agreed upon. These contributions are made at the harvest-time. The cultivator is persuaded to put by at least one-fourth of his income. He can if he likes make deposits for special purposes, such as, for education, marriage, building of a house, or purchase of land. An Agricultural Thrift Society may advance loans to its members not exceeding three-fourths of the total contribution of any member. The member who borrows, so to say, on the security of his contribution, pays a moderate rate of interest, and undertakes to repay his loan to the Society in easy instalments at the harvest-time. The funds of a Society are generally deposited with a Central Bank. Five per cent of the annual profit is carried to the reserve fund, the rest is distributed amongst the members in proportion to the values of their contributions. The Managing Committee conducts the whole affair for the members.

CHAPTER XXVII

LAND MORTGAGE BANKS IN THE PUNJAB

TYPES OF LAND MORTGAGE BANKS

LAND Mortgage Banks have been classified as (1) Co-operative, (2) Non-Co-operative, and (3) Quasi-Co-operative.

(1) *A Co-operative Land Mortgage Bank* is an association of borrowers. Each member pays a small entrance fee to meet the necessary expenses, initial cost of land valuations, and other incidental charges. The association has no capital of its own, but creates credit by the issue of mortgage bonds bearing interest and made payable to the bearer. These bonds are regarded as perfect types of secure investment. Co-operative Land Mortgage Banks endeavour to keep low the rate of interest, and do not aim at profit. The Federal Farm Loan Banks of the United States of America and the Russian Farm Mortgage Mutual Credit Association are illustrative of the Co-operative Land Mortgage Banks.

(2) *Non-Co-operative or Commercial Land Mortgage Banks* are to be met with in large numbers all over the continent of Europe. They are purely commercial concerns, work for profit, and declare dividends. The State in a measure controls their operations in order to ensure that they do not cause hardship to their borrowers, and to make sure that they discharge their obligations to those who invest their money with them. All these banks are modelled after the Crédit Foncier de France. The Agricultural Bank of Egypt also is illustrative of this class of Land Mortgage Banks.

(3) *Quasi-Co-operative Land Mortgage Banks* partake in varying proportions of the ideals and practices of commercial and Co-operative institutions. These associations are formed with share capital on limited liability basis, and their membership is composed of borrowers and non-borrowers. These banks operate over fairly large areas. Each member has a single

vote irrespective of his share capital, and the dividend is fixed at a low figure. The Hungarian Land Mortgage Institute for large and the National Small-Holdings Land Mortgage Institutes for small owners are illustrative of this type of Land Mortgage Bank.

EARLY HISTORY OF LAND MORTGAGE BANKS IN INDIA

In 1863 the Land Mortgage Bank of India, Limited, modelled on the Crédit Foncier de France, was registered in London and started operations in Calcutta, Bombay, and Madras, with sub-agencies in all the principal districts of Bengal, Bombay, Madras, etc. The bank advanced money for a period of seven years at 7 to 8 per cent. The bank flourished for about twenty years and then gradually died away. In 1883 Sir William Wedderburn suggested the establishment of a land bank for Poona, but the suggestion never took a practical form. Sir Frederick Nicholson held (1895) that Land Banks were neither suited to nor needed by the ryots of Madras Presidency. Dupernex, in his *People's Banks for Northern India*, advocated the establishment of such banks for the benefit of the encumbered estates in the United Provinces.

The Committee on Co-operation, 1915, while discussing the possibility of meeting the credit needs of large proprietors, remarked:

"The case of these proprietors has been represented to us, and more than one Registrar has seriously considered the possibility of introducing some form of Co-operation among them corresponding to the Land Mortgage Credit Association or Mortgage Banks which are found on the continent of Europe . . . but we feel that the establishment of well-conceived and well-administered mortgage associations or banks at the instance of the landed gentry of the country, with the help of Government, would be a measure of great value not only to the proprietors themselves but also to the Government, and this fact should in our opinion be borne in mind if applications are at any time made for special concession in respect of such banks."

In 1919 the Finance Member of the Government of India favoured the establishment of Land Banks started and maintained chiefly by local enterprise and supervision. But he was opposed to the Government taking up the establishment of such banks on a large scale.

THE NEED FOR MORTGAGE BANKS

Mr. Strickland has condensed a world of meaning and argument in the following two sentences, which so adequately establish the need for Mortgage Banks.

"The imprudent use of credit by the Punjabi cultivator, and the deplorable tradition whereby the money-lending and grain-lending classes have been led to build up huge claims for debt at compound interest against the agriculturist, have resulted in laying a great load, and an unproductive load, on the land of the Punjab. Whoever is to blame, the borrower, the lender, or the Civil Courts established by the Government, the fact has to be faced, and wide areas of land in the Punjab, as elsewhere in India, are under mortgage to persons who seldom take an active interest in the improvement of agriculture, and are concerned only with their financial operations and their rents."

This load on the land of the country and on the brain and brawn of the country must be lifted. Often the sahukar's loan has swollen to several times its original proportions. The original loan may have been paid many times over, and still the amount due stands so high as to ensure perpetual exploitation and serfdom of the borrower. If economic serfdom is harmful to nations it surely does no good to individuals. It is a wicked system of society that allows such perpetual and dishonest exploitation of the poor at the hands of those who through this very process acquire strength and riches so thoroughly ill-begotten.

UNSUITABILITY OF A PRIMARY CREDIT SOCIETY TO SUPPLY LARGE AND LONG-TERM LOANS

The Primary Credit Society is by its very nature unsuited to the supply of a large and long-term credit. The funds of a Society are generally made up of short-term loans and deposits. Redemption of huge old debts and investments in permanent improvements of land need large sums of money for comparatively long periods. The scanty funds of the Societies cannot reasonably be locked up in such long-term and large loans. Even if a Society has sufficient funds to invest in such loans it will get involved in unpleasant legal proceedings in case of default. A Society wants to develop the character of its members as a security against the loans granted to them, but land mortgage loans depend upon material security.

When a Society refuses to grant long-term large loans to its members, it virtually refuses to advance money to a borrower which his landed property entitles him to. The Society in so doing in a way forces its members to fall into the clutches of the money-lender.

The framers of the original Co-operative Credit Societies Act of 1904 carefully considered the advisability of permitting such Societes to advance long-term credit to their members on mortgage of their land. The question proved one of extreme difficulty. "It was eventually decided to permit mortgage security and local Governments were empowered to regulate it to such an extent as might be found advisable for any Society or class of Societies. . . . The present position is, thus, that land mortgage business can be carried on by Societies registered under the existing Act, unless the Government otherwise direct."

ESTABLISHMENT OF CO-OPERATIVE LAND MORTGAGE BANKS IN INDIA

The need for establishment of Land Mortgage Banks having long been recognized, the first definite pronouncement on this behalf was made at the Conference of Registrars held in 1926.

The Registrars, with the concurrence of the non-official co-operators, adopted a resolution for the establishment of Co-operative Land Mortgage Banks. The Conference adopted the following scheme:

"(1) Mortgage banks based on Co-operative principles are desirable in many parts of India. No transaction should be undertaken which is not economically profitable to the borrower.

"(2) *Objects.*—The principal objects for which loans may be advanced should be:

"(*a*) The redemption of the land and houses of the agriculturists;

"(*b*) The improvement of land and methods of cultivation and the building of houses of agriculturists;

"(*c*) The liquidation of old debts; and

"(*d*) The purchase of land in special cases only to be prescribed in the by-laws. (This provision is evidently intended to prevent land speculation and indiscriminate borrowing to buy land.)

"(3) *Area and Management.*—The area of operations should be the smallest unit consistent with competent management. The imposition of liability on Village Credit Societies or the confinement of mortgage loans to members of such Societies are not recommended, but the bank should consult the Village Societies in the case of all loans to members of such a Society. Punctuality in repayment should be rigidly enforced in Mortgage Banks.

"(4) *Finance.*—A reasonable total of share money should be held by each bank in order to reassure the investing public. In Provinces in which the property can be sold on foreclosure, no loan should exceed half the value of mortgaged properties. No excess liability is required beyond the amount actually borrowed by a member plus his share money. If no excess liability is imposed, the share money of a borrower should not be less than one-twentieth of his loan.

"The minimum loan should be such as to repay the cost of

the transaction to the bank. Each bank should prescribe in its by-laws a maximum loan from time to time according to its financial position. Debentures should be issued by a central financing body in each Province rather than by separate Mortgage Banks."

The Royal Commission on Agriculture expressed substantial agreement with the scheme outlined in the resolution of the Registrars' Conference of 1926. "Such experience of the practical working of Land Mortgage Banks as has been gained since the resolution was passed has not shown the need for any alteration." The Royal Commission on Agriculture made the following recommendations besides endorsing the establishment of Land Mortgage Banks as outlined in the Registrars' Conference:

(1) The guarantee of interest on the debentures of Land Mortgage Banks is the most suitable form in which assistance to these banks can be given by the Government.

(2) Government assistance to Land Mortgage Banks in the form of subscription to their debentures is not recommended.

(3) The debentures of Land Mortgage Banks, the interest on which is guaranteed by Government, should be added to the list of trustee securities under the Trustees Act.

(4) Land Mortgage Banks should only be organized after the most careful preliminary inquiry, and their constitution and working should be as simple as possible.

(5) For some years to come there should be an official member on the Committee of Management of each bank.

The Registrars' Conference met again in 1928 and discussed once again the scheme proposed in 1926 with all the amplifications and amendments suggested by the Royal Commission on Agriculture.

The resolution of the Registrars' Conference of 1928 runs as follows:

(1) The Conference entirely endorses the resolution passed by the Conference of the Registrars in 1926 in favour of the establishment of Land Mortgage Banks.

(2) The Conference is of opinion that Land Mortgage

Banks should be established under the provisions of the Co-operative Acts now in force in British India.

(3) A nominee of Government is necessary on the Managing Committee of a Primary Land Mortgage Bank, except where the interests of the Government and debenture-holders are sufficiently safeguarded by the appointment of a trustee acceptable to the Government.

(4) Government assistance to Land Mortgage Banks in the form of subscriptions to their debentures is recommended while all these banks are in their early stages, and assistance is also recommended in the form of loans.

(5) The guarantee of interest on debentures of Land Mortgage Banks is the most suitable form in which assistance can be given by the Government.

(6) The debentures of Land Mortgage Banks, the interest on which is guaranteed by the Government, should be added to the list of trustee securities under the Indian Trusts Act, 1882.

(7) The Conference is of opinion that Land Mortgage Banks should be organized only after the most careful preliminary inquiry, and that their constitution and working should be as simple as is consistent with adequate safeguards.

THE PUNJAB EXPERIMENT IN CO-OPERATIVE LAND MORTGAGE BANKS

The Punjab had the honour to lead the rest of India in the establishment of Co-operative Land Mortgage Banks. The Jhang Co-operative Land Mortgage Bank was started in 1920. There are now twelve Co-operative Land Mortgage Banks in the Province.

Membership.—Membership of Co-operative Land Mortgage Banks is open to Agricultural Credit Societies and individual owners of agricultural land.

Area of Operations.—With the exception of banks at Jhang and Mianwali, which operate over the whole district, the area of operation of the rest of the banks is limited to a single tahsil in a district.

Objects of Loans.—Loans are generally made for: (1) Redemption of land. (2) Liquidation of unsecured debts. (3) For the improvement of land. (4) Loans for purchase of land allowed in the beginning have been positively prohibited.

Limits of the Loans.—The maximum limit of loan for any member is fixed at thirty times the land revenue payable on the land mortgaged. The maximum limit in the case of one bank stands at Rs. 15,000, and at Rs. 10,000 in the case of four, but the Department now definitely desires to reduce this limit to Rs. 5,000 only.

Duration of the Loan.—Loans were at first granted for five years, the period has now been extended to ten.

Limit of the Loan and the Inquiry.—The limit of loan at first stood at thirty times the land revenue, which recently had been brought down to five times only, and since 1933 practically all lending has been virtually stopped.

The model by-laws provide, in order to secure a margin of safety, that no loan may exceed fifteen times the annual net profit of the mortgaged property. When an application for loan is received a Director and a paid servant of the bank undertake an inquiry into the value of annual profit from the property. A local inquiry into the conditions and productivity of land is undertaken. This committee of inquiry submits an open report to the Directors. One of the members of the committee, usually the Director, submits a confidential report. The maximum assessment of land revenue permitted by Government rules is one-half of the net profit; the by-laws allow this assumption to be made that in the absence of extraordinary and unexpected deterioration of the property, thirty times the land revenue will never be more than fifteen times the net annual profit. When, therefore, the loan applied for does not exceed thirty times the land revenue, a summary inquiry only is made on the spot. If the loan applied for exceeds thirty times the land revenue it is possible that this amount may exceed fifteen times the annual net profit. In such a case a detailed inquiry has to be undertaken. The inquiry is based on revenue records showing the actual crops grown on the land in the last five years, the average out-turn of each such crop in the vicinity of the land on the mortgage of which the loan has to be granted. The prevailing market price of the produce is taken into consideration. This inquiry is conducted by two investigators, as in the first case, and forms the basis of the Director's decision.

DIFFICULTIES AND DEFECTS IN THE WORKING OF MORTGAGE BANKS

(1) *Mania for Purchase of Land.*—Long-term loans for the purchase of land in the beginning were allowed by Land Mortgage Banks in the Punjab. But this tendency to borrow for purchase of land soon developed into a fantastic mania. The rising value of land made the zemindar's hunger for land all the more intense, and this intensity grew more than in proportion to the rise in the value of land. This tendency towards purchase of land made the price of land shoot up; by 1926 it had been realized by the Department that land already stood at an uneconomic price, and it was decided to refuse loans for purchase of land. The borrowers, when their applications for loans for purchase of land were rejected, resorted to mortgaging their existing property in order to buy land and then applied for loans for redemption of land. It was found to be extremely difficult to detect such cases. In 1926 one bank was thus deceived—or should I say the deception was discovered in this one case alone? In 1927 it was decided that no loans should be advanced by any bank for purchase of land which desired to obtain loans from the Government. In spite of this definite prohibition, one bank advanced a loan for purchase of land which under express instructions from the Registrar had to be recalled.

(2) *Directorate: Lack of Ability.*—One of the causes of slow and unsatisfactory growth of joint-stock banking in India is the dearth of Directors possessing the requisite ability and enthusiasm. Joint-Stock Banks draw their Directors from the educated classes. The Directorate of Mortgage Banks is to be drawn

essentially from the zemindar classes, amongst whom it is difficult to find men who are fit to be made Directors of a bank. The educated Punjabi, if he is not a zemindar himself, has very little interest in measures designed to help the cultivator. The bulk of the Directors lack that education and ability which is almost the first essential of the success of a bank. There are some educated Punjabis who are rendering good help to these banks as Directors.

Lack of Loyalty.—As in the case of the Managing Committee of a Primary Society the Directorate of a Mortgage Bank does in various ways misuse its powers to the detriment of the institution. Partiality and favouritism have their full play.

Loans are readily granted to friends and relatives. Preliminary inquiries by Directors on loan applications are generally unreliable. Directors show less of loyalty to the bank and more of dishonest indulgence to the borrowers who are their friends and relatives.

Directorship is a position of honour and may be of great financial satisfaction, and is hence much sought after. One Director of a Mortgage Bank once brought the shareholders to the General Meeting of the bank at his own expense to get elected as a Director. The Directors fight like pleaders to get the loans sanctioned which they have recommended. In the beginning, when Directors could borrow from the bank at will, large sums were borrowed and misused by them. The Registrar proposed in 1928 that loans to Directors should be stopped. Four banks have consequently stopped loans to them. Only one Mortgage Bank allows loans to Directors without any restriction. The remaining half of the banks grant loans to Directors only when two-thirds of the Directors, excluding the applicant, unanimously agree to the loan. But such a sanction by the Directors must also have the written approval of the official member.

(3) *Frauds upon the Banks.*—Members and Directors, it appears, all in a way conspire to perpetrate frauds upon the banks. The borrowers do not always deal fairly with the bank both in borrowing and in making the repayments. The object

of the loan is not always what it is given out to be. Loans for purchase of land can be secured under another pretence. Land is purposely and fictitiously mortgaged to friends and relatives, and money is borrowed from the bank on the strength of such a mortgage.

The Directors' inquiry into the value of assets and previous debts of a borrower is very nearly unreliable. Favourites and followers are shown every indulgence with a view to ensuring their fidelity. The Report for 1928 tells us that in Lyallpur a member took a loan of Rs. 1,400, and within three months applied for insolvency.

In his loan application he had stated that his outside liabilities were Rs. 3,000, but in the insolvency petition he put down his liabilities at Rs. 11,500. The same Report records: "In the same district a Director after inquiry recommended a loan of Rs. 4,400 to an applicant for the repayment of an old debt. The loan was issued shortly afterwards; his other creditors filed an application for insolvency against him, and the loan given to him by the bank is reported not to have been passed on by him to his creditors before the application for insolvency was filed. In other cases borrowers have failed to produce the receipts of their creditors within a reasonable time, which raises suspicion that the money has not been properly applied, in others the receipts produced are not of the same creditors whose names were given in the loan application." So much has been confessed by the Department, but the Department does not always deem it necessary to divulge all that comes to its knowledge. Fictitious receipts have been presented to banks in a number of cases. In fact, as the Report for 1928 tells us, "It seems that repayment of old debts is a convenient plea for incurring a new one." Not only that, I feel the Mortgage Banks have been grossly misused by the borrowers. They have borrowed from the bank for all sorts of purposes, and on all sorts of pretences.

Such frauds seem to be a serious handicap in the development of Mortgage Banks. Sarda Beant Singh, Deputy Registrar, Jullundur, stressed the necessity of penal provisions in the Co-operative Law to punish persons giving false information about their assets and liabilities, and other matters pertaining to land. This, he said, in his evidence before the Punjab Provincial Banking Enquiry Committee, was necessary even when such frauds be not perpetrated by a large number of members, because one member borrowing a large sum of money on the basis of incorrect information may bring the bank into trouble. In one bank a man borrowed Rs. 2,000 on the security of land which was not his. This was discovered after three years.

Practical difficulties have been experienced in three different forms.

(4) *Unacceptability of Cheques.*—A mortgagee to whom the borrower is to make payment for redemption may not always accept a cheque. The borrower is liable to misuse the loan from the bank if the cheque is made payable to him. The encashment of the cheque and payment of debt direct to the mortgagee necessitates the intervention of a Director. While safeguarding one evil it creates another in the temptation that many Directors may not be able to stand.

(5) *Delay in Mutation.*—Mutation of names in revenue records after redemption is as a rule a very tough job. The lower revenue officials, for reasons of their own, look with disfavour upon a redemption proceeding which completes itself with a stunning suddenness and without involving the parties in a prolonged litigation. Special efforts in the form of representations to higher revenue officials are rendered necessary.

(6) *Revenue Records.*—The inquiry into the assets and possessions of an applicant for loan necessitates an examination of revenue records with a view to verifying his statements. The Department complains that copies of revenue records are not to be obtained "with that reasonable promptitude and at the price intended by the revenue rules." The lower revenue staff seems to have thoroughly annoyed the Department of Co-operation. It was suggested by some officials of the Department that banks should be entitled to get copies of revenue

records through correspondence with the revenue authorities, but the Department of Co-operation never made this suggestion to the Government because of "the danger that a person who wished for a copy, but did not really intend to borrow from the bank, might use the bank as a convenience, and needlessly complicate the business." Sardar Beant Singh, Deputy Registrar, in his evidence before the Banking Enquiry Committee, asked for a concession in the form of free access to revenue records. But I think the difficulty referred to above, by the Registrar, could easily be avoided by making the applicant pay double the price for a copy of his revenue records in case he eventually decided not to borrow from the bank.

Period of the Loan.—A mortgage loan is granted for ten years. There is a consensus of opinion within and without the Department that ten years is too short a period to let mortgage loans become a success. The instalments are too heavy to be paid out of savings, and in a number of cases honest borrowers have had to sell their lands to make repayments. The demand for enhancement in the period of loan is universal, and in 1928 Mianwali did actually extend the duration of loans. The Registrar in 1928 did not deem an extension in the duration of payment advisable. He said: "There is danger in this at present, for with an uneducated and unbusinesslike peasantry the benefit obtained by a loan is quickly forgotten, and only the burden remembered with consequent difficulties as to repayment. The period should be extended when punctuality and character and a feeling of benefit is there." Other things remaining the same, the chances of success would undoubtedly be greater than at present if a reasonable extension in the duration of loans is granted.

The Rate of Interest.—Mortgage Banks lend money at 8 or 9 per cent. Money is borrowed by agriculturists, who have to repay it out of the proceeds of their business. This has been recognized to be a high rate of interest which renders borrowing unprofitable. During the last six or seven years the fall in the price of agricultural produce has been very heavy, and consequently it has not been possible for the borrowers to repay without either resorting to money-lenders or selling their lands. It has been found out that in a number of cases in which land has been taken possession of, it will, at the present level of prices, take twenty years to realize only interest due from borrowers. In the canal colonies a plot of land which could be given on lease for Rs. 850 annually, now fetches only Rs. 150.

Defaults.—Every person from whom any sum or principal or interest remains outstanding on the date of demand is reckoned as a defaulter. Postponement in payment is allowed when remission in revenue is granted. Four years of working of the banks introduced the movement to the defaulters. Bad harvests have been recognized as the general cause of default. Borrowers default when they cannot pay. Arbitration proceedings were in 1925 started against the defaulters. But people are known to have defaulted when the Managing Committee for one reason or another shows indulgence to them. In a Mortgage Bank the sympathies of the Directors are with the borrowers and not with the bank. Their position was well depicted by one of the Registrars when he said: "It is not merely that they find it difficult to resist the claims and entreaties of their relatives and neighbours, but in showing indulgence to-day they hope to be treated with indulgence to-morrow."

In the economic crisis through which we are passing defaults are chiefly due to inability to pay. Many have been compelled to sell their lands in order to pay off their debts.

THE RECENT CRISIS AND THE WORKING OF MORTGAGE BANKS

The Registrar held a conference of all the colony Mortgage Banks at Lyallpur in April 1930, to consider the effect of the present economic situation on the colonists and on the working of the Mortgage Banks. The relevant decisions reached were thus summarized in the Annual Report for 1931:

(*a*) As present conditions had reduced the zemindars' surplus to a very small figure, the instalments due from borrowers should be reduced by 50 per cent, and repayments of the balance should be spread over the remaining period of the loan, and the position should be reviewed after three years. Future loans might, if suitable arrangements could be made, be given in approved cases for fifteen years, instead of ten as at present.

(*b*) In future all loans should be limited to five times the land revenue, or Rs. 4,000, whichever was less, instead of the original limits of Rs. 5,000, or thirty times the land revenue.

(*c*) Further, as the object of a bank was to help the borrowers and nobody else, loans for the redemption of land and for the payments of old debts should cease to be given; for the fall in prices had reduced the effective rate on usufructuary mortgages to not more than 5 per cent (while the bank's rate was 9 per cent), and had made it harder for creditors of all kinds to recover their dues; and there was no reason why a bank should harm its members by giving them loans at higher rate of interest than they were actually paying, on the one hand, or on the other helping the money-lenders at its own considerable expense.

The banks that do not operate in the colony areas have more or less conformed to the same course of action, as their local circumstances demand, especially in the matter of reduction of the maximum loan. No loans are being granted at all, and all efforts are directed at making recoveries. Borrowers either sell their lands or go to money-lenders for repayments of the bank loans. There was in fact aroused a feeling of resentment against the harshness of measures adopted by the Department to effect recoveries. The cause of distress that has befallen these banks and the general effect of the depression, that has now assumed the proportions and intensity of a crisis, have been depicted by the Registrar in his Annual Report for 1933 thus:

"The troubles of these banks are in very large measure due to their having been started at an unlucky time. They launched forth into business when high prices and agricultural prosperity were almost at their peak, and loans were given in accordance with the standards prevailing at that time. The depression soon followed, and borrowers have been genuinely unable to meet their obligations in the way of instalments on loans which now assumed three or four times their original value. Moreover, the property held by the banks as security was, and is, no longer sufficient to cover the loans; it has been found that in cases where it has been necessary to foreclose and take over the debtor's lands, the total sum to be derived from them is, at present rate of rent, not even enough to cover the charge for interest, the principal remaining unpaid. This is true particularly in colony areas, unless, therefore, the rise in values comes soon, the banks may have to face considerable losses. In several banks the Directors, now that the issuing of loans has been stopped, take little further interest in their affairs, and the invidious task of recoveries is left to the Managers and the Departmental staff. Of one bank it is caustically remarked that the Directors came 'not to serve but to suck,' and certainly the condition of the bank justifies the comment. The Punjab in this respect must look wistfully across India to Madras, which has recently launched its Mortgage Bank programme, and the banks beginning business in the present condition of low interest rates and reduced values have made an auspicious start." We have in these lines a very realistic description of the working of the banks. It is nothing short of a tragedy that an attempt like this should have come to so serious a trouble. But we must remember that these are abnormal times, and no amount of foresight with which any one of us may be gifted could save the situation. In the case of canal colonies it must be admitted that these banks should not have been started. Zemindars in the colonies could not mortgage their lands, hence there was no question of redemption of land. Land in the colonies being fertile and enjoying irrigation by canal, no large loans for improvement of land were necessary. Since money could be had it was borrowed and mis-spent. The bank in a place like Jhang, where the return for man's effort is so niggardly that the possibility of repayments at such a high rate of interest is indeed very remote, had no prospect of an early success. Whatever the causes, we are facing very unpleasant consequences. Should we then despair and give up the attempt as hopeless? Surely not. Having had more experience and being convinced of the necessity of it, the Department should redouble its efforts at making a success of the Mortgage Banks, which, like so many other forms of Co-operation, the Punjab had the honour to introduce in India. The area of land redeemed will convince each one of us of the usefulness of the effort. One case of redemption of land through Mortgage Banks needs special mention. In Shahpur, a zemindar, with the help of the Mortgage Bank, redeemed his land which had been mortgaged for thirty-six years and repaid the whole amount within a year.

A borrower mortgages his land to the bank when he gets a loan. But the mortgage is without possession. The same land can legally be mortgaged to another creditor, who can have possession of the land mortgaged to him. The other creditor who has acquired possession of the land creates quite a difficult position. This difficulty should be avoided, either by taking possession of the land at the very outset, or by declaring a second mortgage of the land illegal. When the borrower, in spite of all efforts and reasonable extensions, persists in defaulting, the land on the security of which the loan had been advanced is taken possession of by the bank. In a large number of cases such possession has had to be resorted to in Lyallpur. The arbitrator decides that the bank is to be given possession of the land, say, for twenty years. This award is taken to a Civil Court. The Civil Court, accepting the award, intimates the decree to the Revenue Courts asking that possession may be given to the bank. The Revenue Courts generally question the arbitrator's authority to give such an award. The arbitrator should have a very clear idea of the duration of the possession, and in his awards he must specify the period for which possession is to be given.

The arbitrator may merely declare that possession of land

must be given to the bank. Such an award is to be taken to a Collector, who uses his discretion in getting this award executed, and decides the details in his own way. He determines the area of land that must remain in the possession of the debtor for his use, and fixes the period for which possession is to be given to the bank.

RECOMMENDATIONS OF THE PUNJAB BANKING ENQUIRY COMMITTEE CONCERNING MORTGAGE BANKS

(1) There should be no departure from the present policy of cautious advance until the experimental stage is passed.

(2) Loans to Directors should be restricted.

(3) In the experimental stage the period of loan should not exceed ten years; after that stage is passed, it might be extended to fifteen years, subject to special precautions being taken to ensure repayment.

(4) The Committee endorses the recommendation of the Royal Commission on Agriculture, that the debentures of Co-operative Land Mortgage Banks, the interest on which is guaranteed by the Local Government, should be added to the list of trustee securities.

MORTGAGE BANKS AND LAND ALIENATION ACTS

The Central Banking Enquiry Committee has the following recommendation to make:

"In view of these difficulties we recommend that an alteration should be made in the Land Alienation Acts—all legislation which restricts the sale or mortgage or other forms of alienation in the several Provinces is included in this expression—which would give to the Co-operative Land Mortgage Banks the right to take possession of land through foreclosure on default of the payment of the instalment of the loan and to sell it. The sale may be restricted to the agricultural classes according to the provisions of prevailing legislation, and no question of policy in regard to preventing expropriation of these classes is intended to be touched by this particular recommendation."

The very essential point in this recommendation is not clear. The recommendation suggests an alteration in the Land Alienation Acts of the country "which would give to the Co-operative Land Mortgage Banks the right to take possession of land through foreclosure on default of the payment of the instalment of the loan. . . ." Does it mean that when the borrower fails to pay any one instalment of the loan? That can never be the meaning of the authors of the Report. Under special circumstances extensions in the payment of an instalment that falls due have been and ought to be granted. The period and number of extensions is to be determined by the intensity of the operation of factors outside the farmer's control that have made him a defaulter. As the Registrar tells us in his latest Report, "the borrowers have been *genuinely unable* to meet their obligations in the way of instalments." Even under normal conditions, non-payment may be perfectly justifiable, and indulgence must be shown to the borrower. It is only after the borrower's intention to default, in spite of ability to repay, has been established that the right to possession of the borrower's land should be exercised. When the necessity for the exercise of such a right has been established, the process of temporary transfer of land should be summary and independent of any reference to Courts. The final portion of this suggestion is simply shocking. The Mortgage Bank is to be empowered not only to take possession of the borrower's land, but is also to be empowered to sell it! What is the difference, then, between the heartless exploiter of the peasantry, the Punjab usurer, and a Co-operative bank, the moral and Co-operative basis of which are rightly expected to revolutionize the very life of the peasantry in the Punjab?

Such a power is vindictive. When less sweeping measures can ensure the repayment of loan, it is manifestly unjust to deprive the peasant of his means of livelihood, and to make paupers of his heirs. Possession of land for a period during which the loan can be recovered is enough and adequate.

For a temporary benefit granted to the borrower it is unjustifiable in a Co-operative bank to deprive the borrower and his future generations of their permanent source of livelihood. If that is to be the end of it, the farmer must be left in the clutches of the money-lender, where he is certainly safer. The suggestion regarding acquisition and use of authority to sell land mortgaged to a bank in case of default was first made by way of a casual observation by the Honourable Sardar Sir Joginder Singh in 1929. Reviewing the Annual Report for 1929 he remarked: "A Land Mortgage Bank is not the same as a Land Investment Company, but is apt to be regarded as such. That the difficulty is general may be inferred from the fact that in some countries the Directors are compelled to sell the mortgaged property in case of default, and it may prove necessary to impose some such duty here. The Punjab is fortunate inasmuch as a condition empowering the Directors to sell without recourse to Court is legal and permissible, and the introduction of such a condition in all future mortgages deserves to be considered." The first portion of these remarks is to be taken as a timely hint as to the drastic measures, the adoption of which might become necessary. I have given the best of my attention to the second part of the remarks quoted above. All that I know and feel is that the Punjab is fortunate not in having, but in not having, "a condition empowering the Directors to sell without recourse to Court" the land mortgaged by a borrower. We all know that the Land Alienation Act is there, and even a temporary possession of land in the event of default needs the sanction of Court. It is precisely this provision which the Central Banking Enquiry Committee has sought to make in its recommendations. This provision does not at present exist in the Punjab, in spite of the remarks quoted above. The troubles of these banks are in no small measure due to dishonest and inefficient management, and asking for such powers inplies closing our eyes to avoidable mistakes. The official control over the banks in the form of an increase in the nominated representatives as Directors and in the form of greater vigilance on the part of the staff is at present desirable, even at some loss of the Co-operative character of these institutions. The borrrower when he repays his loan reaps the great moral, educational, and financial advantages that this credit bestows upon him. If a handful of inefficient and dishonest members of a Managing Committee cannot learn anything surely the host of honest borrowers ought not to be denied the benefits of the operation of such banks. Such abnormal facilities in recovery wipe off the Co-operative character of the bank, and will drive the cultivator to the money-lender for all kinds of loans to the detriment of the Co-operative movement.

REALIZATION AS LAND REVENUE

There have been definite suggestions in certain very high quarters from outside Punjab that Co-operative Credit may be realized as arrears of Land Revenue. In the Punjab itself there are officials of the Department who desire this provision to be made at least in the case of Mortgage Bank dues. When the Co-operative Movement was started in the Punjab one of the Deputy Commissioners, a very staunch supporter of Co-operation, expressed himself very strongly against advance of loans for payment of revenue. He further held that this would lend itself to misrepresentation, and so it did. Although I do not now after a generation believe in the validity of that argument, yet I share that gentleman's conclusion. The Government dues should never be allowed to be mixed up with any other payments. I have expressed this opinion here, for I know some officials in the Department of Co-operation in other provinces have definitely brought forward this suggestion, although it has not been carried through in a Conference of All-India officials. As recoveries become harder, the disappointed co-operator may and will ask for such a power. Let him feel that his work is that of a missionary and not of a bailiff.

CHAPTER XXVIII

THE NON-AGRICULTURAL CO-OPERATIVE CREDIT SOCIETIES

NEED FOR URBAN CO-OPERATIVE BANKS

CO-OPERATION of sheer necessity has developed in the village. Towns may be said to have been sadly neglected. The Punjab Banking Enquiry Committee wrote in 1930 as follows: "We believe that the small trades and crafts offer a big field for Co-operative enterprise, especially in the smaller towns and townlets. In the Punjab these are particularly numerous, and they are largely unprovided with banking facilities. . . . Only 26 per cent of the towns with a population below 10,000 have any banking facilities at all beyond a Credit Society, often designed as much to help the cultivator as the trader. . . . Much of the business done in the town is not of the kind to suit a commercial bank. The position bears some analogy to conditions in the village. There we have the peasant proprietor, who works with capital partly owned and partly borrowed, but on too small a scale to attract a small commercial bank. His counterpart in the town is the small shopkeeper, who may almost be described as the peasant proprietor of the town. He, too, works partly with his own capital and partly with borrowed, and on so modest a scale that no ordinary bank can handle his business at a profit." The Banking Committee suggested that urban banking should be developed on the lines of the Schulze-Delitzch Banks in Germany and the People's Banks in Italy. In 1930 an inquiry was conducted by the Department to ascertain the number of Credit Societies in towns. The number then was 146. The total number of Non-Agricultural Credit Societies was 870, with a membership of 46,200. The 36,000 townsmen in these Societies were drawn from men in service numbering about 20,000, shopkeepers over 6,000, labourers over 2,000, sweepers about

1,500, and traders over 1,000. The rest of the membership in order of strength included weavers, shoemakers, carpenters, blacksmiths, artisans, dealers, masons, potters, barbers, butchers, oil-pressers, contractors, tonga-drivers, tanners, goldsmiths, water-carriers, washermen, milk-sellers, pleaders, doctors, and teachers. Salaried employees accounted for 55 per cent of the total membership, more than half of whom belonged to the N.W.R. Employee's Society, and most of the others to somewhat similar Societies in Lahore and Simla.

The Non-Agricultural Credit Societies have been classed as Urban and Rural. An Urban Society for the purposes of this classification is one in which the majority of members live in a town, and are not primarily dependent upon agriculture.

It has been noticed that in Societies whose members are such people as shopkeepers there is a tendency to live on borrowed money. It is "seen, in fact, that a fair portion of the credit limit is used as fixed capital and never repaid. . . . I have tried to make them see that it is better to expand a business less quickly, and to build up their own capital, and to acquire a reserve of their own money, than to regard it as normal to live and work on money wholly borrowed, so that the first result of a trade depression, however slight, is an immediate increase of borrowing and debt. But such a gospel is highly unpopular and never followed. Financial independence appears to be a strange idea, and a state rarely desired, and still more rarely seen among this class of people." As I read these lines from the Annual Report for 1929 I seem to appreciate the Registrar's solicitude for the shopkeepers, and he is perfectly justified in sermonizing over the importance of creating their own reserve of capital. I am afraid, however, that the shopkeeper in the Province has well learnt his useful business methods, and if he borrows and is always indebted to his Society our hearts need not melt in sympathy for him, since, as long as borrowed money can be employed with advantage, it is foolish on his part not to borrow. This is trading with

NON-AGRICULTURAL SOCIETIES

(1) URBAN

	1930	1931	1932	1933	1934
Societies	505	533	534	567	591
Members	29,877	37,812	35,026	37,315	39,066
Members who have joined old Societies ..	4,267	5,169	3,480	3,153	—
Demand for the year (lakhs) ..	43	45	37	38	35
Amount recovered by way of principal and interest (lakhs)	43	54	49	48	55
Overdues—					
(*a*) Principal (lakhs)	1·5	1·9	1·9	2·3	1,97
(*b*) Interest (lakhs)	1·9	2·8	3·2	4·3	4,5
Increase in deposits	6	1·5	0·5	1·9	—

(2) RURAL

	1930	1931	1932	1933	1934
Societies	587	578	566	540	529
Members	20,489	16,903	16,641	15,799	15,176
Members who have joined old Societies ..	1,521	1,103	806	1,170	—
Demand for the year (lakhs) ..	15	18	13	10	10
Amount recovered by way of principal and interest (lakhs)	17	13	11	8	7
Overdues—					
(*a*) Principal (lakhs)	2·1	2·6	2·7	1·7	1,47
(*b*) Interest (lakhs)	1·8	2·3	2·7	2·9	3,42
Increase in deposits	1	0·5	−0·5	−0·5	—

capital supplied by the Society. Continuous indebtedness of shopkeepers, who almost invariably do money-lending as well, should in no case be mistaken as a proof of their having no reserve of their own. It simply indicates that borrowing affords them opportunities of such investments which leave them a fair margin of profit, which no money-lender or shopkeeper, much less one who combines both callings, will ever sacrifice.

SOME URBAN CREDIT SOCIETIES

North-Western Railway Co-operative Credit Society was among the earliest Non-Agriculturist Credit Societies started. In 1932 the North-Western Railway Employees' Credit Society had a membership of 3,957 and a working capital of Rs. 5,72 lakhs. By 1933 membership had gone up to 15,229, and the working capital had shot up to Rs. 34 lakhs. Its area of operation now covers the whole of the North-Western Railway. The increase in membership is making supervision of applications for loan thoroughly difficult.

The Telegraph Department Society in 1932 had a membership of 880, and a working capital of Rs. 4,58 lakhs. During the same year the Society advanced 1,600 loans of the value of Rs. 4 lakhs to its members.

Lahore and Delhi-Simla have two groups of Societies whose members are chiefly derived from the employees of the Punjab Government and the Government of India. Simla group of these Societies is doing quite well, and lent to its members during 1932 a sum of Rs. $2\frac{2}{3}$ lakhs. It is interesting to recall now how the Department in the beginning had its doubts concerning the success of such Societies. Mr. Langley in his Annual Report for 1913 wrote as follows:

"Another class of Society about which I feel grave doubts is that confined to clerks. The difficulty of recovering loans is so great that, in my opinion, no Society of this kind should be started unless arrangements can be made to deduct loans from salaries, and unless it is certain that an influential and fairly permanent committee can be secured." The members of these Societies of clerks and salary-earners are required gradually to subscribe large shares and to make compulsory deposits.

Non-Agricultural Credit Societies cover a wide variety. The N.W.R., the Telegraph, and Simla-Delhi Societies are

CLASSIFICATION OF THE NON-AGRICULTURAL CREDIT SOCIETIES

	Urban			Rural		
	1931–32	1932–33	1933–34	1931–32	1932–33	1933–34
A	28	28	46	11	12	19
B	85	99	77	74	88	51
C	372	373	375	407	366	385
D	26	47	54	56	64	75
Unclassified ..	23	19	28	18	10	7

on the one extreme, the other being represented by the small struggling Societies of poor artisans, menials, and labourers. Between these two extremes are the Societies of small traders and business men, some of which are working well and serving a real need as small urban banks. Non-Agricultural Credit Societies are classified as rural and urban. It is for the development of Urban Co-operative Credit Societies that, in accordance with the Registrar's proposal of 1927 and the recommendation of the Banking Enquiry Committee, three Inspectors were appointed in 1933.

CHAPTER XXIX

PRODUCTION AND LABOUR SOCIETIES

THE LAHORE MODEL TOWN SOCIETY

THE fate of the Lahore Model Town Society affords one of the saddest instances of the failure of a magnificent start. Lahore has all the charms and repulsions of a big city. The Lahore Model Town Society was organized in 1920 by Dewan Khem Chand, once the Honorary Secretary of Muzaffargarh Central Bank. The object of the Society was to construct a residential village for the gentry of the Punjab, particularly of Lahore. The Model Town was intended to be built up at Kot Lakhpat, near Lahore, and it was sought to combine a quiet life, away from the nerve-shattering din and bustle of Lahore, with richness in all the amenities of modern life. The Society with its very influential membership at the very start enlisted the active support of the Government. The Government, as a measure of its support to the Society, agreed to sell to the Society the planted area at Kot Lakhpat, covering 1,963 acres, at the exceedingly low price of Rs. 400 per acre. Within a year membership rose to 439, and with the proverbial enthusiasm of an ambitious start the Society announced a prize of Rs. 1,200 for the best lay-out of the town. By 1923 membership increased to 709, and Rs. 70,100 had been paid up in shares and Rs. 1,45,233 by way of instalments of the cost of construction of houses, and Rs. 94,000 had been paid towards the cost of the site.

By 1923 the construction of a tube well had been completed. This well supplied from a depth of 160 feet water which was declared by the Punjab chemical examiner to be fit for drinking. The progress made by the Society by 1924 can best be narrated in the words of the Annual Report for that year.

"The Lahore Model Town Society continues to make steady progress. Membership has risen from 701 to 789; share capital has increased from 70,100 to 78,900, working capital from Rs. 2,19,333 to Rs. 12,39,044. Members have deposited over Rs. 3 lakhs for houses. The balance of the purchase price of the land is shown as a loan from the Government. The plan of the town has been dagbelled on the ground, and the allotment of house-sites has begun, material for construction is being collected, and the building is about to begin. The foundation-stone of the club was laid by His Excellency Sir Edward Maclagan, so that scoffers will now have to revise their opinions. Some sixteen designs for houses are being circulated to members to choose from, and it is hoped that progress now will be continuous and steady. The scheme has aroused great interest, and Dewan Khem Chand can afford to forget the earlier reception which his ideas received."

By 1926 the model town had completed a large club, twelve residential houses, and a number of shops and quarters. A school, a post office, and a library for the use of twelve members, and a total population of eight hundred had been started.

The Report for 1928, while recording the proud achievements of the Society, gives some indication of the dangers ahead. "The Model Town Society is converting 2,000 acres six miles from Lahore into a garden city. With its 849 members (mainly drawn from the upper, middle, and professional classes), its working capital of Rs. 18 lakhs, its fifty-seven residential houses finished or under construction, its club-house, post office, dispensary, tube-well, motor service, and its six miles of metalled roads, it represents a remarkable achievement. But there are dangers ahead. Nearly Rs. 1,75 lakhs is due from members for construction of their houses, about Rs. 1,50 lakhs for their land; and there are also signs of discord."

In 1929 the Society borrowed from the Lahore Central Bank to pay off the Government due. The Annual Report for 1929 records: "Now that, when the Government has transferred the land finally to the Society, as is hoped will soon be the case, the Society will be able to give its members a clear title to the land taken by them, it is hoped the members will be more ready to pay the Society the arrears due from them on account of land purchase and cost of building. As it is, arrears are decreasing. The discord that some members were trying to foster has died a natural death."

This assurance kindles in us a ray of hope. But the very next Report tells us that the Society passed through a critical period owing to careless handling of its affairs and divided counsels. A strong committee was appointed to set its house in order. During 1931, owing to lack of continuity of policy due to too frequent a change in Presidents necessitated by factors beyond the control of the Society, the progress made was not at all satisfactory. But the most important cause is to be found in a "feeling, not unfounded, that the business side of the Society was not being conducted with the efficiency that might reasonably be demanded." This fostered internal dissensions to an undesirable extent.

The latest information available, as the reader must be expecting by this time, is in the form of a funeral oration so solemnly delivered by the Registrar. "The other unique Society is the Model Town Society, which sprang out of a magnificent conception, was lavishly subsidized by the Government, and is now going to wrack and ruin with all the brains of Lahore at its disposal. . . . The founder of the Society, Dewan Khem Chand, was removed from his office during the course of the year. The Society is running at a loss in all its branches, it is frittering away its assets; and its defaulters include some eminent notabilities of Lahore and elsewhere. The Model Town is on the high road to insolvency, but it has at the moment, apart from the magnificent start the Government gave to it, two assets, (*a*) selfless devotion of its present judicial and public-spirited President, and (*b*) the other the latent ability, if exercised, of so many of its members."

The Report for 1934 indicates that the Society is not yet dead. A committee, appointed by the Department, investigated the affairs of the Society, which instead of improving has turned out a source of extreme anxiety to the Department. The Report for 1934 makes the following painful disclosure: "As an instance of the attitude of the members to their

Society may be quoted the case of one, a prominent lawyer, who, having taken full advantage of the Society and incurred large liabilities to it, is contesting payment in the Courts on the ground, among others, that the Society should never have been registered as its members were not men of moderate means. Comment is needless."

Apart from a description of the Model Town Society, under production and labour, the Registrar contributes a very brief but significant note which leaves little room for any elaboration or comment:

"Production and labour Societies are sometimes perilously near the world of sham. There are three fancy Press Societies in Lahore. The English Press, which had to be liquidated in the previous year on account of thoroughgoing mismanagement, but which has been with difficulty revived, a second English Press registered during the current year, which also has a struggle before it, and the Urdu Press, which is running at a loss, and finds prominent politicians bad co-operators."

CHAPTER XXX

HAND-LOOM WEAVING IN THE PUNJAB

THE WEAVER AND THE MIDDLEMAN

THE total number of weavers in the Province was 1,100,000 in 1921. They represent by far the most important industry in the Province. Jalalpur Jattan, Multan, Ambala, Gakhar, Chakwal, Pind Dadan Khan, Dera Ghazi Khan, Hoshiarpur, Ludhiana, and Amritsar are some of the chief centres of weaving in the Punjab. Khaddar, khais, durry, daryai, and lungies are some of the chief forms of material turned out by the weavers. The Punjab weaver is a little conservative but quite a good worker. Given proper training and good looms and credit on more favourable terms, besides facilities for the disposal of his goods, he is bound to prosper.

In the matter of his requisites of production he still willingly or unwillingly works with the old-fashioned hand-loom. The wooden fly shuttle hand-loom is replacing the old small loom in towns. In Jalalpur Jattan District, Gujrat, during the Great War, within a span of four years all the old-type looms were thrown out of work, and the fly-shuttle hand-loom was substituted in their place. These fly-shuttle looms can be made locally in every town, and I presume in villages too, and their cost in Jalalpur Jattan has varied between Rs. 80 and Rs. 30, depending upon the price of wood, iron, and the intensity of demand for these looms. An estimate of its cost given by an expert of the Co-operative Department, and modified by a member of the Punjab Banking Enquiry Committee, is hopelessly wide of the mark. The old-type loom for plain cloth weaving is quite a simple affair, but for check designs in khaisis and other similar material is quite complicated. Another disadvantage of the old-type loom is that its width is very small, and the pace at which it can be worked is slow, hence its ouput is very low. This loom must go, and the sooner it goes the better. Mr. Heath, of the Mayo School of Arts, officer on special duty, Punjab Co-operative Department, believes that the substitution of the new hand-loom for the old will mean more unemployment for the weavers. If while stimulating production we fail to bring about an extension in demand, the result foreshadowed is inevitable. But we must remember that, other things remaining the same, a lower cost of output will tend to bring about an extension in demand.

The second handicap of the weaver is his poverty, which enables the middleman to suck his very life-blood for a little service rendered to him. Much of the hope of his betterment lies in the provision of credit or raw materials on better terms than those on which he gets them now. In no case can he prosper as long as the middleman is allowed to suck him white.

The third difficulty under which the Punjab weaver groans is the absence of marketing facilities. His products are in most cases quite exquisite, but he is poor because of the primitive and defective state of marketing facilities.

Machine-made goods, particularly foreign artificial silk products with their attractive finish and cheap prices, have driven the last nail into the coffin of the weaving industry throughout India.

The deputation of Multan weavers that appeared before the Banking Enquiry Committee, while lamenting the fall in demand for their products, observed: "The reasons were that fashions were changing and local silk manufactures were not appreciated now, and foreign goods imported from Japan, Germany, and other countries were more in demand. The quality of the local-made daryai was not inferior to the imported cloth—in fact it was more lasting—but people now seem to care more for the lustre that the imported cloth has, and which is lacking in their cloth. In addition, the foreign goods are cheaper."

Lack of Adaptation.—Mr. Heath, who has made a special study of hand-weaving in the Province, maintains that much of the misfortune of the weaver is due to the lack of artistic and technical direction. He says: "The artistic sense of the craftsman dies and is replaced by a feeble commercial sense which bids him to counter the demands of the middleman with inferior work and materials until he is powerless to do anything but the cheap work which satisfies the demand." The stimulus for artistic production was formerly provided by patronage, and with the passing off of that patronage has vanished the art of weaving.

For the continuance of this industry it is essential that technical advice be placed at the disposal of the worker. If the weaver's product has lost its artistic quality and the colours he uses are not fast there is no hope of his survival. His products have not much changed in the matter of pattern or design. He is very conservative, or should I say unprogressive. Undoubtedly he possesses little imagination, but given proper facilities and help he shows good common sense. In Jalalpur Jattan people have taken to the production of towels, fringed khaises, and suitings and shirtings of almost every description. Their only difficulty lies in their not being able to give fast colours to their materials and their inability to reproduce complicated designs with the help of their simple looms. A technical weaving school was established there for a number of years, but for no fault of the weavers proved of no use to them.

The Punjab weaver, although on the verge of extinction, has not yet died, and may if looked after be revived with credit to himself and to the Province.

Wages.—The earnings of weavers fluctuate within certain limits in accordance with the type of work they undertake and the demand for their products. The daryai weavers of Multan, the Banking Enquiry Committee state, "earn about 8 or 10 annas per day. Plain work fetches about 8 or 10 annas, flowered about 2 annas more. A cotton weaver would earn about 6 to 10 annas—on fancy cloth about 12 annas. This represents earnings of a family of about five workers. A cotton weaver's family could earn 10 annas per day, but nowadays they are not certain of even 4 or 5 annas." That is the conclusion generally accepted. The amount of wages earned, of course, differs with the nature of demand. In Jalalpur Jattan, when the *swadeshi* movement was at its full swing, a weaver of khaddar with the help of his wooden fly-shuttle loom could earn as much as Rs. 1,2,0, but in this period of depression a weaver can hardly earn 5–6 annas. The fall in demand for the weaver's product has adversely affected the employment of workers in the industry. It has been estimated that the present depression has permanently shunted out 25 per cent of the weavers, and another 25 per cent have temporarily taken to other professions.

THE MIDDLEMAN AND THE WEAVER

The middleman is an essential link between the producer and the consumer, and performs an important function. But the middleman manages to acquire an influence and position in unorganized industries detrimental to the interest both of the producer and the consumer. The middleman's earnings should in fairness be equal to the value of the services he renders. In actual practice, however, we find the middleman dominating the weaving industry to the utter exploitation of the poor hard-working weaver. The following are some of the methods used by the middleman in the Punjab in dealing with the weavers:

Miti or Time Concession.—Weavers usually have no ready money with which to purchase raw materials for their industry. They have consequently, very often, to purchase raw materials on credit. The first great disadvantage of the purchase on credit is that the weaver is compelled to submit to the terms of the shopkeeper, as to the price and quality of the raw material. We all know that the shopkeeper has no mercy for his victims. The weaver must accept the shopkeeper's terms. The seemingly accommodating shopkeeper, while charging more than the market price in advancing raw material on credit, poses as if he is doing a service to the weaver, and graciously grants him usually a fortnight of grace within which the payment will bear no interest. If the payment is not made within the specified days of grace, *invariably* an extra charge is to be paid besides the liability to pay interest at a specified rate thereafter, usually one pice per rupee. The practice is the same throughout the important towns in the Punjab, only the number of days of grace granted and amounts and rates charged are different. The seller of the raw material behaves very much like a monopolist money-lender, and fearlessly practices many of his tricks. In important weaving centres of the Punjab sellers of raw materials for the trade occasionally display unclean account keeping, even in the case of buyers of substantial means, who either on account of their own illiteracy or supreme confidence in the supplier of raw material, cannot or do not keep accounts.

Katoti or Discount System.—Under this system the supplier of raw materials becomes a more substantial partisan in the trade. He is the counterpart, in industry, of the money-lending ahrtee in agriculture. The dealer under this system supplies raw materials and cash to the weaver on the condition that the weaver should deliver the cloth when it is ready to the dealer. For every yard of cloth brought to him, the dealer deducts 1 pice as the profit of his shop at the time of payment. This is one of the very fruitful forms of exploitation of the worker adopted by the dealer.

The Barter System.—Under this system the finished product is exchanged for the raw material. The dealer pays a quantity of yarn equal to the weight of the cloth plus the wages of labour, often calculated at the lowest. This system is adopted often against the independent weavers. But the covetous dealer is only too willing to advance, and the needy weaver never reluctant to raise, a loan. When the independence of the weaver is changed to indebtedness, the relentless dealer holds his prey in an ever-tightening grip.

Pirt Bazaar or Market System.—This system is adopted by the dealers, predominantly in dealing with silk weavers. Under this system of sale, the silk weaver, besides paying brokerage at the rate of 1 pice per yard, is required to forgo

1 yard of silk fabric to the dealer for every 25 yards brought for sale.

The Tombo System or Cash Payment Memo.—After the deductions under the Pirt Bazaar method have been made, the price of daryai or the silk fabric is not to be paid in cash on the spot. Tombos or chits are issued by the dealers, payments for which are to be made after a fortnight from the date of the transaction. Any weaver requiring immediate cash payment must forgo interest at the amount due to him for a fortnight at 6 per cent per annum. Even then part of the payment will be made in cash and the rest of it in kind.

Nine weavers of Multan were examined by the Punjab Banking Enquiry Committee, and they expressed the experience of their class in the following words: "The sahukars do not pay full wages either to their own workers or to weavers who go to them. They know the value of the cloth, and make good profit over it by paying the weavers the minimum for their labour. They give about Rs. 14 for 60 yards as wages. If they use their own yarn and take the cloth to the sahukar, the commission agent takes 2 pice, the middleman 1 pice, and 1 yard the sahukar keeps as *sira* and another for the measuring. For the balance he pays Rs. 1,2,0 or Rs. 1,4,0. This leaves about 2½ annas per day for them."

Sh. Manzoor Ali, Industrial Assistant Registrar, Co-operative Societies, who more than anyone else has an intimate knowledge of the weaver's life in the Province, in his oral evidence before the Banking Enquiry Committee, in answer to a question remarked: "My inquiry revealed that the earnings of weavers are 5 annas, and that of the middleman 8 annas. . . ." This does not evidently imply that the middleman earns 8 annas a day, but that out of every weaver who is in his grip he manages to squeeze 8 annas for every 5 annas that the weaver earns. Since the number of weavers having dealings with one middleman is fairly large, the middleman usually earns quite a substantial sum each day.

Not only that. Since the middlemen are usually persons of means and influence, and being intelligent are quite well organized, they can whenever they feel so inclined make things quite uncomfortable for the weavers or their supporters. One instance of the unfair use of their power of exploitation of the poor was cited before the Punjab Banking Enquiry Committee at Multan. This is how the Banking Enquiry Committee puts it: "Chiragh Din, however, quoted an instance in which he took a piece of cloth to a sahukar, and when he could not get the price he wanted for it he went to another, but the first man sent his servant, who told the second sahukar what his master had offered for it, and so on, to every man to whom he went till he had to return with the cloth unsold with him."

A Necessary Evil.—The observations made by Mr. L. Heath, officer on special duty attached to the Co-operative Department, who has conducted a survey of the weaving industry in the Province, deserve mention here. "Concerning the middleman in the industry," he says, ". . . you can never get rid of him, you can only clip his claws. He has been, and still is, the chief agency for marketing outside purely local demand; he knows a little of the demand, though he has no idea how to stimulate that demand, nor how to create a new demand or a new supply; technically he is as ignorant as the producer, and in this ignorance often kills the goose that lays the golden eggs through squeezing the weaver of his just earnings, the consequent degrading of quality and failure of both the producer and himself. . . ." " The reason the middleman is an evil is not because he is not wanted, but because through the appalling technical ignorance of the weaver and the absence of any organization to help the weaver to improve his standard, or even maintain it, he has a stranglehold upon him."

CHAPTER XXXI

THE WEAVERS' SOCIETIES

Industrial Societies have been established amongst the weavers, shoemakers, tanners, carpenters, furniture makers, dyers, coppersmiths, ironsmiths, and even goldsmiths. But of all these the Weavers' Societies are by far the most important, and deserve a little detailed description.

The Weavers' Societies were the earliest (1911) to be started, and still constitute the most predominant and significant form of Industrial Co-operation. The working and successful management of a Weavers' Society, as compared to a Village Credit Society, presents a more perplexing problem. In a Credit Society an advance is to be made, and if nothing abnormal comes about the Society expects back the loan without much extra labour or worry on that account. Not so in the case of a Weavers' Society. A member of a Weavers' Society is to be given an advance not unoften in the form of the raw material he needs, and we all know the woes of an institution that seeks to put an end to the rapacity of those who supply credit to the poor artisans. But this battle on behalf of the poor whose labour is being exploited has to be fought simultaneously on many fronts. The marketing of the members' goods is a problem of still greater significance and complexity. The goods thus produced have got to be purchased and sold. All this, besides involving a series of very difficult tasks, brings the workers of the Society into exceedingly unpleasant conflict with those who possess power and sit well entrenched in positions of vantage. Mr. Langley depicted the external and internal difficulties of a Weavers' Society in the Annual Report for 1913, as involving "an interference in the established lines of business on behalf of people who are usually quite unable to manage their own affairs or keep their promises. After securing three contracts for these Societies, I have found myself involved in an acrimonious correspondence with three justly incensed individuals, who have not received their goods on the appointed date."

Not only is the weaver hopelessly ignorant of business methods, but the middleman, whose elimination is his chief hope of salvation, has him entirely in his grip. Any effort, individual or organized, on the part of the weavers to free themselves from his grip is not only resented but provokes a storm of opposition, which the weavers with their proverbial cowardice and spirit of submission dare not face. The middleman is often a man of means and influence, and when he feels his best interests are at stake he does not hesitate to adopt means which no honest and God-fearing man would approve of. It has been well remarked by one of the Registrars that the middle-man's "hidden hand is subtle and active in wire-pulling."

Silk Weavers' Societies were registered in Multan in 1921, and the Department records that these Societies immediately upon registration found themselves surrounded by alarming difficulties. The dealers at Multan, upon whom the weavers before the organization of Societies depended for the supply of raw silk and the disposal of the finished products, adopted a hostile attitude. They at once raised their rates for raw silk, and collectively refused to purchase finished goods except at impossible prices. The Societies managed to stand this double and stunning blow by arranging to secure the raw material direct from Kashmir, through the assistance of the Central Weavers' Co-operative Store on the one hand, and through the active assistance of the Department in securing orders for the Societies from the Government, Municipal Committees, and District Boards on the other. But in spite of the backing of a whole Department and the personal influence of the different Registrars of the Co-operative Societies, numerous difficulties and severe disappointments were experienced by the Societies. The following are some of the orders secured by the Department of Co-operation for the Weavers' Societies. Forty thousand durries were supplied to the Army Department through the stores in 1923. In 1924 the Controller of the North-Western

Railway Stores Department placed with the Department of Co-operative Societies an order for 60,000 bastas and 50,000 lungis. In 1923 orders worth Rs. 10,306 were secured by the Sales Depot from the Government and local bodies. The Indian Stores Department ordered gold lungis and kamarbunds worth Rs. 15,000 for Skinner's Horse at Ferozepore in 1926. This attempt at helping the Societies in the disposal of their products still continues, and orders from the Government Departments worth Rs. 8,003 were secured in 1932. If only 25 per cent of the Government Departments and local bodies could arrange to place orders with the Societies for the supply of their requirements these Societies would be working at breakneck speed, and all members of such Societies would be able to improve their lot considerably. But this seemingly simple proposition proved a tough job, for all the vested interests are always willing to conspire against their rival. The subordinate staff that is mostly responsible for placing such orders usually expects some gratification from the contractors. When a rival appears on the scene these subordinates and the contractors put their heads together and by every possible means resist the encroachment of the rival upon their close preserves. This is what some of the Registrars have to say in this connection:

"The aims of the Co-operative Societies are clear and honest dealings, hence they are unable to compete with the ordinary contractors in securing orders by negotiations with the subordinate staff of Government Departments."

"It is almost impossible to obtain orders from district-officers of any department. It is easy to understand the obstacles in the way of an officer who wishes to place his orders outside the neighbourhood of his office. Co-operative Societies will deal only in the open, and supply only at stated prices and the stated quality; they will not send an agent to negotiate orally with persons other than a gazetted officer." Reading between the lines one can easily understand the difficulty of the Department.

The Department of Co-operation adopted every possible means towards the popularization of the products of these

Societies. Samples of the Punjab weavers' work were shown at conferences, exhibitions, and in demonstration trains. The Industrial Inspector attended the All-India Hand-loom Weaving Exhibition held at Patna in December 1921. Participation in this exhibition won for the members of the Weavers' Societies four medals, including one gold medal for the Pind Dadan Khan Silk work, which received high praise.

The samples of Punjab products turned out by members of the Co-operative Weavers' Societies were once again displayed by the Inspector at the Bombay Co-operative Exhibition in 1922. This time the Punjab weavers won five medals, and their work was generally openly recognized to be superior to that of samples from other Provinces.

At a conference of the co-operators held at Lahore in February 1926 the finished goods of weavers, as well as of other artisans, were exhibited. The object of this exhibition was to bring the producer in direct touch with the consumer so as to enable him to study for himself the needs and tastes of the consumer and improve his work in the light of criticism thus offered.

At this conference goods worth Rs. 3,700 were sold. Whenever such conferences have been held the weavers' products have been prominently displayed. The officers of the Department on their tours take with them samples of the Societies' products, and this practice is believed to have stimulated the sale of these goods to the extent of Rs. 16,000 in 1929 and Rs. 20,000 in 1931.

The Department of Co-operation participated in the show organized in the form of the demonstration train in 1927 and sold goods worth Rs. 7,000. The Department rents stalls at fairs, and employs travelling agents for the sale of goods produced by such Societies.

The Department has opened a Sales Depot at Lahore, and some shops for the sale of goods produced by Weavers' Societies. Even *phariwalas*, or hawkers, have been appointed by some Societies to push the sale of their goods. But all this is in these days practically of no avail. Goods cannot be sold unless there is a demand for them. The foreign competition has brought about a change in our tastes, and the demand for home-made goods has fallen. The Department has not been able to do much in this direction. The following significant extract will be read with interest. Malik Fateh Khan Noon, Deputy Registrar, was asked by the Chairman of the Banking Enquiry Committee:

"Would you say that the chief problem in regard to Weavers' Societies was marketing rather than finance?—As far as our Societies are concerned, there is no difficulty in the supply of raw materials, but we cannot succeed in giving them sufficient help for the disposal of their finished goods.

CHAIRMAN: Why is that?—The thing is that it is very difficult to compete with mill-made goods. We did a lot in the days of the *swadeshi* movement, but after that the Societies have been deteriorating regularly.

"During the *swadeshi* movement you had comparatively little difficulty in marketing their goods?—Yes, sir, rather I can say that the members of the Societies were not in need of our help really because they were themselves in a position to dispose of their goods directly.

"Now that they are in need of your help, you are unable to give them much help?—We are trying different methods, and we are of some use to them, but that is very negligible."

PROMOTION OF EDUCATION

In spite of the seeming failure of the Department to be of any real help to the weavers in the Province, the very awakening and a desire for self-improvement that Co-operation breeds is in itself a sufficient reward for the pains that the Department has taken on this behalf. The Department is hemmed in by difficulties on all sides, and if things slacken down a little it is but natural.

As an instance of the desire for self-improvement and a display of the first wave of enthusiasm, it is refreshing to study the following account reproduced from the Annual Report for 1921. If the Department, or people amongst whom and for whom the Department works, could sustain for a decade the flood of enthusiasm with which every new form of Co-operation is adopted, our efforts would yield much more substantial results.

"Five night schools have been opened in connection with the Societies. At present there are seventy-nine pupils, all weavers. The teachers are usually literate weavers or local well-wishers, while the necessary funds are provided by the weavers themselves, with the help of small subscriptions from the villagers. The opening of these schools is a striking testimony to the value of Co-operation in creating a desire for education in a class that has hitherto been content to remain silent in the grip of the middleman. Signs are not wanting that there is a real awakening of the public spirit. The weaver is resolved, if it be possible, to become himself the master of his fate. Many members of the Societies have joined the classes at Government weaving schools, and the improved implements, like the fly-shuttle-loom and warping reel, are now gradually becoming popular."

DEPRESSION AND THE INDUSTRIAL SOCIETIES

The first effects of depression amongst the Industrial Societies were noticed in 1928–29. As many of the members of these Societies deal almost entirely with zemindars, and on credit into the bargain, a poor harvest or low prices for the cultivators' produce adversely affect the interests of the members of the artisans' Societies. Reduced purchasing power of the cultivators, coupled with the competition of mill-made cloth, hit the weavers so severely that on the first symptoms of the present depression the Department observed that the condition of the members of the Weavers' Societies was "getting, on the whole, worse and worse." "Some weavers have given up weaving, while others have relegated it to the position of a subsidiary occupation." Amongst the members of the Society it was a general complaint, as early as 1930, that whatever temporary benefit they had enjoyed had been more than counterbalanced by the general economic depression which set in with the fall of agricultural prices.

The table at the close of this chapter will help to an understanding of the effects of the present depression upon the working of the Industrial Societies. The value of members' goods sold through Societies has progressively gone down from Rs. 2,89 lakhs in 1928 to Rs. 0,48 lakhs in 1933.

The value of material advanced to members has fallen from Rs. 2,94 lakhs in 1928 to Rs. 0,76 lakhs in 1931. The year 1933 shows a little improvement in this respect, and pulls it up to Rs. 1,06 lakhs.

The number of Weavers' Societies has gone down from 197 in 1930 to 187 in 1932. These figures "reflect a general decline in the number of Societies," their membership, working capital, and especially in the value of members' goods sold.

The progressive decline in the volume of work done by the Industrial Societies is indicated by the following:

1920	1922	1926	1927	1933
262	234·6	98	122	26 per cent turnover to the working capital

The stupendous fall in turnover from 262 per cent in 1920 to 26 per cent in 1933 tells a sad tale.

Decrease in Loans advanced to Societies.—The loans advanced by the Co-operative Industrial Bank inevitably decline, as the available figures indicate:

Year	Amount Lent during the Year	Total Amount Lent to the Societies
	Rupees	Rupees
1930	99,800	4,53,000
1931	62,800	4,19,000
1932	40,200	3,83,000
1933	32,915	3,56,531

Recoveries.—The depression rendered recoveries from the members exceedingly difficult. By 1931 it became "necessary for the staff to spend a great deal of its time and energy in efforts to recover money from members who were spoiling their Societies' finances by irregular and inadequate payments." The necessity for recovery led to a detailed inspection of a large number of Societies, and it was discovered, of course quite late, "that they had been granted loans with unnecessary generosity. Accordingly a more reasonable scale was fixed, and more attention began to be paid to recoveries." The latest Report available gives a complete picture of this aspect of the Industrial Societies. "In many cases we find ourselves supporting dead and dying industries, and trying to recover money from men who have not only *no income, but also hardly anv assets.* Again, many of the Societies have the millstones of old and unnecessary borrowings round their necks, and the burden can only be relieved very slowly by steady repayments and very small borrowings. A system of monthly *quistbandis* (instalments) and recoveries has been introduced throughout all the Societies, which is an essential part of the plan to effect this reduction, and it has already had some effect."

Percentage of recoveries from members of Societies was 22 in 1930, and after having risen a little fell once again in 1933 to 23·42 of the total loan outstanding. The percentage of loans repaid by Societies to the Central Industrial Bank fell from 18·25 in the previous year to 15·31 in 1933.

Deterioration.—That there has been an all-round deterioration is a bare statement of fact. I wish statistics concerning a change in classification of industrial Societies were available to prove it, if any proof is still needed. The once famous Multan Societies are under liquidation.

THE SALES DEPOT, UNIONS, AND SHOPS

The Department of Co-operation did at last realize that the only hope of the Industrial Societies lies in the provision of marketing facilities. The much-needed step was taken in January 1929 by the establishment of the Central Sales Depot, Lahore. The object of this depot is to help Societies in the direct sale of their goods, to secure orders from Government Departments and local bodies, and also to help the Central Bank in recoveries by crediting to it direct all sums received on behalf of Societies. In the first year of its existence it sold goods worth Rs. 1,700 only, which figure increased to Rs. 22,413, and once again fell to Rs. 9,300 for 1930 and 1931 respectively. The depot secured orders from the Government Departments worth Rs. 10,306 in 1931 and Rs. 8,083 in 1930. It was hoped that the depot would be of great service to the movement, but unfortunately those high hopes have been dashed to the ground. The selection of the first business manager turned out to be an exceedingly unfortunate one. In the words of the Deputy Registrar, Lahore, "the man was rather dishonest, and *he tried his best to help his father's firm than to do good to our Department.* So we had to remove him." The Report for the year 1932 records as follows: "The Sales Depot had a disappointing year and sustained a loss of Rs. 4,087, which wiped out the profit of the Co-operative Industrial Bank. The main cause of this unfortunate loss was the necessity to depreciate a large amount of old stock which had not been depreciated in the previous year. There was also a theft from the depot, and goods worth Rs. 468 were removed and never recovered." The conclusion arrived at by the Department makes short work of it. The Report for 1933 records: "But the conclusion has now been forced upon us that it is not possible to organize it successfully on the present basis, and a proposal has been submitted after the close of the year under report to close the depot and utilize some of the money now spent upon it in promoting sales of Societies' goods by other methods."

A few Unions in some of the Districts undertook to supply raw material to the members and sell their goods as well. In Jullundur and Hoshiarpur shops for the sale of finished goods were started by the Societies. The Jullundur shop failed after about five months. All arrangements for the sale of weavers' produce seem to have at present collapsed, owing chiefly to a fall in demand for these goods on the part of the public.

The staff for this branch of Co-operation is on a temporary basis, hence discipline is slack, and no serious and permanent effort can be put forth by the staff.

Industrial Co-operation should be taken up as seriously as Agricultural Co-operation. The problem of both these forms of Co-operation is essentially the same. As long as the cottage industries have not been completely crushed by the modern methods of production there will be ample scope for the sympathetic activities of a Co-operative organization. Indeed, a careful organization of the cottage industries by the joint efforts of the Department of Industries and Co-operation can for a very long time prevent the factories' bombardment of the cottage industries. The Industrial Department is well equipped for giving technical training, but cannot be expected to successfully make advances to workers. It would be very much better for the Department of Industries to advance money to poor workers through Co-operative Societies. Supervision of the use of money and making of recoveries cannot with success be ever attempted by the Department of Industries. With the power loom and cheap motive power now available it should be possible to make cottage industries survive the competition of mills. Cottage industries have their own social, economic, and moral justification, and I believe with the Registrar, and I think it was Mr. Strickland, who said: "Our experience tends to show that if only the more educated Punjabi could evince a lively interest in the development of these hand-loom industries, much could be done towards their improvement. The weavers possess character, but need practical encouragement."

The table on p. 339 shows the progress of the Industrial Societies since 1927.

According to the Annual Report for 1934 the number of Industrial Societies stands at 291, of which 171 are Weavers' Societies. The latest classification shows that 14 are in B,

	1927	1928	1929	1930	1931	1932	1933	1934
Number of Societies	188	289	299	320	314	308	300	291
Members	3,666	5,313	5,742	6,047	5,721	5,648	5,243	4,948
Average membership	19	18	18	19	18	18	17	17
Working capital (lakhs of rupees)	4	6	6,70	6,94	6,72	6,21	5,88	5,36
Owned capital (lakhs of rupees)	—	—	1,57	1,86	2,03	2,04	2,01	2,19
Value of raw material advanced to members (lakhs of rupees)	2,48	2,94	1,35	1,22	1,10	0,76	1,06	0,88
Value of members' goods sold (lakhs of rupees)	2,41	2,89	1,35	1,18	1,11	0,81	0,48	0,71
Members deposits (lakhs of rupees)	0,11	0,22	0,38	0,45	0,37	0,29	0,37	0,21

205 in C, and 67 in D Class. Five Societies remain unclassified. Cash advances to members have gone down to Rs. 77,971, and the value of raw material advanced to members is Rs. 87,922 The value of members' goods sold has increased from Rs. 48,000 to Rs. 71,000.

CHAPTER XXXII

THE CO-OPERATIVE INDUSTRIAL BANK, AMRITSAR

THE first problem that the Weavers' Society was called upon to solve was the marked hostility of the middleman towards members of a Society to provide them with yarn. In fact, the immediate problem which such a Society wanted to solve was to check the rapacity of the middleman as it showed itself in advancing loans in cash or kind to the weavers at exorbitant rates of interest. The formation of the Societies saw the middleman quite indignant, and in some cases he downright refused to lend to the members of the Societies. Provision of raw materials to the weavers at reasonable prices meant a real service to them. With the object of placing facilities concerning the supply of raw materials at reasonable terms, the Central Yarn Store was opened in 1915. This developed by 1918 into the Weavers' Central Co-operative Stores, Ltd., Lahore, and was registered as the Central Institution of the Industrial Co-operative Societies, and was shifted to Amritsar in 1920. In 1920 the Store had a working capital of Rs. 1 lakh, and with a turnover of Rs. 6 lakhs earned a profit amounting to Rs. 6,700. In 1924 the working capital increased by Rs. 31,000, and the turnover fell to just half of what it was in 1920, and brought down the profit to Rs. 1,422 only.

FUNCTIONS OF THE STORES

The stores:

(1) Financed the primary Weavers' Societies by making advance in yarn on the receipt of indents;

(2) Advanced cash to Societies for local purchase of yarn on receipt of original invoices;

(3) Accepted repayments in the form of goods as well as cash;

(4) In case of outlying Societies made advances through the Unions which undertook supervision and guaranteed repayment;

(5) Got silk direct from Kashmir for Silk Weavers' Societies;

(6) Co-ordinated the working of Societies.

The store was managed by a Committee of Weavers and had an official manager.

THE INDUSTRIAL BANK

The Weavers' Central Co-operative Store, Ltd., was re-named: "The Co-operative Industrial and Weavers' Bank, Ltd." The object of this change in name was firstly to attract deposits and secondly to undertake financing Industrial Societies other than "weavers" as well. The bank now retains "weavers" as a part of its name merely as an old association. The anticipated expansion in the business of the bank made the Directors of the bank realize the necessity of a separation between financing and trading activities of the bank, and decide to restrict themselves to finance alone. For facilitating trade, particularly the sale of goods, it was to make an independent arrangement in Lahore. The decision in practice assumed the form of the once famous Sales Depot, which by the time these lines appear in print will be dead and gone.

OBJECTS OF THE BANK

The objects of the bank are to facilitate the operations of registered Co-operative Societies of artisans and small industrialists by:

(1) The carrying on of banking and credit business;

(2) The purchase and sale of raw materials for the benefit of the affiliated Societies;

(3) The purchase and sale for common account of the finished products of members of affiliated Societies;

(4) The provision of the implements of the craft;

(5) The supervision and audit of the registered and affiliated Societies;

(6) The provision of educational assistance to the members of such Societies.

MEMBERSHIP

The membership of the Bank is open to registered Industrial Co-operative Societies in the Punjab, the Registrar, Co-operative Societies, Punjab, or a person generally or specially nominated by him, and not more than three individuals who are able to assist the movement by influence or their commercial knowledge.

The liability of each member is limited to double the nominal value of his shares.

COMPOSITION OF CAPITAL:

Capital shall be composed of:

(1) An indeterminate number of shares of the value of Rs. 100 each;

(2) Deposits from members, from other registered Co-operative Banks, Unions, and Societies, and from the public;

(3) Loans as sanctioned by the Registrar.

Each member has one vote. The by-laws require that the Managing Committee shall consist of not less than five persons, besides the three nominated members; in addition to the President, at least two-thirds of the members shall be weavers.

The Managing Committee, amongst other functions incidental to the discharge of its duty:

(1) Fixes, with the sanction of the Registrar, the maximum credit of the Societies;

(2) Decides the terms on, the periods for, and the rates of interest at which loans and advances of raw materials are to be made, and arranges for the recovery of all such loans, advances, and interests;

(3) Decides the terms on and the rates at which implements of the craft are to be supplied;

(4) Decides the terms on and the rates at which the finished product is to be bought and sold;

(5) Decides the terms on and the rates at which deposits are to be received, and arranges for the repayment or return of deposits.

PROFITS

The profits are applied as follows:

(1) Not less than one-fourth must be carried to the reserve fund;

(2) Payment of dividend on shares;

(3) May be spent on any of the following:

- (*a*) formation of a sinking fund, depreciation fund, or building fund;
- (*b*) a rebate on purchase from the Society by members;
- (*c*) a bounty on sales to the Society by members;
- (*d*) the reduction of interest on advances to Societies;
- (*e*) the maintenance of officials for the supervision and audit of the affiliated Co-operative Societies, or for spreading knowledge of benefits of Co-operation, or for the instruction of members of the affiliated Co-operative Societies in methods of the craft;
- (*f*) the provision of educational assistance to members of affiliated Co-operative Societies.

THE POSITION OF THE BANK

We have already seen how during 1930–33 the annual advance to Societies decreased from Rs. 99,800 to Rs. 32,915, and the total outstanding came down within the same period by about 50 per cent.

An idea of the working and position of the bank will be given by the following:

Year	Total amount of loan	Advances made during the year	Profit.	Percentage of the working Capital owned by the Bank
	Rs.	Rs.	Rs.	
1930	4,53,000	99,800	4,211	
1931	4,19,000	62,800	3,448	14
1932	3,83,000	40,200	−844	16
1933	3,56,531	32,915	135	
1934	3,42,670	40,417	5,630	

The Multan Societies have very severely strained the resources of the bank. Every year a large sum of money has had to be written off either on account of the inability of the D class Societies to repay or on account of the losses met with in working the Sales Depot. In the year 1932 alone interest worth Rs. 4,000 had to be written off on account of D class and Multan Societies. The position of the bank in 1934 may be guaged from the following:

Assets		Liabilities	
Co-operative Movement, etc.	345	1. Loans and deposits from members and non-members	3,25,908
1. Cash in hand and Bank	613	2. Loans and deposits from Central Bank ..	78,602
2. Market value of Investments	89,412	3. Loans and deposits from Societies	1,827
3. Loans due by members (individuals).. ..	4,352	4. Share Capital paid up..	30,220
4. Loans due by Banks and Societies	3,54,123	5. Interest due by the Bank	1,349
5. Interest accrued the Bank	19,829	6. Other items	22,180
6. Present value of stock in hand	766	7. Reserve fund	35,713
7. Other items	41,549	8. Other funds, e.g. Building funds, etc. ..	9,215
Total	5,10,644	Total	5,05,012

CHAPTER XXXIII

EDUCATION AND CO-OPERATION

ADULT EDUCATION

GENERAL education is the very basis of all life—religious, moral, intellectual, and economic. The Department of Co-operation in starting night schools for the illiterate adult population of the Punjab rural areas took a much-needed step in 1920. Look at the table of progress, or shall I call it the table of failure, of yet another praiseworthy effort of the Department of Co-operation. It is a table of painful failure, which is bound to breed a sense of utter helplessness in the workers.

Night schools were started in 1920, and for some time, like all new forms of Co-operation in the Punjab, flourished on account of the proverbial enthusiasm of the start. The success of a school depends upon its management, teachers, and the type of students it attracts. Let us see how each of these classes has contributed to the failure of these schools.

TEACHERS

Good teachers, true to the sacred traditions of this noblest of professions, are essential to the regeneration of a country. The establishment of night schools did mean an honest effort at laying the foundations of a better rural life in the Province. But no school can achieve any measure of success where teachers of the right type are not to be found, more so in case of village night schools, where a teacher has to train old rustics —a set of pupils unaccustomed to any discipline and hopelessly unmindful of their work or its ultimate usefulness.

For reasons of economy or self-sacrifice the night school teacher is either the secretary of a local Co-operative Society, any literate cultivator, or, as in most cases, a local schoolmaster. It was supposed that a teacher in a night school would either be working without any payment, or at the most for a small allowance. It was, however, soon discovered that the Societies could not seriously count upon either the self-sacrifice of the honorary workers or the contentment of those accepting small allowances.

The teachers did not, and I should think could not, give their serious thought and attention to this work because the remuneration bore no relation at all to the hardship involved in the greater mental fatigue caused after the day's work. The blank-looking unresponsive dullards ranged round the teacher enhanced his mental worries. The greatest torture for a teacher that I can imagine is to place him amongst confirmed, aged stupids who lack the physical briskness and mental alertness of a schoolboy.

The Department of Co-operation felt that trained teachers were essential, perhaps more essential in the case of adults than in that of the young. Such teachers could not always be had. The lack of good teachers has thus materially contributed to the failure of many an adult school. Thirteen such schools in Gurdaspur and six in Sonipat were closed in one year for the dearth of teachers of the right type. Sometimes when an efficient, self-sacrificing, and sympathetic teacher of a local school has given an exceedingly hopeful start to a school, his transfer saw the end of his labours and sacrifices. His successor is a stranger to the village, presumption goes against him, he may be better than his predecessor, but there is a stampede out of the school. Old men seek and use every such opportunity for throwing off that unpleasant burden of stuffing hard things into their stony heads. But with the old teacher, for one reason or another, they must have suffered it perhaps to the end, for the Punjab farmer appreciates personal relations more than anything else.

PUPILS

Although illiteracy cannot be banished if we neglect the adult illiterate, yet it must be recognized that the old man cannot learn so easily as does the child. The adult pupils at the night schools presented peculiar difficulties. The greatest difficulty these schools had to face was the unwillingness of the pupils to attend a night school after the day's toil. Enthusiasm of the pupils vanishes into thin air soon after its first exhibition is over. Moreover, night schools cannot be run during some months in summer. In some cases the night schools had to be closed after the originators had acquired literacy. That happened at Gurdaspur and Lyallpur in 1922. At a very early stage of the night school movement it was discovered that the school primers written originally for children would not interest the grey-headed pupils. The subjects and the media of instruction should have an attraction peculiar to them. Hence it was decided to invoke the help of the magic lantern and the cinema dealing with agriculture, hygiene, and other subjects of interest pertaining to the Punjab village life. The unsuitability of the primers for the adults was felt to be such an obstacle that new primers for the adults were prepared and introduced in 1927. Unfortunately, since then a progressive decline has set in so far as the number of schools and pupils is concerned. The Education Department in the Punjab appreciates this attempt on the part of the Department of Co-operation, and in 1924 placed a sum of Rs. 5,000 at the disposal of the Registrar to be utilized towards giving monetary help to such schools. In some cases District Boards sanctioned grants-in-aid to these night schools. As the table given opposite indicates, some of the successful adult schools were taken over by the District Boards.

ACHIEVEMENTS

Quite a number of people have obtained their literacy certificates during a little over a decade's experiment in adult schools. People of all professions sat side by side as pupils, and their ages varied between 18 and 60. Not only that. Even father and son could be seen sitting together in such schools. Some perfectly illiterate persons attained literacy enough to work as Secretaries of Unions and independent shopkeepers. An old Numbardar could read for himself the revenue demands which had been a mystery to him for over forty years. In 1926, at a Conference of Adult Schools in Pakpattan, "an aged man, blind of one eye, and seeing imperfectly with the other, was the occasion of a demonstration when he came forward to receive his literacy certificate."

THE ADULT EDUCATION

Year	Total Number of Institutions Registered and Unregistered	Number of Pupils	Literacy Certificate issued to	Schools for Women	Taken over by the District Boards
1921	100	1,783	—	—	—
1922	75	1,122	—	—	—
1924	125	1,766	—	—	—
1925	127	—	400	—	—
1926	269	—	200	8	—
1927	201	4,100	291	6	—
1928	107	—	668	—	66 cancelled as worthless
1929	59	—	293	—	47 cancelled as worthless
1930	26	—	—	—	34 cancelled as failure
1931	17	—	—	—	—
1932	12	318	105	—	—

COMPULSORY EDUCATION

Adult schools were started in 1920, and the Department of Co-operation seemed to be in a mood of atonement for the sins of others. In 1923 it decided to take up another and a more promising position of attack against illiteracy. Old people, for one reason or another, may not, and in a country like India, perhaps cannot, learn. I believe with the Registrar of Co-operative Societies who, in reviewing the working of the adult school, in spite of his hopes and enthusiasm in the beginning, was forced to observe: "I doubt whether the number of those whose life has left their brains in a condition to absorb such knowledge is large enough in a village to support a school." Does it imply the beginning of a realization that we did not begin at the right end?

Compulsory School Societies were started in 1923. These Societies were organized amongst parents who bound themselves, under a penalty of Rs. 50 for default, to send their children to school for a full primary course. The first Society was started in Hoshiarpur with twenty-five parents. Sirsa tahsil organized five Societies with 303 members, and sent 220 boys to school. The one great educational and economic advantage of such an assured supply of boys to the schools is the establishment of a two-teacher instead of one-teacher school.

The Education Department was found more than willing to co-operate with a view to ensure success, and expressed its readiness to start a lower Middle School wherever a Society guaranteed a sufficiency of pupils. This voluntary compulsion seems to have worked extraordinarily well, and the Registrar told us the very next year that wherever schools had been closed for lack of pupils, the complaint was against lack of accommodation. During the same year arbitration proceedings had to be adopted against forty-eight defaulters. Twenty fines were imposed and realized. "The sinners," as the Registrar puts it, "repented after payment and sent their boys to school."

The year 1925 brought yet another proof of the active imagination of the Co-operative Department in the registration of School Societies for Girls. Of course in the case of schools for girls the problem of securing a teacher, as was to be expected, did prove a difficult one. Two of the girls' schools in Montgomery failed in 1926 simply because teachers could not be had. That was not all.

Even all the members, too, did not realize the usefulness of imparting education to that section of humanity which the civilized world calls the "better half." "One of these Societies in Lyallpur fined no less than fourteen of its members for a disloyal agitation against it; the factious plot was suppressed, and the parents sent their girls back to school. It should be emphasized that the action was taken by the elected Committee of the Society, not by the inspecting staff" (Report for 1925).

During 1926 eighty fines amounting to Rs. 1,200 were imposed, but only Rs. 200 were realized. The Department described it as "a tendency to impose heavy fines by way of a threat, and to remit them when the sinners repented." Some Societies, as far back as 1926, showed slackness and took no action against defaulters. Infliction of fines led to the breakdown of a Society in 1927. In 1932 the imposition of heavy fines, in Amritsar, resulted "in the local school being burnt and the books of the Society being stolen." The latest report just issued makes the infliction of fines and their non-realization look like a hopeless farce. During 1933 fines amounting to Rs. 669 were imposed, and the stupendous amount of Rs. 10 was realized. It is exceedingly painful to have to record, as the Report for 1933 indicates: "One Society in Jullundur has gone into voluntary liquidation, as the members of the Committee could not face the displeasure of those who did not send their wards to school, by enforcing the by-laws."

The Annual Report for 1932 observes: "Of the Societies that now remain, the majority are functioning moderately well, if without great enthusiasm. The cause of failure of such Societies is the universal apathy of the cultivator. He is too stupid to understand the necessity of education for his children. But the necessity of utilizing the boy's labour on the farm is very often the only motive of the members' uncharitable resolve. The new by-laws of such Societies allow for this difficulty, supposed or real, in the form of requiring the presence of at least one son in the school where nature has been more generous in granting this gift."

Co-operative Education Societies seem to be dying out, and the Department seems to be well prepared for their burial. The fall in number of Societies and slackness in their operations is nothing extraordinary. Institutions run by the District Boards and the Education Department essentially suffer under

COMPULSORY EDUCATION CO-OPERATIVE SOCIETIES

	1924	1925	1926	1927	1928	1929	1930	1931	1932	1933	1934
Number of Societies ..	45	79	140	158	148	140	116	101	85	84	84
Members	2,630	—	6,728	6,804	7,275	6,814	5,635	4,930	4,017	4,158	4,003
Boys and Girls—											
(*a*) Attending the school	—	—	6,700	6,285	5,734	5,443	4,175	3,398	2,873	2,919	2,519
(*b*) Who should have attended	—	—	—	—	6,162	6,050	5,214	4,215	3,661	4,456	3,087
(*c*) In 3rd class	—	—	—	833	1,008	1,077	725	596	616	511	446
(*d*) In 4th class	—	—	—	592	747	873	624	497	473	442	328
Fines—	—	—	80	99	143	144	128	68	48	64	74
(*a*) Imposed .. (Rs.)	—	—	1,200	1,300	1,398	1,195	1,279	776	538	669	1,141
(*b*) Recovered .. (Rs.)	—	—	200	365	149	205	95	119	52	10	1
Girls' Societies	—	—	5	6	12	10	10	10	9	11	14
Pupils	—	—	—	277	180	303	344	301	303	369	383

the same disadvantages. That is true of India as a whole. Attendance at schools is highly unsatisfactory, and the percentage of those completing their full primary course is hopelessly small. Whenever a real effort at bringing about a lasting improvement in the life of rural India will be made, general education of the masses will be the starting-point. These Education Societies will have to be revived not only in the interest of Co-operation but of education and the much-talked-of Rural reconstruction in the Punjab.

CHAPTER XXXIV

ARBITRATION SOCIETIES IN THE PUNJAB

TEMPERAMENT and lack of education have fitted a Punjab farmer to believe in the efficacy of the direct method of settling his disputes. He literally fights out his disputes before proceeding to a Court of Law. Trivial differences develop into terrible and fatal fights, and end in crushing litigation. Litigation once started serves to fan the spirit of faction, and through sympathy with a party or hostility to witnesses—often hired personifications of falsehood—villages get split up into a number of hostile groups, the existence of which not only shields but positively breeds crime. Litigation is a highly expensive evil that has sapped the very life of our countryside. It has been estimated that the cost of litigation in the Punjab alone amounts to Rs. 12 crores annually, a sum four times the annual revenue paid by the Punjab cultivator. Having practically no reserves to fall back upon, the farmer digs his own grave by running to the sahukar for borrowing in order to meet the expenses of litigation. He borrows, and thus barters all his present and future resources. Thus litigation not only drains away to hopeless and unproductive channels the funds or the credit available to a farmer, but also involves him in self-imposed unemployment. Litigation, for lack of attention, devastates his smiling fields and diminishes his prosperous yields. The countryside in India would certainly be brighter and happier than it is to-day if this colossal waste of money and time could be checked effectively, and the consequent saving in time and money diverted to productive and promising channels. Numerous petty crimes are committed in our villages which can be safely settled in the village itself, and decidedly with greater prospects of reformation of the culprits and with undoubtedly greater deterrent results. In fact one of the speediest methods of reforming rural life in India consists in the setting up in each village of an organization for settlement of certain types of disputes which in the form of protracted and costly litigation that they assume sap the very life of the countryside in India. The Punjab pioneered the establishment of Arbitration Societies for bringing about this much-needed and fundamental reform in our rural life. A study of the working of Arbitration Societies in the Punjab in the present rural uplift age will therefore be quite in the fitness of things.

GENESIS OF THE ARBITRATION SOCIETIES

The Arbitration Societies in the Punjab owe their origin to a suggestion of Mr. M. L. Darling, Commissioner, Punjab, once Registrar, Co-operative Societies, Punjab. In 1917, Mr. Darling put forward the following suggestion:

"The system of arbitration is, of course, only applied to disputes between Societies and their members. In time, probably in some modified form of panchayat, it should be possible to extend it in selected Societies to disputes between individual members. It is commonly asserted that panchayats for settling civil and criminal disputes were at one time a familiar feature of Indian village life. An attempt has lately been made to revive them, and where, as in some cases, they exist by the mutual consent of all concerned they are a peculiarly valuable form of co-operative enterprise. Unfortunately their development in regard to criminal disputes is hampered by the lack of legal status, the recent Act applying only to civil suits. Even if the Act were extended, success on any considerable scale would probably only be possible if close supervision were guaranteed from the outset. For this a special staff would be required, as in the case of the Co-operative Movement, which would have been still-born had not special machinery been created to initiate and develop it. On the other hand, though most of the panchayats informally started exist only in name, the fact that a few of them have survived show the possibilities of this most desirable form of Co-operation."

The Arbitration Societies owe their existence to this suggestion, although the Department seems to have failed to trace the idea to its original source. Mr. C. F. Strickland says: "The idea of Co-operative arbitration was first put forward in local conferences held in the year 1919." The idea with a view to its being translated into practice was really thrashed out at local conferences, as Mr. Strickland tells us. Needless and boundless litigation was recognized to be responsible for a good deal of agricultural indebtedness in the Punjab. Co-operators were unanimous in their demand for the establishment of an organization for settlement of petty disputes outside the Courts. An experimental draft of by-laws was prepared, providing that members of a Co-operative Arbitration Society should draw up a schedule of subjects of all disputes concerning which they undertook to submit to arbitration under the by-laws of their Society. A member had the option of taking his dispute to a court of law either by securing the previous permission of the Managing Committee, or on the payment of a moderate fine even without such permission. The award of the arbitrators after such appeal as the by-laws allowed was declared to be final. On these lines 150 Societies with 16,000 members were registered during 1919 and 1922, and undoubtedly did much useful work.

The legality of by-laws declaring any decision outside a court of law as final was questioned, and a summary order was issued by Lala Har Kishen Lal as Minister in 1922 to dissolve all Co-operative Arbitration Societies in the Punjab. All Societies with a solitary exception were closed down. This one, "appealing to a higher executive authority, obtained a decision that the order of cancellation could not be sustained." This will be easily recognized as the "unkindest cut of all." How deep was the sense of disappointment experienced by all interested in the amelioration of rural life in the Punjab may be gathered from the historic funeral oration delivered by Mr. Calvert, the then Registrar, Co-operative Societies, Punjab.

"For reasons that I have never understood, an order was issued that all these Societies should be closed down. That order has aroused comment and criticism in various provinces. One can, perhaps, imagine what would happen in England if all the arbitration work done by Chambers of Commerce and the big Exchange were suddenly prohibited by a Minister. All reports testify to the genuine sorrow with which the order has been received by members of all castes and grades. There are over 30,000 villages in the Punjab, in 148 of which we had Arbitration Societies, and in over 29,000 of which we had none, so there was ample scope for the development of panchayats under the Panchayat Act, and it cannot seriously be urged that there was any competition. In the 148 villages which have been deprived of a useful means of escape from litigation, there have been set up Panchayats in four only. None of these have yet done any work according to my reports. The remaining 144 have now neither one nor the other.

"Some reports point out that the summary closure of the Arbitration Societies is a big blow to the prospects of panchayats for a very obvious reason. There is a tale of two local notables who were given honorary judicial powers; the ambitious one went about instigating cases and then settling them in his Court; the other, a leading Co-operator, devoted himself to securing amicable relations between disputants without coming into Court at all. The latter was deprived of his powers on the ground that there were no cases within his jurisdiction, while the former has a beautiful record of public work to his credit."

The Arbitration Societies did not thus close down, unwept, unhonoured, and unsung. But the usefulness of their work had so impressed itself upon the Department that an attempt to revive such Societies even in a modified form was believed to be justifiable. The by-laws were revised, and the attempt to declare them final was abandoned. These by-laws were submitted to and approved by the legal authority of the Punjab Government.

The objects of a Co-operative Arbitration Society are:

(*a*) To provide a means for the equitable settlement of

disputes; and thereby to save its members from the trouble and wasteful expenditure caused by false, frivolous, and unnecessary litigation;

(*b*) To provide a means of defence for members against such litigation initiated by others;

(*c*) To secure, when necessary, professional legal opinion for the assistance of members.

Every member on entering the Society pays a nominal admission fee, and through a written agreement undertakes to refer all his disputes with other members to the Society for settlement under penalty that may amount to Rs. 100. The supreme authority within the Society is vested in the general body of members known as the General Meeting. The General Meeting elects a Managing Committee which exercises all powers of the General Meeting. A panel of Arbitrators is also elected from among the members of the Society. A dispute is referred to the Managing Committee, who try their utmost to effect a compromise within a specified time, failing which the dispute is referred to the arbitrators. Usually there are three arbitrators, one of whom is nominated by the Managing Committee, and one is elected out of the panel by each party to a dispute. Appeal against the award of the arbitrators lies to the Managing Committee. Every award has to be confirmed by a Civil Court.

Arbitration Societies have been recognized by the Department as the most difficult form of Co-operation. The Arbitrators have to show vigour and honesty at every step. Once they go wrong they ruin the prospects of every useful activity. Cases have come to the notice of the Department in which people have proved unworthy of the great trust reposed in them. The Report for 1931 tells us that "one Society went wrong and was closed; for it was abused, and caused disturbance in the village; and there have been other instances where absence of complete confidence in the Committee has very adversely affected the health of the Society." The Arbitration Societies have always been discouraged by petty officials and pleaders. Members of an Arbitration Society were hauled up by a hostile Sub-Inspector of Police for unlawful detention of a member. These people suffered a lot without the moral support of the Department of Co-operation being extended to them. The Arbitration Society! Well, all was over with it when its Managing Committee could so easily and effectively be shaken to a realization of its helplessness. Wherever will and honesty are to be found in an adequate measure, mistakes in scope and procedure involve the Societies in failure and disrepute. Some Societies have actually shown a tendency to "usurp the functions and powers of the regularly constituted Courts," and the Registrar in his latest Report remarks that "this must be held in check." But an Arbitration Society to be of real use must, within certain limits, replace a court of law. How long it will take us to produce in our villages men to whom the work can be assigned with perfect confidence is a question an answer to which cannot here be attempted.

Kangra District boasts of more than half of the Arbitration Societies to be found in the Province. The Registrar tells us that this preponderance of Arbitration Societies in Kangra is due to "the simplicity and straightforwardness of the people, the strength of the social tie, and the difficulty and expense of communications." Some of the Societies, particularly Bhidi Society in Sialkot, Thath Ghalwan in Multan, and Muzang in Lahore, and one in Hoshiarpur District, are doing quite useful work. In Hoshiarpur and Multan Districts the Societies successfully decide disputes among Mussulman zemindars and Hindu money-lenders—an achievement which any organization may well be proud of.

An idea of the utility and efficacy of an indigenous organization for settlement of disputes may be had from the following account of its working given by Mr. G. C. Garbett, Chief Secretary to Government, Punjab. This is a translation of the original which appeared in Urdu in *Co-operation,* the Urdu Journal of the Department. "Burhan is a village in the Campbellpur District, situated on the Grand Trunk Road, near Hasan Abdal. Pathans are the owners of most of the land in the village. They are a hopelessly quarrelsome and a highly-turbulent people. The village became notorious for its factions which brought free fights and crime in their wake. Up till 1927, therefore, either the Police kept a vigilant eye over the whole village, or a punitive Police Force had to be stationed at the village, the annual cost of which, Rs. 6,000, had to be paid by the village. In spite of all this crime was on the increase, cases could not either be traced or proved. This brought

ARBITRATION SOCIETIES IN THE PUNJAB

Year	Number of Societies	Members	Average Membership	Number of Disputes Decided	Number of Disputes Decided by Committee	Number of Cases in which the Arbitrator's Awards were enforced through a Court
1927	27	3,000	—	660	—	—
1928	43	6,024	144	787	—	18
1929	44	7,509	170	924	—	18
1930	49	7,822	161	382	172	18
1931	54	8,096	150	371	199	29
1932	72	9,992	139	322	287	22
1933	84	11,768	140	612	295	31
1934	89	15,386	155	917	389	61

poverty and degradation to the village, and everybody's honour was at stake. One day the Tahsildar went to that village and, being tired of their wickedness and machinations, impressed upon them the necessity of putting a stop to that abominable sort of life they were leading. It took him three days to convince the people in the village that nothing but an honest effort on their own part could save them. Their cases, he suggested, must be settled by them in their own village. The entire population agreed to the formation of a panchayat on which would be represented all classes of the people—the high and the low, the good and the wicked. Such a thoroughgoing representation on the panchayat of all classes of the people in the village was deemed necessary with a view to winning the confidence of every class of people. It was more of the nature of an Arbitration Society than of a body the decisions of which would be legally binding upon all. Every member of this panchayat took an oath affirming that he would not show any partiality to his friends or relatives, but would strictly follow the path of justice.

"The very first case this panchayat had to decide was brought forward by a poor widow against the most influential man in the village who was a jagirdar and, to crown all, the very President of the Society. The complaint was that his cattle had damaged the widow's crops. The case was proved after due examination of witnesses. The damage was estimated at Rs. 5, and was cheerfully paid by the President. The panchayat soon won everybody's confidence, and one hundred cases were disposed of in no time. Now all is quiet in Burhan, everyone reaps what he sows. Crime is practically unknown. Every oppressor knows that he will, in view of evidence available against him, soon be punished for his misdeeds. Panchayats have been started in the neighbourhood of Burhan, and much useful work is being quietly accomplished with the once notorious Burhan as the centre of reform."

Disputes of every class arising in Punjab villages were decided by the Arbitration Societies. Such a settlement of disputes brought justice speedy and free of cost to the Punjab villager. Since men living in the same village had a very clear idea of the cause of such disputes, the character of the parties to a dispute and their supporters, besides a knowledge of the sins of each party, their decisions were almost always well balanced.

The Arbitration Societies undertook to settle all disputes arising out of the possession of women, misappropriation of crops, cattle and trespass, insults, hurts, water-supply, succession, possession of land, theft, non-payment of wages, land revenue and rent, breaches of promise, etc. The following are some of the important cases decided by Arbitration Societies, which give us an idea of the usefulness of such Societies in the organization of village life in the Punjab.

The Monzang Arbitration Society in Lahore decided in 1928 a case in which property worth a lakh of rupees was involved. If the case had been taken to a court of law the cost of getting it settled would have at a modest estimate amounted to Rs. 20,000. Similarly, a Society in Gurdaspur decided a dispute over distribution of ancestral property which would have in the normal course of justice involved considerable expense, much inconvenience, and tremendous loss of time.

"In Lyallpur, a lambardar lost his eye in a fight between two parties over a woman; the lambardar did not go to a Court, and the Society got the woman back from Bahawalpur State territory and restored her to her husband."

"In Rohtak one Society decided a case in favour of the plaintiff and the finding was acceptable—when in default of better evidence the plaintiff had sworn to his claim with some Ganges Water in his hand."

The Annual Report for 1930 records: "The most important case decided by an Arbitration Society during the year was one relating to the partition of agricultural land worth Rs. 80,000. The case was particularly complicated owing to various objections raised by mortgagees. Yet in spite of this, partition was effected within three months at a total cost of one rupee. All who are acquainted with the delays and prolixities of a difficult partition case, when handled in the usual way, will have some idea of what the parties must have saved in time, trouble, and expense."

"Another interesting case touched the family affairs of two Kangra chamars. A, after becoming engaged to the daughter of B, spent a good deal on clothes and jewellery for the bride, but at the last moment she was withheld by her father, who hoped for a better price from C. The dispute went before the caste panchayat, but was more than it could manage. A more formal gathering called a Dharam Mandal proved equally ineffective, and it was only when it was brought before the local Arbitration Society that it was settled by the bride being given to A."

In 1931, a member of a Society in Gujrat lost a pro-note

executed in his favour by another member of the Society. The borrower refused to execute a new pro-note, which he had to do when the Committee of the Society decided that he must give a new pro-note. An interesting case was decided in 1932. One person in Kulu divided his property amongst his two sons, who turned him out of their houses after getting possession of land. The Society, when appealed to, decided that a portion of land should be set apart for the old man's maintenance, and must be cultivated by one or other of the sons.

ADVANTAGES OF ARBITRATION SOCIETIES

The Arbitration Society exercises a great educative and moral influence. Even the dullest of persons, when he has faith in the impartiality of judgment and wonderfully prompt and incredibly inexpensive decisions of an Arbitration Society, will not hesitate to bring his disputes to the Society. In fact the presence of an Arbitration Society in a village exercises an unconscious but very certain influence on the mutual settlement of disputes without their presentation even to the Society, for the man in the wrong feels that the case will be decided against him. To some of the Arbitration Societies must, as a matter of fact, go the credit of having introduced an atmosphere of mental tranquillity in their neighbourhood. "In Sialkot the Society at Bhidi enjoys such confidence that it has been asked to settle disputes not only among its members, but among the inhabitants of neighbouring villages, and the same is reported of the large Thath Ghalwan Society in Multan."

INEXPENSIVE JUSTICE

Justice through a court of law is an expensive affair. An award through an Arbitration Society costs practically nothing to the parties to a dispute. In 1932 the Ghazipur Dasti Society succeeded in arranging partition of part of the shamilat in the abadi-deh, the decision involving the exchange of some of the houses. It is estimated that this case, if taken to a Revenue Court, would have lasted at least for a year and "cost about Rs. 1,000." Every case decided by an Arbitration Society means a saving of at least a couple of hundred rupees to the parties. The expense and prolonged period of contest in suits in courts of law has added a proverb to the language in that province, the English version of which would be, "He who wins a suit loses, and he who loses it is done for."

PROMPT JUSTICE

Cases keep on hanging in courts of law for very long periods, sometimes for years together. But an Arbitration Society meets, studies the case, examines the witnesses, and as a local body its members are often already in possession of true facts; the moral worth as well as the social status of every witness and of the parties is known to them—it does not therefore take long to come to a decision, and the decision carries the moral support and embodies the prestige and wisdom of the entire village community, and is this bound to be honoured.

ANTIDOTE TO COMMUNALISM

The Province, due to its peculiar economic features, very often falls a prey to the demon of communalism. Everything that brings different communities together in some practical work where honesty, goodwill and impartial judgment are to be exercised, makes for killing the demon of communalism. An Arbitration Society brings together Muhammadans and Hindus, the former as debtors and the latter as creditors generally. The decisions of the Society are willingly accepted by the parties. These Societies have thus been working even as Debt Conciliation Boards, which, in most of the provinces in India, the Government has as yet failed to establish.

CONSTITUTION AND WORKING OF AN ARBITRATION SOCIETY

The object of a Co-operative Arbitration Society is to promote thrift, self-help, and mutual help among the members, and more particularly:

(*a*) To provide a means for the equitable settlement of disputes, and thereby to save them from the trouble and wasteful expenditure caused by false, frivolous, and unnecessary litigation;

(*b*) To provide a means of defence for members against such litigation initiated by others;

(*c*) To secure when necessary professional legal opinion for the assistance of members.

The supreme authority within the Society is vested in the General Meeting. The Managing Committee is a body annually elected by the General Meeting, and consists of at least five members of the Society who are over the age of twenty-one, and not legal practitioners, or the servants, employees, or agents of a legal practitioner. This Committee includes a President and one or two Vice-Presidents. The members of the Committee are elected for a year, but are eligible for re-election. Meetings of the Committee are held whenever necessary, and for the disposal of any business; the attendance of at least three members is necessary. The Committee exercises all powers of the Society except those reserved for the General Meeting, subject to any regulations or restrictions duly laid down by the Society in general meeting or in the by-laws.

Every member of the Society enters into an agreement with all the members of the Society to refer his disputes with other members to the Committee for settlement or for reference to arbitration. In default he is to pay a penalty, not exceeding Rs. 100. Any member who is aggrieved by an order of the Committee imposing a penalty in case of default may, after depositing the amount of such penalty with the Treasurer, appeal to the next General Meeting, or refer the matter to the Registrar as a dispute between himself and the Committee. A member with the previous consent of the Committee is entitled to institute a suit or make complaint in a court of law concerning disputes which the Society is competent to deal with, or may enter an objection against the filing, enforcement, or execution of an award. A member is entitled to refer a dispute to a court of law, or enter an objection against the filing, enforcement, or execution of an award, in the case of disputes which the Society is competent to try, even without the previous consent of the Committee, but in such a case previous intimation to the President and Secretary of the Society and payment of penalty is essential.

Any party to such a dispute as the Society is competent to hear may apply in writing to the President or the Secretary of the Committee for a settlement of the dispute. The Committee gives a reasonable notice of the time and place, and calls upon parties to the dispute to appear before them. If the Committee fail to settle the dispute by conciliation within one month of the date of the application, they shall call upon the parties to refer the dispute to arbitration.

Every year a panel of trustworthy men is elected from amongst whom arbitrators may be chosen. At such an election at least half of the members of the Society must be present. The panel generally consists of five to twelve men. The parties called upon to settle their dispute through arbitration, unless they settle it privately, sign an agreement to refer it for arbitration either to one arbitrator, who shall be a member of the panel of arbitrators, or to three arbitrators.

Each party is entitled to appoint one arbitrator, and the Committee appoints the third arbitrator from the panel of arbitrators. No party can nominate an arbitrator from outside the panel of arbitrators without the consent of the opposite party and that of the Committee. Each party is entitled to challenge any member of the panel nominated by the Committee, but, if all the members of the panel are challenged in turn, the Committee may nominate the member they consider most suitable and such nomination shall be final. If any party fails to nominate an arbitrator within fifteen days the Committee has the right to appoint an arbitrator on behalf of the party out of the panel of arbitrators.

Any party aggrieved by an award of the arbitrators may, within one month after the award and after depositing with the Treasurer such fee as the Committee may fix, file an appeal in writing to the Committee. The grounds of appeal must be clearly set forth, and the appeal is to be heard and decided on those grounds alone.

An award or a decision on appeal to the Committee shall be final, and an application under paragraph 20 of the Second Schedule to the Code of Civil Procedure to a Court is to be made to have it filed. In proceedings before an arbitrator or arbitrators or the Committee or a commission appointed by the arbitrators to hear evidence no party is to be represented by a legal practitioner. But a legal practitioner may be appointed as a commissioner on a stated point of law, or on questions of fact which call for an examination of official records, or of a local authority, but nothing binds the Committee to accept the decision of such a commissioner. The arbitrators have nearly all the powers of a court of law in the arbitration of disputes, and in every detail follow the procedure adopted in courts of law.

The award is delivered to the President or Secretary of the Committee, and a copy of it to the party or parties in whose favour it is decided.

CHAPTER XXXV

BETTER LIVING SOCIETIES

CO-OPERATION as it works breeds virtues. It sets athinking even the stupid rustic. The intelligent working of the Co-operative Credit Societies soon made the Co-operators realize the fundamental importance of developing all such moral and social virtues which, besides making for collective improvement, have a very great bearing upon economic prosperity of individuals. A study of the life of the Punjab farmer shows that he is very hard-working and honest; is generous to a fault, but on account of lack of education and training has the strangest of notions concerning self-respect and social esteem. If he is ever to improve, side by side with all the efforts at saving him from external exploitation, he must be protected against his suicidal practices in which he willingly indulges. Many Credit Societies forbade wasteful expenditure on ceremonies and unproductive objects. By-laws were passed by Societies to guide their members, and some Societies set up commendable examples. Societies of menials forbade drinking and gambling, and one Lahore Society fined five members for engaging dancing-girls; a form of waste and a tempting source of indebtedness once very common.

In 1925 model by-laws for special Better Living Societies were drawn up and the public feeling was sounded, as the Registrar wanted to proceed very cautiously. The next year, despite the Registrar's desire for caution, fifty-nine Better Living Societies with over two thousand members were working in full swing. This turned out to be the most popular form of Co-operation, and men of all castes and classes—Brahmans, Rajputs, Meos, Ramdasis, and of Criminal Tribes—joined in the movement in their numbers.

OBJECTS OF A CO-OPERATIVE BETTER LIVING SOCIETY

Objects of a Better Living Society as defined in the Model By-laws are:

To promote the economic interests of its members, and more particularly:

(1) To reform bad customs prevalent amongst the members.

(2) To improve the physical, moral, and spiritual condition of members.

(3) To prevent the waste of money, and inculcate habits of thrift.

(4) To teach and practice the rules of hygiene and combat epidemic diseases.

(5) To cultivate the sense of self-respect and resist corruption.

(6) To assist in arrangements for the education of members and their children, and for the organization of games and all useful occupations which render the life of the community more pleasant and liberal.

(7) To promote other measures designed to encourage in the members the spirit and practice of thrift, mutual help, and self-help.

Every member signs an agreement to the effect that he will observe such special rules and practices as the General Meeting may approve; and in the event of his breach of this undertaking he will pay to the Society such fine, not exceeding Rs. 100, as the Committee may impose.

People met and passed resolutions:

(1) Restricting wasteful expenditure on ceremonies to lowest reasonable limits. The scale of entertainment and other charges at marriages and funerals were prescribed to the minimum. Entertainment by dancing-girls and fireworks at marriage parties were prohibited.

(2) Penalizing cattle trespass into the fields of others, an activity which is not treated as a crime in certain parts of the Province.

(3) Forbidding the sale of daughters in marriage; an abomin-

able practice indulged in by certain classes of people well over the whole of the Province.

(4) Forbidding false evidence. This is one of the curses that has befallen the Province. It must be a brave Society, as the Registrar puts it, that undertakes to uproot this evil.

(5) Enjoining temperance and inoculation.

(6) Shopping by women was forbidden at certain places.

(7) In one backward community the eating of dead animals was prohibited.

All resolutions aiming at reform which involve departures from age-honoured practices must be born of inherent and unshakable convictions. Members of Better Living Societies were advised not to make hasty resolves, as it requires unusual strength of character and firmness of will to translate such resolves into practice. Resolutions were discussed at the general meetings, and members were asked to consult their womenfolk before making final decisions. It was in a second sitting that such resolutions were finally adopted.

These Societies are characteristic of the Punjab, although not now confined to this Province. In Bombay and the United Provinces such Societies under different names and with similar objects have been started in recent years.

METHODS AND ACHIEVEMENTS

Resolutions are easy to make, but difficult to live up to. Fines had to be inflicted and realized for breach of pledges in the form of extravagance indulged in celebration at marriages. In certain villages, where some people insisted on the performance of a prohibited rite and presumably turned a deaf ear to all persuasion and agreement, the Registrar records: "I regret to say that they were beaten." In one case sweets that should not have been bought were thrown to the cattle.

The cost of a marriage in Montgomery village, where better living was accepted, came down from Rs. 2,000 to Rs. 300, and in Chunian an average saving of Rs. 1,000 on each of twenty-four marriages in a year was effected. A very interesting incidental effect of these Societies was witnessed in Chunian. "The Chunian Sikhs cut down the ornaments of women from Rs. 3,000 to Rs. 500: the women refused to submit unless their husbands took the pledge of temperance, and the pledge was taken."

The Registrar turned down, in the first instance, a request for the registration of a society for prohibition of smoking in 1927. But when he visited the village personally and "was convinced of the amazing waste of time in smoking in this tribe," he reconsidered his decision, and the Society was allowed. Mention must in this connection be made of an example set by an official of the Department. As the Report for 1927 puts it, "A sensation was locally caused by an Assistant Registrar who, at the marriage of his two brothers, gave spiritual food to the company in the form of three hours' lecture on Better Living and then fed them on a simple diet. The district association of his tribe, including many of the guests, has been converted to support the movement." Better Living has not meant mere reduction in expenses, but it has acted as an incentive to economy and investment. The daughter of a member of a Better Living Society, on being told that she would be given no jewellery, insisted upon a *quid pro quo*, and was given a deposit of Rs. 1,000 in a Central Bank. According to the Reports of the Department, many ladies in Jullundur sold their jewellery and deposited the proceeds in Co-operative Societies. Some Better Living Societies are reported to have succeeded in the most difficult task of persuading the villagers to keep their manure in pits, to refrain from making dung cakes. A village in Ambala is said to have engaged a sweeper for cleaning the streets every day. Every successive Report gives so much of hope-inspiring material that the temptation to reproduce it is held in check by mere considerations of space. The following is typical of a whole lot.

"The activities of these Societies are most diverse. One insists upon inoculation against plague, another has filled three malodorous ponds and set up hand-pumps to facilitate the supply of good drinking water; others distribute quinine and disinfect wells, and two for criminal tribes prohibit the eating of dead animals. Perhaps the most curious is a Society of chamars (near Palwal), which has two rules—one, that members should wash their clothes once a week; and the other, that they should brush their teeth once a day."

In villages where Better Living Societies exist members have undoubtedly improved their ways of life. But as they say the influence of a good example is contagious. The good these Societies can do has attracted and rejuvenated entire village communities. "Two instances are recorded this year in Gujranwala District, where a non-member was induced to celebrate a marriage in his family according to the rules of the Society by the refusal of all the members of the Society to attend unless the wedding were celebrated as their Society demanded."

To everyone acquainted with life in rural Punjab it is as clear as anything can be that an effective working of Better Living Societies will serve as the very basis of prosperous life. Waste in every form has to be stopped. The best and the most effective way of doing it is to make a collective and a co-operative effort. The Punjab social life, particularly in rural areas with all the erroneous notions of *izzat* or respect it involves, has its own peculiarities. A man feels the wastefulness of certain forms of extravagance, yet he dare not neglect the conventions. Death with friends is a festival. When men combine and adopt such new ways of life the reproach of miserliness is gone, and when these measures bring the much-needed genuine relief which nothing else could give, entire communities are taken in.

The rural areas in the Province to-day do not need such a sermon so seriously. When there is no money and none can be borrowed, and when creditors have combined to make a hell of his life, the Punjab peasant cannot afford to be extravagant even if he wishes. May these lessons be remembered when they are needed most, and not merely practised in making virtue of a sheer necessity.

The Punjab farmer, honest and hardworking as he is, needs

more to be taught how to spend than how to earn. Will the Commissioner for Rural Reconstruction set up such organizations in villages where there are no Better Living Societies?

BETTER LIVING SOCIETIES

Year	Number of Societies	Members	Average Membership
1926	59	2,000	—
1927	136	5,350	—
1928	231	8,665	38
1929	289	10,943	37
1930	312	11,610	37
1931	359	13,002	36
1932	430	15,327	36
1933	487	15,338	31
1934	520	18,361	35

It has recently been decided to concentrate on the expansion of Better Living Societies. A special staff of four Inspectors and sixteen Sub-Inspectors has been sanctioned by the Government.

CHAPTER XXXVI

KOT ESTATE SOCIETIES

No account of the growth and working of Co-operation in the Punjab can be complete without a detailed mention of the working of Co-operative Societies in Kot Estate in Attock District. Major Sardar Muhammad Nawaz is an Honorary Assistant Registrar of Co-operative Societies. He received his education at the Aitchision College, Lahore, and later joined the Royal Military College at Camberley, and after completing the course there served in the Army in India for a short time. In 1926 he was elected to represent the Punjab Landholders in the Assembly. The total area of land he owns amounts approximately to 80,000 acres. The value of and income from his estate may be judged from the fact that he pays Rs. 32,000 annually as Land Revenue to the Government. I have made this passing reference to the person of this benevolent chief because he has displayed a rare interest in the Co-operative Movement and the welfare of his tenants. As a study of the working of Societies in his estate will indicate, the Sardar rightly deserves to be held out as a model of benevolent Lordship to the rest of the landed gentry in the Province. All that he has done so far deserves grateful and honourable mention, and I hope as years go by his benevolent activities will win his estate a place in history as a centre of Agriculture, Co-operation, Rural Reconstruction, and progressive Landlordism.

During the minority of the Sardar the estate remained in charge of the Court of Wards, and was ultimately released in 1923. The growth and working of the movement in the estate can be conveniently divided into two periods, 1914 to 1923, and from 1924 onwards. The first Co-operative Credit Society was established at Kot Fateh Khan on October 2, 1914. Fifteen such Societies were started in 1918, and seven more in 1919. The total number of Societies remained stationary up to 1924. The position in 1920–21 was as below:

Number of Societies	Type of Societies	Membership	Working Capital (Rs.)
23	Credit	963	90,201

The working capital included a loan of Rs. 75,603 from the Central Bank, Campbellpur, on the usual rate of interest.

The young Sardar, on assuming charge of his estate, made a very keen and intelligent study of the problems that confronted his tenants whom Providence had placed in his charge. He had a very clear idea of his duties and obligations as a chief and a landlord. His education and the benevolence of his nature have given the Province a landlord of rare virtues and universal sympathies. He studied the Co-operative Movement, and decided to apply this remedy towards curing the malady that had been troubling his people.

Co-operative Societies in his estate were indebted to the Central Bank, Campbellpur, to the extent of Rs. 75,603. The first practical and well-considered step that he took in this direction was to advance Rs. 128,514 free of interest to repay the Central Bank loan and for other purposes. This large sum of money so magnanimously given to the Credit Societies saved them by way of interest approximately Rs. 12,000 annually. He made up his mind once for all to let his people enjoy the manifold benefits of this movement. The benevolent Sardar did everything in his power to encourage the movement. To every one of his tenants who became a member of any Society he either remitted grazing dues, or cartage of his share of the produce to the granaries, or contribution towards the village kamin's (menials) share of the produce, or granted some other similar facility. He wanted not only to emancipate his tenants from the clutches of the bloodsucking money-lenders, but as well to put a stop to that ruinous litigation which, as in other parts of the Province, was quite common there. Hardly had the Sardar assumed charge of his estate for three years when he organized, in 1926, twelve Co-operative Credit Societies, twelve Arbitration Societies, and one Thrift

Society for his employees. Thus the position in 1927 was as follows:

Number of Societies	Type of Societies	Membership	Working Capital Rs. a. p.
49	Credit Union, 1	35	1,29,901 10 3
	Credit Societies, 35	1,845	1,20,972 0 0
	Arbitration, 12	2,003	868 0 0
	Thrift, 1	32	2,224 0 0

He took a very serious view of the state of indebtedness of his tenants to the sahukars, and rightly believed that no scheme of progress was likely to succeed as long as sahukara debts with all their burdens continued. He advanced Rs. 1,50 lakhs more for this purpose, and the entire debt of his tenants was paid off in no time, out of the advances made to the tenants by the Co-operative Credit Societies. The generosity of his nature could have easily paid out the entire sum without imposing any obligations upon the tenants, but he was aware of the moral slackness such a step would produce in the tenants. This sum, too, was advanced free of interest.

The returns to this investment have been as marvellous as the generosity that prompted it. The tenants of his estate are now absolutely free from outside indebtedness. The Sardar's loan, which once stood at Rs. 2,50 lakhs, has in less than a decade been reduced to Rs. 1,17,000. The owned capital has risen to Rs. 17,551. The position at the close of 1933 was as follows:

Number of Societies	Type of Socieites	Membership	Working Capital Rs.
49	The same as in 1927	3,943	2,16,133

The working capital includes Rs. 1,17,000 as the Sardar's loan, in the form of a deposit free of interest. The satisfactory working of the Societies is evident from the fact that out of thirty-five Credit Societies thirty-three are in A and B Classes, and only two are in C Class.

Within a decade these Societies have accumulated an owned capital of over Rs. 17,551. A unique feature of the working of these Societies is that loans are advanced to members free of interest. As a matter of fact, these Societies combine thrift and credit with very great success. Each member pays R. 1 per annum as his share money, which is unreturnable till the member completes his fifty-fifth year of age. Besides the above share money, each member has to pay R. $\frac{1}{8}$ per annum as audit fee contribution, which is indivisible. Each Society pays Rs. 10 per annum to the Punjab Co-operative Union, and Rs. 10 per annum to their own Credit Union. In this way there is always considerable saving under audit fee contribution, and accumulation of share money annually. The Thrift Society of the employees in the estate is permitted to deposit its accumulations in a Central Bank, and the interest thus earned is divided among the members. Even the non-borrowing members are willing to pay annual contributions, as the privileges and facilities granted by the Sardar to the members are far more valuable than the expenses of membership.

ARBITRATION SOCIETIES

The working and success of the Arbitration Societies is perhaps the proudest achievement of the movement in the Kot Estate. It may well serve as a model to all similar Societies working in the Province. All non-cognizable offences and civil disputes amongst the members are disposed of by these Societies. Meetings of these Societies for settlement of disputes are generally held every week. The Sardar's paid servants act as secretaries to these Societies, and keep a record of the proceedings. They observe strict neutrality in the settling of disputes, under severe penalty. The members have been known to appreciate most the benefits of Arbitration Societies which provide them with such a speedy and inexpensive means to justice. The decrees of these Societies are always willingly obeyed and genuinely honoured. There is so much of confidence in the justice dispensed at these courts, so speedily and at no expense, that people from outside the estate having any claims against the members of Arbitration Societies have often preferred taking their disputes to these Societies than taking the same to courts of law. This they do by merely acquiring membership of such Societies. As one of the officers of the Co-operative Department remarked to me, "the actual working of these Societies is worth witnessing, for words will convey but a very poor idea of their marvellous achievement." That pleasure unfortunately has not been mine so far. But fortunately for me, Mr. Darling's delightful description of a meeting of one such Society is available.

"The Sardar rode with me part of the way to show me another of his Arbitration Societies. It was not so good as the last: in fact, it was specially shown as one of the worst, yet it had done useful work for its 234 members. In two years thirty-one disputes had been decided, and only one had been the subject of appeal to the Committee. This one had taxed the Committee beyond its capacity. The facts of the case are these: A had married his daughter at a tender age to B. Five years passed, and the time came to consummate the marriage. This B refused to do, having in the interval married again. A then applied to the Society for redress, and the arbitrators to whom it was referred ordered B either to complete the marriage or pay A Rs. 75. Negotiations between the parties followed but without result. To-day B declared that he was quite prepared to marry the girl, but that A insisted first upon the payment of two maunds of *Gur* and Rs. 35 in cash. The question was—what should be done next? The Sardar was anxious for a speedy decision to prevent the parties going to Court. Before the Arbitration Society was started disputes were settled by the 'Chitdharia' method, that is, by white-bearded elders who used their influence to get the parties to compromise. The Sardar thought we might try the system in this case. Each party selected a panch—one of them, though a Muhammadan, chose a Hindu shopkeeper—and with the consent of both a greybeard with spectacles was chosen as the sarpanch or President of the Court. The case was stated. There was no doubt as to B's claim to the girl, but as he already had one wife, I suggested a formal divorce, for how will you support two? (he was only a tenant with two ploughs). 'The sustainer of all will provide,' was his reply, in the very voice of the fatalistic East. A little later, however, possibly mistrusting divine assistance, he offered to divorce the girl in return for Rs. 200, a modest enough demand in a country in which every peasant girl has a scarcity cash value. The panchayat of three then retired to consider their decision. In less than five minutes they returned and ordered that the girl should be divorced and B paid Rs. 70. A agreed at once, but B jibbed at receiving only Rs. 70. 'What now?' said the Sardar, turning to me. I suggested that if B refused to accept the decision, he should be forbidden *Huqqa and Water*, in fact be ostracized; but the Sardar was afraid that might lead to feud, and there we left the matter."

SOME ASPECTS OF THE MOVEMENT

There were no big money-lenders within the estate itself. Some big money-lenders residing outside the estate and doing business within the estate had the tenants in their grip. As usual, these money-lenders carried on a campaign of misrepresentation against the movement, which has not even yet been relaxed. The tenants were sought to be misled by imputing motives to the Sardar's evident generosity and solicitude for their welfare. The Sardar, it was said, would make serfs of them and take possession of their movable property.

The total indebtedness as estimated at 2 lakhs in 1927–28 has been reduced to about Rs. 1,34,252. The extraneous loan amounts to Rs. 1,17,000, which is due to the Sardar, and the rest of it is from the Societies' own capital. By the time the Sardar's loan is repaid the Societies are expected to have enough of their own capital to meet the needs of their members.

The members get their loans from the Societies free of interest, and hence will not borrow from the sahukar and the sahukar knows that the members of the Co-operative Society have pledged their property to the Societies, hence lending to the tenants means extraordinary risks in recovery which he is too unwilling to take.

The members of Societies make punctual and full repayments under normal conditions. Partial repayments are made in case of unforeseen calamities, in which case postponement of payment is granted. The membership of Societies has increased from 963 in 1912 to 3,943 in 1933. It is a unique achievement of the movement that no member has ever been expelled, nor any Society has ever been cancelled, except the supply store, which had to be cancelled, along with all such Societies in the Province. Since the beginning of the Movement there has been only one case of embezzlement, and in that, too, no member or office-bearer of the Societies, but a Sub-Inspector was involved. He was dismissed.

The true spirit of Co-operation has had an excellent field for play, and has brought out the best qualities of the people. They have developed many moral virtues, and have certainly become more honest and thrifty, and their love of honest dealings and willingness to discharge their obligations to others have made them more prosperous and grateful to their master. The Co-operative Movement in the estate, with characteristics of its own, owes its origin to the benevolence and enthusiasm of the Sardar, and its success to his vigilance and care. Not only has he helped to foster amongst his tenants all virtues that Co-operation breeds, but has himself shown every indulgence to his tenants, and has willingly foregone all customary privileges that go with his position as the chief of such a big estate. To ensure fair dealings so far as his own claims upon the tenants are concerned, he adopts every precaution. His servants dare not harass his tenants on any account. He allows no extortion and no intimidation. He keeps a list of reliable persons in each village in his estate. Three persons out of this list are elected by the villagers. To this Committee

STATEMENT SHOWING THE PROGRESS

Serial Number	Year	Number of Societies	Kind of Societies	Membership	Working Capital Rs. A. P.
1	1920–21	23	Credit	963	90,201 0 0
2	1927	49	1 Credit Union 35 Credit Societies 12 Arbitration Societies 1 Thrift	3,915	2,53,965 10 3
3	July 1933	49	1 Credit Union 35 Credit Societies 12 Arbitration Societies 1 Thrift	3,943	21,16,133 0 0

Serial Number	Year	Central Bank's Loan Rs. A. P.	Owned Capital	Classification A	Classification B	Classification C	Classification New	On Loan Rs.	Deposits of Members Rs.
1	1920–21	75,603 0 0	6,500	8	11	4	—	81,283	8,098
2	1927	20,41,117 0 0	49,848	3	16	6	10	2,00,000	1,556
3	July 1933	1,17,000 0 0	17,551	3	30	2	—	1,34,252	1,139

N.B.—(1) There is duplication of 1,845 members in Credit and Arbitration Societies, that is, 1,845 members have joined the Credit Societies as well as the Arbitration ones.

(2) There is duplication of Rs. 9,189 in the working capital of the Union and of Credit Societies.

of three are co-opted a servant of the Sardar and the tenant himself. This panchayat moves about from field to field in a village, and by mutual consent settles the Sardar's share in the produce. The Sardar readily redresses any grievance of the tenants that is brought to his notice. The solicitude and benevolence of one man have enriched and sweetened the lives of the residents of a whole estate. I have given this broad outline of the policy of one of the noblest chiefs in the Province, as I remarked in the beginning, in the hope that his example may be followed to the benefit of peasantry and agriculture of the Province by those more or less similarly placed.

CHAPTER XXXVII

AUDIT, SUPERVISION, AND INSPECTION

THE NEED FOR AUDIT AND INSPECTION

We must never forget that in India the average member of a Co-operative Society is illiterate, and, like so many of us, forgetful of his obligations. With all his virtues he cannot be trusted to take up the management of the Society in a business-like manner. Illiteracy combined with the general poverty that prevails, in the interest of successful management of a Society makes it absolutely essential that a constant and vigilant scrutiny of the accounts and general management should be a permanent feature of the movement.

Moreover, in the interest of the investing public, it is absolutely essential that every Society holding other people's money should submit to audit whether Co-operative or not. The Act requires that every Society shall be audited at least once a year by the Registrar, or some person authorized by him.

THE MEANING OF AUDIT

The Maclagan Committee, while explaining the meaning of audit, remark: "The terms of the Act expressly require that the audit shall include an examination of assets and liabilities. By this latter we understand not merely the preparation of the balance-sheets of Societies, but also a sufficient check, in accordance with such rules as the Registrar may lay down, of the list of the material assets of the members.

"The audit should, in our opinion, extend somewhat beyond the bare requirements of the Act, and should embrace an inquiry into all the circumstances which determine the general position of a Society. It would, for instance, be the duty of the auditor to notice any instances in which the Act, rules, or by-laws have been infringed; to verify the cash balance, and certify the correctness of the accounts; to ascertain that loans are made fairly, for proper periods and objects, and on adequate security; to examine repayments in order to check book adjustments or improper extensions; and generally to see that the Society is working on sound lines, and that the Committee, the officers, and the ordinary members understand their duties and responsibilities."

The audit of Primary Credit Societies is "intended in the first instance to assure the Government, through whose agency the Societies were formed, that they are developing on sound lines, and only secondarily for the satisfaction of Central Banks or outside investors, who have entrusted money to the movement, and of the Society members themselves."

The audit is State-controlled, and was in the beginning of the movement personally conducted by the Registrar. As the number of Societies increased the Registrar could not undertake this duty, which then began on his behalf and under his authority to be carried on by other officers. In course of time this function has been taken over by a non-official agency, the Punjab Co-operative Union, Lahore, which performs this function on behalf of the Registrar.

The Department of Co-operation in the Punjab has issued standing instructions to Sub-Inspectors to pay special attention to the following points while auditing the Societies:

(1) The figures in the balance-sheet must be compared with the corresponding items in the ledger; and in the case of the following items the comparison must be made with the cash books as well as with the ledger:

(*a*) Loans due; (*b*) loans overdue; (*c*) shares; (*d*) deposits; (*e*) loans due to the Central Banks or Unions.

(2) The balance-sheet should be explained to the Committee and the general features of the audit note to the members. For this purpose a General Meeting should be held on the evening of the last day of the audit.

(3) Any security held by the Society, e.g. Cash Certificates, as well as Deposit Receipts, should be examined to see if they are in order or in proper custody.

(4) The Society's cash balance should, of course, be verified. If there is any deficit a registered notice of demand should be issued to the person concerned and the case reported forthwith to the Inspector. This procedure should always be followed whenever a deficit is discovered and is not at once made good.

(5) The comparison of pass books with the ledger is of special importance. As many as possible should be compared. This should be done in the presence of the members concerned, who should have their accounts explained to them.

(6) A certain number of sureties should be questioned to ascertain whether they understand the obligations, and to prevent the giving of security becoming a mere formality.

No audit is complete unless some teaching is given. Apart from general Co-operative teaching, the Sub-Inspector should see that the Committee understand:

(*a*) The use of the register *haisiyat* and *quistbandi*.

(*b*) Their responsibility for any loss sustained through acts contrary to the law, the rules, and the by-laws;

(*c*) The importance of prompt action against defaulters;

(*d*) How to fix instalments for repayment, and

(*e*) that misapplied loans should be recalled.

The audit note is sent to the Inspector, and a copy of it is to be given to the Society, which should have a separate file for annual audit notes.

THE COST OF AUDIT

With the growth of Societies the cost of audit and inspection grew into a formidable problem. It was decided in 1914 to take from Societies a voluntary contribution of 5 per cent of their annual profits with a view to covering all future costs of inspection. In 1915 detailed rules concerning the establishment and functions of District Unions were framed.

The scheme of launching into existence the District Unions for taking up audit and inspection had to be given up in view of the preference for a Provincial Co-operative Union as suggested by the Committee on Co-operation.

The Committee made the following observations on this behalf:

"The original audit of Primary Societies should in our opinion be carried out by a staff maintained by Co-operative institutions themselves. We deprecate the creation of a new Government agency on a large scale to carry out audit, both because it is undesirable to let loose in increasing numbers a new set of Government officials on the villages, and because the officialization of the work might breed a sense of hostility towards audit generally on the part of the Societies. The staff would indeed be empowered by the Registrar under the Act to undertake audit work, and would remain under his ultimate control; but the appointment, transfer, and dismissal of all auditors should as far as possible be made in accordance with the recommendations of Co-operative institutions, and the pay of the staff should be provided by the movement and not by the Government. Where the Government already finances this staff in whole or in part, its aid may be withdrawn gradually. As long as the pay offered is adequate and the staff such as the Registrar can rely on, we would leave it to each Province to decide in what manner the various Central Banks, Unions, and Societies should combine to entertain the auditors required.

"A common stumbling-block, however, in the case of small and local establishments is the stagnation of promotion and want of prospects, and this can only be avoided by the formation of an audit union for the whole Province, such as has been started in the Central Provinces, by means of which the auditing staff is brought into one cadre under the control of the Registrar. Where this or some similar system is adopted, the cost of its maintenance can be met either (*a*) by a levy *per capita* on all members of Primary Societies, or (*b*) by the distribution of the cost over Societies and Central Banks on the basis of working capital, or (*c*) by a similar distribution on the basis of net profits, or (*d*) by a corresponding rise in the rate of interest.

"In whatever way the money is raised, the system of an audit union on the lines suggested is one capable of development as time goes on. As Societies prove themselves fit to take affairs more and more into their own hands, the degree of control exercised by the Registrar over the non-Governmental staff can gradually be relaxed until ultimately the entire work of making the original audit devolves on the Societies themselves, whose representatives would then be able not only to receive the audit reports, but also to take action on them. That time, however, is still distant."

THE PUNJAB PROVINCIAL CO-OPERATIVE UNION

The Punjab Co-operative Union, after its by-laws had been approved by the Government, came into existence in 1918. By 1920 the Co-operative Union had affiliated twenty-five Central Banks, twenty-three Banking Unions, and forty-six Supply Unions. "The Union wanted to gradually evolve audit, supply, and banking into three definite branches, the last two of which it was proposed to separate into a Co-operative Wholesale Society and a Provincial Bank."

The Union derived its income from the Audit Fund. It consisted of the 5 per cent voluntary contribution out of the annual profits of Primary Societies. This 5 per cent charge was raised to 7½ per cent in 1920. The Central Banks and Banking Unions as well agreed to contribute towards the audit fund. But this voluntary contribution was felt likely to fall short of the requirements of the Union, hence new model by-laws bound "the Societies to pay such fee for audit as the Punjab Co-operative Union may from time to time prescribe." The Union soon realized that even after raising its levy to 7½ instead of 5 per cent it could not meet its growing expenses. In spite of a rise in the contribution the income of the Union did not show much increase, as the profits of the Primary Societies were not rising with any rapidity because (*a*) profits of new Societies in the beginning are very low, and the number of new Societies then was very large, (*b*) old Societies by reducing the rate of interest on their loans were reducing their profits, (*c*) with the repayment of share money after ten years one source of profit disappears. The Union found itself faced with a financial difficulty in 1921, when the number of Sub-Inspectors, whose services were required, was more than the inadequate resources of the Union could maintain. The Union resolved upon three courses of action to meet this financial difficulty. The proposal to approach District Boards in the Province with a view to enlisting their financial support fell through because of the Financial Commissioners' disapproval of it. An appeal was issued to the co-operators, but this on account of the adverse conditions then prevailing did not meet with much success. The appeal brought in Rs. 61,000 in two years. The third course consisted in making a request to the Government for grant-in-aid. The financial stringency was felt so acutely that the Registrar recorded the following, as a shadow of coming events, no doubt: "The scheme whereby Societies contribute 7½ per cent of their annual profits will probably have to be altered, as sufficient income is not forthcoming. It may be found advisable to adopt the plan in vogue in other Provinces, of levying a rate on the working capital."

"A new by-law of the Union passed in 1922 provided against any decrease in the audit fee payable by Societies, if they reduced their net profits by lowering the rate of interest on loans advanced to the members." The audit fee from Societies was raised from 7½ per cent to 10 per cent in 1928, and that high charge on the net profits of a Society still continues.

The Union employs seventy Sub-Inspectors doing audit and supervision, and one hundred and eighty-eight doing audit.

The audit of a Primary Society is undertaken by the Sub-Inspector in the first instance, and wherever possible a second audit is done by the Inspector.

SUPERVISION AND INSPECTION

There has been a good deal of confusion about the functions of audit, supervision, and inspection. Audit at present is undertaken on behalf of the Registrar by Provincial Co-operative Unions, but there is still a confusion as to the institution with which responsibility for supervision and inspection should lie. Concerning the discharge of these three functions there does not exist any uniformity in practice. In some parts of India two agencies handle these three functions, and in some provinces these functions have been clearly taken up each by a separate agency, while in Baroda all the three functions are discharged by the Co-operative Department.

There is nothing corresponding to internal supervision of Societies in India. Supervision and inspection were carried on by Co-operative institutions in the early stages of the movement. As a matter of fact, audit, supervision, and inspection were all combined in the very elementary stages of the movement when Central Banks either did not exist in sufficient numbers or could not afford adequate and competent staff to undertake supervision and inspection. Bombay was first to distinguish between these two functions by entrusting supervision to Local Unions and inspection to Financing Banks. Audit and supervision in the Punjab is undertaken by Sub-Inspectors of the Co-operative Union. There were in 1933, employed by the Punjab Co-operative Union, seventy Sub-Inspectors for audit and supervision, 348 for supervision alone, and 188 for audit only.

THE NECESSITY OF SUPERVISION

The one dominant cause of the failure of Co-operative Societies all over the country has been the lack of adequate supervision. The first requisite of registration is an assurance to the effect that members have understood the theory of Co-operation and the broad outlines of the working of a Co-operative Society. The universal illiteracy of the rural population renders such an expectation exceedingly doubtful. It is hard to find persons with requisite education to work as office-bearers of a Society. It is therefore of the utmost importance that there should be permanent and effective arrangements for supervising the working of Societies.

The successful working of a Society requires a grounding in the principles and methods of Co-operation and elementary banking. However simple at first it might appear, like so many professions the running of a Society needs some practical training. In a country where members are illiterate and office-bearers have had only an elementary education of a very doubtful utility, the necessity of supervision is patent and perpetual. Since the failure of a large number of Societies is directly attributable to the neglect of instruction at the commencement and subsequent slackness in supervision, it is now accepted as an established principle that organization of Societies should never be taken up at a place where properly trained supervision is not available.

MEANING OF SUPERVISION

The Committee on Co-operation describes supervision as follows:

"The work of supervision covers many of the points which have already been included in audit, but in addition it implies the duty of instructing the members in Co-operative principles and the propagation of the movement by the organization of new Societies. Even where it covers the same ground as audit, however, it differs from it in that it aims not merely at testing it to be efficient, and it comprehends the further task of seeing that defects noted at audit have been remedied. The supervisor is concerned to see that the work of the Society is not only business-like and up to date, but genuinely Co-operative. While satisfying himself that the accounts are in good order, and that business is being conducted regularly and prudently, he would refrain from verifying the figures in detail, and would set himself to test the knowledge of the Committee and members, to advise them with regard to difficulties and disputes, to explain and remedy mistakes, and to impress upon them the principles which Societies should always have before them. These functions should in our opinion rightly devolve on the Co-operative institutions themselves." Supervision is a continuous duty. It seeks to make Societies the exact personifications of the principles of the movement. It is the supervisors' duty to ascertain that the members have assimilated the principles of the movement, that the office-bearers have a knowledge of their work, that the provisions of the Act, rules, and by-laws are strictly enforced, that meetings are held at the proper time and business is transacted with a quorum, that all papers are taken care of and books are kept in good order, and that entries in books are made at the proper time. The supervisor is to remain in close and constant touch with the Society so as to insure a parental solicitude for and guidance to the Society which will in due course enable it to grow in that strength and wisdom which makes an independent successful life possible.

The Committee on Co-operation suggested that the expression "inspection" and "inquiry" should be utilized exclusively for the special and occasional operations contemplated by Sections 35 and 36 of the Act. But in actual practice the term inspection has come to denote a definite function allied to supervision and audit. Inspection is an occasional process which seeks to find out whether the Society is working efficiently and properly. In the case of a Credit Society the Inspector is to ascertain that the credit of every borrower has been properly assessed, that loans are covered by sufficient assets, that no undue preference is shown to any borrowers, that receipts and payments are duly forecast, that recoveries are made in time, etc. Inspection is now a recognized function of the Financing Banks.

SEPARATION OF AUDIT AND SUPERVISION

As an experimental measure, it was proposed in 1926 to separate audit from supervision. By such a measure it was sought to secure a more skilled examination of the accounts besides dislodging all suspicions concerning an audit performed by a person who is in a way his own judge. It was hoped, therefore, that besides improved audit it would be possible to detect more readily errors and misconduct of the Sub-Inspector.

The General Meeting of the Union, with the approval of the Registrar, decided to launch the experiment. The experiment extended to three-quarters of the Province in 1930, and, as the Registrar puts it, was "generally regarded as an improvement." In 1931 we were told that the functions of audit and supervision had been separated in over 80 per cent of the Societies. "In most of the areas," the Report for 1931

AUDIT AND INSPECTION OF SOCIETIES

	1934	1933	1932	1931	1930	1929
Due for audit ..	20,477	20,017	19,955	19,736	19,061	17,852
Not audited ..	97	49	105	153	114	125
Inspected by Inspectors ..	19,050	18,755	18,611	18,808	17,500	—
Not inspected for two years ..	—	33	18	15	7	12
Re-audited by Inspectors ..	1,453	1,509	1,492	1,513	1,514	—

tells us, "where separation has not taken place, the backward condition of the region, the number of Societies, and the large areas concerned make separation unsuitable."

The very next year the annual Report springs upon us a new discovery, which has in places necessitated reversion to the combination of functions. "The separation of the functions of audit and supervision, which now covers over four-fifths of the Province, has been maintained as before. A considerable body of opinion is, however, now veering round to the conclusion that the disadvantages attending such separation are greater than the undoubted advantages attaching to it. Under the old system the interest of the Sub-Inspectors was, or would be, fully engaged in all aspects of a Society's work: with separation a measure of intimacy is lost, though the efficacy of audit is strengthened. There have been odd reversions to the old system in circumscribed areas where the volume of work threatened to be too heavy for the existing staff to cope with."

The table indicates that the audit in recent years has been at least so far as numbers are concerned carried out quite adequately. The number of Societies not audited is negligible. For this negligible number of Societies not audited there are valid reasons. Consolidation Societies are not audited because there is nothing to be audited in those Societies. In some cases the Societies could not be audited as their books had been lodged in court in connection with civil or criminal cases. In a few cases there could be no audit of Societies because the books had been "made away with by peccant officers of the Society."

RECOMMENDATIONS OF THE CENTRAL BANKING ENQUIRY COMMITTEE ON AUDIT, SUPERVISION, AND INSPECTION OF SOCIETIES

"Audit, supervision, and inspection of Societies, which are closely allied functions, are now vested in two, and sometimes in three, different agencies, resulting in much overlapping of work and waste of effort and money. After a full consideration of these points, and of the efficiency of the auditing system in European countries like Germany and Austria, we recommend that for the due discharge of the statutory functions of audit special district Unions should be formed to carry out audit, supervision, and inspection of the Societies. The district need not necessarily be an administrative (revenue) district, but it may be an area with a conveniently manageable number of Societies which can be affiliated to the District Union.

"These Unions must be registered under the Co-operative Societies Act, and formed of the Co-operative Societies (Primary, Central, Credit, and Non-Credit) in the area of the District Union. The representation of Societies would ensure local touch and non-official initiative and enterprise. The registration may be withdrawn in case the Union does not discharge its duties properly. The staff employed by the Union shall be recruited from persons certified or licensed by the Registrar, and the licence of an employee shall be liable to be withdrawn by the Registrar for sufficient cause. There must, however, be no interference by the Registrar in the internal management of such a Union.

"There may be specially trained Government officials on the Board of these Unions, which shall consist otherwise of the representatives of the affiliated Societies, and Government officials may also be deputed to serve on their staff. The Staff of these Unions should however be employed and paid for by the Unions. Besides audit, supervision, and inspection of the affiliated Societies, these Unions should also provide practical training to candidates for recruitment to the audit, supervision, and inspection staff of the Co-operative movement. The general work of Co-operative education and propaganda, organization of Co-operative Societies, and expanding the movement should be done by the Provincial Co-operative Institutes. The staff of the Co-operative organizations should consist of men thoroughly trained from bottom to top. It should be a rule that no auditor, supervisor, inspector, or higher officer of a Union shall be employed without having passed the prescribed tests and through a prescribed apprenticeship. There should be close connection between the auditing Union and the Central Banks concerned, by interchange of important reports and statements on Primary Societies, leaving the Central Banks to make such arrangements only for inspection as may be necessary to safeguard their financial interests, such inspection being not only the responsibility but also the duty of the Central Banks.

"The District Unions may be federated into a separate provincial (Apex) Union, or may be affiliated to the existing Provincial Co-operative Institutes as a special branch thereof according to local conditions.

"In the Punjab and in Bihar and Orissa the Provincial Institute employs all the audit staff which works under Government control. The Staff of the Apex Union or the audit branch of the Provincial Institute shall be non-official employees of the Union or Institute. The licensing of the staff by the Registrar shall be on the same lines as for the District Union. The District Unions and the Provincial Co-operative Bank shall be represented on the management.

"The main tasks of the Provincial Union or the audit branch of the Provincial Institute shall be (*a*) supervision of District Unions, (*b*) audit of Central Banks and other Central Associations, and (*c*) audit of Provincial Banks, Provincial Institutes, and other Provincial Co-operative organizations, such as the Provincial Land Mortgage Corporation.

"The expenses of audit of District Unions and of the Provincial Union, or audit branch of the Provincial Institute, shall be met from the contributions of the affiliated Societies (Primary and Central) and subsidies from the Government, which should be pooled to form the resources of the Provincial Union or audit branch of the Provincial Institute."

CLASSIFICATION OF SOCIETIES

With a view to ascertaining the standard of working of Societies, classification of Societies was taken up first in 1916. The Report for that year records: "During the year a beginning has been made in classifying Societies according to their merits: relegation to the lowest or D class will practically amount to a threat of liquidation, and if at the next annual inspection no improvement is shown, it is intended that these shall be wound up. This will result in a temporary increase in the number of Societies under liquidation, but the steady elimination of the failures will not only raise the general standard, but will enable the staff to devote more time to those for whose ultimate success there is a greater hope."

Societies have been classified as A, B, C, and D according to the measure of success and independence with which they are conducted. An A class Society is independent of all external help, either from the official staff or the staff of the Punjab Co-operative Union, and is merely audited. A B class Society must keep its own accounts, prepare its crop demands, loan applications, and arbitration references, recover its own dues, and enforce its own awards against defaulters, and is expected to perform these functions with the mere advice and general

CLASSIFICATION OF AGRICULTURAL CREDIT SOCIETIES IN THE PUNJAB

(*Percentage*)

Class	1917	1918	1919	1920	1921	1922
A	9	11·5	11	13	13	10·5
B	28	33·8	36·5	40	41	36·5
C	40	38·5	38	35	38	45·5
D	23	16·2	14·5	12	8	7·5
Class	**1923**	**1924**	**1925**	**1926**	**1927**	**1928**
A	7·2	6·2	6	4·25	3	2·1
B	31	31·3	30·5	26·25	22·6	18·6
C	54·2	55	56	62	70·25	73·6
D	7·6	7·1	7·5	7·5	4·15	5·5
Class	**1929**	**1930**	**1931**	**1932**	**1933**	
A	2·02	2·05	1·9	1·8	1·9	
B	16·6	15·08	13·2	11·4	10·79	
C	75·3	76·6	76·3	76·4	76·1	
D	5·9	6·2	8·5	10·3	11·19	

encouragement of the staff. A C class Society is one which cannot perform these functions without the help of the Sub-Inspector. It is in fact in various stages of tutelage. It is a bad Society capable of improvement. A D class Society is the last thing tolerable. It exists in various stages of decay. It is virtually on the margin of liquidation, from which process it is proposed to save it with the utmost care and exceptional treatment if it be possible.

The classification of Societies is a very sure indication of the success of the movement, provided it is not itself based upon low standards of work and indulgent optimism of the classifier.

The schedule on page 396 compiled from the annual reports, not without considerable mathematical performances on account of lack of uniformity in the method of its expression adopted by the Department, indicates the various phases of this aspect of the movement.

We have to remember here that all Societies were not classified each year. The number of Societies left unclassified was, however, never large. The Registrar, while attributing the deterioration of Societies to stricter classification, wrote in 1928 as follows:

"My impression is that the rapid advance of the last three or four years has led to some deterioration of quality in the older Societies. The present policy of consolidation and less rapid advance will, I hope, arrest this." Since 1928 the deterioration has been abnormally high owing to the effect of the recent depression.

The Report for 1934 records: "The continuance of the depression has had the inevitable effect of pushing more Societies into the lowest class. Percentage of A and B Societies to the whole is now 12½. . . ."

CHAPTER XXXVIII

EXECUTION OF AWARDS UNIONS

THE Co-operative Agricultural Credit Society monopolized the attention of the early organizers of the movement in India. Even now the Agricultural Credit Society dominates the field, and perhaps rightly so. Unfortunately the Punjab peasant even now to all outward seeming looks upon the Society as a cheap money-lending agency. A member of a Co-operative Society, according to the principles of the movement, is to be a man of character, in the widest sense possible. In India the movement had mainly to depend upon the moralizing influence of its own growth upon the members. That hope has been amply justified. The movement still exercises that influence over the members who secure admission to the Society even as a cheap money-lending concern. The members of a Credit Society, therefore, in some cases do, for reasons sound and unsound in regard to payment of loans, take up an attitude which only suits a sahukar to tolerate, or even to encourage.

The problem of default by members of a Credit Society made its appearance in 1911, when a few suits had to be filed against certain members who had, in accordance with the guiding principles of the movement, been turned out of one or two banks undergoing the process of reorganization on a firmer basis. Within a couple of years after this it became evident that default by members of a Credit Society was growing more frequent. Both the Societies and the Department, being new to the task, as well as in their anxiety to avoid getting a bad name, sought the assistance of the Inspectors, and occasionally of the Deputy Commissioners, to make the recalcitrant members realize the desirability of paying the dues of the Society. It was felt that moral pressure and persuasion by the members of the Society had in cases proved of no avail. Arguments with money-lenders and defaulters can possibly have little effect. A solitary defaulter, whom nothing else could move, had to be sued for the recovery of a loan in a court of law. The Report for 1914 tells us that a few Societies had been obliged to sue recalcitrant members for advances made to them.

By 1915 default and the necessity for proceeding against defaulters became a permanent feature of the working of Societies. The need for arbitration was felt on account of a colossal waste of time of the representatives as well as of the funds of the Societies. But perhaps more than this, it was the hostile attitude of the Munsifs and their subordinates which the Co-operators wanted to escape. That attitude unfortunately continues even after the coming in of arbitration procedure. An idea of the waste of time and funds of the Societies may be formed from the fact that in 1933 nearly 23,000 cases were referred to arbitration, which means such a large number of representatives of the Societies would, in the absence of arbitration, have to waste their time in attending courts, the attitude of which is still far from fair, and a description of the nature and extent of which appears in the chapter on "Opposition." It was felt that moral force at the command of Societies should in all cases be used in a more effective way. Arbitration outside a court of law, in the first instance, was the remedy suggested, and adopted. In 1915 fifty-five applications were admitted for arbitration. The number of defaulters increased so heavily in 1916 that 1,000 cases were referred to arbitration. The arbitrators were then frequently able to secure payment; because when an award was given it was not hastily taken to court, since it was the practice to allow the defaulters time to pay up. Sometimes the arbitrator would yield to the prayers of the debtor and grant postponement of a decision till the next harvest. That the claims of the Societies were always genuine is borne out by the fact that in 1917 out of a total of 7,540 awards only one was given against the Societies, presumably because of some technical mistake in procedure or account-keeping. In the year 1917 13,000 people were proceeded against for the recovery of a total sum of Rs. 16,80,000. Nearly 2,800 awards had to be filed in courts.

"Arbitration" authorizes the Registrar or his nominee on his behalf to decide the disputes arising between the Societies and their members. This means avoidance of a stupendous waste of time and money. But the decision of an arbitrator becomes effective only when it has been ratified by a court of law. Working of arbitration for a whole decade suggested that the Societies were reluctant to take the awards to courts for the realization of their dues. Not only that. In the beginning even remarkable unwillingness to initiate proceedings against defaulters was observable. This unwillingness is born of a feeling of pity for the neighbours and the disinclination to file awards in courts is due, in the words of the Registrar, "to the vexatious proceedings or absence of proceedings in court."

Within a decade of its initiation, the difficulties in the way of arbitration rendered this right practically of no importance. In 1932 over 12,000 awards had to be taken to the courts. If arbitration pure and simple were to be resorted to over 12,000 representatives of the Societies would have to attend the courts, with all discomforts, besides the huge expenses that such a procedure involves. Representatives of the Societies dreaded attending the courts; for, besides waste of their own time, their ignorance of law and procedure, especially with hostile sub-judges, would make the whole task unpleasant for them. The work of the representatives of Societies suffered from the following defects:

(1) No reliable record of the case for ready reference;

(2) Imperfect account-keeping;

(3) Reliable statistics could not be produced at inspection;

(4) Chances of dishonesty due to lack of proper audit;

(5) Chances of the officers of the Department remaining ignorant of this aspect of the movement in absence of regular accounts on this behalf;

(6) A colossal waste of time and money. Sometimes the Societies got so seriously involved in litigation with their

members that all constructive work suffered heavily, and cases had to be taken to the High Court;

(7) The representatives of the Societies were subjected to innumerable and uncalled-for sufferings by the petty officials of the Judicial Department as described in the various annual reports of the Department.

The defects and difficulties grew quite grave within a decade of the start of arbitration. In 1925 the co-operators of the Province realized the futility of individual effort in this direction, and the necessity for collective action forced itself upon their notice. Although, as the Report for 1929 puts it, "according to the strictest principles they should not perhaps exist, but as things are, they are a useful concession to weakness," yet their existence is a positive proof of the imagination and adaptability possessed by the Punjab co-operators.

The first Co-operative Union for the Execution of Awards was established at Dinga, District Gujrat, in 1925. Lyallpur followed next year, and thus a beginning was made. The first mention of such Unions was made in the Annual Report for 1928. "Most Districts have organized, or are organizing, Co-operative Unions for executing the awards of their member Societies." By 1929 their number went up to twenty-one, and in 1932 it was thirty-four.

THEIR WORKING AND DIFFICULTIES

The Report for 1928 tells us that these Unions are unquestionably useful, for the execution of awards requires a knowledge of legal procedure which is beyond the Committee of an ordinary Society. The Report for 1931 observes: "They are of varying qualities, for it is naturally difficult to get good superintendents and bailiffs, and the work of execution, never quickly done, drags on and on. One of their chief difficulties, that of providing themselves with funds to carry on with, has been solved by the grant to them of loans without interest by central institutions in whose interest they are working. The overhauling of the whole system of recovery through execution has begun to be considered. The Report for 1932 makes brief but pointed reference in the following words: "Of these Unions it is doubtful if more than half a dozen are working satisfactorily. Everywhere there is the same difficulty of finding reliable superintendents and agents, and the same complaint of malpractices and lack of co-operation of bailiffs." Many of the old defects and difficulties are still there, and the Department has still to exercise an anxious watch over those connected with this work. These Unions have now acquired a notoriety, and the member Societies do not quite like the hardships in which the execution of awards involves their neighbours. It is significant that in 1933 over 2,500 awards could not be taken to the courts by the Unions because of the Societies being unable to pay the necessary expenses. The Department, as well, is inclined to send an award to a court of law only in the last resort. When the award has actually been sent to a Union, the interest of the superintendents and assistant superintendents lies in having the award executed through a court of law.

OBJECTS OF THE UNION

The objects of the Union are:

(1) To promote the economic interests of its members, and more particularly to execute arbitration awards on behalf of Co-operative Societies, especially member Societies, and thus to save them from unnecessary expense and trouble;

(2) To perform liquidation work entrusted to it.

Membership of the Union consists of Societies, and such individuals who join with a desire to serve the Unions as Honorary Secretary or Joint Secretary, or in any other way. Members have to pay an admission fee of R. 1.

A Union for Execution of Awards undertakes through its officers to take awards to the courts, and after getting these ratified to have the decreed amounts realized.

The amounts realized are credited to the accounts of the member Society. A Society applying for membership of the Union sends along with such application a letter of authority for the Union on its behalf. The Union is thus authorized to file, defend, or compromise a suit, or get the decree executed on behalf of the Society. A Society pays a sum of Rs. 5 as an advance for expenses of the case for every award that it sends to the Union. It undertakes as well to meet all expenses incurred by a Union during the pendency of all such cases. A member Society also pays to the Union a specified rate of commission, usually 5 per cent, on recoveries. The rate of commission to be thus paid is decided upon by the arbitrator while giving the award, and is subject to the approval of the Registrar.

A Union often employs a clerk, a superintendent, and an execution officer. The officers defend the cases and arrange to have the decrees realized. If the funds of a Union permit, it borrows the services of a bailiff from the judicial Department with a view to facilitating the realization of awards. But the salary of such a bailiff has to be paid in advance. These mighty little bailiffs have in their own interests set at naught the efforts of a beneficent Department. A detailed account of their misdeeds appears in the chapter headed "Opposition."

A word about the arbitrator is essential in this connection. Whenever a dispute arises between a Society and any of its members, the Society applies for arbitration. The Registrar appoints an arbitrator. The debtor appoints one man as his representative, and the Society nominates its own representative. All papers and books concerning the dispute are placed before the arbitrator, whose business it is to see that no mistake has been committed, or no deliberate fraud has been practised. The arbitrator announces his award, against which an appeal lies with the Registrar, within one month of its announcement. If the debtor honouring the award pays the amount due, that is the end of it. If the debtor refuses to abide by this award, anyone, even a non-member, may be authorized by the Society to take the award as an attorney to a court of law. Arbitrators are usually appointed every year by the Department. An arbitrator has similar power as a court of law. The award cannot be questioned by a court of law, which is required to ratify it so as to give it the status of a legal decree.

If, however, the Court is convinced that the arbitrator has for one reason or another made a serious mistake in giving the award, it is authorized to return the award for reconsideration.

The Unions now are experiencing the same difficulties as did the individuals at the hands of the courts in the pre-Union days. A good deal of such complaints is bound to disappear with the advent of the new era in the judicial life of the Province. The Chief Justice of the Province, the Honourable Sir Justice Douglas Young, has set himself to eradicate the evil of corruption and all vexations caused to the public in general by the ever-exacting subordinate staff of the Judicial Department. Another grievance of the Unions against the courts in the Province concerns the payments made by a Union. The Union pays the usual court fees when it institutes awards in the court. The payments thus made include remuneration for the services of bailiffs. But if the volume of work requires the services of a whole-time bailiff exclusively for the work carried on by the Union the bailiff's salary has to be paid by the Union in full, and in advance into the bargain, the rest of the charges standing unabated. Surely there is an element of double charge which can easily be avoided. The Department of Co-operation once applied for permission to appoint their own bailiffs wherever the volume of work made it necessary. The High Court did not see its way to granting this request.

The volume of work handled by these Unions is increasing, and the interests of this Department deserve a more sympathetic consideration. The Department would gain substantially by some well-deserved concessions the High Court may deem fit to grant. In certain places the volume of work and the need for speedy justice necessitates the appointment of honorary or special sub-judges.

A NEW LINE OF WORK

Nearly all Execution Unions pay their employees 3½ per cent commission on recoveries; 1½ per cent is spent in meeting other expenses of the Unions. This system of payment, it is believed, acts as a stimulus to the workers of the Union. Unfortunately the best hopes of the originators of the Unions have not been realized. A new scheme for the working of the Unions is under contemplation. Nay, the scheme has been already put into operation in the Attock District as an experimental measure. Under this scheme the execution work is to be entrusted directly to the executive branch of the Department.

Each Sub-Inspector is to be a Superintendent of Execution for his jurisdiction. A Court Inspector will be responsible for instituting and conducting cases in courts. The Sub-Inspector, with the help of a bailiff, will be required to perform the duties now assigned to Execution Clerk. Such a scheme is fraught with dangers, and is likely to react upon the already diminishing popularity of the Department. Why should not more attention be paid towards nipping the evil in the bud? Why not find out the causes of default and remedy the defects in the working of Societies?

CHAPTER XXXIX

LIQUIDATION

LIQUIDATION connotes the winding-up or dissolution of a Society or firm by settling with the debtors and creditors and apportioning the assets towards the payment of liabilities. Each shareholder thus knows what profits he is entitled to or what amount he is to make good.

A Society can only be brought under liquidation if its registration has been cancelled by the Registrar under Section 39 or 40 of the Act. The Registrar will only cancel registration under Section 39 if he is of the opinion that the Society ought to be dissolved. Under Section 41 of the Act, on cancellation a Society ceases to be a body corporate and the attribute of a separate entity from the individual members composing it, which it had acquired under Section 18 of the Act, vanishes. The Society loses its privilege of settlement of disputes through arbitration, and becomes amenable to stamp duty, registration fee, and assessable to income tax. Prior claim for the recovery of certain debts from its members cannot stand, and the entire shares and interest of members in the capital of the Society become attachable. The Registrar is not bound to liquidate every Society which he cancels. For a number of reasons he may decide not to appoint a liquidator. If a Society has paid all its liabilities, and there are competent members in it who can take care of themselves, then such a Society may continue to exist as an unregistered body. A liquidator is generally appointed to safeguard the members from the evil effects of liquidation in civil courts.

In Bombay and Burma the order of winding-up may precede the cancellation of a Society. In that case the Society retains the privileges during the winding-up stage.

CANCELLATION OF A SOCIETY

Cancellation of a Co-operative Society may take place:

(1) As a result of an inspection of the Society by the Registrar made of his own motion;

(2) As a result of an inspection made at the instance of the collector;

(3) As a result of an application by the Committee or one-third of the members;

(4) On the Society proving to be unable to pay its debts;

(5) At the request of three-fourths of its members; and

(6) On its membership declining below ten.

The Registrar could exercise his power of cancellation:

(*a*) On proof that a certificate of registration has been obtained by mistake or fraud;

(*b*) On proof that a Society exists for an illegal purpose;

(*c*) On proof that a Society has violated any of the provisions of the Act, such as persistent lending to non-members;

(*d*) When it has ceased to exist (if it does not commence business for a year);

(*e*) On the proof that there is no hope of eventual solvency or progress. It is desirable that the Registrar should exercise his power of cancellation in the following cases as well:

(*f*) For indulgence in activities other than Co-operative and economic;

(*g*) When the Society is merely a one-man show;

(*h*) When overdues are mounting up and there is little hope of recovery except through coercion;

(*j*) When well-to-do non-borrowing members are retiring in order to escape the effects of liability;

(*k*) When office-bearers have embezzled or misappropriated considerable sums and are about to alienate their effects;

(*l*) A D class Society, when it shows no improvement for two years.

THE POWERS AND FUNCTIONS OF A LIQUIDATOR

Where the registration of a Society is cancelled under Section 39 or Section 40, the Registrar may appoint a competent person to act as liquidator of the Society.

A liquidator so appointed enjoys the following powers:

(1) If necessary, the liquidator may institute suits for the recovery of sums due to the Society. This he shall do on behalf of the Society by his name of office.

(2) The liquidator shall proceed to determine the assets and liabilities of the Society as they stood at the time of the cancellation of its registration, and shall determine the contributions to be made by the members and past members, respectively, to the assets of the Society. He shall also determine by what persons and in what proportions the costs of liquidation are to be borne.

(3) The liquidator shall investigate all claims against the Society, and subject to the provisions of the Act shall decide questions of priority arising between claimants.

(4) The liquidator is entitled to issue a summons to any person whose attendance is required either to give evidence or to produce documents. He may compel the attendance of any person by issue of a warrant for his arrest through the civil court exercising jurisdiction in the area in which the Society operates.

(5) The liquidator sends all such processes for service to the civil court having jurisdiction in the area in which service is effected. The court shall proceed as if such processes had been issued by it, and shall return them to the liquidator with a report of service.

(6) The liquidator shall make an order noting the names of members and past members of the Society and the amounts to be realized from each as contribution under clause (*b*), Sub-section (2) of Section 42, and as costs of liquidation under clause (*d*) of the same sub-section. This order shall be submitted to the Registrar for his approval, and he may modify it or refer it back to the liquidator for further inquiry or other action.

(7) A copy of the order as finally approved by the Registrar, accompanied if necessary by a list of the property of each member or past member against whom the decree has to be enforced, shall be filed in the civil court having local jurisdiction to be enforced as laid down in clause (*a*), Sub-section (5) of Section 42.

(8) If the civil court is unable to recover the sum assessed against any member or members, the liquidator may frame a subsidiary order or orders against any other member or members to the extent of the liability of each for debts of the Society until the whole amount due from the members is recovered, and these orders shall be executed in the same way.

A liquidator is no permanent member of the Department. He is appointed by the Registrar when the services of a liquidator are needed. By a recent notification of the Department a liquidator is required to furnish a security of Rs. 2,000. He is not paid any fixed salary, but payment is made to him on commission basis ranging from 5 to 10 per cent. Usually he is paid 5–10 per cent on an ascending scale on the basis of recovery.

On cancelling the registration of a Society the Registrar may publish, in such manner as he thinks proper, a notice requiring claims against the Society to be submitted within one month to him or to such person as he may name as liquidator. All liabilities recorded in the books of any Society shall be deemed *ipso facto* to have been duly notified.

When the Registration of a Society is cancelled, the Society ceases to exist as a corporate body:

(*a*) In the case of cancellation in accordance with the provisions of Section 39, from the date the order of cancellation takes effect; (*b*) in the case of cancellation in accordance with the provisions of Section 40, from the date of the order. On cancellation a Society forfeits all its rights and privileges under the Act and the rules. Shares become liable to attachment, and the members become liable to immediate repayment of the debts they owe to the Society.

When the registration of a Society is cancelled under Section 40 of the Act, or when no appeal is preferred against the order of cancellation passed under Clause 2 of Section 39 of the Act, or where such an appeal has been dismissed, the liquidator shall forthwith take charge of the books, cash balance, and other property of the Society. This implies that a liquidator cannot take charge of a Society's books and assets before the time allowed for appeal has expired or the appeal has been rejected.

In practice this procedure creates a good deal of difficulty. The opinion in the Department favours the appointment of a liquidator immediately a Society is cancelled so that the time taken by the appeal is not utilized by the members in destroying the books of the Society or misusing the cash. I feel the difficulty could be avoided by empowering the Inspector to take charge of the books and cash of the Society, which he may hand over to the liquidator when one is appointed.

That the possibility of destroying the books of the Society or the refusal to hand them over to the liquidator is genuine is borne out by facts. This happened at Kalay Wali in the Sialkot District, where the Treasurer, who was in charge of the books, backed by the members of the Committee, refused to produce the books, and was convicted for one year when he was prosecuted by the Department.

THE MANNER OF MEETING THE CLAIMS

The liquidator, on assuming charge of the books, adds up the interest to each principal borrowed by the Society, and the total thus arrived at is henceforward treated as the principal borrowed.

The first charge on recoveries made by the liquidator comprises the expenses of liquidation, the liquidator's fees, and the audit fees. The claims against the Society are then met in the following order:

(1) Dues of such creditors as have advanced to the Society on some security;

(2) The principal payable to all creditors;

(3) The interest payable to all creditors;

(4) The share money of the members will be returned.

The rest of the amount recovered may be spent according to needs, but all these creditors will be paid in proportion to the total due to them, and each one of them will be paid his share in full before the next in order is paid.

DIFFICULTIES IN LIQUIDATION PROCESS

The following difficulties have been experienced in the liquidation of Societies:

(1) *Delays.*—Liquidation is not a simple process. Different forms of litigation, such as insolvency of members or mere indifference of the court, may hold up proceedings for long periods. At one place one court wanted four months' time for serving an ordinary summons sent by a liquidator. In one case a legal practitioner, acting on behalf of the liquidator, received certain payments, but did not file the suit in court. As many as fifty-one cases of his neglect were brought before the court of inquiry, but no action was taken against him. In 1925 it was found that sixty cases had been dragging on for four years or more. In some cases liquidation could not be completed even in ten years.

(2) *A Vain Attempt.*—In some cases liquidation is resorted to at a stage at which realizations have been rendered well-nigh impossible. Some cases present exceptional difficulties. In 1928 it was found that the Hoshiarpur Union had liabilities amounting to Rs. 22,960, and almost no assets. Another Society consisted mainly of professional beggars, who managed to avoid every warrant of arrest.

(3) *Dishonesty of Liquidators.*—It is exceedingly unfortunate that liquidators sometimes show a remarkable lack of honesty. Many liquidators have had to be removed. Some of them even go to the extent of refusing to hand over the books and accounts. In 1931 one liquidator, who was wanted on a charge of dishonesty, absconded with most of the books of the Society. The number of liquidators guilty of dishonesty is as follows:

1928	1929	1931	1932	1933	1934
6	9	3	4	7	3

Now that the Department demands from every liquidator Rs. 2,000 by way of security, it is hoped cases of dishonesty that defy even the authority of the Department will be rare. Liquidators have been known to squeeze money out of the members of a Society on grounds of partiality in apportioning contributions.

CONCERTED OPPOSITION AND CRIMINAL RESISTANCE

Members combine not only to give no information concerning the custody of books, but do sometimes adopt a criminally aggressive attitude. The following instances will illustrate the point. In 1925 one liquidator was assaulted and badly wounded. His assailants were sent to jail for two years. In the same year an Inspector had to use his pistol in order to protect the liquidator from assault. In yet another case in the same year prosecution for assault on the liquidator had to be instituted. In 1930 an Inspector and his party who went to a village for attachment of property were attacked. Three of the culprits were sent to jail for a year. In the same year and in the same district, Ferozepore, a liquidator was saved from being attacked by the timely but accidental arrival of the local Sub-Inspector of Police.

HOW CONTRIBUTIONS ARE TO BE DETERMINED

The liquidators' task consists in determining the assets and liabilities of a Society at the time of its cancellation, and in fixing contributions that each member past and present shall pay towards the liabilities of the Society. "Contribution" means the amount payable by a member as such, and does not include debts payable to the Society. Contribution in reality means the unpaid portion of the liability. No contribution can, therefore, adequately be required from the members in case of a limited liability Society with a fully paid-up share capital, unless it be held that dividends have been paid without being earned, and they may in such a case be recovered. It is not clear what principle the liquidator is to follow in an unlimited liability Society with share capital. Should the contributions be uniform or in proportion to the number of shares held? The liquidator should not in calculating contributions take notice of the share capital of each member. When members have already lost their share money, it would be unfair to make a greater levy on one who has already borne the greater loss.

It appears more equitable that contributions should be levied at a uniform rate so far as possible, and not in proportion to the number of shares. Shares were purchased by the members not with a view to making money, but with a view to helping the Society. The Act, the rules, and the by-laws all discourage the spirit of profit-making. No considerations of the liquidator's convenience should be allowed to encourage such a procedure. When all, the rich and the poor, were equally responsible for the management of the Society, it is only desirable that the ultimate burden should be equally divided. But if the rich have already by misuse of their power contributed to the failure of the Society, they ought to be suitably punished in the form of greater contributions.

If any sum remains outstanding, even after all possible effort has been made, the liquidator may with the Registrar's approval order the amount to be made good by any one member. The Department has not been very fortunate in the matter of selection of liquidators, and it is highly desirable that the liquidator should be a retired official, and the workers in the Department seem to believe that these contributions should be realized as arrears of Land Revenue. The experience of the Provinces with this provision is not encouraging, and I feel the Government dues should never be allowed to be mixed up with any other repayments.

CAUSES OF LIQUIDATION

The following causes lead to cancellation or liquidation of Societies:

(1) *Bad Start and Insufficient Supervision.*—From the very outset of the movement extreme caution in starting a Society and the necessity for honest and effective supervision were impressed upon the workers in the Department. But in their misguided zeal to swell the numbers of Societies organized, the workers of the Department neglected all the sound principles of organization, and did little to exercise adequate supervision over and give proper guidance to such Societies as had been started. As early as 1908, the Registrar had to record as follows: "The most unsatisfactory feature in the history of the movement so far has been the large number of Societies that have died at birth, or been wound up after a brief and inglorious existence. In most cases misguided official zeal has been the cause of this fiasco."

Year	Number under Liquidation at the beginning of the Year	Number of Societies Cancelled	Number of Societies of which Liquidation was finished	Under Liquidation at the end of the Year	Amounts Outstanding	Recovered during the Year
					Lakhs of Rs	Lakhs of Rs.
1934	965	189	103	1,051	—	—
1933	873	219	126	965	—	—
1932	736	338	198	873	—	—
1931	582	355	201	735	—	—
1930	520	333	273	579	—	—
1929	486	277	194	518	—	—
1928	379	336	277	436	—	—
1927	259	310	203	375	—	—
1926	182	—	248	259	—	—
1925	317	—	187	307	—	—
1924	271	—	225	264	—	—
1923	—	—	129	231	—	—
1922	—	—	73	226	3,52	2,61
1921	—	—	109	153	2,29	1,28
1920	—	—	86	168	2,66	1,99
1918	200	—	—	—	—	—
1917	104	—	—	—	—	—

(2) *Usurpation of Power and Dishonesty.*—It happens quite

frequently that power in a Society is usurped by a single member or a number of members. Invariably in such cases this power is misused, with the result that large sums are borrowed and not repaid. Not only that, frauds and misappropriations come in, and soon all is over with the Society.

The loss to depositors and financing institutions has been as follows:

Year	Loss to Depositors	Loss to Financing Agencies
	Rs.	Rs.
1932	250	11,914 Principal
		10,842 Interest
1933	181	10,166 Principal
		3,877 Interest
1934	229	2,225 Principal
		1,769 Interest

The number of Societies brought under liquidation has increased from 271 in 1924 to 873 in 1933. The number of Societies whose liquidation has taken more than four years has risen from 79 in 1930 to 190 in 1933. In Rohtak in 1933 out of 91 Societies under liquidation 38 had been lingering for over five years, whereas 9 had been cancelled quite a decade ago. This is so because liquidation is an unpleasant as well as a dangerous job, and honest people have not been found to undertake it. The cost is very high. In 1933 the cost of liquidation rose to 16¼ per cent. In some districts liquidation was entrusted to special Sub-Inspectors, but "the system has on the whole made neither for cheapness nor effectiveness."

CHAPTER XL

DISHONESTY

No study of the movement can have any claim to completeness unless it has revealed all aspects of it. I am attempting a brief description of this evil, not in the Department, but in the movement. I should, however, like to make it perfectly clear that in giving this brief survey I have to express in very unequivocal terms my appreciation of those at the helm of affairs in the Department, but for whose love of fair play we would have seldom known anything about this phase of our character, which implies, be it said to our shame and sorrow, a lamentable lack of business honesty. The Department of Co-operation and Co-operative principles are not to blame for it. Dishonesty, especially when it yields an income, is a human weakness that man will never conquer. The circle of my readers will necessarily be limited to educated and intelligent persons, and I have every confidence that whatever follows in this chapter will be studied and utilized in the spirit in which it is written and will not be used to the detriment of the movement.

INSTANCES OF DISHONESTY AND THE ACTUAL AMOUNT LOST

I wish the public at large had been taken into greater confidence so that some of us could at least satisfy a curiosity for statistics regarding this aspect of Co-operation in the Punjab. Figures for all years and all cases have not been published. I reproduce the following from the Annual Reports with a view to forming an estimate of the total money lost through embezzlements, a very inadequate estimate, of course, in the absence of data which the Department has evidently decided to treat as confidential.

1913. A fraud on the Jullundur Central Bank occurred during the year, but in the criminal case which ensued guilt could not be proved against any particular person. One President of a Village Bank was convicted of misappropriation of the Society's money and sentenced to imprisonment.

1914. At least three cases of embezzlement or misuse of money by officers of Societies have come to light. In one the delinquent was convicted and sentenced to imprisonment; the second case is under inquiry. The third is on the border-line of the criminal and will probably be settled without prosecution.

1915. Two instances of misuse of a Society's money came to light which appeared to be of a criminal nature and prosecutions were instituted. In one case prosecution failed owing to the death of the principal witness. The other is still under inquiry.

1917. The Registrar writes: "It is with great regret that I report several cases of dishonest misappropriation amongst the staff and the workers. The worst cases were those connected with the Co-operative shops for sale of produce at Pattoki and Akalgarh. The Manager of the former was sentenced to three months' imprisonment and Rs. 1,000 fine. At Akalgarh the villainy was more widespread. One man was sentenced to eighteen months' and another to six months' imprisonment and five accused were discharged or acquitted. Dishonesty was extensive and the result of the prosecution was not very satisfactory."

A particularly sad case was that of a man in Jullundur District, who in the early stages of the movement rendered great help. He was President of a big Society, was later appointed honorary Sub-Inspector, and finally given a paid post. Apparently he thought he could cheat a depositor of Rs. 800 and so took the money and entered it as repaid. When inquiries were being made and the facts were coming to light he again made entries in the books and showed part of the money as redeposited. He was convicted on three charges of breach of trust and forgery and sentenced to seven years' imprisonment.

One Treasurer of a Society in the same district was sentenced to six months' imprisonment for misappropriating the balance to his own use, while another on a similar offence got one year's imprisonment.

On similar charges a Secretary in Lahore District was convicted and sentenced to one year's imprisonment and Rs. 500 fine. A Vice-President in Ferozepore was fined Rs. 100, a Treasurer in Lyallpur was fined Rs. 400, and a President in Ambala was fined Rs. 100. A Sub-Inspector in Ambala was sentenced to three months' rigorous imprisonment for embezzling Rs. 600, which he had collected for the Central Bank. Two Presidents and two Treasurers were acquitted. Some of the staff have had to be dismissed, and in other cases it was considered advisable to prosecute.

1921. Two cases of prosecution for criminal breach of trust ended in conviction. One Inspector seems to have embezzled money. A heavy embezzlement of Rs. 10,000 took place in Karnal Central Bank.

1922. Two Sub-Inspectors misappropriated money. A paid Secretary of an Ambala Society misappropriated Rs. 880, and the case was sent to the police for prosecution.

The Reports for 1910 to 1922 have in general nothing on record except a shower of well-merited praise for the Junior staff of the Department. The Report for 1923 reveals a lurking suspicion in the mind of the writer, which a careful reader cannot fail to detect and interpret as "morning shows the day." Mr. Calvert says in this Report: "The Inspectors are somewhat even. One or two have fallen out, unable to maintain the high standard of honesty demanded in a Department which is trying to found credit on integrity." Concerning the Sub-Inspectors the Report says, "a few had better seek easier life elsewhere." Reading between the lines one can easily guess what must be coming next. "The Inspectors, on the whole, have done well. A few proved unworthy of the task, and are being dealt with." This casual remark in the next Annual Report displays the last year's hesitancy to lift the veil from the scenes that need best be concealed from the public gaze.

The Report for 1925 was prepared by Mr. Strickland, and concerning the recurrence of embezzlements, he says: "I know of no complaint against the staff paid by Government. . . . Sub-Inspectors also betray a trust which should never be placed in them. They are strictly forbidden by the Punjab Co-operative Union to handle money on any account, but Societies press them to do so, with regrettable results. One or two have been dismissed after repayment, others must be prosecuted."

Let us pass on to the next Annual Report of the Department prepared by Mr. Strickland. " . . . Four Sub-Inspectors have been dismissed for financial irregularities, three are under inquiry. Five have been prosecuted and three convicted, the sentences varying from a fine of Rs. 300 to three and a half years' imprisonment. The offences are not of the past year but relate to previous years. Nineteen office-holders of Societies have come under inquiry, of whom fourteen have been prosecuted and ten convicted." The Report for 1927 tells us: "Two Sub-Inspectors of the Punjab Co-operative Union and seven office-holders of Societies have been sentenced to imprisonment for terms varying from three months to two years. One Secretary who had embezzled Rs. 400 was released as first offender, having made good the defalcation. Two Sub-Inspectors are being prosecuted, with one Circle Secretary, one Execution Agent, and eight office-holders, other cases are under inquiry . . . in one case a Sub-Inspector was sentenced (on four counts) to five years' imprisonment and a fine of Rs. 800. Such sentences are needed, for in the last four years about fifty Sub-Inspectors have been involved."

Ten Sub-Inspectors who proved unsatisfactory were dismissed in 1927.

1926. "A trusted Secretary in Hoshiarpur, knowing that he was about to die, made away with Rs. 18,000, in the few months following the audit, in order to provide for his wife and children."

1927. In a Hoshiarpur Union, another Secretary was responsible for embezzlement of Rs. 27,000.

1929. The President of a Society embezzled Rs. 13,000. The Manager of a Commission shop misappropriated Rs. 5,000.

1931. A Mortgage Bank lost Rs. 10,000 and a Central Bank was relieved of Rs. 3,000. In a branch of a Central Bank clerks embezzled Rs. 890. In Amritsar District another Society lost through embezzlement nearly Rs. 17,000.

1932. "Embezzlements in the Lyallpur, Jaranwala, and Gojora shops have had a damaging effect on the shops at large. A sum of Rs. 2,466 had to be written off as bad debts and the estimated amount of bad and doubtful debts incurred in a variety of ways Rs. 23,000. One of the main reasons for the troubles which have fallen upon the Lyallpur shop was the practice of the late Manager doing business with the Society's money and purchasing bad stuff and mixing it with members' produce. The President of the shop, after failing to attend any meeting, has become a sadhu."

Hafizabad shop lost Rs. 295 in 1928 over the boycott in that year owing principally to the carelessness of the Manager. During the year 1928 three Managers had to be dismissed for dishonesty. In 1927 an employee of the Hafizabad shop disappeared after misappropriating Rs. 2,000. In 1928 the Munim of the same shop absconded with Rs. 1,040, and the next year it was the Manager's pleasure to disappear with a sum well over Rs. 5,000.

During 1929 seven Sub-Inspectors were dismissed and five were reverted. The Report for 1930 records as follows: "The dishonesty of many of those connected with the movement was dealt with at length last year, and little need be added except that it still gives cause for serious reflection." The Report for 1931 gives some indication of the prevailing state of affairs: "If one may speak from the moral and not the legal point of view, then it may be said that the above figures bear hardly any relation to fact. For there are countless cases in which moral obliquity appears, though a criminal court would not take cognizance, and Civil proceedings, even if successful, would be fruitless, for money once spent is with difficulty recoverable."

1933. Cases of dishonesty increased from 269 in 1932 to 437. Two hundred persons were involved. In point of sums involved the most conspicuous cases were the embezzlement in the Civil Secretariat Society, Lahore, amounting to about Rs. 30,000,

TABLE INDICATING THE GROWTH OF DISHONESTY IN THE WORKING OF THE PUNJAB CO-OPERATIVE SOCIETIES

	1926	1927	1928	1929	1930	1931	1932	1933	1934
Total number of Societies ..	—	—	318	262	377	362	269	423	299
Primary Societies	—	—	311	237	362	349	256	423	278
Central Institution	—	—	7	25	15	13	13	14	21
Total number of persons involved	—	—	170	175	171	159	146	200	141
Inspectors	7	—	1	—	—	1	—	1	—
Sub-Inspectors	—	4	26	26	24	15	10	7	8
Liquidators	—	—	6	9	—	3	4	9	3
Execution Agents or employees	—	9	7	8	17	27	15	—	22
Office-holders of Societies ..	19	—	118	123	121	96	103	143	97
Secretaries and clerks	—	—	10	8	16	16	7	12	—
Bailiffs	—	—	2	—	—	—	—	—	—
Cases of Criminal proceedings started	—	94	—	83	58	75	83	152	82
Cases of conviction	—	13	—	35	50	34	46	—	—
Acquittals	—	13	—	7	10	12	13	—	—
Cases pending	—	—	—	41	—	1	—	—	—
Cases withdrawn or compromised	—	13	—	—	—	—	10	—	—
Members of societies involved ..	—	—	—	—	—	—	5	—	—

and that in the Gurgaon Central Bank involving nearly Rs. 18,000. Fifty-five cases were started in Sialkot alone, where the accused included three zaildars and one sufedposh, and the officials of the Department were far from guiltless.

1930. Reviewing the working of the Co-operative shops, the Report records: "During the year two Managers had to be suspended for dealings that appeared to be dishonest, and a cashier was convicted."

1933. The Manager at Toba Tek Singh shop embezzled in 1932 a sum of Rs. 47,000. Lyallpur had to face a bad debt half of which was due to embezzlement by the late Manager. "There is another black spot at Sangla, which has been wrecked by the debt owed by its late lessee amounting to Rs. 74,000."

The total loss due to embezzlements and dishonesty in other forms, as I have calculated it, since 1915, in cases where figures are given, amounts to over Rs. 2,34 lakhs. Of this amount a certain percentage—very low percentage—it has been possible to recover. The annual average over the last twenty years works out at Rs. 12,000.

I should like the reader to have the official view of the matter. The Registrar writes in the Annual Report for 1929 as follows: "The brighter side is of course the very large sums in circulation, the very large number of people who handle them, the very small amounts which generally make up each transaction, and the smaller proportion of people, amounts, or transactions involved in the cases. All that is possible for the Department to do is, I believe, being done to combat the evil. On the other side, we need a stronger public opinion against such practices and a desire in the community to bring offenders to justice. I, personally, should like to see a lessening of the tendency on the part of the people, co-operators and others, and sometimes courts, to lay all the blame for these occurrences on us."

DIFFICULTIES IN DEALING WITH CASES OF EMBEZZLEMENT

Cases involving moral obliquity are countless, but of such a criminal court would take no cognizance. On the other hand the Registrar is convinced that cases go to criminal courts that are not really criminal. "For instance, audit may reveal that certain items of receipt were not credited in the cash or in the books of a Society. This omission may well have been pure forgetfulness, or carelessness, but the person responsible for it, when asked about it, denies it stoutly from a queer sense of *Izzat*, or sometimes from fear, and even, on the spur of the moment, automatically asserts that the case is false, and has been made up at the instigation of someone or other because 'there is a party against him.' Then, the facts being obvious from the documents, there is no alternative to prosecution. And thus a few moments of forgetfulness end in a long trial, much expense, general unpleasantness, a set-back for some Society, and jail for one who in the beginning was innocent of criminal intent."

The greatest difficulty experienced in bringing the culprit to book is the dilemma in which the Committee finds itself. The Department and the Committee are anxious, in the first instance, to realize the amount embezzled. When the money lost has been even partially recovered the members of the Society are exceedingly reluctant to proceed against the culprits, who are their friends, relatives, or neighbours. Whereas if prosecution is resorted to promptly, the chances of recovering the amount lost often disappear.

THE WAY THEY DO IT

I give below a few of the instances of embezzlement and dishonesty as practised by office-bearers of Societies and the staff of the Department.

One Sub-Inspector used to earn a lot of money by befriending the money-lenders and their victims simultaneously to his own great financial advantage. "Well, Sahukar Sahib," he would say to the money-lender, "M is so poor. How can you hope to recover your money? Why not strike a balance and get only as much as he can pay? If you do not avail of the opportunity that I offer you, well, your money is lost." "All right, sir," says the sahukar, "I will accept Rs. 300 for Rs. 500 that he owes me." "Well said, Sahukar Sahib, I will use all my power to let this realization be made possible," says the Sub-Inspector. He calls the debtor, who is a member of a Society, and says to him, "It is in your interest to pay off the sahukar. Borrow from the Society. Save yourself the exorbitant dues of the sahukar and in easy instalments pay off the Society. Moreover, I can persuade the sahukar to grant you a substantial remission. You owe him Rs. 500 and he will grant you a reduction of a hundred rupees." "This is quite good, sir, I agree to it." M is debited with Rs. 400 in the books of the Society, the sahukar realizes Rs. 300 in full settlement of the debt, and the Sub-Inspector is richer by a hundred rupees. This man had to pay a severe penalty when his nefarious ways came to the notice of the Department.

A Sub-Inspector received Rs. 246 from a Society on March 12, 1930, for depositing in a Central Bank. The Central Bank received Rs. 155 only on March 23rd.

The Central Bank sent a receipt for Rs. 155. The case was reported to the higher authorities. Fearing action against him, the Sub-Inspector sent the balance per money order to the Treasurer of the Society. He was hauled up for having wrongfully kept the money in his custody for two and a half months. In the meanwhile he had secured from another Society a sum of Rs. 138, which he had wrongfully kept in his own custody for four months. This he had not paid to the Society but had got debited to the account of a member whom he had given a pro-note for an equal sum. For a number of similar offences, after being given a chance to make good these losses, he was hauled up and sentenced by a court to rigorous imprisonment for one year and nine months.

A Treasurer realized Rs. 2,000 from some members and informed the authorities that he had given this money to the Sub-Inspector for payment to the Central Bank and he had not done it. This clever Treasurer was sentenced to rigorous imprisonment for two years and a fine of Rs. 1,000.

Another Secretary conspired with a member to rob the Society of a sum of Rs. 300. This member wanted to transfer

Rs. 300 of his debt to his son. The son was shown to have borrowed Rs. 300, which the Secretary deducted from the cash in hand and manipulated the books to show that this member had repaid Rs. 300. One year's rigorous imprisonment and a fine of Rs. 150 for each was the sentence passed in this case. A member of a Society conspired with a dismissed Inspector to defraud a Central Bank of Rs. 200 on the strength of a false pro-note. One year's rigorous imprisonment for each was the sentence passed.

A Treasurer of a Society, under liquidation, misappropriated Rs. 153 and failed to make good the loss. He was fined Rs. 100 and awarded imprisonment for one day.

The Secretary of a Credit Society did not enter a sum of Rs. 562,10, repayment of instalments by a number of members. He also used to get bonds signed for larger sums than were borrowed by illiterate members. He tampered with the figures during a departmental inquiry so as to reduce the sums involved. The balance still unaccountable he showed as debt advanced to him and his father. He was sentenced to different terms on five different counts.

The President of a Society embezzled Rs. 1,000 and was sentenced to seven years' imprisonment.

Embezzlements are by no means confined to the working of Co-operative Societies. No institution in the Province can claim to be immune from corruption and dishonesty in its multifarious forms. Joint-Stock Banks managed by men of education and means have probably a worse record in this respect. A number of people in all walks of life will always misuse their opportunities. Instances of embezzlement are to be met with in the Co-operative Department in other Provinces as well. The average co-operator, however, in view of the huge sums and colossal numbers involved, is to be commended for his standard of honesty, which may well be the envy of other Departments and institutions. Neither is the Province as a whole to be stigmatized for corruption and dishonesty. The tendency to misuse opportunities is the same all the world over, and some of the most civilized countries are the worst offenders in this respect.

CHAPTER XLI

THE EFFECTS OF THE DEPRESSION UPON CO-OPERATIVE SOCIETIES IN THE PUNJAB

DETERIORATION OF THE SOCIETIES

FALL in the payment of dues by members swells the overdues of the Societies and naturally adversely affects their classification. The action of the Department in combining A and B Societies for purposes of classification and giving total numbers

Year	Total Number of Societies Classified	A	B	C	D
		Percentage	Percentage	Percentage	Percentage
1926	—	4·25	26·25	62	7·5
1927	—	3	22·6	70·25	4·15
1928	12,049	2·1	18·6	37·6	5·5
1929	13,512	2·02	16·6	75·3	5·9
1930	14,548	2·05	15·08	76·6	6·2
1931	15,311	1·9	13·2	76·3	8·5
1932	15,763	1·8	11·4	76·4	10·3
1933	15,956	1·9	10·79	76·1	11·19

instead of percentages has not helped to clarify the situation. In order to bring out more vividly the state of deterioration of the Societies by comparison with previous figures, I have had to subject the available statistics to a number of processes in order to reduce them to a common form.

A little more of a mathematical patience and practice and I can tell you that the fall in A and B class Societies amounts to 55·29 and 58·13 per cent respectively. The rise in C and D class Societies has amounted to 22·58 and 49·2 per cent respectively.

Looked at from another point of view, we see that A and B

class Societies now number about 12 per cent only—a sad commentary on the achievements of a whole generation.

CASUALTIES

In spite of the stupendous deterioration and very great care in handling Societies, the casualties have been very abnormal, as the number of Societies cancelled and brought under liquidation in recent years indicates:

Year	Number of Societies Cancelled	Number of Societies under Liquidation at the end of the Year
1923	—	231
1924	—	264
1925	—	307
1926	—	259
1927	310	375
1928	336	436
1929	277	518
1930	333	579
1931	355	735
1932	338	873
1933	219	965

The Report for 1932, while recording some improvement on this behalf made by Kangra, remarks: "Elsewhere the agricultural depression and the fall in prices have contributed to a general deterioration, in spite of the fact that recoveries have been good in the circumstances. The rapid rise in the number of D Societies is serious enough on the above showing but the actual position is really worse. There are a few Districts, notably Gurgaon, in which many or some Societies which according to the rigour of the rules should be classified as D have been classified as 'C poor,' e.g. in Gurgaon the 'C's' are 523, 'C poor' 176, 'D' 123 out of 853 Societies all told, D denoting those Societies which have two years' Central Bank interest in arrears or in which the accumulated interest against members exceeds three years' interest on the loaned-out capital, or standing for some element of danger on account of anticipated bad debts."

NUMBER OF AGRICULTURAL SOCIETIES

Some indication of the effect of depression on the number of Agricultural Credit Societies can be had from the following figures:

Year	Number of Agricultural Societies	Increase during the Year	Number of Societies Cancelled
1930	16,125	657	—
1931	16,297	172	209
1932	16,247	50	218
1933	16,268	21	144

For the first time an actual decline was recorded in 1932. Liquidation was eschewed as much as possible. ". . . even many of the weakest Societies are being given the chance of keeping alive, and maintaining their heart, if they can."

MEMBERSHIP OF AGRICULTURAL CREDIT SOCIETIES

In spite of all efforts directed at increasing the membership in these Societies, there has been noticeable in recent years not only a diminution in annual increase but an actual fall.

Year	Annual Increase in Total Membership	Net Decrease
1927	—	—
1929	100,293	—
1930	28,000	—
1931	16,453	—
1932	15,458	−5,024
1933	16,405	−2,707

The Registrar wrote in 1930: "The policy of persuading old Societies to bring in good new members has been continued and in three years has resulted in the addition of 100,293 co-operators. We must not forget the many thousand casualties—last year nearly two thousand in Lyallpur alone—to be set off against this."

No doubt the restricted financing of the Societies left no attraction for the new members to join, and defaulters had to be pruned, "but in addition, particularly in the south-east of the Province, there has been noticed a tendency for members owing small loans to clear their accounts and quit. Gurgaon, for example, reports a decrease of 861 members . . . it simply means people have got disheartened for the time being, nature being too harsh. The considerable loss of membership in Lyallpur is partly due to the niggardly way in which Societies there were financed by their central institutions."

The Report for 1933 observes: ". . . in spite of fairly steady influx of new members to old Societies (16,405 during the year), the tendency of members to leave their Societies after paying up their dues continues and there is a total decline in membership of 2,707, a number which, though disappointingly large, is considerably less than the decrease of 5,024 recorded last year. In many Societies it is unfortunately the good members who are apt to go, either from fear of the enforcement of unlimited liability or because owing to the default of their fellow-members their Society's credit with the Financing Bank is reduced and they are unable to get loans which they really need and to which their individual credit should entitle them. In Gurdaspur District there have been as many as 554 voluntary withdrawals, in Montgomery 455, and in Lyallpur 913."

REFERENCES TO ARBITRATION

As the effects of depression began to be felt references to arbitration became more frequent—the figure jumped from 15,195 to 26,849 in the short span of four years and so did the number of awards which had to be taken to the courts. The amount claimed as well exactly doubled in four years. The year 1933 shows a sudden decline in all the three figures. But it does not imply that the necessity for such an action is over.

Arbitration leads to execution of awards, which is a very difficult problem. "It may be said, and it has been said, that these and similar occurrences show that Societies and the Co-operative staff are exercising undue harshness in exacting debts from debtors who are already desperate from sheer need.

REFERENCES TO ARBITRATION

	1929	1930	1931	1932	1933	1934
References to arbitration	15,195	17,496	24,462	26,849	22,992	15,180
Awards taken to courts	6,773	8,509	10,678	12,016	11,938	7,561
Amounts claimed (lakhs of rupees)	35	38	59	70	57	39

The situation in this respect obviously requires very careful handling, but it is unfair to form a conclusion adverse to the movement without a very full knowledge of the circumstances in each case. It is by no means always the man who is least able to pay who is most violent in resistance and outcry." (Report for 1932.) The occurrences alluded to above refer to an attempt at suicide, the murder of an execution agent and that of the nephew of a zealous President.

It is these painful occurrences and the increasing unwillingness of the members to help Societies against their friends and relatives and the growing disinclination of Committees to pay for executions, that made the Department take to milder measures. In 1933 over 2,500 awards could not be taken to courts because the Societies concerned did not remit advances to the Unions to meet necessary expenses. It was, as well, realized that "extreme coercive measures, such as sending defaulters to jail . . . show that the expense of such measures is generally disproportionate to the amount recovered."

In the light of this background and the reasons advanced

by the Registrar in his Report for 1933, we can easily account for the huge fall in figures concerning arbitration. The reason for this decrease is, according to the Report for 1933, "that Societies have been more inclined to follow the policy of recovery by gentle and persistent persuasion rather than by resort to legal methods of compulsion; under present circumstances there is little doubt that such a policy is a wise one, but it is to be feared that it has also covered a number of cases in which the Committees of Societies have been unwilling to proceed against influential members or their own friends who are in default."

REPAYMENTS

The Co-operative Credit Societies draw their members almost entirely from agriculturists, any fall in whose cash incomes must inevitably be reflected in their diminished capacity for repayment. The abrupt and continuous fall in the income of

DISTRICT PERCENTAGES OF RECOVERIES

District	1930–31	1931–32	1932–33
Gurgaon	3	3·2	2·5
Hissar	5	4·2	2·77
Rohtak	6	4·2	4·2
Karnal	6	3·77	5·92
Multan	36	27·9	25·7
Kangra	34	26·6	27·5
Montgomery	—	23	20
Rawal Pindi	—	23	18
Jhelum	—	21	19
Hoshiarpur	—	20	20·5
Jullundur	—	19	19·5
Lyallpur	—	17	—
Attock	—	17	—
Muzaffargarh	13·1	16	18·8
Shahpur	—	12	—
Ferozepore	—	7·3	8·7
Ludhiana	—	16·5	18·3

the agriculturists has, therefore, expressed itself in a very great fall in the recoveries, as the following figures will indicate:

	Percentage of Repayment of the Principal Outstanding		Percentage of Repayment of the Principal Outstanding
1926 ..	.. 35	1931 ..	.. 16
1927 ..	.. 34	1932 ..	.. 16
1928 ..	.. 33	1933 ..	.. 13
1929 ..	.. 28	1934 ..	.. 14
1930 ..	.. 23		

REPAYMENTS TO PRIMARY SOCIETIES BY THEIR MEMBERS

(*Lahks of rupees*)

	1928	1929	1930	1931	1932	1933	1934
Principal ..	1,52	1,55	1,42	1,12	99	90	93,67
Interest ..	54	60	62	62	68	63	60,63
Total repaid ..	2,06	2,15	2,04	1,74	1,67	1,53	154,30

REDUCTION IN LOANS GRANTED

(*Lakhs of rupees*)

	1929–30	1930–31	1931–32	1932–33	1933–34
Loan advanced during the year	216	140,25	79,6	79,22	90,84
Loan outstanding at the close of the year ..	691	718	691	—	—
Average debt per member	143	144	141	—	—

While studying the figures for recovery we have to remember that the Department riveted all attention upon recoveries and all other activities were practically at a standstill. Coercive methods such as have earned a bad name for the movement in certain areas were adopted. These measures were resented and a reference to this had to be made in the Annual Report for 1933.

"An inquiry has been made into the extent to which coercive measures have been applied in recovering the dues of Societies. These show that in the whole year 494 debtors (about one member in a thousand) were committed to the civil jail, and of these the greater number were soon released; an inquiry made during the year showed that at one time the total number in jail was ninety. Of the 494 cases mentioned, however, it is a fact that more than half were in the four Districts of the Province, and inquiries are being made in regard to the high proportion of arrests in these Districts."

RESTRICTIONS ON LOANS

While all possible efforts were being devoted to the recovery of loans, it was thought advisable to restrict borrowings by the members. With this restriction in view the credits of members and Societies were greatly reduced and instructions were issued by the Department to advance loans with greater circumspection and for productive purposes alone. This restriction brought down the annual loan of the Societies to the members from Rs. 216 lakhs in 1929–30 to Rs. 79,6 lakhs in 1932, as the table given above indicates.

CENTRAL CO-OPERATIVE BANKS AND THE AGRICULTURAL DEPRESSION

Contraction of Loans.—The Central Banks were not willing to advance loans to Societies on the old liberal scale, and side by side with effecting recoveries thought of restricting the loans to Societies. The Central Banks advanced to the Societies as follows:

1929–30	1930–31	1931–32
Rs. 192 lakhs	Rs. 105 lakhs	Rs. 49 lakhs

"Speaking broadly lending business was only half in 1930–31

of the volume of the previous year, and that half has now dwindled to half again." Societies were unable to borrow because of the restriction on loans, delays in repayments, and positive defaults.

Year	Number of Societies that did not borrow during the year	Number of Societies that had not borrowed for the last two years	Number of Societies which exceed their Maximum Credit Limit
1932	11,035	8,608	4,218
1933	11,668	9,625	—
1934	12,083	11,157	—

Societies not assessed to demand numbered 1,614 in 1931 and 1,871 in 1932. Figures for 1933 show that 8,037 Societies defaulted in respect of payment of principal and 5,921 in respect of payment of interest. Corresponding figures for 1934 are 7,251 and 6,645.

Difficulties in recoveries were experienced. While reviewing the Report for 1932 the Ministry of Agriculture observes: ". . . It is inevitable, though the Registrar of course is right in deploring the fact, that recovery in the present circumstances should be difficult, with the result that Sub-Inspectors have had to devote a disproportionate amount of their time to the unpopular rôle of the bailiff."

BAD AND DOUBTFUL DEBTS

Debts from D class Societies and Societies under liquidation are classed as bad and doubtful. The following table illustrates the growth of bad and doubtful debts:

Year	D Class Societies	Societies under Liquidation
	Lakhs	Lakhs
1931	32,09	8,80
1932	42,4	12,28
1933	48,28	15,95
1934	59,25	17,28

This rapid growth of bad and doubtful debts is alarming when we remember that during 1920–29 only Rs. 60,000 had to be written off as irrevocable. Now the amount of bad and doubtful debt stands at Rs. 64,93 lakhs and the possibility of loss on this score is painfully apparent.

MORTGAGE BANKS

Defaulters.—Out of the twelve Mortgage Banks in the Province only two, Shahpur and Bhalwal, had no defaulters. In the rest of the banks, out of 1,589 borrowers 620, or 39 per cent, were in default in 1930. In addition to those who defaulted, 291 borrowers had their instalments postponed.

	Number of Defaulters	
	1930	1931
Gurgaon	193	155
Sonepat	27	21
Nariangarh	12	50
Gujranwala	62	64
Toba Tek Singh ..	14	14
Sheikhupura	52	45
Mianwali	24	91
Jhang	121	121
Lyallpur	93	93
Samundari	22	22

In view of the seriousness of the situation, a conference of all the colony Mortgage Banks was held at Lyallpur in April 1931. The decisions of the conference have been reproduced in the chapter on Mortgage Banks. Relevant extracts from recent reports are produced below:

"Sheikhupura has had to take possession of land in three cases; but there are borrowers who have steadily refused to pay anything at all ever since they got their loans, as far back as four years."

GURGAON.—"The year's recoveries of principal are lower than last year, and are only 3 per cent of the amount that was on loan at the beginning of the year. . . . But the interest unpaid represents nearly twenty-two months' interest on the money out on loan. In Gurgaon Bank, out of 251 debtors, fifteen have paid their loans in full. But the manner of repayment makes one wonder how far the aims, objects, and character of a Mortgage Bank, and the true meaning of a loan, have been realized. All these loans have been paid before due dates. Six debtors sold land; three mortgaged land; two 'raised money on females'; one borrowed from his relatives; one loan was repaid three days after it had been taken; one borrower died and the money was recovered from his heirs; and one repaid out of his own income." "Land Mortgage Banks . . . show a small profit; but they have been badly hit by the collapse of prices of agricultural produce; it has been found necessary to relieve the borrowing members of part of their burden by reducing the instalments; new loans are being restricted, and old loans are being recovered with difficulty."

Report for 1932.—"Mortgage Banks (twelve) have been struggling to collect their dues and there has been no fresh business to speak of. . . . The mortgage burden has been found to be disproportionately heavy in comparison with the value of the estate. . . . In spite of a halving of the instalments in colony areas, there has been a *bona-fide* inability on the part of many borrowers to meet their loan obligations . . . the present catastrophic fall in prices is straining their resources and their morale equally."

"The tale of default has increased. The increase in default in the Lyallpur District . . . is notable and depressing. The number of defaulters all told was 1,071, and with the exception of 395, all of them were proceeded against in one way or another. Thirty-nine defaulters were put in jail, and the possession of borrowers' land was taken in thirty-six instances, generally for twenty years . . . overdues have more than doubled. . . . Execution proceedings were taken in hand in 546 cases of default. The resultant amount recovered was

Rs. 52,853 at a cost of Rs. 4,287, or a ratio of 1 : 12, though in 261 cases it was not found possible to effect any recoveries at all." Even in the most successful banks borrowers had to be proceeded against and sent to jail.

Report for 1933.—"No branch of the Department's activities has been so seriously affected by the recent depression as the Mortgage Banks. . . . Now loans have assumed three or four times their original value, while the property held by the banks as security is no longer sufficient to cover the loans."

"Only one Bank—Gujranwala—has issued any loans during the year, and these loans were three in number, of a total value of Rs. 3,784. . . . Over dues have shown only a small increase to Rs. 4,30 lakhs in the year under report. . . . As a result of the year's working there is a loss of Rs. 33,000.

"The Lyallpur Mortgage Bank has during the year taken possession of debtors' land in sixteen cases out of a total of 150 defaulters; six have been put under arrest. The Jhang Mortgage Bank shows a comparatively high number of arrests, fifteen . . . In the rest of the banks the total number of civil arrests is only five; no other bank has taken possession of any debtor's land during the year.

". . . The depression soon followed and the borrowers have been genuinely unable to meet their obligations in the way of instalments on loans, which now assumed three or four times their original value."

INCREASE IN INSOLVENCY AND RESORT TO MURDER

The Report for 1932 records:

"In some districts petitions for insolvency are becoming increasingly frequent as a method of escaping obligations to Societies, and in Gurdaspur, where 124 such petitions were filed, the Deputy Registrar described it as a menace to the movement. From Gurdaspur comes an account of persistence in avoiding payment worthy of a better cause: a debtor first filed a petition for insolvency, which after nine months' consideration was dismissed; he then threw himself down a well; extracted from this he beat his head against a stone, hoping in both these cases to involve the Execution staff in criminal proceedings; it has finally been necessary for the police to charge him with attempted suicide.

"It is in the South-East Punjab, where conditions are hardest, that the greatest difficulties have been experienced, and execution proceedings had even had as their sequel the murder of an Execution Agent and of the nephew of a zealous President."

Execution and liquidation proceedings are unanimously hampered by all.

RELIEF

The acute depression has given a very rude shock to agriculture in the Province and the Societies have naturally been concerned to afford as much relief as possible. The following steps have been taken in this respect:

(1) Demands have been fixed at a very low level so as to facilitate and adjust repayments to the capacity of the members.

(2) Rebates of interest to punctual repayers.

(3) Rates of interest have been reduced wherever and as far as possible.

(4) Share instalments have been lowered.

(5) In some Societies in which shares were non-returnable, by-laws have been amended making them returnable and share-money has been adjusted against members' loan accounts.

(6) All Central Banks have reduced the rate they charge the Societies on money lent to them.

(7) Most of the banks allow a rebate on repayment of interest by Societies.

(8) Central Banks have been advised to suspend interest and receive payments from D class Societies as capital.

(9) Such Primary Societies as have no outside liabilities have been permitted to forgo interest on the sums due from their members.

CHAPTER XLII

OPPOSITION*

MONEY-LENDERS AND CO-OPERATION

SOME of my readers may fret and fume at the determined and vehement opposition displayed against the Co-operative movement by money-lenders, as the following account will illustrate. Exceedingly regrettable as some of the forms which this opposition assumed may be, its exhibition is perfectly natural. Whatever the ultimate academic aim of Co-operation may be, it remains a fact that in its commencement it simply appeared to the money-lender a rival lending agency. Agriculturists present a unique field for exploitation by money-lenders, and any agency that steps in to disturb the sahukar's monopoly will naturally have to bear the brunt of their opposition, which can show no respect to principles however exalted and motives howsoever ennobling. The following account represents an abridged history of their attitude towards the movement, and is based upon the observations made in the Annual Reports of the Department. I wish I had more time and assistance at my disposal to collect more material on this subject, for the material in the Reports makes bare reference to the activities of the money-lenders against the movement.

Karnal was one of the five districts originally chosen for experiment. The storm of misrepresentation and opposition began in this district first. The money-lenders were responsible for a widely-spread rumour that whoever joined a Society would be sued at once on either a real or fictitious claim and treated with the greatest severity allowed by law against unfortunate judgment debtors. The Annual Report for 1905 records that "in more than one instance this opposition combined with threats of false cases was sufficient to stop the establishment of possible Societies."

* Italics throughout this chapter are the author's.

The opposition became much more marked as the experiment advanced. According to the Report for 1907, "Opposition by money-lending classes has been universal. It varies according to the success of the movement. Thus in Gurdaspur and Jullundur it has been most marked." The money-lender has always treated the establishment of Co-operative Societies as a trepass on his special preserves. In the early stages of the movement he tried to prevent their establishment by misrepresenting the object of the movement. The Report for 1907 records as follows: "He tries to persuade the villagers that *Co-operative Societies are formed by a designing Government to appropriate their hard-earned savings.* He tells the borrowers that *if they do not repay their loans punctually their land will be sold without delay or confiscated by Government.*" Intimidation of indebted members by means of threats to worry them by legal proceedings often succeeded in preventing them from joining a Society. The Report for 1908 records: "The opposition experienced at the hands of the village money-lender continues and grows more widespread as the Co-operative Movement extends. Misrepresentation is the most deadly weapon that the money-lenders possess. . . . *One of my Inspectors has been followed in many villages in Jullundur by a money-lender opponent,*" obviously for counteracting the Inspector's propaganda for establishment of Societies. Misrepresentation and intimidation proved quite effective in strangling the movement in many a place that offered brilliant prospects of success. The opposition began to organize itself with the spread of the movement. The Report for 1908 records that "in the Garshankar tahsil a private company of money-lenders with a capital of Rs. 2 lakhs is said to have been formed *to prevent the establishment of Co-operative Credit Societies by every conceivable means.*"

The relevant portion of the Report for 1908 opens thus: "The movement still meets with hostility, to some extent organized, not only from the professional sahukars, but also from the Muhammadan Shylock of the land-owning class."

Hitherto the opposition consisted in organized campaigns

in the form of misrepresentation of the objects of the movement and of the motives that brought this movement into being, and of intimidation of the agriculturists already in the grip of the sahukar. The superior cunning of the sahukar now hit upon another plan to keep the zemindars in his grip. The Report for 1909 records that "*Money-lenders have in some instances refused to take payment of old debts, just as they often refuse to accept redemption of mortgaged land.*" How flagrantly unjust it is, yet the sahukar for one reason or another still follows this practice. The then Registrar felt the hopelessness and helplessness of such a situation, and thought that legislation was required to meet such a refusal. He was perfectly justified in putting forward such a suggestion, which unfortunately did not receive the support of the Government. Every honest man will heartily endorse the Registrar's opinion when he says that *it is inequitable to compel a man to remain in debt when he is able and willing to pay.*

What in the beginning of the movement were considered mere threats and sheer attempts at intimidation materialized with the growing success of the movement. In the beginning the threats had the desired effect, but when over five years of experience demonstrated to the zemindars the various advantages of the movement, and they stood convinced of the necessity of joining the movement, and mere threats proved ineffective, the sahukar went a step forward in demonstrating his power and influence, which unfortunately the Societies were not in a position to counteract. We cannot but sympathize with the Registrar, who was a helpless witness to the various attempts at strangling the infant Societies he was ushering into existence. The Registrar, in his Report for 1911, remarks: "One objectionable feature, however, has been brought to my notice as having sprung up in nearly all districts in which the movement is making headway, and is I think worthy of mention. It is this, *that not infrequently when a zemindar, owing money to a money-lender, joins a Society and gets a loan, his creditor puts him into court and gets a decree against him, not payable in instalments, as is usually the case, but in a lump sum,* the idea, of course, being that the Society will have to find the money. This idea is more often than not fallacious, but the principle underlying the order is unfair to the Societies, and should, I think, be discountenanced."

No more effective method of dealing a blow at the promising infant and of causing a flagrantly dishonest and exceedingly uncalled-for embarrassment to a poor tiller of the soil just struggling to organize himself for economic betterment could be devised. We have just noticed that the money-lender refused to liberate a debtor by accepting payment of his dues when the debtor was willing and able to discharge his obligations to him. At one time it suits his interest to adopt this seemingly incredible course, and he does it. At another he hits hard by making a poor cultivator discharge immediately his obligations which, under normal course, for the unfortunate victim's exploitation he would fain and often does pass on to his sons for further realization.

The opposition of the money-lenders to the establishment of the Co-operative Credit Societies expressed itself in yet another form. So far, besides other tactics, we have seen them refusing to accept payment of their dues, or compelling wholesale immediate payments. This time they invented quite a new trick. Now they refused to lend to the inhabitants of those villages where Societies had been formed or were likely to be started. The money-lender finances a whole village, the Society cannot undertake wholesale financing of the village.

The Report for 1912 records: "Reference has been made in two previous Reports to official opposition. This, I regret to say, still continues, and is to be met with chiefly in Munsifs' courts. The Munsifs as a body are recruited largely from the money-lending or small shopowner classes, so that many of them have a class prejudice against the Village Banks. *This is shown in the vexatious and even illegal action towards parties who happen to be members of Co-operative Societies, and by insulting treatment of them in court.* It is not an uncommon practice for a money-lender to put some members of a newly started bank into court with the object of frightening the other members, who are also on his books, from joining the Societies. *Once the client is in the court many and various are the ways in which a hostile Munsif can persecute him. There are very general complaints in some parts, and I propose to bring such cases to the notice of the chief court.*"

Any comment upon and elaboration of the above is evidently needless.

This evidently was designed to punish to submission the whole of a village community. It can easily be imagined that the activities of the advocates of Co-operation must have brought upon them the displeasure of an ignorant and enraged peasantry with whom the sahukars' seductive and apparent favours were the only basis upon which a miserable life could be dragged on. The Annual Report for 1913 records: "For instance, in part of the Gurdaspur District the money-lenders carried their hostility so far as to refuse advances even in villages in which there was no bank, because they were convinced that banks would be started in them before long." The hostility of the money-lender to the Co-operative movement gained in speed and force with the growth of the movement in its early stages. The Report for 1913 records: "During the past year there has been a certain amount of organized hostility on the part of money-lenders . . . but while it lasts it is extremely troublesome to the infant Societies. It is, of course, to be expected that these little tyrants of the fields should bitterly resent being withstood by a hitherto submissive clientele."

To crown all previous performances, the money-lender did not hesitate to use his silvery bait wherever he thought it would work well, and we know a silvery bait not only works well but works wonders.

The Report for 1915, a decade after the commencement of the movement, states: ". . . but the Societies have to contend with individual opponents. *The most to be feared are those who entice away prominent members from their allegiance, or even bribe whole Societies by promises of reduced interest and other concessions.*"

The hostility of the money-lender towards the Co-operative movement has consisted in misrepresentations of the objects and methods of the movement, intimidation of the debtors, dragging the debtors to courts and demanding wholesale immediate payments, refusal to accept payment of debts, refusal to advance loans to entire villages with reasonable prospects for the growth of Co-operation, and finally in meanly enticing away prominent members of Societies. Can we, therefore, not say that the money-lenders in the Punjab left no stone unturned in their effort to nip the movement in the bud?

The Money-lender's Kith and Kin.—We have so far witnessed the money-lender's all-pervading and intense opposition to Co-operation. As if the money-lender with all the advantages of superior intelligence, wealth, and power was no match for the infant Societies growing up, his class and his kith and kin instinctively came to his help. He had now the power of law at his back, which in the Punjab has always been used to his advantage. For the purposes of this book I cannot do better than quote the findings of the Registrars, who, I have reasons to believe, never fully disclosed the material at their disposal.

"Opposition from some other quarters cannot be treated so lightly. *I could quote an instance where two officials of a Government Department have set themselves to injure the prospects of their subordinates, who have given help to Rural Societies, and there are other instances of active opposition on the part of officials.* I shall, in future, bring such cases to the notice of the Government" (Annual Report for 1909).

One E.A.C. evicted one of his tenants who joined the village Society—such was the unpardonable nature of his sin. Members of the Punjab Civil Service, in the words of the Report for 1917, "*afford ground for the belief that their feelings favour the local usurer.*"

Talking about the opposition of the money-lender to the Co-operative movement, the Annual Report for 1910 records: "*It becomes objectionable when their sons and relatives in an official capacity cannot conceal their feelings.*"

We have already noticed that the sahukars, in the early stages of the movement, dragged the poor cultivators to courts and secured decrees against them for immediate and full payment of debts. On the part of the Munsifs, this cannot but be interpreted *as a deliberate misuse of official power to the benefit of one class and the disadvantage of the other*. This unfortunate, and I should like to say deliberate, misuse of official power was not confined to the preliminary stages of the movement. The Report for 1921 records: "It might be possible to mention a few cases of misuse of official power. . . . In one case an order by an officiating Deputy Commissioner had to be reviewed, and a remark by him expunged from a zaildar's book; a Munsif refused to acknowledge the legality of the Government rules excluding Civil Courts from dealing with disputes, but gave way after causing trouble, and another case had to be referred to the Honourable Judges."

The same Report tells us that "*A Head Master of a middle school was compelled to vacate his post by local sahukars because he refused to cease to help some local Societies.*"

Could vindictive meanness go any further? While every fair-minded man will condemn the sahukars' action against the Head Master, let us for a moment pay a heartfelt tribute to the spirit of self-sacrifice displayed by him.

The Registrar tells us that some Inspectors prepared lists of people, in 1922, who had been opposing the movement. The names of these people, however, were not disclosed. In his Report for 1923 the Registrar remarks as follows: "Mere lack of interest is to be expected, but definite antipathy towards the movement deserves further remark. . . . This being granted, it does appear that officials who definitely oppose the movement should receive very summary treatment."

When the consolidation of holdings was taken up in all seriousness the Registrar had to record: "*Quanugoes and patwaris are as a rule ranked by the staff with baniyas as the natural enemy.*" One Subdivisional officer refused to sanction mutation of land as a result of consolidation. He brought the entire work in this *illaqa* to a standstill. Higher authorities had to be moved, and this official had to be transferred by the Government to some other place.

Now that the elementary stage is over the courts find it possible to harass the members of Societies and subject them to many hardships and disadvantages in dealing with disputes and arbitration awards filed with them. It is exceedingly regrettable to find Civil Courts thus evidently taking sides against a movement which is perhaps the only hope of the Province's economic salvation, but the success of which would stop the agelong exploitation of the unfortunate victims of the sahukars. The Report for 1918 records: "Practically every district report contains complaints against the Civil Courts, and several instances have come to light of conduct which it would be difficult to excuse. Most Munsifs are ignorant of the law of arbitration, and many know little of liquidation work. Attempts to convince them that the decree must be in accordance with the award are rejected with contempt. In some cases we have been compelled to seek aid from Appellate Courts, and though we win in the end, this is not the best way of teaching Munsifs that the Civil procedure code is binding on them. In some courts there seems to be an idea that we are infringing their jurisdiction, and resentment is shown against the idea of arbitration without the intervention of the court. In execution proceedings there is great room for improvement, the Naib Nazir and the Bailiff are almost universally dishonest, and we have either to condone bribery or see our decrees unsatisfied." This by itself is sufficiently clear, but would admit of some explanation. I wish I could have access to the files of material in the Registrar's office, which unfortunately are treated as "Confidential." Anyway, one thing seems perfectly clear; now that the cultivator is brought to court by a Society and not by a sahukar, the Civil Courts begin to show him some indulgence, evidently not with a view to helping him, but obviously with a desire to embarrass the Societies and to imperil the working of the movement so far as it lies in their power.

The Report for 1920 has a similar story to record. "The

complaints against the subordinate Civil Service Staff come from every District." The chief difficulty is due "partly to the vexatious proceedings or absence of proceedings in court; when a man is performing honorary duty he does not like to be made to wait about all day only to be asked for a bribe and abused at the end of it." It is a sad commentary upon the ways and methods of petty-minded officials who in their zeal misuse their authority to the detriment of such a movement. This uncharitable treatment extended to the Co-operative movement by presiding officers of Civil Courts becomes contagious and all connected with such courts refuse to discharge their duties honestly in cases where Co-operative Societies are concerned. "The worst obstacle is the bailiff. In one case, at least, an order of dismissal resulted from a well-founded complaint. In another case, corruption was reported to the Munsif, who, after due inquiry, reported it to the senior sub-judge, who in turn *finding the bailiff guilty, only warned him.*" Here is a complaint openly made by the head of a Government Department against the behaviour of officers of another Department. Do such attempts amount to shielding corruption in the subordinate staff, or purposely depriving those connected with another Department of the right and facility allowed by law? Who will solve this riddle? I wish it were possible for me to make public all such cases in the light of which certain conclusions would be irresistible and unassailable. Here are some specific cases mentioned by the Department. "In one case there were forty infructuous hearings in two years against a man of property, in another forty-two hearings spread over three years yielded nothing."

The Report for 1917 records: "Unfortunately the old opposition still persists amongst a few Munsifs of a particular class, and has led them into courses actually illegal . . . but there is still room for improvement in the attitude of some courts towards a movement which is not only replacing litigation by arbitration, but is aimed at uplifting the economic position of the people."

The wily bailiff, whose services are needed in connection

with execution proceedings, has proved to be too much for the Co-operative Department. The Report for 1926 is itself elaborate enough to let us feel the power of this mighty little man. The Registrar says: "Hitherto we have been allowed in several districts to pay for special bailiffs, and have been required also to pay commission fees on goods auctioned by these men who were maintained at our cost. I represented that since Societies expect a bailiff to carry out without further charge the duty for which he is paid, and this is distasteful to many bailiffs, we should be allowed to offer our own candidates for employment, or pay a higher salary to a regular bailiff. The order actually passed, however, is that bailiffs executing Co-operative awards are to be changed every month. *Each bailiff therefore shall suffer only one month, and we shall suffer all the time.* One bailiff took a gratuity of 10 annas from a defaulter and gave him a receipt. *The receipt was produced, with a request for severe action before the sub-judge, who warned the offender.*"

"A sub-judge surprisingly held, in a Civil suit by a surety from whom recovery had been made in lieu of an insolvent debtor, that the insolvency of the principal released the sureties. His judgment was upset on appeal."

The Report for 1927, discussing the difficulty of the Co-operative Department regarding the change of bailiffs every thirty days, records: "The order of the High Court, directing that bailiffs who execute warrants on behalf of Co-operative Societies shall be changed every month, has deprived the special bailiff (for whom we pay) of all value. Knowing that Co-operators will not satisfy his demands, the bailiff does the minimum possible in his short period of affliction." This is but a hopelessly inadequate review of the state of things. I leave it to the fair-minded reader to frame his own conclusions on the material supplied by the various Registrars who, I have reasons to believe, have withheld more voluminous and damaging material than they have permitted to see the light of day.

CHAPTER XLIII

ASSISTANCE

WE have now left behind us the storm of opposition still raging in all its fury, only the Department has evidently stopped taking or making any note of it. Co-operation for its success presupposes amongst other things a public-spirited and generous enthusiasm on the part of its workers, and real sympathy and devotional support of every citizen worth the name. As the movement began, it did secure a certain amount of support from public-spirited workers, but as it grew the proportion and intensity of external support weakened. One of the reasons for the comparatively poor support of the movement in rural areas is the lack of people really capable of helping the movement. An enthusiasm for such a movement presupposes a certain amount of mental and social development which does not exist in the Punjab. Anyway, at the commencement of the movement the assistance was not entirely lacking, and those who quite a generation ago gave their time and energy to the furtherance of this movement deserve an honourable mention in the history of Co-operation in the Province.

The first person to deserve such mention is Sardar Hira Singh, of Panjwar Society, concerning whom the Registrar records in the first Annual Report of the Department as follows: ." . . the whole credit will be due to Hira Singh. His assistance has been invaluable. He stayed with me some ten days in camp and delivered four excellent addresses. He has offered to give his services free to help and advise any new Society in the neighbourhood. I have great pleasure in bringing his services to the notice of the Government. Unofficial assistance of this kind will contribute enormously to the success of the scheme."

ASSISTANCE OF THE PRESS

In the beginning of the movement the Mussulman vernacular Press in the Province lent very great help to the cause of its furtherance. The Press itself was in a very elementary stage of development, but it acquitted itself in a manner that left nothing to be desired. The *Zemindar* rendered commendable services in this connection, and these services met with the warmest approval and the sincerest appreciation of the Department. The Registrar in his Annual Report for 1907 records: "I have been fortunate everywhere in receiving most valuable assistance from the true leaders of public opinion, and from the native Press. The *Zemindar* newspaper especially has taken great interest in the movement, and its lucid and sympathetic articles have been most useful in spreading information on the subject among zemindars in the Central Punjab. To Munshi Siraj-ud-Din, the editor, especially my thanks are due."

The *Zemindar* has always been a friend of the zemindar. This policy of the founder of the *Zemindar* has been more than maintained by a valiant son, who commands a place of honour amongst the leaders of thought and action in Mussulman India.

The *Watan*, of Lahore, another Urdu weekly like the *Zemindar*, rendered every help to the movement. The Registrar in his first Annual Report records: "The *Watan* also by its broad-minded articles on interest has done much to remove the prejudices of Muhammadans against a scheme of which the main object is to relieve them from the clutches of the interest-seeking money-lender. I should be obliged if the copies of my Report be sent to the editors of these two newspapers." The Registrar was rightly so confident of the support of the vernacular Press for the movement that, continuing his remarks, he said: "In fact I would suggest that copies of my Report be sent to the editors of all vernacular newspapers in the Punjab as I feel sure that, whatever their attitude may be on other matters, they will bring favourably to their readers' notice a scheme of which the object is the material and moral improvement of the Punjabi zemindar." This was an excellent idea, and I believe can even now be followed with great advantage.

The village headmen, safed-poshes and zaildars helped the movement, and their help was recognized.

In the Annual Report for 1908 the sympathies and assistance of the vernacular Press meet with the usual acknowledgment and appreciation. The *Zemindar* and the *Watan* are particularly mentioned.

Regarding the contribution of the *Watan* towards the furtherance of the movement, the Report records: "The editor of the latter (*Watan*), who has written a broad-minded book (sale price, annas 10) on the morality of Muhammadans taking interest, presented me with forty copies for distribution. They have had an excellent effect." As regards the activities of the *Zemindar*, the Registrar records: "The editor of the *Zemindar* prints periodical pamphlets on agricultural improvements, which, he suggested, might be circulated to Co-operative Credit Societies. Though these pamphlets are full of useful information, I am doubtful whether the ordinary villager would derive much benefit from them. The educated ought to subscribe individually." What Molvi Siraj-ud-Din, the founder of the *Zemindar*, thought essential in 1908, and concerning the wisdom of which course Mr. Wilberforce, the then Registrar, felt doubtful, carries the support of subsequent events, and is at present recognized as of fundamental importance, and similar pamphlets and now even books are being published in large numbers by the Department itself.

Workers in the movement were awarded titles, the first one, that of Sardar Sahib, going to Sardar Narain Singh, of Tibbus Bank, in 1908. Certificates of approbation of the Punjab Government were also awarded.

Everyone will agree with the Registrar when he says: "The true pioneers of the movement are the gentlemen who by the establishment and efficient management of good Societies set an example to others. A successful concrete example has far more effect on villagers than any amount of persuasive argument. For instance, the success of the establishment of five Societies among colonists in Lyallpur recruited from the same zail."

The Province as a whole was exceedingly different in its mental and political make-up and outlook from what it is to-day. The influence of the Government officials was immensely greater than it is now, more particularly in rural areas. The poor cultivator of the soil even now feels that the patwari is a mighty man, who must be feared and obeyed. He recognizes that the Tahsildar and the Sub-Inspector of Police personify the power of the Government, and their favours and frowns may make or mar the careers of men and positions of families. This is a self-evident truth, and the inhabitants of the rural areas have learnt this lesson exceedingly well, and tend consciously or unconsciously to mould their activities in conformity with this belief. The influence of the Government officials, whose wishes, express or otherwise, must instinctively be honoured by the leaders of rural areas, was almost incalculable a generation ago. The then Registrar, like everyone of us, knew this, and counted upon the support these Government officials could lend. Some of them, of course, rendered every help as a matter of duty. Such help should always be counted as assistance to a sister Department of the Government. I will be giving copious extracts from the Annual Reports, but I do feel that Government officials as a class did not show, with few exceptions of course, that enthusiasm for the movement which it deserves. In a way the position still requires considerable sympathetic treatment at the hands of those representing different parts of the machinery of government in the Punjab.

The Registrar in his second and third Reports of the Department recognized the help he had received at the hands of the Government officials, and in his Report for 1908 came out with a list of Tahsildars and Extra-Assistant Commissioners who had helped him. But an embarrassing experience at the very outset of the movement, I believe not the only one of its type, made him quite cautious. Official help was badly needed, as no start could be made without their active support and moral assistance. The Registrar wrote in 1909: "The help of Government officials, if properly directed, is still more useful than any other, and I am arranging to obtain it as much as possible." It was the following incident that put the Registrar on his guard in the matter of receiving official help. He had this experience in the Karnal District at the very commencement of the movement in 1905. "These Tahsildars received some excellent instructions from the Deputy Commissioner, but entirely misunderstood their purport. They thought that it was a Government order that Societies should be started everywhere, and without the least comprehension of the nature of the scheme proceeded to take energetic and active measures. The Tahsildar of Kaithal explained to a large meeting of the zaildars and lambardars that the Registrar was arriving shortly and that before his arrival they must each send in applications to be entered. In the other three cases the coerced contributors were practically all in debt, and naturally saw no advantage in borrowing Rs. 50 or Rs. 100 at 27 per cent from a money-lender to finance a Society in which they took no interest, and of which they had no knowledge. The misguided action of the Tahsildars has to a certain extent discredited the scheme in Thanesar and Kaithal."

The next year the Registrar recorded: "Officials are taking growing interest in the movement. Their help, always valuable, is mostly so when the work is being started in a District."

Syed Iftikhar-ud-Din, an E.A.C., identified himself with the movement, and, in the words of the Registrar, "lost no opportunity of pointing out its advantages to the people." But the Registrar in the same Report in which he singles out Syed Iftikhar-ud-Din for mention, remarks: "The number of officials who are genuinely interested in the Village Banks is indeed small." Eight years after its establishment the Department had to record that there were only "a few influential supporters outside" the movement.

Certain Government officials regarded the movement as

opposed to their interests. The officials must be reckoned as dangerous opponents. The Registrar records in his Report for 1914: "Some lesser officials see in the members of these Societies a growing spirit of independence which they feel conflicts with their authority and interest. One or two appear to think that the Co-operative Credit Societies tend to form an *imperium in imperio* in the Districts, and to become something outside the ordinary District administration." I respectfully make a gift of this extract to Mr. F. L. Bryane, the pioneer of the Rural Reconstruction Movement in India, who now worthily fills the position of Commissioner, Rural Reconstruction, Punjab. What happened twenty years ago in regard to the Co-operative movement is likely to repeat itself, if there is the remotest chance of disturbing the monopolists of official power. But I have ample faith in the Commissioner's power as compared with the helplessness of a Registrar of Co-operative Societies more than a score of years ago. This, however, is in passing.

The Registrar tells us in 1916: "That the Central Banks owe their success to the devoted public spirit of a few gentlemen. . . . Amongst the members of primary societies are many enthusiastic workers who constitute the basis for an optimistic view of the future of the movement." The Registrar by that time had found out: "That the person who wields most influence, and who is trusted by the villagers, is most frequently unknown to the District staff, while the lambardars are often counted amongst our opponents."

Since the movement was by that time only a decade old the Registrar's mention of such staunch internal supporters of the movement does not seem to indicate that the number of such enthusiastic workers was in any way comparatively large. The Annual Report for 1917, while telling us that some Deputy Commissioners have evinced a practical sympathy with the movement, complains against the indifference of the Punjab Civil Service. Their open or veiled opposition to the movement has already been mentioned. It is refreshing to have to record in the words of the Annual Report for 1917 that

"Indian police officers and retired military officers are giving valuable help." Indian police officers and military officers generally do not belong to the money-lending classes of the Province. Opposition from such classes would have been unchivalrous, and it is a pleasure to confess that these classes fulfilled our highest expectations in the assistance of a movement directed to the uplift of the downtrodden. The movement in its present stage does not stand in need of such help as was essential in the beginning, but even now retired military officers, wherever they have taken up this work, are doing it with characteristic devotion and honesty of purpose. Mr. Darling in a recent Report mentions the case of a sixty-year-old retired military officer in the Attock District walking about forty-two miles both ways to attend a meeting organized by a Central Bank.

Official help from Deputy Commissioners and Tahsildars was not always lacking, and under normal conditions is not now much needed. But on the basis of the material available the conclusion is that Government servants as a class, particularly those in the Civil, did more to injure the movement than encourage it.

Mr. H. Calvert did much to organize his Department, and succeeded in putting more life and vigour into those who were already there, and brought more ability and enthusiasm into the Department in the form of new recruits. The success of a Department like this depends upon the worth of its own representatives. Regarding his own workers, Mr. Calvert wrote in 1923: "They are a body of men of whom the Province ought to be proud. They developed the real constructive sense that aspires to work for distant ends, even though the immediate results seem small and slow of growth."

Any official assistance in the form in which it was needed at the commencement is no longer necessary. The attitude of those who in one way or another still misuse their official power to the detriment of the movement must needs be mended.

The movement for its growth and consolidation needs as ever the honest and devoted efforts of the workers of the

Department, and more sacrifice and honesty on the part of those engaged in running the movement.

HONORARY STAFF

Major Sardar Muhammad Nawaz Khan, of Kot Fateh Khan, Attock District, is the only Honorary Assistant Registrar in the Province. He is a Punjab chief who has set an enviable example in honestly looking after the welfare of those whom Providence has been pleased to place under his wise and sympathetic charge. He finances as well as supervises the forty-nine Societies in his estate. An account of the working of the Societies in his estate appears elsewhere in these pages. The number of Honorary Inspectors, some of whom do useful service, stood at ten in 1930, and is now declining. There are only three Honorary Sub-Inspectors whose work is in the latest report described as being "on the whole a very notable contribution to Co-operative activity."

More than this staff, it is the actual workers who are needed badly. The movement for its success and expansion needs more of actual, honest, and intelligent workers—Presidents, Secretaries, and others. There is a dearth of capable men for running the Societies. In towns of the Province we come across a number of retired officers who can take up any type of honorary work, and amongst the Hindus any kind of social service is willingly and with benefit taken up by such retired officials. Few such people are to be found in villages, hence there is a great difficulty in finding intelligent and sympathetic workers for the movement. People who are capable of taking up this work in rural areas are generally poor, and consequently lack that spirit of self-sacrifice and zeal which is so essential to the success of the movement. Not only that. The number of those who wish to manipulate their position for personal ill-gotten gains is not quite negligible.

A popular misconception must in this connection be corrected. It is sometimes erroneously believed that schoolmasters and ministers of religion do not play their part, as in Europe, in assisting Co-operation in the village. An inquiry was conducted in 1928, and the result indicated that this reproach is not entirely justified. Schoolmasters and mullahs were found to be working as Secretaries in a large number of Societies. The latest figures for such honorary workers are not available. "The movement owes these gentlemen a debt of gratitude, for many of them are working honorarily, and the rest are receiving a very modest allowance for their services."

	Number of Societies	Secretaries
1928	1,188	Schoolmasters
	877	Mullahs
1929	1,383	Schoolmasters
	963	Mullahs*

* Report for 1928.

CHAPTER XLIV

ACHIEVEMENTS

PROVISION OF CAPITAL AND SAVING IN INTEREST

Without the provision of capital no economic development is possible. But it is not the mere provision of capital, but the adequate provision of capital on reasonable terms that helps the economic development of a country. The sahukar has lent large sums of money to the cultivator, but he is a blood-sucker. The terms on which he supplies capital are calculated to carry on a reckless exploitation of the industrious son of the soil. Co-operation has not only supplied large capital to the cultivator, but has supplied it on very humane and reasonable terms. "Reckon up the mere value of money," says Wolff, "which this Co-operative mint has drawn from the capitalist market, traders, and wage-earners, distributing it judiciously at the very points at which there was the greatest need for it, and at which it promised to prove most productive, dividing it according to the requirements of each case, watching over its employment, and then, after having given bread to the eater and seed to the sower, gathering it all up again with scarcely any loss and with adequate interest." Again, "it has brought money to many a spot thirsting for it, generally in the right way, it has replaced hopeless insolvency by the solvency already attained, or else in prospect; there are at any rate hundreds, probably thousands, who have by the aid of this powerful ally effectually liberated themselves from the usurer's yoke; there are villages in which the *mahajan* and *sowcar* now find their occupation gone. The institution has accordingly inspired new hopes with the debt-burdened ryots and opened them a way to higher existence." There is more than mere beauty and force of language in these quotations from the pen of a celebrated writer and a world-renowned co-operator, but unfortunately this description is yet very premature. We can, however, form an estimate along these lines, which since it has not been attempted is well worth trying. The establishment of the Co-operative Credit Societies has been a source of immense saving to the Punjab cultivators in the form of low rates of interest to be paid as against the heartless exactions of the money-lenders. Take the Report for 1933, the latest available at the time these lines are being written: "The amount of capital actually in circulation among Societies, excluding money interlent, is about 12,73 crores. . . ." The Committee on Co-operation say: "We may fairly assume that the saving on each loan given out by Societies during the year to the agriculturists has at least amounted to 10 per cent. . . ." If all payments are taken into consideration this estimate has to be acknowledged as fairly true. Reckon it up and you find that the Punjab co-operators save Rs. 12730,000 a year, a sum which represents nearly 32 per cent of the annual land revenue of the Province. The total agricultural debt of the Province has been reckoned at Rs. 135 crores. If this entire amount had been borrowed from the Co-operative Societies the annual saving on interest alone would have amounted to Rs. 13½ crores, a sum which, if wisely utilized, would transform the very face of the Province within five years. If Co-operation could yield no other benefit, this one alone is sufficient to command every possible effort on our part to replace sahukara credit by Co-operative credit.

ENCOURAGEMENT OF SAVINGS

Co-operation breeds many virtues. By enforcing the productive use of a loan and its punctual repayment it awakens in the co-operator a desire for a successful business life. With the growth of the Co-operative credit the love of hoarding is dying out, and people are developing the habit of investment. The amount of capital actually in circulation in 1933 was Rs. 12,73 crores, out of which Rs. 0,12 crores was in the form of loans from Government granted almost exclusively for

Mortgage Banks. The rest of Rs. 12,61 crores was made up as follows:

	Crores
Paid-up share capital	1,95
Reserve fund	2,38
Deposits	7,28

Taking the Agricultural Societies alone we find that for 1932–33:

	Lakhs
Shares amounted to	1,10
Reserve funds	2,30
Profits	34

Deposits in Agricultural Credit Societies for 1933 amounted to about Rs. 75 lakhs alone. But it cannot be denied that for the movement as a whole the entire sum of Rs. 12,61 crores represents a substantial effort at inculcating the habit of thrift amongst co-operators and others. The depositors include all classes, and the virtue of thrift and saving has been preached with satisfactory results even among women and children.

GROWTH OF EDUCATION

Co-operation is in itself an educative medium of considerable importance. Illiterate persons who live up to the standards of the movement develop great practical common sense which has a greater economic value than mere literacy. Co-operation did arouse in the people a strong desire for general education, and the Department of Co-operation has long since been helping the establishment of Societies for Education. Adult schools and schools for children have been working for about fifteen years, and quite a large number of pupils have acquired literacy certificates through both these types of schools. Members of the Compulsory Education Societies undertake to send their children to school under pain of a penalty. These Societies have helped the cause of education in rural Punjab, and have thereby prepared the ground for investment of effort in every good cause. In 1933 there were eighty-four Compulsory Education Societies with 2,919 pupils on the roll. There were eleven Societies exclusively for the education of girls. This form of Co-operation has unfortunately shown an alarming deterioration, and needs immediate attention and joint effort on the part of the Departments of Education and Co-operation, whose activities can with advantage be supplemented by the District Boards. From 1925 to 1932 the number of literacy certificates for the six years for which figures are available comes up to 1,957. This is a great step forward in a country where one may travel for miles without meeting a person who can read or write a letter.

MORAL ADVANTAGES

As the main standard of admission to a Society is a man's character, Co-operation has helped the formation and elevation of character amongst those who have come under its influence. Co-operation has not only moulded the character of members unconsciously, but has consciously exerted a considerable influence in reclaiming bad characters. Drunkards and gamblers have reformed their ways. "What can be done by Co-operation in a village community is exemplified by the history of a Sikh village near Amritsar. This was formerly full of bad characters, the people were poor, many of them drank, their cattle were weak, and their land mostly mortgaged. In this village the Co-operation Society is now seven years old. The people no longer drink, no one is on security, the cattle are strong, and much land has been redeemed. Equally healthy is the growth of sound public opinion among the members of the Co-operative Societies. From one Punjab village comes the story of a member who made a regular income out of perjury. The Directors of a Local Union got the other members to expel and excommunicate him. The perjurer repented, took a public oath in the village mosque, and was readmitted" (*India in 1919*).

In Gurgaon District a Committee considered that a man

spent too much time in the mosque, and therefore his maximum credit limit was reduced to Rs. 30 only until he "bestirred himself over his fields." In one case in 1920 a Society expelled a man for abduction. He was acquitted by the court, presumably on mere technical grounds, but the Society did not forgive him. In one village gambling was very popular. The inhabitants of that village wanted to start a Society, but it was not allowed to be started until the prospective members gave a written agreement that gamblers would not be admitted. "The distinction smote the non-members, who in a few months gave up gambling and applied for membership." The virtue of punctuality is fostered widely and in various ways. Report for 1920 tells us, "Gurgaon Society fines its members for absence from monthly General Meetings, and contributes the receipts to the mosque fund." The same Report states: "Several Inspectors report cases of people giving up a criminal career in order to qualify for membership." In one village where there were three Societies one member, on being expelled from his Society for gambling, applied to the other two for admission, but was given a stout "No." In one case the President of a Society was found gambling. He was taken to task by the members, and was readmitted only after taking an oath to give up the habit. In one case a member was convicted of theft, and his brother wanted to borrow money from the Society for meeting the expenses of an appeal, and we are told the Committe had the good sense and courage to refuse the loan on the ground that the man was really guilty. In two cases in 1921 members were fined for giving false evidence before the arbitrators.

We are told that members of a Purbia Society in Lyallpur gave up drink entirely. Those who know the Purbias will realize that their abstinence is the greatest achievement of the movement. A drunkard was expelled from one Society, and another in another Society was threatened with fine as penalty for a second offence.

In one village a bad character induced the inhabitants of his village to start a Society. A Society was started, but he was not allowed membership. He got together some more persons and organized a second Society, but in that venture, too, he was refused membership.

BETTER LIVING AND SOCIAL REFORM

Wasteful expenditure on ceremonies is a social evil which no individual effort is capable of suppressing. Uncalled-for and colossal expenses on deaths, marriages, and births have ruined the Punjab peasantry, yet no individual dare defy the conventions of the community. Co-operation sets people thinking, and being combined in a group their courage is doubled, and their resolution to set an example to the rest of the community make of them pioneers of social reform. Whatever of social reform, thrift, and better living in rural Punjab is to be witnessed to-day is the direct result of the growth and understanding of the spirit of Co-operation. At an early stage of the movement it was realized by the workers in the movement that the Punjab cultivator is not only to be supplied with cheap and controlled credit, but he must as well be made to realize that checking of waste is, if not more, at least equally important. In some cases the Co-operators organized associations for bringing about social reform, in others they adopted by-laws in Credit Societies providing the eradication of many social evils as one of their objects, and later on separate Societies in the form of Better Living and Arbitration Societies developed to foster some specific object of great social and economic value. The co-operators have tried with a measure of success to check extravagance, litigation, and objectionable ways of living. Dancing-girls are no more employed at marriage parties, and the use of fireworks has been very nearly completely abandoned. In 1920 a Moharar of the Lahore High Court who issued invitations to a ceremony on gilt-lettered cards was fined by his Society for extravagance. A considerable number of Societies have definite by-laws aiming at the abolition of extravagance. Large marriage parties are a thing of the past, and are not entertained for a number of days at the girl's house.

The entertainment is of a very simple and inexpensive kind. In one case people who insisted upon extravagance, when they failed to listen to arguments, were beaten. In one case sweets that should not have been bought were thrown before the cattle. Members of one Society refused to join a marriage party of non-members unless they agreed to do away with all forms of extravagance, as decided by the members of the Society.

Thrift is the basic virtue of a prosperous nation. This virtue the Department of Co-operation has tried to foster as far as possible. The growth of non-agricultural Thrift Societies is indicated by the following table:

	Number of Societies	Membership	Amount of Saving
			Rs.
1923	72	1,164	25,000
1933	1,146	21,708	13,89,000

Efforts have been made to check litigation by the imposition of fines on those who give false evidence, and by the establishment of Arbitration Societies. The number of Arbitration Societies is eighty-four, with a membership of nearly twelve thousand. The highest recorded number of disputes decided was 924 in 1929. Co-operation has affected the life of the people in almost all its phases. "Besides rules directed to this end," says the Report for 1933, "Societies have adopted others for village sanitation, compulsory vaccination and inoculation, ventilation of houses, prohibition of opium and (in two *Jat* Sikh villages) of illicit distillation, cleanliness of clothes and person, etc. Practical measures have also been taken to protect crops from stray cattle and pilfering humans, and to promote physical culture by wrestling matches."

The attitude towards beggars has changed. A Hissar Society ejected from the village eleven professional beggars when the economic and moral significance of beggary was explained to them. One village has disallowed the entry of beggars in it.

Another village has decided to give alms only to such beggars as are allowed to enter the village by the village *granthi*.

SHARE OF WOMEN IN THE MOVEMENT

In 1920 in the Society of chak 102 R.B. Patti Musalmana, the President, died leaving a minor son. His widow was elected President at the General Meeting, and the Annual Report for that year proudly records the Registrar's great appreciation of the way in which she discharged her duties. The Report says: "She takes an active part in the work, attending meetings, making recoveries, and managing the Society. She also personally shows the accounts, etc., to the staff. Her success is indicated by the fact that the Society is in class B. Her name, Musammat Hakim Bibi, deserves to be placed on the record."

Women are members of Men's Societies in a number of cases, and in some it is virtually the wife of the President who serves the Society. Co-operation is spreading gradually amongst women in the Punjab, and there are eleven Sub-Inspectresses and one lady Inspector to help the growth of the movement. There are 189 Women's Societies with a membership of 3,393, and a working capital of Rs. 1,86 lakhs. These Societies are inculcating in the females and children of the Province a love of thrift and better living—an investment of effort and money which over long periods is bound to yield very substantial results.

SICKENING STARVATION TURNED INTO SMILING PLENTY

The following account of the miraculous powers of Co-operation and the honest and humane efforts of the Punjab co-operators is given by Sardar Bhagat Singh, Assistant Registrar. We are sure the Department has wrought numerous such miracles whose brilliance is all the more genuine for not having been used by the publicity enthusiast.

"I was stationed as an Inspector at Karnal in 1918, and used often to roam about in rural areas where the civilizing influence of man seems to have left untarnished the workmanship of God. In one of my rambles I passed, one afternoon, by the side of a well, the scanty equipment and the deserted appearance of which proclaimed the poverty of its owner. I went to the hut close by, and a sickly, starving cultivator coughed aloud and looked up to me. His appearance betrayed not only his physical infirmity and mental distress but disclosed equally clearly the anguish of his soul.

" 'What ails you?' I inquired of him. 'Sheer hunger, sir,' was his determined and stunning reply. This was more than I expected. I sat down by his side to console him in his distress. Seeing me thus visibly moved, he began narrating his story.

" 'My name is Allah Bakhsh. My father, who was quite a well-to-do zemindar, died six years ago. I had to spend Rs. 250 on the ceremonies gone through at the death of my father. My father had left me Rs. 200, and Rs. 50 I borrowed from Shaikh Mohd. Ibrahim. Soon after this I had to borrow once again Rs. 300 towards the expenses of my sister's marriage. Mohd. Ibrahim, the indulgent money-lender, once again so willingly came to my help. A succession of bad harvests rendered it difficult for me to pay the land revenue even. Mohd. Ibrahim volunteered to help me out of the difficulty once again. One of my bullocks died last year, and in the sowing season I had to purchase on credit a bullock for Rs. 80, which in cash was hardly worth Rs. 50. The courteous money-lender has grown strangely callous now, and holds out a threat to drag me to a court of law in case of non-payment. The seller of the bullock wants payment. Underfeeding has undermined my health; my children are starving, and my bullocks have deteriorated for the lack of fodder. How can I plough, and what can I sow?'

"I consoled him for a while, and then quietly suggested to him that it was all due to his own improvident and foolish ways of life, and that there was still a way out. 'Well,' he said, 'God alone can change my condition now. All is over with me.' It took me some time to shake off his mental distress and inject some hope into his broken heart. I asked him to bestir himself and to make up his mind to practice thrift, and to save at least one-fourth of his income. I made a number of calculations for him, and found that he could with a little external help and strict economy in his expenditure still be redeemed to solvency and prosperity. He promised on oath to follow my directions, and the very next day I visited his village and in due course started a Co-operative Credit Society there. I explained to them all the causes of their poverty and the way out. All made serious promises, and Allah Bakhsh was a member of this Society, the by-laws of which provided for compulsory deposits.

"Each member had promised that he would (1) practice thrift; (2) borrow only for productive purposes; and (3) make production more efficient.

"Allah Bakhsh had been fired with a desire to regain his lost prosperity and peace of mind. He often consulted me as to the methods he should adopt in practising economy on certain special occasions. I left Karnal after two years, and was retransferred to Karnal after five long years. Allah Bakhsh was the first man to greet me at the railway station, Karnal. He invited me to his place, a poor farm with a deserted well, where seven years ago my rambles had led me. I was very impatient to see for myself the result of my experiment in redeeming many a lost family. I went to Allah Bakhsh's village the same afternoon. To my agreeable surprise and utmost satisfaction the entire scene had changed. The broken thatched hut had given place to a pukka room in the fields, and the deserted well of seven years ago had been so extended as to allow the working of a double *rahat.* The green fields of tobacco and sugar-cane produced a beautiful contrast to the dismal background of seven years ago so fresh in my memory.

"Allah Bakhsh told me with a feeling of pride that Mohd. Ibrahim, the magnanimous money-lender, had left the village. All cultivators had joined the Society, and had no external transactions. Their deposits had swelled to Rs. 6,000, and Allah Bakhsh alone was responsible for Rs. 2,000 out of the total deposits. Allah Bakhsh had been elected President of the Society. The village had a school for children, people had reformed their ways, and were both happy and prosperous. I left the village late in the evening, but the transformation of this village, whenever I recall it, yields me a supreme spiritual satisfaction."

The above is an English rendering of an Urdu article which appeared in the *Co-operation* of Lahore. Some friends have suggested that it is merely a story. The names may well be fictitious, but no one who knows anything about the working of the movement will doubt its authenticity.

Co-operation is a vital force which, under the peculiar circumstances prevailing in this country, needs for its expression the sympathies and powers of a Sardar Bhagat Singh combined with the energy and will of an Allah Bakhsh. It is this combination that will bring about the desired transformation within a generation. The problem of the Department is to find a Bhagat Singh, and that of the Government so to extend its ameliorating activities as to redeem every Allah Bakhsh before he is lost for ever. As the Government and the Department must do their duty, let us lift our hats to Sardar Bhagat Singh and Allah Bakhsh, who combined to banish sickness and poverty and brought instead profound peace and smiling plenty to the peasantry of the Punjab.

REDEMPTION OF OLD DEBTS

The Jhang Mortgage Bank, the first Co-operative Land Mortgage Bank in India, was organized in 1920. The number of Land Mortgage Banks in the Punjab now is twelve. These banks supply long-term credit to the agriculturists, and have been a source of considerable use to the zemindars and have redeemed many an honest zemindar from the jaws of certain economic death. Since their start the banks have advanced nearly Rs. 33¼ lakhs. The total amounts advanced up to 1930 for different purposes were as follows (the figures cannot be brought up to date for the subsequent loans have not been very clearly classified):

	Lakhs of Rupees
Repayment of old debts	14,47
Redemption of land	14,70
Improvement of land	2,17
Purchase of land	0,19

The total area of land redeemed through these banks amounted to 21,338 acres up to 1930.

AGRICULTURE

CONSOLIDATION OF HOLDINGS

Holdings in the Punjab are small and scattered, and these defects besides leading to frequent quarrels in our villages and a huge loss of area in the form of too many boundary lines make progressive agriculture an impossibility. Co-operative Consolidation of Holdings was initiated in the Punjab, and has achieved marvellous results. The area of land under cultivation has increased, the number of disputes has diminished, rents have gone up, and land revenue has increased, 2,020 wells have either been newly constructed or have been brought back into use after having been discarded—proud achievements which alone entitle the Department to the lasting gratitude of the cultivator. A few instances will not be out of place. In one place an area of 4,173 acres scattered into 1,099 blocks has been consolidated into fifty-eight blocks. One owner had his 875 acres scattered in 194 blocks over ten villages, consolidation has given him a single block in one village. In Ghazikot one owner had 31 acres divided into forty fields scattered in twenty-six places. He received Rs. 6 as rent per acre. Consolidation gave him one solid block, and the same tenants paid him Rs. 10 as rent per acre. In 1924 it was possible to bring under cultivation 27,000 acres of land which excessive fragmentation had thrown out of cultivation. New adjustment of land in certain places has so considerably increased the area under cultivation that the farmers have set apart tracts of land for the digging of manure-pits, for grazing-grounds, for gardens, for school buildings, for playgrounds and graveyards. The use of better implements has been rendered possible, and improved methods of irrigation have been adopted. In 1933 there were 101 Societies working for Consolidation of Holdings in the Punjab, and 62,052 acres had been consolidated, with the result that over 91,000 fields had been converted into nearly 15,000 blocks.

Any scheme for the economic regeneration of the cultivator who neglects his craft is sadly incomplete. The Department of Co-operation at a very early stage of the movement devoted its attention to the improvement of agriculturists. The staff of the Department acquires necessary information concerning purely agricultural problems through agricultural training classes. For starting Milk-recording Societies members of the Department were sent for training to Karnal and Bangalore. The Department is thus well equipped with people who are competent to give lessons in agriculture to cultivators. In co-operation with the Department of Agriculture, the Department of Co-operation in the Punjab has helped the cultivator to understand the utility of adopting improved implements for and methods of agriculture. The Societies have helped fruit growing, sugar-making, lac growing, and joint cultivation.

The number of Stock-breeding Societies has increased from twenty in 1923 to 136 in 1933. These Societies have instilled a desire in the members to improve the stock and to dispose of such cattle as impose an uneconomic obligation upon them. The cattle belonging to the members of such Societies always win prizes at cattle shows, and command a premium on the current price. Unfortunately these Societies have deteriorated a good deal. Milk-recording Societies have helped the members to carry on scientific tests as regards the quality of their milk cattle. A beginning was made in cattle insurance, but unfortunately has not met with much success.

CO-OPERATIVE MARKETING

Co-operation has not only sought to redeem the cultivator from the throttling grip of the money-lender, but it has made an efficient producer of him, and it has also taught him to market his produce with greater benefit to himself. Co-operative Commission Shops have been started with a view to saving for the cultivator that which is unduly taken away from him by the rapacious middleman. The establishment of these shops means substantial profit to the seller of the produce. These shops save him a good deal in commissions, deductions, and a number of other unjustifiable charges, besides the numerous tricks that are played upon him in order to rob him of his due share in the price of his produce. There are twenty-three Commission Shops with 30,338 individuals and 1,269 Societies as members.

SANITATION

Co-operation has made the conservative farmer awake to a realization of his responsibility to himself, and he is surely though slowly changing his outlook. He is filling up ponds, distributing quinine, learning the value of pure water, and in various ways showing an inclination to grasp everything good that comes his way.

INDUSTRIAL CO-OPERATION

The Department has not entirely neglected the artisan. A number of Industrial Societies have been started. They seek to redeem the artisan from the clutches of the money-lender-middleman, who provides credit only at his own terms, and purchases the finished product at prices which swell his profits and crush all life and energy out of the artisan.

CHAPTER XLV

RURAL UP-LIFT MOVEMENT AND THE PANCHAYATS

NO account of the economic, moral, and social life of rural Punjab can lay any claim to completeness without a description of its Rural Up-lift Movement and its Panchayats. The Panchayats seek mainly to provide inexpensive and speedy tribunals of justice for petty village disputes; whereas the Rural Up-lift or Rural Reconstruction Movement aims at an all-round and simultaneous overhaul of life in the countryside.

The Punjab has been singularly fortunate in having amidst its officials a few at least who have shown a sincere solicitude for the people of the Province, and a sympathetic and practical handling of the problems of a downtrodden and friendless peasantry. The names of Strickland, Calvert, and Darling will for ever be engraved upon the memories of grateful Punjabis, and will live in the history of the Province as being those of men great in their different spheres of work. But F. L. Brayne, of Gurgaon fame, the present Rural Reconstruction Commissioner, will be remembered as the Voronoff of India. In 1921 he was the Deputy Commissioner of Gurgaon, where he started his rural up-lift or rural reconstruction work, which is now an all-India movement, and has won a place as a special Department of every Provincial Government. The Government of India has in its budget for 1935–36 set apart a sum of Rs. 1 crore to be distributed amongst different Provinces of the country for taking in hand the reconstruction of rural India.

The Punjab Government deserves to be congratulated warmly on its timely establishment of a Department of Rural Reconstruction, and on its rare good luck in having the author of the Gurgaon Scheme as the first Commissioner of its new venture in nation-building.

What is rural reconstruction? It is not hard to understand.

A study of the life and conditions in rural areas throughout India reveals quite a distressing state of things. Men are poor in spite of richness in their surroundings. They are poor but extravagant. They are in the throttling grip of the sahukar and the landlord. They respect the educated, but shun education.

Rural up-lift seeks to study the causes of poverty and distress in rural areas, and by combating these causes aims at building up a new rural civilization for India.

Rural reconstruction schemes involve a study of the man from various points of view. We study his occupation, his personal, family, and social life, and seek to eliminate the causes of his distress.

A study of agricultural methods reveals that the Punjab peasant, like the rest of his kin in India, is hopelessly ignorant of scientific and modern methods of production. He uses practically no scientific and chemical manures, is unaware of the value of rotation of crops, his implements are antiquated; in practice, he attaches no importance to the seed he sows, his methods of irrigation are as primitive and costly as are his methods of harvesting and thrashing grain. All this is enough to make him a bad farmer in spite of his proverbial industry, endurance, and immense capacity for quiet suffering.

His cattle constitute his very limbs, but he is ignorant of their value to him, and instead of being a source of wealth to him they are one of the chief causes of his distress and indebtedness. He keeps such large numbers of animals that he cannot feed adequately. He is indifferent to their quality, and is ignorant of their physical needs. He makes them drink at the dirtiest of village ponds. When they fall ill he does not easily move; and if matters come to a head he clips their ears or brands them with red-hot iron, and as a last resort invokes the spiritual healing powers of the village priest or the mullah.

It is very seldom that he takes his sick cattle to a veterinary assistant, who may be living only a few miles away. In epidemics he rarely, if ever, believes in precautionary measures. His fatalistic attitude towards life, born of his profound ignorance, dictates no urgent course of action to him, even in case of epidemics that carry away millions of men. The decree of Fate cannot be altered, and Death will not be postponed through precautions. That is his unshakable belief, which, unfortunately, in the form of his refusal to adopt precautionary measures, proves fatal to his interests and dangerous to those of the society in which he lives.

He is incredibly indifferent to the necessity of stock-breeding, and thus allows the mixing of worthless bulls with his herd of cows. This results in the production of a very inferior type of cattle. Being illiterate and ignorant, the idea of maintaining milk records of his cows and buffaloes is not acceptable to him.

Study his person and you find in him strange combinations. He is what his dull, unchanging surroundings have made him —conservative, illiterate, ignorant, suspicious, jealous, fond of litigation, incapable of making a sustained effort for his own improvement, extravagant, a confirmed borrower, industrious, honest, simple, confiding, devoted to his benefactors, hard to teach, fond of his occupation, an extreme lover of land, incapable of making even small sacrifices for large issues, and willing to sustain huge losses for contemptibly small issues.

Cleanliness of person, house, and village—the less said about it the better. He lives in a house full of rats, where people lie huddled together in winter, sleeping two or three in a bed, with scanty protection, and very often in unhealthy dingy cells where cattle are kept for the night, and in which the floors remain saturated with urine and dung. If you ask a farmer why he sleeps with his cattle in the same room, he says because it is so warm there.

He seldom washes his clothes, and a vast majority of them have never had the luxury of using soap in their bath. In illness and epidemics they display that fatal ignorance which characterizes their attitude towards the cattle.

This is due both to their ignorance and to the complete lack of medical assistance in rural areas. They suffer patiently and long, and naturally have greater trust in the local *hakim* than in a physician who has had the benefit of education in a medical college. It is more the lack of medical assistance than anything else that is responsible for this attitude. The entire medical facilities, health-promoting activities, and preventive measures are monopolized by the towns, and the rural areas are virtually treated as plague spots in our country which must for the very lives of us be avoided.

Children are not taken care of. They are kept dirty and ill-clad. Vaccination is avoided. All preventive measures are feared as a challenge to the will and majesty of God.

It is inconceivable what great hardships women undergo during confinement. In every village the *dai* or midwife is a low-caste woman, sometimes a sweeperess, steeped in supreme ignorance and abominably dirty. Recently a woman from a village was brought to Aligarh after five days of heroic struggle in confinement. The results would have been disastrous but for the sturdy life of the peasant woman that makes delivery a less serious affair than it is with the town-bred delicate women of India.

The peasant is illiterate, but loath to send his children to school. Illiteracy, conservative surroundings, and lack of intercourse with the changing world outside give him a mental make-up incapable of even seeing efforts directed towards his good in their true significance. Mr. Brayne says: "The biggest problem of all, I find, is the people themselves. They do not want to improve themselves, and, therefore, everything one does in the village fades away as soon as one turns one's back and goes away. It is easy enough to pick a man up when he is lying down, but if the man himself does not want to stand up you can only keep him up by hanging on to him all day and night. This is the villager."

His notions of social honour and obligations never allow him to practice thrift, but impose upon him the evil of an uncalled-for extravagance on ceremonies. He gets the bad looks of his brotherhood if he does not more than reciprocate the entertainment he has received. Strange notions of self-respect impoverish not only his body and mind, but embitter his very soul. He suffers all this with an almost divine patience. Life in the villages is not at all attractive. The same routine of work goes on year in and year out. His finances are borrowed from sahukars, whose unscrupulous methods and exorbitant rates of interest break his very back. He is obliged to sell under conditions and at rates which serve to enrich his exploiters. His holdings are small and fragmented.

He has a low standard of living which he is seldom ambitious enough to change. The Punjab peasant is poor, and in the strangling grip of the sahukar. He likes to meet his obligations, and up till quite recently no one seemed interested in his betterment; the neglect of the educated classes in this respect being almost criminal. The farmer is the foundation of society. He has, in the Punjab, borne the burden of the heavy structure supremely well. It is time therefore that this foundation was reinforced, or else the entire structure will collapse.

But the future is not without hope. Pioneers like Mr. Brayne, whose remarkable book, *The Re-making of Village India*, ought to find its way, directly or indirectly, into every village community in the land, have pointed the way of regeneration. The Rural Reconstruction movement is a direct attempt at rejuvenating the countryside; but in fixing our hopes upon it, let us always remember that education is the very foundation upon which all beneficial movements must be built. The Punjab peasant is illiteracy personified. Therefore we must not build upon sand. The present generation being incorrigible, let us capture the future farmer, and by preparing this ground, ploughing it deep and broad, sowing a good seed, and arranging for perennial irrigation, let us reap an inexhaustible harvest in the days to come. Change the mentality of the child and the Punjab will change; otherwise success will be short-lived and insignificant.

THE PANCHAYAT

The Panchayat is an old institution for settlement of disputes that had vanished with the advent of the new order of things in this country. The alarming increase in litigation in the Province, and the consequent waste of time, money, and energy, which a poor peasantry can ill afford, made a revival of the institution a matter of supreme necessity. The Punjab Village Panchayat Act, which provided for the establishment of Panchayats consisting of members or Panchs elected by the people of a single village or group of villages, was passed in 1921.

The main object of the Act is to provide a locally elected Committee for the settlement of petty civil and criminal disputes in villages so as to provide an organization which offers the advantages of a court of justice without the attendant waste of time and money, and much more without that bitterness of feeling that feeds upon and in its turn breeds litigation.

The supplementary functions of a Panchayat embrace all such activities which tend to promote the peace and progress of the village and its general improvement—such as the construction and maintenance of wells, tanks, drains, roads, the health of the village, the taking up of patrol duty on night, regulation of turns and duration for the use of canal water. The optional duties of the Panchayat comprise the improvement of agriculture, agricultural stock, cottage industries, maintenance of libraries, the prevention of nuisances, and the supervision of the conduct of patwaris and other petty officials.

The Panchayats were slow to come, and in a conference of officials and non-officials held in Lahore in 1926 it was decided to appoint Panchayat officers with a view to popularizing the establishment of Panchayats. Since 1926 the number of Panchayats has gone up, although local jealousies and feuds or the lack of qualified men to serve on the Panchayat were responsible for a number of casualties.

Years	Number of Panchayats
1924	240
1926	300
1928	371
1930	733

Fees and fines, besides a few voluntary contributions, form

the only sources of revenue of a Panchayat, although in a few cases village and special rates may also be imposed. By 1929–30 the number of Panchayats rose to 733, and the number of civil and criminal cases disposed of during that year came up to 3,657 and 10,540 respectively.

CHAPTER XLVI

DEFECTS AND DIFFICULTIES OF THE MOVEMENT

CO-OPERATOR'S IGNORANCE OF THE OBJECTS AND PRINCIPLES OF THE MOVEMENT

"The aim of the Credit Society is to afford cheap credit, and by so doing to reduce the total indebtedness of the members." This remark, bringing out the object of a Credit Society, was made by the Honourable Lala Har Kishen Lal, Minister for Agriculture, in an official review of the Annual Report for 1922.

This remark betrays either an indifference to the interests of the movement or a lamentable ignorance of the role of Co-operation in the economy of a country. Fortunately the interests of the movement then were safe in the able and powerful hands of Mr. Calvert, who made it a point to explain in his next Annual Report the aims and objects of Co-operation to all those who looked upon a Credit Society as a mere cheap lending agency. Referring to the above remark, Mr. Calvert said:

"With great deference I would remark that I should be very sorry indeed if any of my staff held that view, and would be surprised if any of the members gave expression to it. . . . The mere reduction of indebtedness and the provision of cheap credit are not our objects. What we do aim at is the provision of sound, well-controlled credit for productive purposes and the replacement of unproductive debt by productive borrowing."

The Honourable Sardar Sir Jogindar Singh, Minister for Agriculture, in his official review of the Annual Report for 1929 remarked: "The principles of Co-operation are now widely known, and it is their practical application which can secure satisfactory results." It is a matter of common knowledge that there is an almost universal ignorance of the principles of Co-operation. Only a few educated persons outside the circle of university teachers, or those actively associated with the movement, have attempted to acquire a knowledge of the objects and the working of the movement. It goes without saying that a knowledge of the principles of Co-operation is the very basis of the movement, and that it cannot be expected in a people where literacy is an exception. A Punjab cultivator in 70 per cent of cases cannot count up to one hundred. Do we expect such people to learn and remember principles of Co-operation? Is it not curious that a predecessor of the Honourable Sardar Sir Jogindar Singh should have had such an unscientific notion of the object of Co-operation? Need we then blame the illiterate cultivator who is mentally incapable of learning and remembering things after having learnt them.

Anyone who knows the stuff of which the members of an Agricultural Co-operative Society are made will never be prepared to subscribe to this view. In a vast majority of the Societies all that the members know about the Society is that it is a *sarcari* bank, and its purpose is to advance cheap loans to the members. The situation was rather tersely summed up by a Sub-Inspector, who was admonished by the Circle Registrar on finding that the members of a Society did not know the main principles of organizing and running a Credit Society. This Circle Registrar was himself once in that very circle a Sub-Inspector, and had thus been responsible for teaching the members. The Sub-Inspector quietly replied, "Sir, many a Sub-Inspector has risen to Circle-Registrarship in his endeavour to teach these rustics, but with no results." This admirably sums up the incapacity and indifference of the average member to bother himself with a knowledge of the theory and practice of Co-operation. Amongst those who have a practical knowledge of the working of these Societies he must be a bold man who claims, like Sir Jogindar Singh, that the knowledge of the principles of Co-operation is common, but for those who believe more in the written word I have an authority to quote. The minister in charge of the Department made this statement in 1929; whereas Mr. Darling, the Registrar, remarks in the Annual Report for the following year:

". . . during my touring in 1928–29 I was forcibly struck not only by the lack of understanding on the part of the general body of members in most of the districts traversed, but still more by the inability of the ordinary Sub-Inspector to teach." One more piece of evidence from the Department in support of my view and I have done. The Report for 1933 records: ". . . Even so, the general level of Co-operative knowledge among members of Primary Societies remains very low, and the work of Sub-Inspectors is often lax and perfunctory."

This lack of Co-operative knowledge, on the face of it, may be due either to the negligence of the staff or incapacity and indifference of the average member. There are only two parties to this bargain, and the blame cannot but lie on one or both of them. The Punjab peasant is proverbially ignorant and hopelessly unmindful of even his own interests. He therefore needs a good deal of repetition in order that ideas and schemes may percolate into his slow-moving mind. His incapacity to learn, combined with his indifference, makes things very difficult for those whose duty it is to teach him.

An officer of the Department went to inspect a Society. A General Meeting was held, and the members were asked the following questions with a view to testing their knowledge of the working of the Society: (1) Why do you lend on personal security and not on the security of property? (2) What are the advantages of unlimited liability? (3) How can you minimize the dangers of unlimited liability? (4) What is the obligation of the members during the period between the advancement and the repayment of a loan? There was profound silence—an unmistakable sign of ignorance.

The officer took the Sub-Inspector to task for not having given them the required teaching. The Sub-Inspector pleaded their incapacity and indifference as the cause of their ignorance. The officer then began explaining the objects and methods of a Society to them; and when, after an hour's lecture, he once again tested their knowledge, he found that they had not gained anything from his teaching.

As to the responsibility of the Sub-Inspectors, it looks very much as if overwork and the unresponsive character of their dull pupils make them relax their efforts. The Punjab Banking Committee, presided over by Mr. Darling, while admitting that lack of teaching is at the very root of the defects in the working of Co-operation in other Provinces, remark: "That Co-operation in the Punjab is a movement and not a mere organization—we had ample evidence of this on tour—is an indication that much teaching must have been given. But it is possible that it has not kept pace with the very rapid development of the last ten years." Mr. Darling in the Annual Report for 1930, writing on the "teaching of members," says: ". . . but before this can be done there must, I fear, be a considerable outlay upon teaching and training if only to remedy the deficiencies of the past. To say this is in no way to reflect upon those who laboured in the past, for the Co-operative field is essentially one in which circumstances are continually changing and experience increasing."

A CHEAP MONEY-LENDING AGENCY

A Co-operative Society seems to have been mistakenly understood by all as a rival to the money-lender. The Department also seems to have adopted at the very outset the line of least resistance. A study of the agriculturist's problems revealed that he was being exploited by the money-lender—and the position has not changed after a whole generation of the working of these Societies. With that mental background and to the entire neglect of other vital problems touching the poverty and prosperity of agriculture, the average Sub-Inspector felt that the object of Co-operation was to replace the money-lender. The co-operator's most favourite theme was to decry the sahukars' methods with a view to capturing his clients. "Do not borrow from a sahukar, borrow from the Society," sums up the actual argument of the Sub-Inspector and the object of the movement as interpreted by him.

Now, after thirty years, a rude shock has made all co-operators realize that what they had been preaching was only half a truth. The cultivators liked the advice, and began acting up to it with a vengeance. They borrowed from the Society as long as the Society could afford to lend; and they then turned to the sahukar. During the Great War, and for some years subsequent to it, prices rose; and with them the cultivator's power to borrow. They borrowed indiscriminately, and high prices enabled them to make repayments. This made the Department feel that Co-operation was getting planted in the very soul of the peasantry. How one wishes it were so! The depression has exposed the Societies in their true colours, and the Punjab official co-operator has realized in practice that the original sermon was a dangerous half-truth, and that the Society had been hailed by an indebted peasantry as a cheap money-lending agency established by a beneficent Government for the welfare of the Punjab cultivator. The Department now is out to preach the lesson of thrift, and seems to have withdrawn its attractive argument which had served a whole generation. It is a pity that this movement should have been so hopelessly misunderstood by the people, but as long as the peasant with his mental make-up, moral standards, social obligations, and sense of values does not undergo a change for the better, the prospect of any lasting improvement will continue to be as remote as ever.

DISSENSIONS

A village is usually split up into factions, and members of factions in an Indian village are incapable of combination, even for the advancement of their own interests. Whenever a Society is run by members belonging to different factions the Society is bound to suffer seriously. Common interest is sacrificed at the altar of dissension, and all manner of unco-operative tactics are adopted to discourage the members of the weaker faction. They are not given loans for their legitimate needs; they are pressed more severely for repayment; in fact, their stay in the Society is sought to be rendered exceedingly difficult. In one Society, the General Meeting of which I attended, one member was being unduly pressed for repayment, although his record was commendable. He told the Inspecting Officer that his adversaries wanted to turn him out of the Society; and as I witnessed the proceedings—the charges and the replies—I felt that a good man was being put to trouble evidently for reasons unconnected with the working of the Society. Dissensions sap the very life and spirit out of a Society and hasten its collapse as nothing else could ever do. A house divided against itself cannot stand long; this is true of any Society where dissensions prevail; and dissensions are a normal feature of our village life.

PURPOSE OF THE LOAN

The Annual Report gives a striking analysis of the objects for which loans are advanced to the members of Agricultural Co-operative Credit Societies. Those who know the inner working of these Societies allege that loans are granted for specified and approved purposes, but that no watch is generally kept over the use to which they are put. Not only that, there are positive complaints that the Presidents and Secretaries tutor the borrower with a double purpose in view, if he happens to be a more honest man than they are. The real object of the loan is concealed, firstly because the Society will not lend for unproductive purposes, secondly because the Society, with an eye on the future, prefers to lend for such purposes as help to facilitate recovery. An unproductive loan will, therefore, be shown to have been incurred for, say, the purchase of cattle. Such a transaction enables the borrower to get his loan, although it is not his intention to buy any cattle with the money. Should he default in repayment, the Society is able to realize its dues by taking possession of the debtor's cattle, in execution of an award to be obtained in due course. Thus, through a flagrant neglect of the principles of Co-operation, and through dishonesty, is the real message of the Societies destroyed. Those who know things from the inside will not deny the existence of such practices, the volume of which it is difficult to assess, but the practice of which it is equally hard to disbelieve or deny.

By stating that their loans were needed for "redemption of debt" people are known to have borrowed in canal colonies expressly for payment of revenue. Being smart people, they knew that a loan for payment of revenue has to be paid back in six months, whereas one for redemption of old debt may continue for three years. Members of the Delhi R.T. and R.M.S. Societies have borrowed substantially for medical aid. A private inquiry from the members brought out the fact that a loan sought for "medical aid" was never refused. Hence the device.

The very low figures showing amounts borrowed for ceremonies and litigation are very hard to accept as strictly true. Co-operators have not given up litigation, nor do they spend such small amounts on ceremonies. The only alternative explanation, besides the Society's refusal to lend large sums for such purposes, is to be found in the favours that a money-lender is ever willing to show to these needy cultivators.

THE PERIOD OF THE LOAN

A Credit Society is fundamentally incapable of advancing long-term loans. Wherever Primary Societies have taken to advancing long-term loans they have invariably failed. Societies advancing for short periods have very often been successful. The Departmental Inquiry of 1916 into the causes of failure of Societies disclosed that loans had not always been granted for short periods. In practice, however, extensions and fictitious repayments may convert a short-term loan into a long-term one. The mental make-up of the cultivator renders it difficult for him to appreciate the difference between the two types of loans. When his loan is a short-period loan he feels nobody ought to object to any renewal of the loan, as long as he is willing enough to honour his obligation in that connection. It is the money-lender's favourite form of exploitation for which the farmer seems to have developed a profound fondness.

UNDESIRABLE MEMBERS

With the rapid expansion of the movement the quality in the matter of membership was sacrificed, with the result that men morally and socially undesirable and economically insolvent got admitted into the Societies. Some of them were bad characters who could not reform their ways, but had entered the Societies with the positive intention of making money out of a movement aiming at the betterment of the honest and struggling poor farmer.

In some cases these undesirable persons took the management in their own hands, to the utter disrepute of the movement and at the cost of the simple-minded peasants, who joined a Credit Society with feelings of gratitude and relief. In some Societies the majority consisted of undesirables, and consequently awards, executions, and liquidations had to follow; and the staff of the Department, in a number of cases, was resisted and assaulted, books were burnt, and huge sums were misappropriated, to the utter disgrace of the movement. In one case beggars were admitted into a Society, and could not be traced when required to meet their obligations.

NON-PAYMENT OF A LOAN

The farmer borrows and hopes to escape repayment by some unthought-of stroke of fortune. When the time for repayment arrives, even if he has money enough to repay, he wishes to spend it otherwise and delays repayment. He never seems to realize that repayment is to his advantage, and that delays will help to drown him in debt. In the repayment of a Society's debt sometimes the psychological effect is very great. The office-bearers, their friends and relatives do not wish to repay punctually, both as a matter of right, and as a display of their power in the Society. This infuriates others, who refuse payment simply because those able to repay have not done so. Apart from this cause, the habit seems to have been fostered in the farmer by the money-lender; and the farmer feels it extremely difficult to shake off this evil, even when he is dealing with the Credit Society. The Report for 1916 observes: "The village money-lender is inclined to invest his capital in long-term loans, and so long as his heavy interest is paid he is content to let the principal run on. This is the only kind of money-lending with which most Punjab agriculturists are acquainted, and it is no easy task to teach them proper business principles."

MISMANAGEMENT

A Society is virtually run by the Managing Committee. If this Committee consists of honest men, who guide the Society wisely and impartially, and are not selfish and dishonest, the success of the Society may be assured. When these men do represent, as they should, the honesty, integrity, business capacity, and intelligence of the Society, the Society can be expected to work on sound lines; for these few people can grasp the principles of Co-operation, and, even if the rest of the members are mere fools, they can at least be guided by the Committee to borrow for productive purposes and to repay punctually. Unfortunately, in a large number of cases, even good management has not been possible; and a good deal of our misfortune can be traced directly to the mismanagement by the Committees. The Registrar caused an inquiry to be made into the causes of failure of a hundred Societies. He wrote in the Report for 1918: "Mismanagement, which accounts for the highest figure (33 per cent), means a bad Committee. Either the Committee as a whole is selfish and grasping, or makes reckless advances, or it allows everything to be done by one man who is lazy, self-seeking, or dishonest. A bad President will always, sooner or later, wreck a Society unless he can be changed, which in this country is not always possible." I wish we had a more detailed description of the mismanagement by the Committee. Usually a Society is an entirely one-man show. The most influential persons monopolize the offices, and the members, in spite of all the assurances of the Department, dare not question the authority of office-bearers, even when they are oppressed. Whenever they feel the conduct of an office-bearer must be brought to the notice of the officers of the Department, they hesitate to do it, through fear of consequences on account of the intimate relations that are supposed to exist between the officers of the Department and those of the Society.

The office-bearers of Societies have been known to have grossly misused their power and position. They figure most prominently among those whose dishonesty is a blot on the character of the Punjab co-operator. Unfortunately, when such people are prosecuted, the members of the injured Society do not support the case, either through sympathy or foolishness or fear of making enemies of them; and a court of law being sometimes more a court of law than of justice, people are on technical grounds able to rob wholesale from Co-operative Banks and build themselves beautiful bungalows to live in. By the arguments of a good vakil, and the judgments of learned judges, the whole movement is getting a bad name. Two cases in which sensational Central Bank embezzlements were alleged have recently ended in this disappointing manner; and it is not difficult to see what an adverse effect such unsuccessful prosecutions have upon the cause of Co-operation and public honesty.

Just a little as to how bad management spoils Societies. A Society may be in the hands of one man, or a whole clique of office-bearers who follow the same policy. Where such is the case it is quite possible that no General Meeting is held; the President and the Secretary coming together and taking decisions by themselves. When a prospective borrower of the opposite faction needs money and the loan is granted to him, various means are adopted to delay the payment. "Money has not yet been received." "You will get it of course." "What is the hurry?" "Come after a week." These replies clearly indicate to the borrower that the machines are jammed and need lubrication. They are just a hint that the money is available for him as soon as he agrees that a certain percentage should be deducted for the responsible officials.

Moreover, in some cases deductions other than the above "commission" are sought to be made. In a certain District the President of a Society entered a sum of money as having been paid to a school of which, too, he happened to be the president. This in fact had never been paid to the school. In another case a borrower came late in the evening to make a repayment. "All right, the entry will be made in the morning." Repayment was shown as having been made after a month. The interest on this amount was charged to the borrower and pocketed by the office-bearer. Similarly, advances are made to very poor people; the sureties and the office-bearers charging them heavy commissions for their good offices. Deductions have also been known to be retained from the dividends payable to members.

The President and other office-bearers, whenever they are corrupt, make a good deal of money in the process of recoveries. A member is sent for and asked to make repayment, and if he offers something by way of illegal gratification an extension is granted. If he is unable to pay, and belongs to a rival faction, steps are taken against him. Awards, decrees, and executions follow, and people lose all faith not only in the Society but even in the movement.

In some cases men in charge of the management have taken to private money-lending, and their knavery is unbounded. When they feel that a client is in a hopeless position and their money is in danger, they forthwith admit him into the Society. He is advanced money from the Society, and by this means payment of his private debts is secured. The Society thus accepts a virtual pauper as a member, who, whenever it suits him or the dishonest management, is declared an insolvent or a defaulter. One President of a Society borrowed Rs. 3,000 from the Society. After some time he transferred Rs. 2,000 of his liability to his brothers; despite the fact that he was a rich man with a large balance in the District Central Bank, and that his brothers owned no property. He knew that they would never be able to repay the debt, and that the amount would have to be written off. It was a clever device on the part of the President to get rid of his rightful burden.

A Society or a bank when it fails leaves many dishonest office-bearers and leading members very rich and prosperous. In some cases the office-bearers have admitted menials within the Societies, simply with a view to borrowing money for personal use whenever their credit limit had been exceeded. There does not seem to be any device that human ingenuity can invent which has not been used by a dishonest management.

It is gratifying to note, however, that such practices are not common, otherwise by this time the entire movement would have collapsed. It is the ignorance and stupidity of the average member that has rendered such a successful exploitation possible. Not only that. When the culprits are hauled up by the Department for frauds and embezzlements the members of the Society or bank, being neighbours and relatives of the accused, out of a feeling of false pity or for fear of future embarrassment, make the Department's position hopelessly weak by their refusal to tender evidence against them.

FICTITIOUS REPAYMENTS

Says the Maclagan Committee on Co-operation: "An insidious and dangerous irregularity is the practice of allowing renewals based upon fictitious repayments. The practice consists in showing an outstanding loan in the accounts as fully repaid, and sanctioning on or about the same date a fresh loan of the same amount, actual repayment either not taking place at all or being made purely as a formality." Fictitious repayments are effected in every Province, and it seems with more experience better methods have been evolved. The practice fortunately is not common, but on the other hand it is not totally absent. Repayments are not only effected in the manner explained by the Maclagan Committee, but a more original method has been evolved. The debtor unable to pay is asked to bring in a friend or a relative who is a member of the Society and willing to have the debt transferred to his name. The amount is entered as repaid, and is shown as issued to another member. In some cases the process is believed to have gone on for a long time, from one member to another, on the strength of mere book entries. Such malpractices can easily be checked by the Sub-Inspector.

The same manipulation of figures is resorted to by superintendents who are out to realize money from actual defaulters. Without actual payment being made the debt is renewed—to the benefit only of the superintendent, whose commission on recoveries, no doubt, swells.

CHAPTER XLVII

A FEW SUGGESTIONS

START CO-OPERATIVE SOCIETIES ONLY WHERE THEY ARE NEEDED

Great care should be taken in starting a Co-operative Society of any type. Theoretically the demand for a Society should come from the people, and a Society should never be imposed upon an unwilling area. Societies are known to have died an inglorious death at places where the initiative came from the official side. Co-operation for its growth and working presupposes a realization of the disadvantages of individual weakness and waste, as well as an effective appreciation of the benefits of honest combination. In the past, at certain periods, speed in organizing Societies and in swelling their numbers seems to have been the one great failing of the Department. For a fairly long time the object of the worker of the Department seems to have been the mere organization of a Credit Society. The selection of a suitable area of operation, the habits, customs, needs, and character of people, their intelligence, business capacity, the extent of their indebtedness, and all other essential points of interest and economic importance must be clearly studied before a Society is started.

MEMBERS OF THE RIGHT TYPE

After a locality has been scrutinized with a view to the organization of a Society, the selection of members commands our utmost attention. The fall of a Society is almost invariably due to undesirable membership. Members may be poor, but they must be men of tried honesty and character.

Men of the most undesirable type have joined the movement, the straitened circumstances of which cannot but be attributed to the unsuitability of members in a large majority of cases.

Based as the movement undoubtedly is upon character and business, if it gets the right type of people to work it can never come to grief. Care in the selection of members not only in the beginning but ever afterwards is a matter of the most fundamental importance. There should be launched an extensive campaign against undesirable members, who must be made to mend their ways or leave the movement.

SUPREME NECESSITY OF TEACHING

The average Punjab peasant is ignorant and illiterate. It is because of his incapacity to safeguard his own interest that the movement must combine expansion with consolidation. A successful Society is a great economic and a moral lighthouse, and nothing but a flood of light from that house will bring millions of ships struggling in surging seas to the harbour of safety. The material at our disposal cannot be radically changed in a short duration, and therefore needs intensive and perpetual teaching and inexhaustible sympathy.

Even the illiterate peasant is capable of learning the broad principles with surety, and of acting upon them with certainty. As lack of education has failed to develop character in him, he needs frequent reminders and sometimes timely rebukes. His difficulty at present, as I understand it, is that his indifference to the necessity of a knowledge of Co-operation and working of a Society has not been conquered. If the Punjab peasant can remember his prayers in Arabic he can learn and remember broad principles of Co-operation in his own language. A knowledge of Co-operation, of the by-laws, rights, and obligations in a Society will make better members. Hence better Societies. Suitable material for the use of members does not at present exist. Pamphlets and books will have to be written for the use of the half-literate Secretaries and Presidents, who must also take part in teaching the members, at least to the extent of reading out books and pamphlets to them. The Sub-Inspector's area of duty will have to be curtailed.

SELECTION OF MANAGING COMMITTEES

The Managing Committee is virtually the Society. Every possible care should be taken to enlist able, intelligent, honest, and business-like members to form the Managing Committee. It is the Managing Committee that makes or mars a Society. Men of the same family should not be allowed to acquire a majority. Supervision should be rendered more exacting in the case of Managing Committees.

SIMULTANEOUS ALL-ROUND DEVELOPMENT

Over 80 per cent of the Societies in the Province are agricultural; and of these 90 per cent are Credit Societies. Credit Societies are essential; and most people competent to pronounce a judgment believe that a Credit Society is the very foundation of Co-operation, and that no other form of Co-operation is likely to succeed in a locality and amongst people where Co-operative Credit has failed. I believe the Central Banking Enquiry Committee share this view. There is a good deal of truth in the idea. We are rich in experience and knowledge.

Co-operative Credit is as important to-day as it was thirty years ago. We know that the provision of this cheap and controlled credit, if we can call it so, has certainly failed to bring the required transformation in the rural economy of our country. Our business is to find out all the points of waste and leakage in our agricultural economy and to make an effort to stop them up simultaneously.

The cultivator is an inefficient producer, a great borrower, pays high rates of interest, is exploited very badly in the process of marketing his produce, and keeps a large number of useless cattle. His holdings are fragmented and scattered, and he is incredibly extravagant and wholly illiterate. It is, therefore, of the utmost importance that he should be treated, not in parts and at different periods, but as a whole and simultaneously. Amongst an extravagant people, whose social customs involve heavy expenses and extreme thriftlessness, no Credit Society can ever succeed of itself.

We must not build on sand. Co-operative Credit Societies have merely been used by the cultivators as cheap money-lending agencies; and during the last thirty years they have thought fit to utilize this increase in credit agencies towards enhancing their indebtedness. They have borrowed from the money-lender and the Society. Repayments to the Society have been made by borrowing from the sahukar, who in his turn has been paid by means of the accommodation provided by the Society.

Thrift and Better Living Societies cost very little and are easy to run. They should in my opinion always precede the establishment of a Credit Society. When a Credit Society has been so established, its success is certain; and where a Credit Society has acquired a certain measure of success, all other forms of agricultural Co-operation should be forthwith tried, so as to secure the maximum good in the minimum period, thereby imparting to the cultivator's life that completeness and charm which economic independence and moral development alone can ensure.

Thrift and economy are the very essence of a prosperous nation, and indispensable to an agricultural economy. Credit Societies have been most successful amongst Arains, a thrifty class of people. Arains and Jats of Jullundur and Hoshiarpur are thrifty, and have proved successful co-operators in their own districts and in the colonies. The Sialkot Jat is a spendthrift fellow, and therefore a bad co-operator everywhere.

MORE SUPERVISION AND BETTER AUDIT

If Societies come to grief in a large number of cases this implies slackness of supervision and unsatisfactory audit. Frequently the Sub-Inspector in charge of supervision has a large number of Societies to look after. In a country with such difficult and slow means of communication in its rural areas as ours has, this often makes it impossible for him to realize what is expected of him. The Sub-Inspector and the auditor are rightly blamed for not doing their work with a due sense of responsibility, when we recall the many embezzlements that have come to light long after their having actually occurred. But if we are to be fair, the area under the supervision of a Sub-Inspector must be substantially curtailed, so as to make an honest and intensive attempt at supervision possible.

Auditors need a stricter control. A second audit should be carried out in at least 50 per cent of the Societies; and whenever an auditor is believed to have failed in the discharge of his duty, he should be taken to task and his promotion should entirely depend upon the efficiency with which he discharges his duties. Such of the auditors whose work the Department has reasons to believe is unsatisfactory should not be allowed to continue in service. The area of work entrusted to an auditor must also be cut down to limits of safety and efficiency.

HELP TO D CLASS SOCIETIES

Liquidation, like weeding and pruning, is essential to sound growth, but its frequency is a slur upon the movement; and, although invariably the responsibility for the winding-up of a Society rests with the Committee and the members, it somehow gets shifted on to the Department. Liquidation gives a severe set-back to the movement. The neighbourhood comes to believe that the movement itself is incapable of yielding satisfactory results in practice.

Not only that. The liquidation of a Society involves such hardship for members that, taken along with the dishonesty of liquidators, it makes the peasantry abhor the movement. One liquidator decided that a certain man employed in military service was to pay Rs. 4,000 as his contribution. This man was at the time posted at Lahore Cantonment; and his only fault had been his admission to his Village Society. The liquidator, for reasons best known to himself, transferred, it appears, the entire burden on to the shoulders of this unfortunate man. The military authorities came to his rescue; and through the intervention of Mr. Dod, the then Registrar, who acted promptly in the matter, the fair name of the movement was saved.

All persons are not in the position of the man just referred to, and do not even know how to begin protective action. It is therefore a matter of the utmost importance to save a Society when it is going to the wall; for by so doing one is not only saving the Society, but is saving the movement too. A D class Society should be taken charge of by the Department. The Committee must be suspended. The Society should be worked carefully by someone on behalf of the Department. Undesirable persons should be expelled. When it gains sufficient strength the Society should be handed over to a new Committee of Management.

EDUCATE THE FUTURE CITIZEN

The best method likely to give lasting and more successful results consists in educating the schoolboy. Before, however, the schoolboy can be so handled with advantage, his teacher must first be taught. The Department of Co-operation, in collaboration with the Department of Education, must prescribe a simple course in Co-operation and Rural Economics for training classes in Normal Schools; so that such teachers, when they go to village schools, are not complete strangers to the beneficial movements in the Province. Urdu Readers for village schools should contain, in intelligible language, information in broad outline about the reform of rural economy. It is these very boys whose inclinations and tastes, if developed along right lines, will form the very foundation of a progressive Punjab.

Nor can we afford to neglect the schoolboy in cities. He is being neglected in the same way in which his father and grandfather were neglected. No progressive Society can afford to do this. He must also be roped in.

All this effort presupposes the provision of excellent, intelligible, and up-to-date books and pamphlets on Co-operation, dealing with the special conditions prevailing in the Province.

Here once again education and Co-operation must combine. The Punjab Co-operative Union can get it done easily and quickly. Let there be no teacher in any town or village school who is ignorant of what Co-operation has done and is capable of doing for the economic and moral development of the Province.

CO-OPERATORS' DAY A PUBLIC HOLIDAY

That Co-operation is a movement the right understanding and widespread adoption of which is the speediest way to national prosperity goes without saying.

The average citizens' ignorance of Co-operation is amazing, and the enlistment of his interest is indispensable to the growth of the movement. Co-operators' Day deserves to be celebrated with much greater enthusiasm than it receives at present.

The declaration of Co-operators' Day as a public holiday throughout India will be incalculably beneficial to the movement. Every school and college should observe that day by holding a meeting.

Side by side with this, co-operators and their sympathizers should take it upon themselves to flood the Press of the Province with contributions on particular aspects of the movement. Propaganda for Co-operation should in fact be made intense and widespread during the week preceding Co-operators' Day.

In every Province the Provincial Co-operative Union should take it upon itself to get an annual address written by some authority, official or non-official. This address should be ready in time to reach every meeting in the Province, where it should be read out. The development of broadcasting will make it possible to celebrate this day with great benefit. This celebration should become the greatest uniting force in the Province.

DISTRICT OFFICERS

It is exceedingly unfortunate that District officers and other officials as a class have failed to show that interest in the amelioration of the agricultural masses which ought to be the concern of every well-wisher of the Province. Unfortunately the mental make-up of the rural areas makes nothing effective without the sympathetic attitude of the Government officials. It is absolutely essential, therefore, that the District officers be reminded of their duties towards popularization of Co-operation, with due regard to the soundness of its growth. The Departmental examinations of the executive officials in the Province should have a paper on "Rural Economy of the Province."

THE PUNJAB COLLEGE OF CO-OPERATION AND RURAL ECONOMY

The Punjab's system of training the future staff of the Department occupies a place of honour amongst similar institutions in the country. The training class at Gurdaspur is certainly an achievement to be proud of. But it has over-lived its usefulness now. Thirty years of Co-operation in the country have created a history of their own. The world at large has made rapid strides towards progress in training co-operators. The scope of study has widened and future plans of development necessitate extensive research into rural, economic, and social problems. The Rural Uplift Movement stands in need of a large number of workers trained in the essentials of Co-operation and the various branches of rural economy. If a movement is to succeed, it must have well-trained workers; there ought to be a ready supply of Educational Inspectors who could be sent from place to place, either for imparting instruction to workers in the ranks or for supervising classes. The Central Banking Enquiry Committee has suggested the establishment of provincial colleges of Co-operation, together with an all-India college.

In view of the finances needed, it would be advisable for the Punjab, Delhi, United Provinces, and the North-West Frontier Province to combine and start such a college at Delhi, which would serve these four Provinces at first, and might ultimately be raised to the status of the all-India college suggested by the Banking Committee.

The Punjab has the enviable distinction of having pioneered for the rest of the country in many forms of Co-operation. It has led the way in practical research into rural problems, and has started a Rural Uplift Movement that has won handsome praise everywhere. Might not this Province then serve as the basis for the establishment of a college that has long been overdue, and thus retain its honoured position in the country?

STAFF CONFERENCE

The junior staff of the Department ought to be taken into greater confidence by the officials of the Department. The Sub-Inspector is the Department personified. You may have even a Raffeisen as your Registrar, but with the present scale of your business he will be a hopeless failure if the field staff lacks intelligence or the will to perform its duties honestly. The weakness of the movement, the ever-changing problems that arise and the methods for tackling these problems cannot be understood and handled by the Department without making full use of the knowledge and experience of the Sub-Inspector. It is, therefore, exceedingly essential that the Department should take the Sub-Inspector more into its confidence. If he is given a sympathetic and honest hearing, he will make such disclosures as will startle any writer of magnificent and inspiring Blue books.

HIGHER GRADES FOR THE STAFF

The two greatest nation-building Departments in India labour under a very great disadvantage. The teacher and the Sub-Inspector of the Co-operative Department do not command that social esteem and influence which are accorded to their low-paid companions in other Departments. It is unfortunate in the extreme that a Society at large, on account of its peculiar environments, has so far failed to honour suitably these worthy servants of the public. It remains a fact that people seeking employment would prefer a low-paid Sub-Inspectorship of Police to an Inspectorship of Co-operative Societies, because of the greater social esteem and additional benefits that go along with the former. I cannot forget an incident I witnessed about fifteen years ago, when an Inspector of Co-operative Societies in my own District was housed while on tour in a place which was a disgrace according to any decent scale of values. An ordinary constable of police would have been better housed than this honest servant of the people, whose official tours—as I can personally vouch for—left nobody the poorer. A Sub-Inspectress tells me that while on tour board and lodging constitute a very formidable problem for ladies holding her position, and that, too, amongst a people who will receive a sheer stranger with utmost hospitality, and feel proud of the lavish entertainment they offer to a head constable of police or to a patwari. The physical inconvenience involved in the Sub-Inspector's work is very considerable, and at a certain season of the year almost unbearable. It is no wonder that low pay and these disadvantages help to kill all ambition and aspiration towards a life dedicated to the service of people not the least bit responsive. I have met in a number of Districts the Sub-Inspectors of the Department; and I feel the Province ought to be proud of these highly-intelligent people, who, in spite of their disadvantages, may still be ranked as the foremost workers in the field of nation-building. In the interests of the Department and of the movement, I feel it is absolutely essential that these patient and honest workers should be given greater leisure and less work, so as to improve their efficiency. Continued hard work and low remuneration tend to sap the very life of man. In every rank of its officers the Department needs men of ability and sympathy; and while sympathy and service you may get free of charge, for ability you will have to pay a price.

SPEED-UP THE SPREAD OF CO-OPERATION

In 1933 there were 17,726 Agricultural Societies in the Province. The recent depression and its adverse effects do not inspire much hope as to any possible increase. Let us put the number at 18,000. The number has been reached in thirty long years—a whole generation, a period in which nations are known to have risen and fallen. Calculated over this long period it means 600 Societies a year, or fifty Societies per month throughout the Province, i.e. less than two Societies each District every year. Surely he must be a brave man who warns us against the too rapid growth of Co-operation in the Province. Take mere numbers alone. There are about 35,000 villages in the Province. At the rate of the average of the last thirty years it will take another thirty years to give one Co-operative Society to each village in the Punjab. Is not such a calculation alarming, when all are agreed that the growth of Co-operation is the only way out of the extremely unpleasant situation into which the countryside has been allowed to drift. Sixty long years just to give one Society to a village! The Punjab Banking Enquiry Committee, on the average of the last five years, calculated in 1930 that at the rate of one thousand Societies per year every Punjab village will have a Society within fifteen years. But this Committee had calmly assumed that 15 to 20 per cent of the villages will for one reason or another be found to be either unfit or unwilling to have a Co-operative Society. Surely this is unfair. Unless a village is entirely inhabited by the criminal tribes there is every hope of starting a Society in it. Why? The Department has started Societies amongst the criminal tribes as well, no doubt with a fair hope of success.

As against the anticipated increase of a thousand Societies a year, the growth of Societies during the last four years works out at about 125 a year. This slow progress is due to the effects of the depression that has held the Province in its grip for the past five years. Extension of the movement needs money; and at present the major portion of what the Government spends seems to benefit only the smallest number. If it must deny the rural areas medical aid and the luxury of a foolproof radio set, must it deprive them as well of more education and Co-operation? The Province spends a great deal upon its Departments of Agriculture and Industry, and squanders a lot of money on higher education (to swell the number of discontented B.A.'s). But its expenditure upon the education of the rural areas and the growth of Co-operation in the countryside is pitifully inadequate. Let us hope a better sense of values will dictate a radical change in the spending of our resources. More money means more men and a speeding-up in the pace of Co-operation. Given good workers in adequate numbers, speed in growth will not affect the efficiency of the Department. Growth of Co-operation must be simultaneous with the growth of education. Unless Co-operation is given the fullest encouragement and is allowed to play its part in the solution of economic problems, the bases of which are mental and moral, the statesmen of the next generation will find the vast majority of the population either reduced to the position of serfs, who are a disgrace to humanity, or starving rioters and rebels, who are a menace to the peace of the Province.

A REVIEW OF THE POSITION

Thirty long years have passed. The movement has grown in volume and variety. The Province has had the proud privilege of guidance by a set of sympathetic and incomparably brilliant Registrars. But it is time we should fully realize the extreme inadequacy of the movement as a method of revitalizing the peasantry of the Province, which is the pride of our country. Most of the Provinces have already taken stock of their position in this respect. It is a mistake to believe that we need no review of our achievements and obstacles.

A critical review of the working of the movement has long been overdue. Let the problem of the movement be studied with a view to a future programme for education and Co-operation; for therein lies the only hope of ensuring the existence of a sturdy peasantry (now on the verge of collapse). Hasten the appointment of a Committee on Co-operation; and thus enable the Province to avoid the mistakes of the past, and have a progressive plan for the future. The United Provinces, Burma, Madras, and the Central Provinces have had the working of their respective movements inquired into by committees of experts. The interests both of Co-operation and of the Punjab demand that such an inquiry should be held without any further delay.

THE REGISTRAR

The Registrar is the guiding spirit of the movement in a Province; and the popularity and progress of the movement is almost entirely determined by the Registrar's ability, enthusiasm, and influence. The Punjab owes the volume and richness of its movement solely to its incomparably brilliant Registrars—Messrs. Strickland, Darling, and Calvert. The future of Co-operation depends upon the support the Provincial Governments give to the Registrar, and the measure of interest with which the Government of India decides to guide the movement. Co-operation is a transferred subject, and in a considerable measure its progress will also depend upon the attitude of the minister in charge of the subject. It would, therefore, be damaging to the interest of the movement to place it at the mercy of a money-lender.

The Registrar, however, should always be the very soul of the movement; and in places where the Registrar is a misfit the movement is not likely to flourish. But no Registrar, with all his brilliance, will ever be able to achieve anything unless he feels that his position commands an influence and esteem (together with financial inducements) such as he would have in any other position open to him. It is, therefore, of the utmost importance that the selection of the Registrar should be made with all possible care. Once the selection has been made and the incumbent of the post has given every satisfaction, it is the duty of the Government to see that he does not jeopardise the chances of his promotion. It is not difficult to find men who do not hanker after executive power, and are prepared to dedicate their lives to the uplift of the poor. But when they are found, chances of legitimate promotion should never de denied them. This does not imply, however, that a Registrar, after ten years of meritorious service in the Department, should be offered a higher post in some other branch of the administration, where the richness of his experience in this line of work is lost to the Province. The Registrar, Co-operative Societies, Punjab, holds a position of unique importance and trust. It is now in the fitness of things that Co-operative Departments in all Provinces should be overhauled so as to arrange for the promotion of a Registrar of Co-operative Societies to the rank of Commissioner, Co-operative Societies. The Department of Co-operation is the most beneficial, and in fact a major Department of the Province, upon the sound and speedy working of which depends the prosperity of the Province in no small measure. The Punjab Government has no reason at all to refuse the pay and position of a Commissioner to an experienced Registrar, when it has created a Commissionership for Rural Uplift. Rural uplift is a part of the programme of Co-operation, and it is doubtful if the creation of this rival agency will ultimately be of good to both the movements. No Province can afford to lose a good Registrar; and his ability and experience ought always to be available in the interest of the development of every Province. Therefore it would be wise to raise such an officer to a Commissionership, and either give him the sole charge of this rural reconstruction work, or place one or two kindred departments under him. He would thus be retained in Co-operative service, and work in peace and contentment. Failing this, every Registrar would be compelled to behave like the civil bailiff on duty with a Union for the Execution of Awards, ever ready to slip away at the first opportunity that offers itself. Officers below the rank of a Registrar, capable of being selected for the Registrarship, should be chosen with the utmost care; and they should not be allowed to continue in the Department when lack of ability or inclination render them unfit for such duties. It is manifestly unjust to the movement that a man who has no faith in Co-operation should be put at the helm of affairs.

GOVERNMENT EXPENDITURE

The Government expenditure on the movement is sadly inadequate to say the least. Co-operation is the most beneficial department in every province, and needs ever increasing care and financial assistance. The expenditure invested in the movement will repay itself in many ways.

CHEAP MONEY

Apart from actual expenditure in the movement, the Government should now raise large sums of money at the present low rates of interest and earmark the same for investment in the movement. It should be a long-term loan which can be applied through proper channels and with due safeguards towards consolidating the movement and accelerating its pace. The investment will turn out beneficial to the country and remunerative to the Government.

INDEX